The FALL and REDEMPTION of CONSCIENCE

A Reformed Biblical Theology

"Andrea Ferrari draws 'conscience' out of the theological purgatory where it had been languishing. Following the lead of the late John Webster, Ferrari offers some possible avenues toward a renovation of this theme, which had been vehemently set aside by Karl Barth and others in the last century due to its 'bridging' and mediating function between the Creator and the creature. Conscience is not just *conscientia*, an inner faculty to form judgments, it is also (following Calvin) *sensus*, a kind of subjective, immediate awareness. This study is an interpretation of conscience that pays close attention to the Scriptures and that frames this theme in a Trinitarian and covenantal way. An impressive achievement!"

—**Christophe Chalamet,** professor of systematic theology, University of Geneva, Switzerland

"With theological insight and spiritual maturity, Andrea Ferrari provides something we've needed for a long time: a Reformed theology of conscience. Ferrari offers a compelling argument that conscience is a recurring theme in the Old and New Testaments and that conscience must be understood in the context of theology proper, anthropology, and soteriology. This is an enriching study that will be foundational for all future Reformed reflection on the topic."

—**David VanDrunen,** Robert B. Strimple Professor of Systematic Theology and Christian Ethics, Westminster Seminary California

"A richly Reformed and biblical study of conscience—as created, fallen, justified, and perfected. Ferrari shows how important conscience is for the Reformed tradition, beginning with John Calvin, whose position differs in intriguing ways from Thomas Aquinas's. This superb study fills a notable gap for students of Christian anthropology and ethics."

—**Matthew Levering,** James N. Jr. and Mary D. Perry Chair of Theology, Mundelein Seminary

"Building on the traditional Reformed framework of creation-fall-redemption, Andrea Ferrari formulates a constructive doctrine of conscience. Well-attuned to developments in systematic theology, his book carries real potential application for Christian ethics, particularly in our increasingly relativistic world. Ferrari's historically informed and theologically grounded project helps the church articulate a more robust account for why we are without excuse before the Lord and in need of the saving gospel of Christ."

—**Harrison Perkins,** pastor, Oakland Hills Community Church (OPC), Michigan; author of *Reformed Covenant Theology: A Systematic Introduction*

"With this thorough study on a neglected topic in present-day Protestant theology, Andrea Ferrari has reflected on the biblical and theological significance of the conscience for Christian anthropology. Intertwining exegesis and biblical theology, Ferrari locates the subject in robust Trinitarian and covenantal frameworks, and dialogues with the most important voices in the Protestant tradition—from Calvin's *sensus divinitatis* to John Webster's seminal essay 'God and Conscience." Contrary to intellectualist notions (like Aquinas), Ferrari expounds a perceptual and intuitive explanation of the conscience that better fits the biblical account and human experience. With this study, Ferrari has not only provided a state-of-the-art academic monograph but also a constructive way forward to appreciate the relevance of conscience for Protestant theology as a whole."

—**Dr Leonardo De Chirico,** lecturer in historical theology, Istituto di Formazione Evangelica e Documentazione, Padova, Italy

"Though he doesn't mention it, Ferrari exposes the shortcomings Krister Stendahl's 1963 influential essay 'The Apostle Paul and the Introspective Conscience of the West,' insisting that a full-orbed biblical picture of conscience is less about guilty subjective interiority than the constant awareness, before God, of our human covenantal vocation, its privileges and responsibilities. Here is a properly theological account of conscience as created, fallen, redeemed, and perfected that will be of interest not only to introspective Westerners, but to people of every tribe and nation."

—**Kevin J. Vanhoozer,** research professor of systematic theology, Trinity Evangelical Divinity School, Illinois

"Theological interpretation of Scripture has made tremendous strides over the past two decades, and Ferrari's work exemplifies its maturity. With careful attention to traditional literary, linguistic, and exegetical tools yet guided and enriched by psychological, philosophical, and—above all—theological categories and insights, this biblical-theological treatment of conscience demonstrates the depth and promise of theological interpretation for hearers of God's word. Old Testament specialists in particular will appreciate Ferrari's sensitivity to their field and will benefit not only from the content of his theological synthesis, but also from an illustrative and compelling method that refuses to divorce theology from exegesis."

—**R. Andrew Compton,** professor of Old Testament, Mid-America Reformed Seminary, Dyer, Indiana

The FALL and REDEMPTION of CONSCIENCE

A Reformed Biblical Theology

ANDREA FERRARI

STUDIES IN HISTORICAL AND SYSTEMATIC THEOLOGY

The Fall and Redemption of Conscience: A Reformed Biblical Theology
Studies in Historical and Systematic Theology

Copyright 2026 Andrea Ferrari

Lexham Academic, an imprint of Lexham Press,
1313 Bay St., Bellingham, WA 98225
LexhamPress.com

You may use brief quotations from this resource in presentations, articles, and books. For all other uses, please write Lexham Press for permission. Email us at permissions@lexhampress.com.

Unless otherwise noted, Scripture quotations are from the Scripture quotations marked (ESV) are from ESV® Bible (The Holy Bible, English Standard Version®), copyright © 2001 by Crossway Bibles, a publishing ministry of Good News Publishers. Used by permission. All rights reserved.

Scripture quotations marked (NASB) are from the New American Standard Bible®. Copyright 1960, 1962, 1963, 1968, 1971, 1972, 1973, 1975, 1977, 1995 by The Lockman Foundation. Used by permission.

Scripture quotations marked (NIV) are from the Holy Bible, NEW INTERNATIONAL VERSION®. Copyright © 1973, 1978, 1984, 2011 by Biblica, Inc. Used by permission. All rights reserved worldwide.

Scripture quotations marked (NJPS) are from *The Jewish Study Bible: Featuring The Jewish Publication Society TANAKH Translation*. Oxford University Press, 2003.

Print ISBN 9781683598725
Digital ISBN 9781683598732
Library of Congress Control Number 2025943780

Lexham Editorial: Todd Hains, Allisyn Ma, Erin Mangum, Mandi Newell, Abigail Stocker
Cover Design: Fanny Palacios
Typesetting: ProjectLuz.com

25 viii / US

To Cristina, my better conscience

CONTENTS

Foreword xi
Acknowledgments xv
Prayer for Those with a Tormented Conscience xvii
Introduction 1

Part 1: Created Conscience 27
1. The Manifestation of Conscience 31
2. The Function of Conscience 57
3. The Nature of Conscience 69

Part 2: Fallen Conscience 91
4. Fallen Conscience as Nonphysical Perceptual Awareness 93
5. How Conscience Is Fallen 135

Part 3: Redeemed Conscience 159
6. The Preparation of Conscience 161
7. The Regeneration of Conscience 171
8. The Justification of Conscience 189
9. The Sanctification of Conscience 207
10. The Perfecting of Conscience 227

Conclusion 239
Bibliography 249
Subject Index 271
Name Index 287
Scripture Index 291

FOREWORD

In works of anthropology in general, and theological anthropology in particular, the human conscience always makes an appearance. The conscience is, after all, an intrinsic aspect of what it is to be human; it is crucial for the reflexive sense of the self, and its exercise is linked to a whole range of factors—rational, affective, and ethical. It is little wonder that the conscience appears at a host of critical junctures in Scripture, across passages containing dramatic narrative, theological instruction, and ethical counsel. Yet for all its centrality to being human and its presence in holy Scripture, the conscience has seldom been the focus of sustained attention in theology, and in recent works in particular it has been somewhat neglected—something of a poor relation.

It is into this dearth that the present work of Andrea Ferrari makes its appearance. Ferrari—a scholar, teacher, and pastor with decades of experience—takes the relatively disregarded topic of the conscience as the central focus of his book and proceeds to offer an outstanding conspectus of biblical wisdom and theological insight on the subject in a work that is not only academically rigorous but pastorally aware. In so doing, he not only sheds light on one of the most interesting and complex topics in the history of theology; he constructs a highly persuasive theological account of how to conceive of conscience today.

There are three features worthy of particular note at the outset. First, Ferrari recognizes the need for a faithful account of the human conscience to have appropriate foundations—not to be free-floating and speculative but to be wisely grounded in unshakeable truths. For this reason, Ferrari bases his account on exegesis and analysis of Scripture, drawing in the process on a whole range of texts from the New Testament and the Old. The latter point is worthy of close attention: eschewing the danger of seeking reference to human conscience only in verses where a particular technical term appears (such as *suneidesis* in the New Testament), Ferrari attends to several important passages in Scripture where the *substance* of human conscience is clearly in view, and thus ranges widely across both the Old and the New Testament. The result is an understanding of conscience that is attentive to the whole sweep and the various phases of salvation history and to the unfolding of the history of the covenant. This canonical basis allows Ferrari to ground his account of conscience even more deeply—in the relationship between the Triune God and the created human being. And further, Ferrari takes the bold step of suggesting that the covenantal awareness and vocational responsiveness that are intrinsic to conscience are, in some manner, reflective of the inner life of the Trinity.

Second, Ferrari not only attends to the unfolding story of the covenant between God and human beings, but he is sensitive to the different ways in which conscience is manifest and the different functions with which it is vested across history. This multifocal attention is evident in the structure of the work. As one might expect, much of Ferrari's focus is on the conscience in fallen and redeemed human beings, in the course of which he engages deeply both with the relevant scriptural material and with the subsequent theological tradition. However, he also frames these proximate inquiries within explorations of the less attended themes of created conscience and perfected conscience. These fresh explorations manifest some of the most innovative and generative work in the book, as Ferrari seeks to understand how conscience would have functioned for our first parents and how it will function in the heavenly realms. The benefit of this wide-lens perspective is that his account of conscience avoids being circumscribed by merely ethical concerns, which is a standing temptation for those who hear the trope of human conscience invoked. In place of such a restrictive account, Ferrari offers a full-orbed and holistic depiction of conscience as covenantal awareness and vocational responsiveness.

Third, Ferrari insists that to think about human conscience faithfully is to be directed to think principally not about the self but about God. Ferrari evidences a deep awareness of the Christian tendency to focus on introspection and of the consequent danger of confusing the objective reality of salvation for the inward experience of assurance. He also recognizes the tendency in contemporary society to focus similarly on the interior self, on its instincts, intuitions, and feelings. If such well-trodden but erroneous paths of spiritual narcissism are poorly framed or are left unchecked, the end result can only be unhappiness. As a counterpoint, Ferrari insists that the conscience is always directed—and is always directing the human being—to God, the Lord of the covenant who has created it, who redeems it, and who will perfect it. It is in God that the assurance and peace of conscience lies, which is the desire of the pilgrim on earth and the reality of the saint in heaven. It is only within the assurance provided by this covenant framework that the scripturally mandated requirement to reflect upon the self can faithfully proceed in the conscience. Far from being a quest for the true self, the task of the human conscience is that of turning to God, of attending to his presence and vocation.

The above sketch of three compelling features of this account offers but a preview of the delights of the whole. There will, of course, be room for readers to dissent from the readings and the arguments both large and small that Ferrari presents in this volume. But it is to be hoped, at the very least, that this book stimulates further work on this worthy topic and, beyond this, that it illumines those who read it. At one point in his *Institutes*, John Calvin reflects that the task of the theologian is "not to divert the ears with chatter, but to strengthen consciences by teaching things true, sure, and profitable."[1] In my view, this work of Ferrari on the theology of conscience happily fulfills this task; may other readers also find their consciences strengthened by it.

Professor Paul T. Nimmo
King's Chair of Systematic Theology
Divinity – King's College
University of Aberdeen
Aberdeen
Scotland
June 2024

---

1. John Calvin, *Institutes of the Christian Religion*, 1.14.4 (164 in LCC edition).

ACKNOWLEDGMENTS

I would like to express my gratitude to several people who have assisted with the completion of this work. The late John Webster was very kind in responding graciously to my emails and offering his advice in the early stages of my dissertation prior to his untimely death. Rev. Zachary Keele, Pastor of Escondido Orthodox Presbyterian Church, and Professor David VanDrunen of Westminster Theological Seminary in California read some parts of my dissertation and sharpened my thinking, for which I am grateful. Rev. Charles Tedrick, Dean of Students at Westminster Theological Seminary in California, read the whole work enthusiastically giving thematic insights and stylistic guidance.

My supervisor, Professor Paul T. Nimmo, has been a constant source of inspiration and encouragement. He has been always available, prompt, meticulous, and sharp in his questions, observations, and corrections. At the same time, his academic competence and precision have always been accompanied by a humble, respectful, and pleasant attitude. Without his help—especially in the final stages of the work—my English would have been much worse and the contents of the dissertation much more confusing.

PRAYER FOR THOSE WITH A TORMENTED CONSCIENCE
—

In the name of the Father and of the Son and of the Holy Spirit. Amen.

O Lord, you have searched me and known me!
You know when I sit down and when I rise up;
    you discern my thoughts from afar.
You search out my path and my lying down
    and are acquainted with all my ways.
Even before a word is on my tongue,
    behold, O Lord, you know it altogether. *Psalm 139:1–3*

Without your aid, O Lord, our conscience has no power to discern the judgments of your will. And as your eyes have beheld our imperfection today, we beseech you, make us whole, that we would desire to pursue perfect righteousness. Pardon our transgressions, show mercy upon our ignorance, and forgive our sins. Grant us your power to love what you command and to desire what you promise. We waste away on account of our tormented conscience, O Lord, fearing that our ignorance has led us into sin or that our will has driven us headlong into unrighteousness. We beseech you, we pray to you, that whatever offense we have caused today, by your forgiveness we would be granted remission of our sins, and that clinging firmly to your word, we would forgive those who have sinned against us as we have been forgiven, and that all who confess their sins to you would receive everlasting life. Through Jesus Christ, our Lord, who lives and reigns with you and the Holy Spirit, one God, now and forever. Amen.[1]

---

1. The prayer "Without Your Aid, O Lord" above has been adapted from a seventh-century Spanish prayer called *Nulla est, Domine*. (It was used to close local councils. The original Latin can be found in H. Schneider, *Die Konzilsordines des Früh- und Hochmittelalters* [Hahn, Hannover, 1996], 184–85.) It shows the spirit in which Christians have prayed through the centuries and—most importantly in our case—the vital place of conscience in Christian piety and theology. The penitential character of this prayer identifies the limits, the struggles, the sorrows, and the needs of human conscience while, at the same time, asking for the balm of God's forgiving and justifying grace to heal a fearful and guilty conscience. This prayer can be used to meditate on and examine our own conscience before the Triune God.

INTRODUCTION

In the history of Christian anthropology, conscience has always played an important role. Even though pastors and theologians have approached their discussions on conscience in particular historical and social settings, in different geographical locations, with diverse styles, purposes and distinctive nuances of meaning, assigning to it a more or less prominent role in their theological anthropology, there has been a remarkable continuity in their interest in this human phenomenon. And because it is a *human* phenomenon, we find a similar interest outside the boundaries of a Christian interpretation of reality not only across other religious traditions but across distinct eras, cultures, and philosophies.[1] Indeed, Paul Strohm begins his short introduction to conscience by saying that "the variable yet durable phenomenon called conscience has outlasted epochs and empires, credos and creeds."[2]

For John Calvin, the human conscience was so important it was to be the main target of theological work: "The theologian's task is not to divert the ears with chatter, but to strengthen consciences by teaching things true, sure, and profitable."[3] By contrast, in contemporary Christian thinking, there seems to be a general neglect of conscience. An instance of this inattention is *The Ashgate Research Companion to Theological Anthropology*, in which considerable consideration is given to self-consciousness but very little is said

---

1. Jayne Hoose, ed., *Conscience in World Religions* (University of Notre Dame Press, 1999); H. Jaeger, S. J., "L'examen de conscience dans le religions non-chrétienne et avan le christianisme," *Numen* 6.3 (1959): 175-233.

2. Paul Strohm, *Conscience: A Very Short Introduction* (Oxford University Press, 2011), 1. For a similar judgment, see Richard Sorabji, *Moral Conscience through the Ages* (Oxford University Press, 2014), 215.

3. John Calvin, *Institutes of the Christian Religion*, ed. John T. McNeill (Westminster, 1960), 1.14.4.

theologically about conscience.⁴ As early as 1963, Paul Lehmann highlighted in a significant footnote the theological decline and fall of conscience:

> A full-length study of what has happened to conscience in the Western cultural tradition is overdue. A carefully documented and sufficiently comprehensive account of what might be called "the shape of conscience," i.e., of an interpretative framework other than that offered by moral theology in which the ethical nature and behavioral effectiveness of the conscience might once again be clearly and persuasively understood, is not at hand.⁵

More recently, Paul Ricouer asserted that a "theology of conscience remains yet to be done" adding that "few contemporary theologians have undertaken to reinterpret the phenomenon of conscience."⁶ Similarly, the late John Webster felt the need not to abandon conscience to "the anthropological captivity of the church and its moral theology," and asked, "What kind of repair work is needed to accomplish the theological renovation of conscience?"⁷ He answered, "We best articulate a Christian theology of conscience when we refuse to isolate it and treat it as a phenomenon in itself. Instead, we need to expound it as one feature within a larger moral landscape."⁸ According to Webster, this larger landscape is "the moral field of the gospel," for the appropriate context for a theological discourse on the reality of conscience is "the drama of salvation."⁹

This book, therefore, is based on the premise that there is a need in Christian thought to recover a compelling theology of conscience.¹⁰ As hinted

---

4. Joshua R. Farris and Charles Taliaferro, eds., *The Ashgate Research Companion to Theological Anthropology* (Ashgate Publishing Limited, 2015). I only found a passing reference to conscience (167).

5. Paul L. Lehmann, *Ethics in a Christian Context* (Westminster John Knox, 2006), 327-28.

6. Paul Ricoeur, "The Summoned Subject in the School of the Narratives of the Prophetic Vocation," in *Figuring the Sacred: Religion, Narrative, and Imagination*, ed. Mark I. Wallace (Augsburg Fortress, 1995), 273.

7. John B. Webster, "God and Conscience," in *Word and Church: Essays in Christian Dogmatics* (T&T Clark, 2001), 233.

8. Webster, "God and Conscience," 233.

9. Webster, "God and Conscience," 257. This conclusion is shared by Roman Catholic theologian Matthew Levering, *The Abuse of Conscience: A Century of Catholic Moral Theology* (Eerdmans, 2021), 207.

10. That this is a "felt" need is evidenced by the publication of *Christianity and the Laws of Conscience: An Introduction*, ed. Jeffrey B. Hammond and Helen M. Alvare (Cambridge University

at above, in comparison to the theological past it seems that at present the conscience has almost disappeared from contemporary doctrinal and even pastoral concerns. It appears to be an essential theological endeavor for the present day to provide such a theology of conscience, and it is precisely this endeavor that this book undertakes. In particular, its purpose is to ground theologically the experience of human conscience in an ordered construal delineating its essential and immutable mediating character in the relation between the Triune God and human creatures. In order to accomplish this task, a renewal and a theological and pastoral rehabilitation of conscience is needed in the light of its eclipse in systematic, moral, and pastoral Protestant theology in the twentieth century, demonstrating at the same time a measure of continuity between patristic and medieval theology on the one hand and the Reformed tradition on the other in their respective conceptions of conscience.[11] To this end, the book aims at constructing a theology of conscience within a framework governed by God's Trinitarian and covenantal presence and action in the world, and it will locate the reality of conscience—and of theological anthropology in general—in a derivative position, subordinate to the study of God's being, purpose, presence, and action. Seeing human history as covenantal history—that is, as the history of the drama of redemption—I will consider conscience as a perceptual awareness and as a spontaneous responsiveness that is integral to the human person. In the process, I will explore the importance of a biblical and theological understanding of conscience with regard to contemporary thinking.

In order to offer a preliminary delineation of the theology of conscience that will be developed, the remainder of the introduction proceeds in three sections. First, to demarcate the field of inquiry, it offers four methodological coordinates within which the Christian discourse on conscience will be developed within this thesis, and it will indicate some of its most significant

---

Press, 2021). This remarkable volume differs from the present theology of conscience in that it is chiefly historical, interacting with Scripture and theology in relation to the most important moments of Christian history and to Christian thinkers and their reflection on natural law.

11. For a general overview of the eclipse of natural theology (and of conscience) in Reformed theology in the twentieth century, see Stephen J. Grabill, *Rediscovering the Natural Law in Reformed Theological Ethics* (Eerdmans, 2006), 1–53; John V. Fesko, "Introduction," in Geerhardus Vos, *Natural Theology* (Reformation Heritage Books, 2019), xvii–ixx; Bruce P. Baugus, *The Roots of Reformed Moral Theology: A Study of the Historical Background of an Ecclesial Tradition of Moral Instruction* (Reformation Heritage Books), 2022.

conversation partners. Second, it explains what contributions in constructing a comprehensive theological discourse that aims both to articulate a Christian explanation of conscience and to challenge the present negligence of this important theological topic. Third, it presents an outline and a summary of the way in which the topic will be developed in the chapters that follow.

THEOLOGICAL APPROACH

There are four methodological presuppositions that guide this inquiry—a theology of conscience must be articulated in a way that is biblical, theological, Trinitarian, and covenantal. After I introduce these, we will explore some of the key conversation partners that aid in pursuing this theological approach.

A BIBLICAL THEOLOGY OF CONSCIENCE

To start, the theology of conscience needs to be placed within the interpretative framework of the gospel, namely within the context of the drama of salvation as narrated by the Bible. Within this gospel framework, the theology of conscience is first of all *biblical* because the words of the Old and New Testament constitute the essential source of God's revelation of himself and of the meaning of his work in creation and redemption. This correlation between the words of the Bible and the works of God derives from the belief that "God ... by his very nature, acts by speaking."[12]

This biblical approach is a deliberate effort to follow the historical and dramatic unfolding of the gospel following God's own explanation of what the Father has purposed in the Son and accomplished by the Spirit. In this regard, Donald Carson warns against the peril of elaborating a theological interpretation of Scripture that is disconnected from history—of having a theology that does not refer to what actually happened, implying that certain historical events are accessible only by faith.[13] On the contrary, a scriptural explanation of conscience facilitates a theology that is integrated with human history. According to Geerhardus Vos, in the Bible we have "the actual embodiment of revelation in history,"[14] such that, as Michael Horton observes,

---

12. Timothy Ward, *Words of Life: Scripture as the Living and Active Word of God* (InterVarsity Press, 2009), 22.

13. Donald A. Carson, 'Theological Interpretation of Scripture: Yes, But ...," in *Theological Commentary: Evangelical Perspectives*, ed. R. Michael Allen (T&T Clark, 2011), 189-90.

14. Geerhardus Vos, *Biblical Theology: Old and New Testaments* (Eerdmans, 1948), 6.

"God's speech does not merely interpret history; it creates it."[15] Thus, a biblical discourse on conscience rooted in the historical nature of biblical revelation will be essentially realistic, not appealing—as Webster writes—"to natural religion and morality as anterior (and in important ways superior) to positive theological teaching."[16]

God's act of speaking, which shapes the historical and dramatic character of Scripture, indicates that the Bible is not just a "thing," a text to be critically scrutinized, dissected, and judged by the autonomous self. Considering the meaning of the Greek verb δράω, Kevin Vanhoozer observes that "a drama is a *doing*, an enactment."[17] In the words of the Bible, God *exhibits* his personal presence so that the self is summoned and called to respond before him.[18] The dramatic character of Scripture reverses the dynamic: the Bible critically scrutinizes and judges the self, portraying its story within the framework of the Bible's larger story.[19] Therefore, a discourse on conscience following the historical trajectory of the Bible explains conscience as a human response within redemptive history that is experienced within the actual movement of that history.

A THEOLOGICAL THEOLOGY OF CONSCIENCE

Given the exegetical and hermeneutical difficulties caused by the scarcity of biblical material concerning conscience, some people might think it would be better to have just a phenomenological or theoretical approach that avoids interpretative problems and conceptualizes God's truth about conscience

---

15. Michael S. Horton, *The Christian Faith: A Systematic Theology for Pilgrims on the Way* (Zondervan, 2011), 123.

16. John B. Webster, "Theologies of Retrieval," in *The Oxford Handbook of Systematic Theology*, ed. John Webster, Kathryn Tanner, and Iain Torrance (Oxford University Press, 2007), 10–11. On the importance of reading the Bible as the history of redemption, see Michael S. Horton, *Covenant and Eschatology: The Divine Drama* (Westminster John Knox, 2002), 99–120.

17. Kevin J. Vanhoozer, *The Drama of Doctrine: A Canonical-Linguistic Approach to Christian Theology* (Westminster John Knox, 2005), 37.

18. For a development of the concept of "semantic presence" and "communicative interaction," see Kevin J. Vanhoozer, "God's Mighty Speech Acts" and "From Speech Acts to Scripture Acts," in *First Theology: God, Scripture and Hermeneutics* (InterVarsity Press, 2002), 127–203; Ward, *Words of Life*, 20–95; Timothy Ward, *Word and Supplement: Speech Acts, Biblical Texts, and the Sufficiency of Scripture* (Oxford University Press, 2002), 75–136.

19. Horton observes that "the contemporary reader or hearer is not an aloof spectator who merely grasps, but an actor in the drama itself who is grasped," (*Covenant and Eschatology*, 206). On the implications of the reading/hearing event as a divine summons, see Horton, *Covenant and Eschatology*, 191–219.

in the form of general propositions. By contrast, I will attempt to read the story narrated by the Bible integrating it into a systematic construction of a theology of conscience. In doing so, I pay attention to a danger that Carson identified as follows:

> If one rightly concludes that there is a central storyline to the Bible and tries to use it in ways that enrich our theological understanding of Scripture, it does not necessarily follow that one is reading that storyline richly as well. Moreover, failure to do so will have deleterious effects on the theology we construct as a result of our (flawed) understanding of that storyline.[20]

As observed above, it is necessary first to grasp the biblical storyline for the purpose of developing a theology of conscience. But, in order to read the dramatic storyline richly, its systematic implications have to be understood, delineated, and built up as they are made known in the storyline itself. And since the principal source of theology remains God's revelation in Scripture—both in its historical character and in its doctrinal content—we must pay attention to these implications for, as Carson indicates, they might be veiled behind various literary genres and linguistic and metaphorical frameworks.[21]

Accordingly, this book will endeavor to develop a *theological* discourse on conscience, integrating the biblical story of conscience with the central doctrines of God, Christ, the Spirit, and creation and new creation, offering at the same time a more systematic treatment of conscience.[22] This approach helps to avoid proof-texting and atomistic tendencies while building a theology

---

20. Carson, "Theological Interpretation of Scripture," 206.

21. Carson, "Theological Interpretation of Scripture," 206. Webster warns against separating historical and analytical intelligence, explaining that Christian theology is a joint venture of exegetical and systematic reasoning. He writes, "What is amiss here? Partly is that the irreducibility of Scripture can be compromised by treating prophetic and apostolic discourse as raw material rather than *interim terminus* of systematic theological intelligence. Partly, again, it is allowing too much weight to concepts and logical anatomies as improvements upon Scripture. But there is also a certain neglect of the ineffability of the ontological principle of theology, a reluctance to allow the incommunicability of God's self-knowledge to chasten analysis, a softening of the distinction between attaining and comprehending, a desire to pass too soon beyond the ectype." Webster, "Principles of Systematic Theology," in *The Domain of the Word: Scripture and Theological Reasoning* (T&T Clark, 2012), 148.

22. For some reflections on striking a balance between a dramatic and a systematic approach to theological construction, see Donald A. Carson, "Systematic Theology and Biblical Theology," in *New Dictionary of Biblical Theology*, ed. T. Desmond Alexander, Brian S. Rosner, Donald A. Carson, and Graeme Goldsworthy (InterVarsity Press, 2000), 89–104.

of conscience by combining the historical character of Scriptures with its doctrinal implications.[23] In this endeavor, I will also retrieve[24] the witness of historical theology rather than engage in what Webster has called an "anthropology of enquiry" with its "rejection of citation in favour of enquiry."[25] The historical theology will serve the purpose of addressing contemporary issues in a literary form "generally governed by the fact that the Christian worlds of meaning are shaped by biblical, creedal and doxological texts and by the practices which both carry and are themselves carried by those texts."[26] This approach is heuristically helpful, for after so much energy has been spent engaging critically the past from the perspective of the present, theology also needs to engage critically with the present from the perspective of the past.

A TRINITARIAN THEOLOGY OF CONSCIENCE

The biblical and theological discourse on conscience set forth here will be necessarily *Trinitarian*, for the revelation of the Trinity is the foundation of the Christian faith. The doctrine of the Trinity is not just one aspect of Christian teaching comparable to others in importance; rather, it is like the ground in which everything else is rooted or the trunk from which all branches shoot forth. Consequently, this theology of conscience will be God-centered, Christ-focused, and Spirit-interpreted.[27]

Once again, Carson warns about the need to "integrate trinitarian thought into a doctrine of Scripture, with implications for its interpretation."[28] In this respect, Timothy Ward develops a theological analysis of the relationship between each divine person and the words of the Bible. For Ward, the

---

23. For a contribution on reintegrating biblical and systematic theology, see Horton, *Covenant and Eschatology*, 220-64.

24. On "retrieval theology," see Webster, "Theologies of Retrieval," 583-99; Michael Allen and Scott R. Swain, *Reformed Catholicity: The Promise of Retrieval for Theology and Biblical Interpretation* (Baker Academic, 2015).

25. John B. Webster, "Theological Theology," in *Confessing God: Essays in Christian Dogmatics II* (T&T Clark, 2005), 14, 16. On Webster's notion of theological theology, see Michael Allen, "Toward Theological Theology: Tracing the Methodological Principles of John Webster," *Themelios* 41.2 (2016): 217-37.

26. Webster, "Theological Theology," 20.

27. On the place of the doctrine of the Trinity in Christian theology, see John B. Webster, "*Rector et iudex super omnia genera doctrinarum*? The Place of the Doctrine of Justification," in *God and the Works of God*, vol. 1 of *God without Measure: Working Papers in Christian Theology* (T&T Clark, 2016), 159-75.

28. Carson, "Theological Interpretation of Scripture," 205.

Scriptures are the words of the Father's promise, the words fulfilled in the Son who is the Word, and the God-breathed words of the Spirit.[29] He concludes that Christian thought and practice originate from the reality of the Triune God who makes himself known in the words of the Bible. Similarly, in a stimulating integration of Trinitarian thought into a doctrine of Scripture, Fred Sanders proposes a "prosoponic exegesis," namely a Trinitarian rereading of the whole Bible to identify the divine persons throughout the economy of salvation.[30] Sanders's integration presupposes the primacy of the doctrine of the Trinity over the doctrine of revelation:

> In the fullness of time, God did not give us facts about himself, but gave us himself in the person of the Father who sent, the Son who was sent, and the Holy Spirit who was poured out. These events were accompanied by verbally inspired explanatory words; but the latter depended on the former. ... It is not quite enough to say that the doctrine of the Trinity is a revealed doctrine. That could situate the locus on the Trinity within the locus on revelation, constraining the doctrine of God by the doctrine of revelation. But the doctrine of revelation must already be dictated by a reality we can only define as Trinitarian in its material contents (an account of salvation history as an economy of God's self-revelation in the Son and the Spirit) before it can be generalized or formalized. The doctrine of the Trinity is the doctrine that norms and forms the doctrine of revelation itself.[31]

Sanders's conclusion is that "even Scripture is ordered under the missions," culminating in the incarnation and Pentecost, which redemptive activities cause us to move "back to antecedent processions" so that the "inside knowledge" of the Trinity has been "made public in the fullness of time by the only ones who could make it public: the insiders," who "bore witness to themselves and each other in the process of saving the outsiders."[32] Since the biblical drama of salvation narrates the story of the one Triune God creating in the person of the Father, redeeming in the person of the Son, and

---

29. Ward, *Words of Life*, 51–94.
30. Fred Sanders, *The Triune God* (Zondervan, 2016), 215–37.
31. Sanders, *The Triune God*, 40, 41–42.
32. Sanders, *The Triune God*, 69, 97, 74.

perfecting in the person of the Spirit, a Trinitarian discourse on conscience will place anthropology as subordinate to the revelation of this Triune God who—in the beautiful words of Vos—is "the one supreme reality from whom all other things [including conscience] derive their significance."[33]

In this regard, Webster observes that "what is said theologically of humanity is said after what is said of God as creator, saviour and perfecter," and therefore, "theology will be required to begin its talk of conscience with talk of God, Father, Son and Holy Spirit."[34] This approach avoids treating conscience merely in terms of morality and as autonomous by showing that it derives its truest significance from the supreme reality of the Triune God. Moreover, this approach will protect from the danger of limiting God's relation to creation by focusing too exclusively on the Father, or on the Son, or on the Spirit.

A COVENANTAL THEOLOGY OF CONSCIENCE

Building upon the foundation of Trinitarian thinking, I will develop a biblical and theological doctrine of conscience using the guiding superstructure of covenant.

Since the Trinitarian being of God is the archetype of all life, Meredith Kline notes that God called into existence a covenantal kingdom order that was not superimposed on a temporally or logically prior noncovenantal state.[35] Indeed, the psalms about nature show that the whole creation is to be summoned by the Lord of the covenant to respond in such a way as to glorify its creator (see Pss 93–99; 114:7; 148).[36] When God called creation to life by the

---

33. Geerhardus Vos, "Our Holy and Glorious God," in *Grace and Glory: Sermons Preached in the Chapel of Princeton Theological Seminary* (Banner of Truth, 1994), 259.

34. Webster, "God and Conscience," 254, 251. For a demonstration of the depth and scope of renewed interest in Trinitarian theology, see *The Oxford Handbook of the Trinity*, ed. Gilles Emery and Matthew Levering (Oxford University Press, 2011).

35. Meredith G. Kline, *Kingdom Prologue: Genesis Foundations for a Covenantal Worldview* (Wipf & Stock, 2006), 14–21; Kline, *Images of the Spirit* (Wipf & Stock, 1999), 39–56. Marvin A. Sweeney thinks that the genealogical framework of Genesis for the history of Israel serves the purpose of relating the covenant with Abraham and Sarah to the context of creation, and he adds that this "is crucial to establishing the eternal covenant of YHWH with creation and Abraham/Sarah in particular." *TANAK: A Theological and Critical Introduction to the Jewish Bible* (Fortress Press, 2012), 68.

36. John Owen refers to the covenantal order of creation by calling it "law of our being," "law of nature," "covenant of creation," "law of creation" or "covenant of nature," in "An Exposition of the Epistle to the Hebrews with Preliminary Exercitations," in *The Works of John Owen* (Banner of

power of his Word (see Ps 33:6–9), that Word was already in itself a covenantal call for all creatures. Ward asks, "What, according to the Bible, is in fact going on when God speaks?" and he answers that God's speaking activity results in "*his establishment of the covenant.*"[37]

Both Vanhoozer and Horton propose in a similar manner that we approach Scripture "as covenant document"[38] or "as covenant canon."[39] According to Vanhoozer,

> The canon, seen in the light of its connections to the covenant, is much more than a theological slide rule or criterion for true propositions. It has a properly soteriological purpose as well. The notion of covenant document helps us to put the canon into proper perspective, with regard to form and content alike. As to content, Scripture depicts the history of God's covenantal relations to humanity, including those communicative acts—promises, warnings, commands, consolations—that witness to what God was doing in Christ. As to form, the canon is an authoritative and binding witness to the fact, and the terms, of the covenant relationship. *The canon is thus the instrument through which the Spirit of God ministers and administers the covenant today.*[40]

The theme of the sacred bond of the covenant takes precedence over and gives meaning to other important themes in Scripture, holding together its documents, genres, and topics. In this sense, redemptive history is foremost the history of God's covenantal relation to humanity, and all other important theological topics that traverse Scripture derive their meaning from this

---

Truth, 1991), passim 18:326–408. Owen refers particularly to the human person as the image of God, explaining that a "covenant belonged to the law of creation" and that "the law of creation had a *covenant* included in it, or inseparably annexed unto it" (*The Works of John Owen*, 18:337, 406). On Owen and the covenantal nature of the life of creation, see Carl R. Trueman, *John Owen: Reformed Catholic, Renaissance Man* (Ashgate, 2007), 67–76. Other Protestant divines thought that a covenant was not inherent in but an addition to creation; see Joel R. Beeke and Mark Jones, *A Puritan Theology: Doctrine for Life* (Reformation Heritage Books, 2012), 221–24.

37. Ward, *Words of Life*, 20, 22.
38. Vanhoozer, *The Drama of Doctrine*, 115–50.
39. Horton, *The Christian Faith*, 151–85.
40. Vanhoozer, *The Drama of Doctrine*, 139.

central reality of God creating, redeeming, and consummating a covenantal relation with humanity.[41]

This covenantal structure of the Bible constitutes the scaffolding that will be used to construct a *covenantal* theology of conscience, because human history and experience are essentially covenant history and covenant experience.[42] Accordingly, this book retrieves the continuity of covenantal theology in Christian doctrine[43] in its correlation with the reality of conscience and does so with particular attention to classical Reformed theology and to developing its understanding of conscience as interwoven with the doctrines of the so-called covenant of redemption, covenant of works, and covenant of grace.[44]

---

41. Horton writes that a "biblical-theological understanding of covenant ties things together in systematic theology whose relations are often strained: ecclesiology (the context of the covenant), theology proper (the covenant maker), anthropology (the covenant partner), christology (the covenant mediator), soteriology (the covenant blessings), eschatology (the covenant consummation)," (*Covenant and Eschatology*, 17).

42. This approach allows the development of what Marc Cortez defines as a "theocentric anthropology" that recognizes "the importance that God has placed on the human person in establishing humanity as the objects of his covenantal relationality and eschatological purposes." *Theological Anthropology: A Guide for the Perplexed* (T&T Clark, 2010), 5. Jon D. Levenson writes that identifying God as the Lord of the covenant "stands guard against any effort to depersonalize God" in the theological enterprise, *Sinai and Zion: An Entry into the Jewish Bible* (HarperCollins, 1985), 53. Similarly, Webster states, "Theological talk of human nature and destiny does not refer to abstract, a-historical entities but to the identity acquired by subjects as they act and are acted upon in the reciprocit[y] of relation to God [in] the ways of God with humankind, emerging in the life and practices of covenantal fellowship." Webster, "The Human Person," in *The Cambridge Companion to Postmodern Theology*, ed. Kevin J. Vanhoozer (Cambridge University Press, 2003), 227.

43. See J. Ligon Duncan III, "The Covenant Idea in Irenaeus of Lyons: An Introduction and Survey," in *Confessing Our Hope: Essays Celebrating the Life and Ministry of Morton H. Smith*, ed. Joseph A. Pipa and C. N. Willborn (Southern Presbyterian Press, 2004), 31–55; Peter A. Lillback, *The Binding of God: Calvin's Role in the Development of Covenant Theology* (Baker Academic, 2001); R. Scott Clark, "Christ and the Covenant: Federal Theology in Orthodoxy," in *A Companion to Reformed Orthodoxy*, ed. Herman J. Selderhuis (Brill, 2013), 403–28; Andrew A. Woolsey, *Unity and Continuity in Covenantal Thought: A Study in the Reformed Tradition to the Westminster Assembly* (Reformation Heritage Books, 2012).

44. Theologians such as F. Turretin, C. Hodge, and H. Bavinck integrated the dramatic approach of covenant theology in their respective systems. See Francis Turretin, *Institutes of Elenctic Theology* (P&R Publishing, 1992, 1996), 1:569–90, 2:169–270; Charles Hodge, *Systematic Theology* (Eerdmans, 1989), 2:117–29, 354–77; Herman Bavinck, *Reformed Dogmatics* (Baker Academic, 2004, 2006), 2:564–79, 3:193–232.

CONVERSATION PARTNERS

The chief conversation partners will be theologians (past and present) sympathetic to the Reformed tradition since I will explain the phenomenon of conscience within the framework of redemptive history as articulated by classical Reformed theology. The primary ones are the late John Webster, John Calvin, Herman Bavinck, Michael Horton, and Simeon Zahl, and the way in which each of these figures has influenced the current project deserves concise mention.[45]

The present investigation of conscience could be considered a tribute to the work of the late John Webster.[46] Indeed, the catalyst for developing this theological theme came from the reading of Webster's essay, "God and Conscience," which this introduction has already referred to a number of times. It might be said that my endeavor is an attempt to put flesh on the skeleton assembled by Webster. Besides the copious references in the footnotes to Webster's many essays, it should be pointed out that in the brief but penetrating article "God and Conscience" Webster attempts to build his own, albeit brief and provisional, theology of conscience upon a Trinitarian foundation, shaping its form by a redemptive orientation and an eschatological trajectory.[47] Placing conscience within the framework delineated by Webster avoids isolating and relativizing the phenomenon of conscience, as well as keeping it anchored to an explanation of reality as the history of humanity in fellowship with God the Father, the Son, and the Holy Spirit.[48]

---

45. Attention will be devoted also to scholars outside that theological tradition and an effort will be made to take seriously the advice of Cortez, according to which "theological anthropology should be involved in constant dialogue with ... other [anthropological] disciplines," such as cultural anthropology, philosophy of mind, psychology, sociology, and neuroscience, even though it "cannot simply adopt whatever results are produced by these other anthropological disciplines," (*Theological Anthropology*, 6).

46. On Webster's theology, see Ivor J. Davidson, "Introduction," in John B. Webster, *The Culture of Theology*, ed. Ivor J. Davidson and Alden C. McCray (Baker Academic, 2019), 1-42; R. David Nelson, Darren Sarisky, and Justin Stratis, eds., *Theological Theology: Essays in Honour of John Webster* (T&T Clark, 2015); Michael Allen and R. David Nelson, eds., *A Companion to the Theology of John Webster* (Eerdmans, 2021); Jordan Senner, *John Webster: The Shape and Development of His Theology* (T&T Clark, 2022).

47. For an overview of Webster's theological anthropology, see Michael Allen, "Toward Theological Anthropology: Tracing the Anthropological Principles of John Webster," *International Journal of Systematic Theology* 19, no. 1 (2017): 6-29.

48. In this regard, this book responds to Michael Allen's observation according to which Webster's "early nod to the significance of a moral psychology recast in light of the economy of sin and redemption was never quite addressed, and we still await with bated breath the

John Calvin will be another constant point of reference. Although Calvin does not develop a systematic discourse on conscience, in his sermons, commentaries, treatises, letters, and in the *Institutes*, conscience is constantly present.⁴⁹ In particular, I will retrieve Calvin's understanding of conscience as *sensus*, primarily as a *sensus divinitatis* and derivatively as a *sensus divini iudicii*. Calvin's notion of this natural awareness of God will be compared with the intellectualist conception of conscience by Aquinas in an attempt to show that a perceptual and intuitive explanation of conscience better fits the biblical account, human experience, and soteriological participation.

Following Calvin and the Reformed tradition, Herman Bavinck devoted considerable attention to conscience throughout his career, even though his *Reformed Dogmatics* contains only a few references to it.⁵⁰ There are two particular aspects of his understanding that will be important for the present theology of conscience. The first is that for Bavinck the doctrine of creation is not the chief location in which to place the reality of conscience. In an assertion that will be pondered later, Bavinck affirms that "before the fall, strictly speaking, there was no conscience in humans."⁵¹ For Bavinck, then, a theological consideration of conscience can only begin with the doctrine of sin and, therefore, within the context of soteriology.⁵² The second—and more positively received—is that Bavinck considers conscience to be, as it were, the place in which a sinner subjectively experiences justification, and

---

delivery of such an anthropological contribution that attends to the principles of theology and does so across the full swat of divine economy" ("Reason," in *A Companion to the Theology of John Webster*, 141).

49. See Randall C. Zachman, *The Assurance of Faith: Conscience in the Theology of Martin Luther and John Calvin* (Westminster John Knox, 2005), 89-248.

50. See Herman Bavinck, "Conscience," *Bavinck Review* 6 (2015): 124-25, https://bavinck institute.org/review/tbr-6-2015/ (originally published in 1881), accessed on June 1st, 2021; Bavinck, *Reformed Ethics: Created, Fallen, and Converted Humanity* (Baker Academic, 2019), 1:165-214; Bavinck, "Foundation of Psychology," *Bavinck Review* 9 (2018), https://bavinckinstitute.org/tag/psychology/ (originally published in 1897), accessed on June 1st, 2021. Also relevant is the chapter by Bavinck on "Revelation and Religious Experience" in *The Philosophy of Revelation* (Baker Books, 1979), 203-41.

51. Bavinck, *Reformed Dogmatics*, 3:173.

52. Similarly, for Calvinist (Dutch) philosopher Hendrik G. Stoker, sin and evil are the fundamental presuppositions that explain conscience: "We do not have the right, in principle, simply to label as 'conscience' any of those moral phenomena highlighted by knowledge or mental urges as such. On the contrary, only those moral phenomena that are founded on the essential existence of (possible or real) evil have the right preeminently ... to be called conscience." *Conscience: Phenomena and Theories* (University of Notre Dame Press, 2018), 145 (see also 211-43).

he develops this theme more precisely and comprehensively. Consequently, I will devote considerable space to his treatment of these matters, (humbly) correcting Bavinck's perspective regarding conscience as an exclusively postlapsarian reality and expanding his insights about subjective justification.

Among contemporary theologians, Michael Horton stands out as he updates classical federal theology in his covenantal anthropology.[53] Even though Horton mentions conscience only occasionally, his work is important because he so resolutely places humanity within the larger reality of a covenantal ontology, such that in Scripture "we begin not with the metaphysics of being but with YHWH of the covenant."[54] Revealing himself as covenant Lord, God shows that he "wills to enter into a relationship with his creatures" and "the covenant is the context in which that becomes possible."[55] Horton insists that God's covenant lordship is universal, embracing all people as well as history and nature, for revelation is "the story of God's covenant with *creation*."[56] In relation to conscience, this covenantal context is important because it shapes an "understanding of human nature before and after the fall in terms of covenant theology."[57] Horton considers conscience—as one capacity of human beings—to be a prerequisite of covenantal personhood. Consequently, this book will interact with this covenantal anthropology by explaining the phenomenon of conscience as caught within the dynamics of the relation between God as covenant Lord and the human being as covenant servant.

Another contemporary theologian with whom I will interact significantly is Simeon Zahl. His work will become important when considering conscience and the personal and subjective experience of salvation. Besides some essays that will be referred to later, in his recent work on the Holy Spirit and Christian experience,[58] Zahl investigates religious affections and

---

53. Michael S. Horton, *Lord and Servant: A Covenantal Christology* (Westminster John Knox, 2005).

54. Horton, *Lord and Servant*, 10.

55. Horton, *Lord and Servant*, 48.

56. Horton, *Lord and Servant*, 69. Horton qualifies what he means as follows: "While the concept of covenant cannot carry the entire burden for an account of the God-world relationship, it provides a context in which both otherness and union, transcendence and immanence, can be concretely articulated," (*Lord and Servant*, 66).

57. Horton, *Lord and Servant*, 93.

58. Simeon Zahl, *The Holy Spirit and Christian Experience* (Oxford University Press, 2020).

conscious religious experiences. Even though he refers to conscience only occasionally—and usually quoting other theologians of the past—his exploration resonates both with Calvin's notion of the *sensus* and with Bavinck's understanding of conscience as the place of the subjective realization of justification. Considering the cognitive impact of the doctrines of the gospel, Zahl reflects on their "affective salience"[59] in arousing and bringing to awareness affective responses, proposing that particular theological metaphors, concepts, or doctrines are objects of consciousness capable of engendering a personal response.

CONTRIBUTIONS

The main contributions I hope to add in this book to this conversation are: an account of conscience based on the whole of Scripture; a specific analysis of conscience in the Old Testament; an investigation of conscience as a created reality; and a reorientation of conscience away from the self and toward God.

A COMPREHENSIVE ACCOUNT OF CONSCIENCE BASED ON THE WHOLE OF SCRIPTURE

The first contribution is a theology of conscience developed in a comprehensive (rather than fragmentary) way with reference to the drama of redemption balanced between the two poles of protology (creation) and eschatology (new creation). This canonical location and redemptive trajectory determine the major contribution of the book, namely the elaboration of the doctrinal theme of conscience on the basis of Scripture.

Surveying existing literature, it seems that a theological interpretation of conscience that follows the whole Bible's plot line and takes into account the variegated nature of Scripture's genres is lacking. There exist concise and fragmentary approaches to the theme common in the works of biblical

---

59. Simeon Zahl, "On the Affective Salience of Doctrines," *Modern Theology* 31.3 (2015): 428–44.

studies such as commentaries,⁶⁰ essays,⁶¹ and philological works.⁶² At the same time, there are minor and necessarily peripheral treatments in systematic theologies⁶³ and theological anthropologies,⁶⁴ as well as the narrow focus in historical investigations.⁶⁵ The specific claims of these various works will be treated at appropriate places in the chapters that follow. In contrast to these confined explorations, this work offers a comprehensive and full-orbed biblical account of human conscience.

A SPECIFIC ANALYSIS OF CONSCIENCE IN THE OLD TESTAMENT

A second and subordinate contribution of this book is that it attempts to provide a penetrating investigation of conscience in the Old Testament. Examining existing literature, the presence of conscience in the Old Testament—if noticed at all—is treated cursorily and often inaccurately.⁶⁶ The main reason for this lack of attention seems to be the fact that the Hebrew language does not have a term corresponding either to συνείδησις or *conscientia* ("conscience"). Yet the absence of a word in a language does

---

60. For example, Charles E. B. Cranfield, *A Critical and Exegetical Commentary on the Epistle to the Romans*, vols. 1-2 (T&T Clark, 1975, 1979), 1:155-63, 2:452-53, 2:667-68; Anthony C. Thiselton, *The First Epistle to the Corinthians* The New International Greek Testament Commentary (Eerdmans, 2000), 340-41, 639-44.

61. For example, Bruce F. Harris, "ΣΥΝΕΙΔΗΣΙΣ (Conscience) in the Pauline Writings," *Westminster Theological Journal* 24, no. 2 (1962): 173-86; Margaret Thrall, "The Pauline Use of Συνείδησις," *New Testament Studies* 14 (1967): 118-25.

62. For example, Philip Bosman, *Conscience in Philo and Paul* (Mohr Siebeck, 2003); Claude A. Pierce, *Conscience in the New Testament: A Study of Syneidesis in the New Testament, in the Light of Its Sources, and with Particular Reference to St. Paul, with Some Observations Regarding Its Pastoral Relevance Today* (SCM Press, 1955). For a survey of conscience in Paul, see Robert Jewett, *Paul's Anthropological Terms: A Study of Their Use in Conflict Settings* (Brill, 1971), 402-60.

63. For example, Bavinck, *Reformed Dogmatics*, 3:32, 132, 156, 170, 173, 198; 4:203, 219, 225, 248.

64. For example, Gerrit C. Berkouwer, *Man: The Image of God* (Eerdmans, 1962), 168-77. Wolfhart Pannenberg devotes more space than usual to conscience as he attempts to critically appropriate a nontheological anthropology to develop a nondogmatic anthropology that nonetheless might be relevant to theology. *Anthropology in Theological Perspective* (T&T Clark, 1985), 265-312.

65. For example, Timothy C. Potts, *Conscience in Medieval Philosophy* (Cambridge University Press, 1980); Zachman, *The Assurance of Faith*; Stephen G. Gabrill, *Rediscovering the Natural Law in Reformed Theological Ethics* (Eerdmans, 2006).

66. For example, *Christianity and the Laws of Conscience* starts with a chapter on conscience in the New Testament and mostly neglects conscience in the Old Testament, except for the chapter by David Vandrunen, "Conscience and Natural Law in Scripture," which contains a short section on conscience in the Old Testament; see Helen M. Alvaré and Jeffrey B. Hammond, eds., *Christianity and the Laws of Conscience: An Introduction* (Cambridge University Press, 2021), 42-50.

not itself prove that something is unknown or even nonexistent.⁶⁷ Indeed, something—even experiences and concepts—may exist but be called by different names or even remain nameless.⁶⁸ Although it is admitted in the literature that the Hebrew Bible does not neglect absolutely the experience of conscience, it is usually affirmed that it is within Greco-Roman culture that a clear notion of conscience was born and that, in particular, it is with Paul that the Christian notion of conscience originated because in the Gospels the word does not occur. However, from a biblical and theological perspective, this approach appears to be somewhat reductive.⁶⁹

In this regard, Vanhoozer posits the following exegetical principle: "Interpreters should strive for literacy rather than letterism. What is interesting theologically happens on the level not of the letter, nor of the word, but rather of the whole text. In other words, it is not the word/concept alone, but the word/concept as used in the context of the literary whole."⁷⁰

---

67. Philosopher Ray Jackendoff believes that thoughts and concepts remain neutral in respect to the particular language that gives them expression. A language may have words for some things while another language may lack those terms. According to Jackendoff, this is the case of Eskimo languages, which have a number of words for different types of snow while lacking a generic term to refer to snow itself. *Patterns in the Mind: Language and Human Nature* (Basic Books, 1994), 185–86. In a captivating comparison between spoken languages and sign languages, Jackendoff observed that even though in certain cases signs may partially portray that to which they refer, usually the form of the signs is not determined exclusively or even primarily by what they signify (*Patterns in the Mind*, 83–100). Similarly, while συνείδησις and *conscientia* are linguistically close in meaning to the reality they portray, in the Old Testament the meaning of conscience is not primarily conveyed by words and expressions that are strictly close to the way in which people experience it.

68. In this regard, Stoker writes, "No more than the lack of certain names for colors in Homer's writings would indicate that those colors had not yet been perceived in Homer's time does the absence of a consistent word for 'conscience' indicate that it was not experienced. It is often the case that, even in the development of language, the best-known things are precisely those that receive no special name" (*Conscience: Phenomena and Theories*, 296).

69. Webster observes that a theology of conscience "will be free from the illusion that the history of conscience can be studied lexically, by simply tracing the history of terms," ("God and Conscience," 250). Criticizing the idea of a "discovery" of the concept of conscience by Christianity, Antonia Cancrini stresses that even if scholars could ascertain that certain documents were the first in which the term conscience appeared, that would not guarantee that that was actually the first time when this phenomenon manifested itself. Cancrini interestingly observes that the notion of conscience is already present in the Greek world before the coinage of a specific term to refer to it. *Syneidesis: Il tema semantico della "con-scientia" nella Grecia antica* (Edizioni dell'Ateneo, 1970), 9–15, 38 (translation mine).

70. Kevin J. Vanhoozer, "Introduction: Hermeneutics, Text, and Biblical Theology," in *New International Dictionary of Old Testament Theology and Exegesis*, ed. Willem A. Vangemeren (Paternoster, 1996), 1:40.

Contemporary scholars—such as Barr,[71] Silva,[72] Cotterell and Turner,[73] and Carson[74]—have labored to give substance, nuance, precision and depth to this model of biblical literacy. What this means in practice here is that the exegetical and theological task resolutely refuses to jump at once to the language and conceptualities of the Greeks or of the Latin theologians of the Middle Age but rather constructs its discourse with material taken chiefly from the whole Bible. From the perspective of the confession of God as "the Father almighty, creator of heaven and earth," it would seem strange to act as if prior to Greco-Roman culture or Latin theology the Bible had nothing to say about such a fundamental human experience as conscience.[75] Therefore, a theology of conscience should be deprived of any predetermined ideas and should paint a picture with the colors of the canonical revelation of God as the triune covenant Lord: creator, redeemer, and consummator.[76]

---

71. James Barr, *The Semantics of Biblical Language* (Oxford University Press, 1961).

72. Moisés Silva, *Biblical Words and Their Meaning: An Introduction to Lexical Semantics* (Zondervan, 1983).

73. Peter Cotterell and Max Turner, *Linguistics and Biblical Interpretation* (InterVarsity, 1989).

74. Donald A. Carson, *Exegetical Fallacies* (Baker Books, 1996).

75. Historically, this jumping to Greek and Latin languages has robbed patristic and scholastic thinking on conscience of the necessary Trinitarian and redemptive framework. Oliver O'Donovan makes the following observation: "The difficulty with the patristic conscience is the absence of reflection on the relation of this inner discourse to the Paschal mystery. The application to the conscience of the death and resurrection of Christ, as in Hebrew and I Peter, drops out of sight, so that the encounter with God often seems to be removed from the trinitarian field of vision that characterizes patristic theology otherwise." Similarly, scholastic discussions on conscience "are only remotely attached to Scripture; to which we may add that they have a very narrow base in patristic tradition, too." *The Ways of Judgment* (Eerdmans, 2005), 305. Evaluating the discussion on conscience of medieval theologians, Potts writes, "The first item to be recorded is the surprising lack of attention which they pay, when we consider that they were professional theologians as well as philosophers, to biblical material on conscience," (*Conscience in Medieval Philosophy*, 61).

76. Although in his valuable work C. A. Pierce rejects the fallacy of a Stoic origin of the New Testament concept of conscience, he does claim that it was Paul that introduced it into Christianity. Giving superficial attention to the Old Testament's vocabulary and metaphorical and analogical language, according to Pierce, the Pauline understanding of conscience is not to be looked for in the technical language of philosophers but rather in the Hellenistic popular speech at the beginning of the Christian era. He claims that Paul derived the concept from his opponents in Corinth. Even though it is true that the word "conscience" did not originate in the biblical world of the Old Testament, Pierce comes to the wrong conclusion that conscience is one of the few Greek words of the New Testament that have not had imported into them a coloring from the Hebrew experience and outlook of the Old Testament (*Conscience in the New Testament*, 13-20, 54-60). Ceslas Spicq thinks the exact opposite: "In reality this evolution [of the concept of conscience], due to the Pauline genius, depends more on the moral conceptions of Israel than on the doctrines of the Philosophers. ... We can conclude that the Pauline conscience

Nevertheless, the problem of the different ways in which humans explain their experiences in their respective languages and cultures cannot be avoided and poses some intriguing questions. Is it plausible that human beings in the past did not experience or understand the phenomenon of συνείδησις or *conscientia* just because those specific words were not present in their cultures? Could it be that the belief and the *forma mentis* of people in the Old Testament coincided so much with their language that, not having a corresponding word for συνείδησις and *conscientia*, it was impossible for them to know about conscience? Is the attempt to find the reality of conscience in the Old Testament a reading back into earlier literature a late use of words and concepts from different languages and cultures? If not, is conscience a present reality in the Old Testament, even though the ways in which the prophets spoke about it do not correspond linguistically and culturally to the way in which the apostles spoke about it?[77]

This book answers the last question affirmatively, because conceiving of the significance of a certain reality (such as conscience) does not depend on the language or on the words used. While there is certainly a legitimate and useful (albeit limited) biographical and lexical approach to the term "conscience,"[78] in constructing a theology of conscience there must be reference to

---

is a mature fruit of the Israelite morality." "La conscience dans le Nouveau Testament," *Revue Biblique* 47 (1938): 55, 78-79 (translation mine). Some scholars also disagree with Pierce concerning the origin of the term "conscience" in popular speech; see Cancrini, *Syneidesis*, 56-57. These remarks show the inaccuracy of Sorabji's statement: "Until St. Paul, sharing knowledge with oneself about wrongdoing and divine law remained separate ideas" (*Moral Conscience through the Ages*, 20).

77. Carson concludes that the biblical meaning of concepts does not derive merely from the presence, shape, or the components of certain words. Meaning is not dependent upon set words. That being the case, the conceptuality of people in the Old Testament must not be so restricted by their language as to make impossible for them to conceive of conscience. Indeed, even though they use different vocabularies and conceptualities, all languages can refer to the same meaning, and for this reason, all meanings can be expressed in any language; see *Exegetical Fallacies* (Baker Books, 1996), 32, 44-45, 54, 62. Robert W. L. Moberly engages a similar linguistic problem when he deals with the apparent lack of sin language in Genesis; see *The Theology of the Book of Genesis* (Cambridge University Press, 2009), 70-87. It is noteworthy that Mark J. Boda recently wrote a 622-page book on sin in the Old Testament: *A Severe Mercy: Sin and Its Remedy in the Old Testament* (Eisenbrauns, 2009). For the "lack of" *imago Dei* language in Scripture, see Cortez, *Theological Anthropology*, 15, and for the "lack of" the specific usage of the term "providence," see David Fergusson, *The Providence of God: A Polyphonic Approach* (Cambridge University Press, 2018), 19-21.

78. As an example of the limits of an etymological approach, Stoker points out the "extraordinary fact" that both συνείδησις and *conscientia* fail to convey a reference to or an indication of the reality of "antecedent (anticipatory) conscience," (*Conscience: Phenomena and Theories*, 22).

the whole covenant canon to understand the theological meaning of this phenomenon in all its depth. And although a theological account of conscience will interact with the history of cultures and with the development of their languages and conceptualities, it will do so with a deliberate view of incorporating history and lexicology into the larger context of redemptive history.

AN EXPLORATION OF CONSCIENCE WITHIN THE CONTOURS OF THE DOCTRINE OF CREATION

A third contribution is that this theology of conscience is developed with reference to the doctrine of creation for the simple theological reason that "from [God] and through him and to him are *all things*" (Rom 11:36, emphasis added). From the perspective of the Christian confession, all things in the universe derive their origin, nature, and end from God—the one who out of the plenitude of his own Trinitarian life freely called into existence a cosmos other than himself. As noted by Webster, "All being and occurrence that is not God is to its very depths *ex nihilo*."[79] To talk about conscience beginning linguistically, culturally, or phenomenologically impoverishes theology, especially in its contemplation of God as creator of all that is. Such methods risk implying that conscience is primarily an *invention* of the Greeks and the Romans, or of Paul, instead of a *creation* of God. Approaching conscience in this way greatly weakens conscience's relation to God or even utterly disengages it from that relation.

If a theological theology has for its object "God the Holy Trinity and all other things relative to God,"[80] from the perspective of the doctrine of creation, the argument that we cannot locate conscience in Genesis 1 and 2 seems rather fallacious. Theologically, human conscience—even as experienced in different cultures and explained through different terminologies—must be grounded in the reality of God and known, elucidated, and experienced *coram Deo*. It is therefore fundamental to maintain the central place of the object of theology, namely the Triune God, and all things in relation to him.

Given that conscience is part of God's external works of creation, in some manner—as Webster claims—it "arise[s] from and correspond[s] to his inner

---

79. John B. Webster, "Love Is Also a Lover of Life: *Creatio Ex Nihilo* and Creaturely Goodness," in *God and the Works of God*, 100.

80. John B. Webster, "What Makes Theology Theological?" in *God and the Works of God*, 213.

life ... from himself God gives himself."[81] Because of this, the phenomenon of conscience can be properly understood only by looking at the one from whom it came and who gave it. "Conscience," explains Bavinck, "is not my fabrication. ... Thus it cannot be explained from within myself but points to an authority above me that has been given to me as a law of my personality. ... God himself is the last factor of the conscience. This law of the personality points back to him as the Legislator."[82] It will be considered later how and why conscience points back to God and to him as legislator; for now, it is important to see that with God as the creator and donor of conscience it is fundamental to begin not by considering conscience in itself but rather by contemplating God, as the one who made and gave conscience.

This God who created conscience is the one we know as Father, Son, and Spirit, not in the immanent perfect life of the Trinity but in the economic dimensions of creation, redemption, and consummation.[83] For this reason, a fundamental theological assumption is that conscience is properly explained first of all in light of the reality of the Father's creation and only subsequently in light of the Son's redemption and in light of the Spirit bringing to perfection the life of creation into the new creation. That is, we understand conscience theologically as we grasp first the meaning of the purpose of creation, then the nature of the salvation brought about by redemption, and finally the blessed hope of perfected holiness in consummation.[84]

A REORIENTATION OF CONSCIENCE AWAY FROM THE SELF AND TOWARD GOD

A fourth contribution of this book is that it subordinates the investigation of the phenomenon of conscience to soteriological categories. Against the backdrop of the contemporary fascination with the self, the construction of a theology of conscience on the foundation of the Trinitarian works not

---

81. John B. Webster, "Life in and of Himself," in *God and the Works of God*, 23.

82. Bavinck, "Conscience," 124–25.

83. Not in an absolute sense, because from the revelation of God in the economy we are enabled to say something of the inner life of the Triune God, reaching back from the missions, to the persons, to the relations, and lastly to the processions; see John B. Webster, "Trinity and Creation," in *God and the Works of God*, 83–98.

84. In speaking of the economy, the present work considers the *ad extra* works of creation, redemption, and consummation not as *exclusively* assigned to Father, Son, and Spirit, but given their indivisibility, they are ascribed to the divine persons only *distinctly*.

only of creation but also of redemption and consummation helps to avoid the self-absorption and spiritual narcissism that originate from the reduction of the gospel to conscience and of God to self. A theology of conscience should pull people out of themselves, causing them to look to God rather than the other way around. Thus, the present work will explain the nature of conscience as determined by the realities of the covenant, especially by God's Trinitarian life. In particular (and without attempting to give a full definition of conscience prematurely), it will be argued that—retrieving Calvin's notion of *sensus divinitatis*—conscience is to be understood in terms of a perceptual awareness that in concurrence with other human capacities always points human creatures to God.

Speaking of conscience's orientation toward God, it should be noted that in the Christian life there is always the peril of inverting the places of objective salvation and subjective assurance, making the former dependent on the latter. As noted by Luca Baschera, in spite of their initial criticism of the penitential and sacerdotal system of Roman Catholicism, "towards the end of the sixteenth century there arose among Protestants a new interest in casuistry … that responded to new needs and brought along also some changes."[85] According to Webster, one change was that the conscience became "the place of subjective certainty of salvation [through] … intense self-examination against the norms of Scriptural commandments, casuistically applied"; this in time "reinforced the individualism of conscience."[86] In light of the ever-present danger of mere moralism, keeping the gospel history central will maintain a discourse on conscience that is subordinate to God's action. It will thus be in accordance with the "classical Reformation insistence on the priority of divine acquittal," for in Christian theology, conscience, as Webster notes, "can never be the location of a serene process of self-review."[87]

---

85. Luca Baschera, "Ethics in Reformed Orthodoxy," in *A Companion to Reformed Orthodoxy*, ed. Herman J. Selderhuis (Brill, 2013), 546.

86. Webster, "God and Conscience," 256. This individualistic restriction appears, for example, in William Perkins, "A Discourse of Conscience," "The Whole Treatise of the Cases of Conscience," "A Case of Conscience, the Greatest that Ever Was," in *The Works of William Perkins*, ed. Joel R. Beeke and Derek W. H. Thomas (Reformation Heritage Books, 2019), 8:1–94, 8:95–440, 8:595–638; see also Beeke and Jones, *A Puritan Theology*, 909–45.

87. Webster, "God and Conscience," 256–57. In his uplifting *Discovering the Joy of a Clear Conscience* (P&R Publishing, 2012), Christopher Ash presents a contemporary example of this tendency; although he tries to keep the gospel central, his equation "conscience is what I know to be true" (122) has the propensity to lead us to focus our attention on how we feel about ourselves

Nonetheless, the inward and subjective dimension should not be neglected. Therefore, attention will be devoted to the inner self as well: conscience will be considered not as a faculty or organ that works in isolation, as if human capacities and powers could be dissected and analyzed independently from one another, but in its interaction and concurrence with other human competencies.[88] In particular, in the section treating the soteriological implications for the conscience, the subjective, self-conscious, and experiential aspects of conscience will be explored to show how the self is made a partaker of salvation.

OUTLINE

This book will follow the classic Reformed understanding of the progression of redemptive history and of human nature in its fourfold state.[89] I will consider in the first section *created conscience*. Chapters 1 to 3 will be respectively concerned with the manifestation, function, and nature of conscience. In attempting to offer a comprehensive account of conscience in the whole of Scripture, concentrating specifically on the way in which the Old Testament speaks of conscience, in these first three chapters I endeavor to prove that conscience should be first understood in the light of the doctrine of creation and in prelapsarian terms. The goal is not just to show that the Scriptures do indeed speak of the reality of conscience according to the Hebrew idiom and its specific mode of expressions; it is to show that the theological implications for locating conscience in the context of the doctrine of creation are important for realizing that created conscience is fundamental in originating, mediating, and developing the covenantal communion between God and human beings. Moreover, and most importantly, being a constitutive part—along with other human capacities—of the *imago Dei*, conscience reflects something of the inner Trinitarian life of God himself, for from himself God

---

rather than on what God has declared about us in the gospel. On the problem of the individualism of conscience, see the exegetical and theological comments by Thiselton on 1 Corinthians 4:3–5, (*The First Epistle to the Corinthians*, 438–44).

88. As previously noted, by attempting to address the need "to expound a moral psychology" in an exegetical and theological analysis of conscience within the context of the economy of God's grace, it allows us to further develop the theological anthropology sketched by Webster (Allen, "Reason," in *A Companion to the Theology of John Webster*, 145).

89. On the ordering of biblical anthropological topics within the context of the progress of redemptive history, see, for example, the classical work of Thomas Boston, *Human Nature in Its Fourfold State* (Banner of Truth, 1964).

gives himself. This is fundamental in order to understand that what explains most deeply the nature of conscience is not the reality of the fall and of human sins but the essence of the God of the covenant.

In the second section, chapters 4 and 5, we will consider *fallen conscience*, exploring the fall, condemnation, and corruption of conscience. These chapters consider conscience in the context of a larger discussion on the whole human person, with all her properties, to be holistically understood as the *imago Dei* (rejecting a strictly "structural" understanding of the *imago*). Offering a specific definition of conscience as it operates in concurrence with other human capacities, I draw on Calvin's notion of *sensus divinitatis*, which defines conscience primarily as a nonphysical perceptual awareness that is reciprocal in its functions—that is, as a basic awareness of God that is capable of perceiving his covenantal presence and vocation and only derivatively capable of moral perception and reflection. In its final part, this second section will investigate how that basic personal and covenantal awareness has been corrupted from its original integrity, losing its innocence and its capacity for true self-knowledge and accurate self-scrutiny.

The third section will cover *redeemed conscience* and will devote attention to the spiritual renewal of conscience and its participation in the dawn of the life of new creation. As Christian conscience struggles in the time of the already-and-not-yet, it awaits the world to come in which it will be brought to perfection by God himself. Chapters 6 to 9 will examine the experiential reversal of the noetic effect of sin upon conscience, considering such reversal in affective and evaluative terms, showing that it results in a renewal of conscience's capacity for spiritual sensibility. This renewed sensibility is worked out by the Spirit and experienced in the regeneration and the subjective justification of conscience. At this juncture, the rather subtle distinction between objective and subjective justification will be dealt with. In general, it will be argued that active or objective justification refers to the *extra nos* dimension of justification—that is, to justification as related to the *forum divinum* and to the objective work of Christ and its objective effects. On the other hand, passive or subjective justification refers to what happens *in foro conscientiae*—that is, the personal realization of the gift of Christ's imputed righteousness *in nobis*. Going back to what was said earlier on about the manifestation of conscience, in the final part of this third main section, I show how a covenantal and Trinitarian conception of conscience has profound pastoral implications and applications in that in sanctification conscience experiences three progressive reversals: the soothing of guilt, the appeasing of shame, and the calming of fear, resulting in the abandonment of hiding.

The fourth and final section will contemplate *perfected conscience* at the time of consummation at the eschaton, and chapter 10 will explore the perfection of conscience in terms of heightened awareness. After an explanation of the notion of "heightened awareness," according to the classical concept of *visio Dei*—that is, in terms of an expanded and clear new perception of God—the perfecting of human conscience will be compared to the perfection of Christ's human and covenantal God-consciousness. This in turn will flow into a consideration of how the ectypal experience of perfected human conscience will become an expression of the archetypal Trinitarian mutual awareness and reciprocity.

Part 1

CREATED CONSCIENCE

Speaking of "created" conscience is exegetically and theologically challenging. The difficulty is that only Genesis 1 and 2 describe a prelapsarian context and the rest of the exegetical material belongs on this side of the fall. So the question arises: how is it possible to speak of conscience in light of the doctrine of *creatio ex nihilo* when both Old and New Testaments apparently say nothing about its creation and refer to it only in regard to the doctrines of sin and salvation? Some prominent theologians even assert that before the fall there was no conscience. It is certainly true that conscience—as we experience it now east of Eden—manifests itself clearly in the context of the miseries of the fall; however, it remains the case that conscience is *essential* to being human. By contrast, some theologians speak as if conscience were not intrinsic to human creatureliness. For example, Bavinck writes:

> Immediately after the fall ... human conscience was aroused. *Before the fall, strictly speaking, there was no conscience in humans.* There was no gap between what they were and what they knew they had to be. Being and self-consciousness were in harmony. But the fall produced separation. ... Human conscience is the subjective proof of humanity's fall.[1]

Likewise, Bonhoeffer writes, "Before the fall there was no conscience."[2] These assertions seem to imply that conscience was not bestowed on humanity at creation. However, other theologians think otherwise. For example,

---

1. Bavinck, *Reformed Dogmatics*, 3:173 (emphasis added). In his theological ethics, Bavinck similarly considers conscience in his reflections on *sinful* humanity: "[The] presence of a conscience requires sin as its basis," (*Reformed Ethics*, 1:205).

2. Dietrich Bonhoeffer, *Creation and Fall: A Theological Interpretation of Genesis 1–3* (Macmillan, 1966), 81.

Webster insists that in "speaking of conscience by speaking of God, Christian moral theology will emphasize (1) that conscience is a *created* reality,"³ and Edward A. Dowey Jr. affirms that "conscience is an element of the subjective revelation of God, the Creator, *given in the created order itself*, not in Scripture. It is a universal endowment, part of man as man."⁴

It appears somewhat unnecessary to affirm that conscience was not part of God's creation *ex nihilo*, and it seems more plausible that before the fall conscience was already operating, albeit only in a positive mode. Drawing on the classical distinction, conscience can very well be conceived at work both as *conscientia antecedens* (prospective) and *consequens* (retrospective)⁵ even prior to the fall, if *only* in relation to what was pleasing in God's sight and thus independently of personal sin and evil. In other words, before the fall conscience could be *only* a good conscience as it did not *yet* have any relation to sin and guilt. That is a different thing than asserting in absolute terms that before the fall there was no conscience.

According to the Christian confession, God created *ex nihilo* all things (visible and invisible), imparting to them the properties, capacities, and dispositions they needed to be what they were created to be. As Horton observes, in the creation account "we encounter two distinct types of divine declarations: the fiats of *ex nihilo* creation ... and God's command to creation to put forth its own powers with which he has endowed it and within which the Spirit is operative. ... We may put these two types of speech acts in the form of 'Let there be ...' and 'Let it become what I have worded it to be.'"⁶ Having been created to act freely according to their own aptitudes, human creatures have

---

3. Webster, "God and Conscience," 251.

4. Edward A. Dowey Jr., *The Knowledge of God in Calvin's Theology* (Eerdmans, 1994), 56 (emphasis added).

5. Generally speaking, the *conscientia antecedens* refers to a normative judgment in relation to the righteousness of an action before or in concomitance to its enactment, while the *conscientia consequens* is a normative judgment of approval or condemnation subsequent to an action performed; see Rudolf Hofmann, "Conscience," in *Sacramentum Mundi: An Encyclopedia of Theology* (Herder and Herder, 1968), 1:411–14.

6. Horton, *The Christian Faith*, 345. Similarly, Owen refers to the second kind of divine declaration as follows: "Every creature of God hath in its creation *a law of operation* implanted in it, which is the rule of all that proceedeth from it, of all that it doth of its own accord." "The Nature, Power, Deceit, and Prevalence of the Remainders of Indwelling Sin in Believers," in *The Works of John Owen* (Banner of Truth, 1966), 6:303–4.

had the capacity to perceive and understand things religiously and morally from the beginning, drawing on their faculty of conscience.

After the fall, conscience certainly manifested itself but not as a new disposition that did not previously exist. While conscience was active before the fall as a positive witness to harmony in relation to God, after the fall, it began to function in the contrary as a negative testimony to disharmony in relation to God, manifesting itself as a negative awareness.[7] And indeed, the Bible speaks often of conscience in the light of sin and salvation. Despite the fact that Scripture apparently says very little—if anything at all—about conscience in light of creation, it should not be forgotten that as God gave to the soil the power to bring forth by itself vegetation through a natural process, so he gave to humanity the ability to bring forth by itself religious and moral awareness as needed through conscience. I, therefore, propose that conscience was also created *ex nihilo* and has been present in Scripture—and humanity—since the very beginning.

In this first part of the book, starting with God as the creator, conscience will be considered especially in the Old Testament (though the New Testament will be referred to from time to time) and the material will be divided into three chapters: the first is about the *manifestation* of conscience and will attend to the reality of conscience in general; the second investigates how conscience's manifestations are indicative of its *function* in creation; and the last will consider how the way in which conscience functions according to specific modalities in creation raises questions about its *nature*. It should be noted that there will be a progression: the chapter on the manifestation of conscience, which shows that conscience is a reality, collects the exegetical raw material that allows for a conceptual movement in the following

---

7. In his theological ethics, Bavinck states that the "consciousness of having to do something or of having done something was naturally present in Adam before the fall, just as the *syntērēsis* was," (*Reformed Ethics*, 1:199). This assertion shows that fundamentally Bavinck embraces a Thomistic understanding of conscience. This matter will be treated in greater detail later. For the present, it is interesting to note that this distinction between *syntērēsis* and consequent personal consciousness allows Bavinck to affirm that while "*syntērēsis* was certainly present in Adam," conscience is "first negative, a consciousness of having done wrong," (*Reformed Ethics*, 1:205). Although Bavinck thinks that Adam's consciousness of having acted morally cannot be called conscience before the fall, he instinctively feels that he cannot utterly sever conscience from the doctrine of creation and in a rather condescending manner he observes the following: "Nevertheless, we may state it somewhat popularly that Adam ... had a conscience," (*Reformed Ethics*, 1:206).

chapter on its function, in order to understand how conscience works; then the degree of conceptualization and systematization will increase when the analysis of conscience explores why conscience functions as it does. At that point, the previous findings on the manifestation and function of conscience will be grounded in the larger fields of theological anthropology and especially theology proper in an attempt to show that the nature of conscience is ultimately determined by who God is.

1

THE MANIFESTATION OF CONSCIENCE

A fundamental exegetical question has already been raised above: how and when does Scripture—particularly the Old Testament—show the presence of conscience? We must address this question before we can explore the topic of this section, the *created* nature of conscience. The function and nature of *created* conscience will be taken up in the two chapters that follow. The present exegetical survey will proceed in two parts. It will consider, first, the variety of linguistic expressions employed by the Old Testament to speak of the experience of conscience—specifically, the heart, the kidneys, the hands, and the feeling of guilt. Then it will explore the way in which the Old Testament refers to the conscience not only explicitly by employing specific words, idioms, and metaphors but implicitly by describing the ways in which it is subjectively experienced in guilt, shame, fear, and in the desire to hide.

THE HEART MANIFESTING CONSCIENCE

Since language expresses our knowledge of reality, it seems best to begin by considering the words, idioms, and metaphors in the Old Testament that refer to what has been described later in history by the nouns συνείδησις[1] and *conscientia*. In general, there is a consensus among scholars that in the Old Testament the terms "heart" (לֵב) and "kidneys" (כְּלָיוֹת) at times refer specifically to conscience.

---

[1]. It is debated whether to translate the term as "conscience," "consciousness," or "self-awareness"; see Thiselton, *The First Epistle to the Corinthians*, 640-44. On the nuances of the meanings of συνείδησις, see C. S. Lewis, *Studies in Words* (Cambridge University Press, 1960), 181-213; Cancrini, *Syneidesis*; Wendell Willis, "Conscience in the New Testament," in Alvaré and Hammond, *Christianity and the Laws of Conscience*, 26-37.

Starting with לֵב, the Old Testament employs the metaphor of the "heart" as a wider reference to the inner person as a whole, the self.² As Aubrey Johnson observes, the heart is that which "approximates to what we should call 'mind' or 'intellect' [and] is frequently employed by metonymy to denote one's thought."³ As will be explored later, in discussing the relation between conscience and other human capacities, since reason and conscience assist each other, in Scripture the term "heart" is applied to both. That is why it might be said that the heart is the seat of conscience, even though it remains distinct from thinking. Indeed, the heart manifests the inmost thoughts of human beings, their deepest wishes, their most intimate feelings, their self-consciousness as well as their self-awareness in relation to God.⁴

Even though the Old Testament has no word for "conscience," nonetheless, "the phenomenon [of conscience] is seen as one of the many promptings of the human heart"⁵ and is related to one's religious and moral self-consciousness. Alex Luc argues that in the Old Testament לֵב is to be translated "in some instances 'chest' and 'conscience.' "⁶ According to Hans Walter Wolff, "The heart is always recognized as being an inaccessible, hidden organ inside the body," therefore "numerous sayings about man presuppose this view, which takes its starting point from the anatomical position of the heart," and at times the term "comes to take on the meaning of 'conscience.' "⁷

One of the most explicit texts that shows conscience at work in the Old Testament is 1 Samuel 24:4-5: "David arose and stealthily cut off a corner of Saul's robe. And afterward David's heart struck him, because he had cut

---

2. See John Goldingay, *Israel's Faith*, vol.2 of *Old Testament Theology* (InterVarsity Press, 2006), 555.

3. Aubrey R. Johnson, *The Vitality of the Individual in the Thought of Ancient Israel* (University of Wales Press, 1964), 77. It should be noted that the language of the Old Testament explains "the vitality of the individual" starting not from a scientific description, or from linguistic usage, but from daily experience.

4. According to Peter Cotterell, words do not have a single basic meaning but always have a range of meanings since they are "more or less effective symbols attached to referents, and each such attachment is in some sense a unique use of the word and the common or basic meaning or theme of words must not be allowed to conceal the possibility of some quite unpredictable departure from it." "Part IV: Semantics, Interpretation, and Theology," in *New International Dictionary of Old Testament Theology and Exegesis*, 1:149.

5. Jonathan Gorsky, "Conscience in Jewish Tradition," in Hoose, *Conscience in World Religions*, 130.

6. Alex Luc, "לֵב," in *New International Dictionary of Old Testament Theology and Exegesis*, 2:749.

7. Hans Walter Wolff, *Anthropology of the Old Testament* (SCM Press, 1973), 42-43, 51.

off a corner of Saul's robe."[8] A similar manifestation of conscience occurs when David orders the numbering of the people of Israel: "But David's heart struck him after he had numbered the people. And David said to the LORD, 'I have sinned greatly in what I have done. But now, O LORD, please take away the iniquity of your servant, for I have done very foolishly' " (2 Sam 24:10).[9] Commenting on these two passages, Wolff states, "The reason given for the 'beating' of the heart in the respective contexts shows that the writer does not mean the beating of the heart, either in the psychological sense, or in the sense of excited emotions; what is being described is the reaction of the ethical judgement formed by the conscience."[10]

It is not surprising that in the book of Psalms—memorably described as "an anatomy of all the parts of the soul" by Calvin[11]—we find regular usage of the metaphor of the heart, which at times refers specifically to conscience.

In Psalm 4:4 people are exhorted as follows: "Ponder in your own hearts on your beds, and be silent." Robert Alter explains: "The auditors of the poem are exhorted to tremble as an act of conscience that will dissuade them from acts of transgression, then commune with themselves in the solitude of their beds and speak no more."[12] Another instance, Psalm 17:3, offers the following confession: "You have tried my heart, you have visited me by night, you have tested me, and you will find nothing; I have purposed that my mouth will not transgress." Calvin writes:

> It is, therefore, as if David had said, O Lord, since the darkness of the night discovers the conscience more fully, all covering being then taken away, and since, at that season, the affections, either good or

---

8. The NIV translates 1 Samuel 24:6 as "David was conscience-stricken," while the NJPS translation reads, "David reproached himself." In his translation, Robert Alter offers: "David was smitten with remorse," emphasizing the religious and moral expression of David's heart. *Ancient Israel—The Former Prophets: Joshua, Judges, Samuel, and Kings—A Translation with Commentary* (W. W. Norton, 2013), 381.

9. The NIV translates 2 Samuel 24:10 as "David was conscience-stricken after he had counted the fighting men," and the NJPS translates: "David reproached himself." Alter's translation is: "David was smitten with remorse," highlighting David's "cogent sense of moral agency and moral responsibility," (*Ancient Israel*, 583).

10. Wolff, *Anthropology of the Old Testament*, 51; see also David G. Firth, *1 and 2 Samuel*, Apollos Old Testament Commentary (Apollos, 2009), 544–45.

11. John Calvin, "The Author's Preface," in *Commentary on the Book of Psalms* vol. 4 in *Calvin's Commentaries* (Baker Books, 1996), xxxvii.

12. Robert Alter, *The Book of Psalms: A Translation with Commentary* (W. W. Norton, 2007), 10.

bad, according to men's inclinations, manifest themselves more freely, when there is no person present to witness and pronounce judgment upon them; if thou then examines me, there will be found neither disguise nor deceit in my heart.[13]

In Psalm 51—one of the so-called penitential psalms—the supplicant opens himself up to God. He asks to be washed and purified, and he confesses, "I recognize my transgressions and am ever conscious of my sin" (Ps 51:3 NJPS). The resultant sense of need for inward purification brings the supplicant to petition: "Create in me a clean heart, O God, and renew a right spirit within me" (Ps 51:10). Wolff clarifies: "In Ps. 51:10 the guilty man joins his plea for a pure heart with the request for the new creation of a pure conscience, meaning that his life should take its bearings from the conscience. The prayer that follows for a 'steadfast spirit' adds the wish for the enduring power to implement to a corresponding degree what the conscience has perceived."[14] This supplication is further elucidated by the concepts of brokenness and contrition: "The sacrifices of God are a broken spirit; a broken and contrite heart, O God, you will not despise" (Ps 51:17). According to Alter, "Here there is an arresting new emphasis on an inward condition of contrition," namely "a person's remorse over past actions."[15] Both the broken spirit and the contrite heart indicate the presence of religious and moral self-awareness. Even though at times the qualities of the heart may be religiously or ethically neutral, it might be plausibly said that in Psalms the metaphor of the heart (and of the human spirit, even though less frequently[16]) is at other times an implied similitude referring to the workings of conscience, such as when the psalmists speak of a "pure heart" (Ps 24:4), the "upright in heart" (Ps 11:2), a heart that is "blameless" (Ps 119:80), or "steadfast" (Ps 57:7).

On other occasions the metaphor of the heart becomes a manifestation of a lack of conscience, such as when the fool expresses a religious and moral judgment in his heart, saying, "There is no God" (Ps 14:1). Alter comments, "The thrust of this line ... is not a philosophical question of God's existence

---

13. Calvin, *Commentary on the Book of Psalms*, 4:238.
14. Wolff, *Anthropology of the Old Testament*, 52.
15. Alter, *The Book of Psalms*, 183.
16. The human spirit as manifesting conscience might also be found in the phrase having "no deceit" (Ps 32:2).

but the scoundrel's lack of conscience, his feeling that he can act with impunity, because he thinks he need not fear divine retribution."[17] Moreover, the heart can be "like fat" (Ps 119:70) and people can "harden" their hearts (Ps 95:8; see also Exod 7:3; Prov 28:14).[18]

A couple of examples from wisdom literature may evidence further the relation between heart and conscience. Job—the non-Israelite from Uz in the East—was a God-fearing person who confessed, "I hold fast my righteousness and will not let it go; my heart does not reproach me for any of my days" (Job 27:6). The situation in which Job's heart expresses itself is that of a reflection on ethical righteousness and, according to Delitzsch, "Heart is used here as the seat of conscience, which is the knowledge possessed by the heart, by which it excuses or accuses a man."[19] In the book of Ecclesiastes, the heart is synonymous with the self and refers to the thinking and discerning activity of the self. The preacher, Qohelet, constantly ruminates on wisdom and folly, speaking about them in or with his own heart (Eccl 1:17). In his search, as Qohelet ponders what takes place under the sun "in its time" (Eccl 3:1–8, 11), he is torn by the difficulty of the task since the human being is not able to discern God's works from the beginning to the end (Eccl 3:11). However, as he closes his meditation about the problem of justice and injustice (Eccl 3:16), he comes to a sure conclusion: "I said in my heart, God will judge the righteous and the wicked, for there is a time for every matter and for every work" (Eccl 3:17). The heart therefore bears witness to individuals that there will be a time for the righteous judgment of God (Eccl 3:1). Thus, Qohelet recognizes the awareness of the heart in relation to God and his justice, and

---

17. Alter, *The Book of Psalms*, 40. There is a relation in Hebrew between the verbal root meaning "to wither" and the name "scoundrel" or "fool," in the sense that the fool is one in whom the vitality of a religious and moral conscience has withered and decayed so that he becomes literally "un-conscious," namely without conscience.

18. Even though the "lacking" heart in Proverbs is usually associated with the mind or the head, to indicate someone who lacks sense, it may alternatively be referred to as conscience, especially when it is associated with some form of religious and moral evaluation (see Prov 6:32; 11:12; 12:11; 15:21; 24:30).

19. Franz Delitzsch, "Biblical Commentary to the Book of Job," in *Commentary on the Old Testament* (Eerdmans, 1986), vol. 4, 2:68. In his commentary on Job, Marvin H. Pope translates לֵב as "conscience," *Job*, The Anchor Bible (Doubleday, 1965), 187, 190. Noticing the similarity with the language of the LXX—which employs the verb σύνοιδα preceded by the reflexive pronoun ἐμαυτῷ Gerd Theissen suggests in a footnote that Paul might have been thinking of this passage when he wrote, "My conscience is clear" (1 Cor 4:4 NIV); see *Psychological Aspects of Pauline Theology* (T&T Clark, 1987), 61.

although he is not explicitly thinking in terms of moral self-awareness, he is doing so implicitly because he subsumes all things under the authority of God's justice—not only other people but also himself.[20]

THE KIDNEYS MANIFESTING CONSCIENCE

Another important term that indicates the presence of conscience in the Old Testament is כְּלָיוֹת, or "kidneys." Robert Chisholm writes, "Several passages view the kidneys as the seat of one's moral character. As the Creator of this moral/ethical center (Ps 139:13), God examines it to discover one's true attitudes and motives and to determine one's appropriate reward or punishment."[21] Wolff similarly argues that "next to the heart, the kidneys are the most important internal organ in the Old Testament [and] are the one organ referred to particularly in Ps. 139 as being created by God (v. 13)"; moreover, when the term refers to human beings "more frequently the kidneys are the seat of conscience."[22] It must be noted that both scholars highlight that God is the creator of conscience. Even though some understand כְּלָיוֹת in Psalm 139:13 as a synecdoche just for the inner organs of the body,[23] the term can be taken to point to the whole of the human person, including all her inner and spiritual dispositions. As creator, God's knowledge is so exhaustive and all-embracing that if he knows perfectly the mysteries of the body, he surely knows perfectly the mysteries of the kidneys, or in other words, the conscience.[24]

Since God is the creator, he is the one who searches the hearts and kidneys of people (cf. Pss 7:9; 26:2; Rev 2:23). Commenting on Psalm 26:2, Calvin affirms:

> The distinction which some make here, that *the heart* signifies the higher affections, and *the reins* [kidneys] those that are sensual (as they term them) and more gross, is more subtle than solid. We know that the Hebrews understood by the term *reins* [kidneys] that which

---

20. It is particularly important to note that Ecclesiastes indicates that the heart works in a dialogical manner. This observation will be expanded later in discussing conscience interacting with other human capacities and especially with language.

21. Robert B. Chisholm, "כִּלְיָה," in *New International Dictionary of Old Testament Theology and Exegesis*, 2:656.

22. Wolff, *Anthropology of the Old Testament*, 65.

23. See John Goldingay, *Psalms*, vol. 3, *Psalms 90–150* (Baker Academic, 2008), 633.

24. That seems to be the understanding behind the NJPS translation: "It was You who created my conscience."

is most secret in men. David, therefore, conscious of his innocence, offers the whole man to the examination of God.[25]

Besides manifesting this consciousness of one's own innocence, the kidneys also give expression to a sense of admonishment: "My conscience [כִּלְיוֹת] admonishes me at night" (Ps 16:7 NJPS). We encounter again כִּלְיוֹת with reference to the conscience in Psalm 73:21-22: "When my heart was embittered, and my conscience stabbed with pain, I was a dolt and knew nothing, like cattle I was with You."[26] Asaph here confesses his sinful envy, anger, bitterness, and especially unbelief, recognizing that because he made room for such attitudes he felt afflicted all day long.[27]

THE HANDS/PALMS MANIFESTING CONSCIENCE

Another part of the body indicating the activity of conscience in the Old Testament is the hand (יָד), or the palm (כַּף). Even though these terms are used more often in relation to activities and to the exercise of strength, power, and dominion, they also refer to inward attitudes and dispositions, such as aggressiveness (Num 20:9-11), boldness (Exod 14:8), deliberation (Num 15:30), hopelessness (Isa 13:7), resoluteness (1 Sam 23:16), loyalty (Gen 14:22), and generosity (Ps 16:11).[28] What is relevant here is that, as noted by Johnson, the hands/palms are "occasionally ... subject to a moral judgement and so may be referred to in ethical terms," and in such cases, it "is idiomatic as a means of denoting one's state of innocence or one's positive righteousness."[29] Thus,

---

25. Calvin, *Calvin's Commentaries*, 4:439.
26. Alter, *The Book of Psalms*, 255.
27. See John Goldingay, *Psalms*, vol. 2, *Psalms 42–89* (Baker Academic, 2007), 412. The prophet Jeremiah adopts the language of Psalms to give expression to the inner and more emotional aspect of the work of conscience (Jer 11:20; 12:2; 17:10; 20:12). In a theologically dense and humbling description of the depth of human corruption, Jeremiah affirms on the one hand the incapability of human beings to fathom the depth of their own sinful condition and on the other hand—like David in Psalms 139—the infallibility of God's knowledge of their inner state (Jer 17:9-10). The workings of heart and kidneys show the presence of a conscience that answers God's searching of the heart and testing the kidneys. According to the prophet, God's *action* in searching the heart and testing the kidneys *activates* personal conscience.
28. See Johnson, *The Vitality of the Individual*, 50-58.
29. Johnson, *The Vitality of the Individual*, 62, 63.

when some sort of religious or moral evaluation is expressed concerning the hands/palms, it presupposes the activity of conscience.[30]

When God came to the pagan king Abimelech, for example, imposing the death sentence upon him because he had taken Abraham's wife (see Gen 20:3), Abimelech justifies himself, saying, "In the integrity of my heart and the innocence of my hands I have done this" (Gen 20:5; cf. Pss 24:4; 73:13). It is important to observe here the presence of both "heart" and "hands" along with the corresponding dual evaluative movement: first, the inward dimension of the heart is examined, and second, the outward conduct of the hands is tested. Abimelech's conscience, operative in a consequent mode, declared a verdict of innocence.

Meanwhile Job, in his piercing and excruciating self-evaluation, tries to descend as far as he can into the inner recesses of his own conscience. In the context of a legal disputation in chapter 9 (see Job 9:3a), finding himself summoned before the court of divine justice, Job desperately examines himself. He is open to his friends' "wisdom" as he agonizingly attempts to justify himself before God while they make him feel guilty (see Job 8:3-6). Submitting himself to a conscientious and thorough scrutiny of heart and conduct, Job recognizes the disparity and the gap between human justice and God's demands: "How can a man be in the right before God?" (Job 9:2). He apparently agrees with the common understanding of God's righteous retributive justice. However, Job feels himself to be innocent (see Job 9:20-21), and confused about this common understanding of God's justice, he comes to the following conclusion: "It is all one; therefore I say, 'He destroys both the blameless and the wicked'" (Job 9:22). In the end, stressing the uselessness of testing his conscience, he employs the metaphor of clean palms, implying that their status corresponds to the status of his whole being: "If I wash myself with snow and cleanse my hands with lye, yet you will plunge me into a pit" (Job 9:30-31a). Once more, the metaphor of the hands/palms becomes the vehicle that brings the reader to a natural and instinctive recognition of the spontaneous religious and moral evaluations deriving from the hidden activities of conscience.[31]

---

30. In the New Testament, Pilate washing his hands is an emblematic act involving conscience (see Matt 27:24).

31. The same thorough scrutiny of conscience and conduct reappears in chapter 31, where Job compares his inward attitude to that of Adam: "Have I covered my transgressions like Adam,

THE FEELING OF GUILT
MANIFESTING CONSCIENCE

Having considered some of the more explicit terminology pointing to the presence and reality of conscience, the difficult but intriguing usage of the verb אָשֵׁם or אָשַׁם [32] must now be given attention, as there is scholarly debate about the meaning of אָשֵׁם and its possible relation to conscience. Jay Sklar writes:

> The translations that have been proposed for אָשֵׁם within the priestly literature fall into four categories: (1) "to be/become guilty," "to incur guilt," "to be/become liable for guilt"; (2) "to feel guilty"; (3) "to realize guilt"; and (4) "to suffer guilt's consequences."[33]

The difference depends on whether the verb is understood as referring to objective guilt, as in the case of (1), or as indicating some sort of subjective experience as a consequence of guilt, as in the case of (2), (3), and (4). A number of scholars have noticed that the traditional objective meaning is problematic at least in Leviticus 4:13-14, 22-23, 27-28, and 6:2-5. Therefore, they have felt compelled to find a different, subjective understanding of the verb.[34]

These Leviticus passages consider the case of someone who sins unintentionally, such as the whole community, or the leaders, or the common people:

> Now if the whole congregation of Israel commits error and the matter escapes the notice of the assembly, and they commit any of the things which the LORD has commanded not to be done, and they become guilty [אָשֵׁם]; when the sin which they have committed becomes known [יָדַע], then the assembly shall offer a bull of the herd for a sin offering and bring it before the tent of meeting. (Lev 4:13-14 NASB)

---

by hiding my iniquity in my bosom?" (Job 31:33 NASB). The statements, questions, and "ifs" in this chapter constitute Job's final protestation of innocence and are a reflection of the testing of his conscience and thoughts. Here, Job once again refers to the image of his palms to which no blemish clings (Job 31:7; cf. Deut 21:5-6; 1 Sam 12:5; 24:11; 2 Sam 22:21; Pss 7:3, 8-9; 18:20, 24; 24:4; 26:2; 73:13; Isa 1:15; 59:3, 6; Ezek 18:8; Mic 7:3).

32. In the Hebrew Bible, the most common form of the verb is אָשֵׁם, even though אָשַׁם is also found. Conventionally, scholars usually refer to the verb in קַל פָּעַל.

33. Jay Sklar, *Sin, Impurity, Sacrifice, Atonement: The Priestly Conceptions* (Sheffield Phoenix, 2015), 25.

34. Nobuyoshi Kiuchi, *The Purification Offering* (Sheffield Academic, 1987), 31-34; Jacob Milgrom, *Leviticus 1-16*, Anchor Yale Bible Commentaries (Yale University Press, 1991), 339-45; Sklar, *Sin, Impurity, Sacrifice, Atonement*, 24-43; Boda, *A Severe Mercy*, 62-64.

When a leader sins and unintentionally does any one of all the things which the LORD his God has commanded not to be done, and he becomes guilty [אָשֵׁם], or [אוֹ] his sin which he has committed is made known [יָדַע] to him, he shall bring for his offering a goat, a male without defect. (Lev 4:22-23 NASB, modified)

Now if anyone of the common people sins unintentionally in doing any of the things which the LORD has commanded not to be done, and becomes guilty [אָשֵׁם], or [אוֹ] his sin which he has committed is made known [יָדַע] to him, then he shall bring for his offering a goat, a female without defect, for his sin which he has committed. (Lev 4:27-28 NASB modified)

Contrary to the impression that may be given by the above translations, these verses do not indicate an objective condition of guilt; they explain what must be done when the community, a chieftain, or an ordinary person passes from a lack of awareness to a state of consciousness in relation to sin.[35] As Sklar observes, "This of course leads to the question: How can an offering be brought for a sin that is hidden from—or otherwise unknown to—the sinner?"[36]

The movement from unawareness to subjective consciousness of sin is especially clear in Leviticus 4:22-23 and 27-28, where it may occur according to two different modalities. The use of the conjunction אוֹ—translated above "or"—shows that a chieftain or a person who sins may become aware of guilt through one of two distinct occurrences, namely אָשֵׁם or יָדַע. The second modality is easier to understand: יָדַע is the subjective "knowing" rendered to the sinner by someone else in the community. Boda writes: "The use of ידע reveals that, although each member of the community needed to be vigilant in recognizing guilt, there was a role for the broader community to play in the

---

35. Leviticus 4:3 deals with the sins of the anointed priests, but nothing is said about their becoming aware of guilt. Milgrom observes, "The text does not even state that his error was committed inadvertently!" This raises a question about whether the verbs אָשֵׁם and יָדַע, which appear in 4:13-14, 22-23, and 27-28, are missing here. Milgrom's conclusion is that "there is no choice but to infer that these things [אָשֵׁם and יָדַע] are taken for granted" (*Leviticus 1-16*, 232).

36. Sklar, *Sin, Impurity, Sacrifice, Atonement*, 24.

identification of sin."[37] What remains to be elucidated is whether אָשֵׁם is to be understood as feeling guilty, realizing guilt, or suffering guilt's consequences.

Before addressing this matter, there is yet to be considered the case of someone sinning intentionally. Leviticus 6:2–5 speaks of a person who deceives his neighbor, steals from him, oppresses him or lies to him:

> When a person sins and acts unfaithfully against the LORD, and deceives his companion in regard to a deposit or a security entrusted *to him*, or through robbery, or *if* he has extorted from his companion, or has found what was lost and lied about it and sworn falsely, so that he sins in regard to any one of the things a man may do; then it shall be, when he sins and becomes guilty [אָשֵׁם], that he shall restore what he took by robbery or what he got by extortion, or the deposit which was entrusted to him or the lost thing which he found, or anything about which he swore falsely; he shall make restitution for it in full and add to it one-fifth more. He shall give it to the one to whom it belongs on the day *he presents* his guilt offering. (Lev 6:2–5 NASB)

Since it is obvious that this is an objective guilt, what is being said is not that the sinner is or becomes guilty. This person knows his guilt because he acts in a deliberate manner (cf. Num 5:6–7). The problem thus surfaces again: what sort of subjective experience is being described with אָשֵׁם? Sklar writes, "What then prompts the sinner to return what was stolen and to bring the guilt offering? It cannot simply be their guilt, as the translation suggests, for the sinner would be aware of their guilt from the outset. Some other factor must be involved."[38] Yes, but what factor?

Noting the distinction between the expressions אָשֵׁם and יָדַע, Boda understands the meaning of אָשֵׁם to refer to some kind of subjective experience:

> Between committing and sacrificing for sin there are two possible actions. The one possible scenario is clear: someone makes known to the sinner the infraction. This suggests that the other option is

---

37. Boda, *A Severe Mercy*, 65. In this regard it should be noted that in Leviticus 4:23 and 28 יָדַע is in the passive form, suggesting that sin can be made known to the sinner by someone else.

38. Sklar, *Sin, Impurity, Sacrifice, Atonement*, 32.

correlate but not identical, the simplest option being that *the sinner comes to know his/her guilt on his/her own.*[39]

Unfortunately, Boda does not pursue this explanation further.

Jacob Milgrom, however, takes a step beyond this. He believes that one's own realization of sin derives from an accusing conscience that has legal force. Commenting on Leviticus 6:4, he remarks, "The defrauder, embezzler, robber, and the like are quite aware of their guilt. It is their conscience that subsequently disturbs them," and a little later he adds:

> Thus, contrary to usual translations, *'āšām* without an object does not refer to a state of guilt; rather, in keeping with its consequential meaning, it denotes the suffering brought on by guilt, expressed now by words such as qualms, pangs, remorse, and contrition. *'āšām* would then mean to be conscience smitten or guilt-stricken, and henceforth it will be rendered as "feel guilt."[40]

On his part, Sklar wonders if אָשֵׁם referring only to conscience is a reading that is too restrictive of the action and states that "Milgrom's arguments reveal that, at most, he opens up the *possibility* that אָשֵׁם could refer to emotional suffering."[41] Sklar thinks that the misery caused by guilt should not be limited to inward spiritual and psychological suffering but understood more broadly. Quoting an example to substantiate what he means—namely, David perceiving the reality of sin through a famine in 2 Samuel 21:1—Sklar concludes: "This is the same situation envisioned by the use of אָשֵׁם in the priestly texts: an unknown sin has been committed, and the sinner becomes aware of it *only* because of some sort of suffering that results from the sin."[42] Boda cautions similarly that the meaning of אָשֵׁם must be considered more broadly, observing that when a sinner comes to recognize sin by himself, it is difficult to tell if this involves feeling guilt or if it is prompted by the external consequential miseries of sin.[43]

---

39. Boda, *A Severe Mercy*, 64 (emphasis added).
40. Milgrom, *Leviticus 1–16*, 338, 343.
41. Sklar, *Sin, Impurity, Sacrifice, Atonement*, 38.
42. Sklar, *Sin, Impurity, Sacrifice, Atonement*, 40 (emphasis added).
43. Boda, *A Severe Mercy*, 64. However, when he later writes about confession of sin considering Numbers 5:6–7, Boda seems to narrow his own understanding, affirming that אָשֵׁם should be explained in terms of remorse: "For deliberate sins there is the added requirement that

However, it should be noted that Milgrom recognizes that conscience can be veiled under various responsive emotions and physical reactions:

> The ancient did not distinguish between emotional and physical suffering; the same language describes pangs of conscience and physical pain (e.g., Jer 17:14; Pss 38:2-11, 18-19; 102:4-11; 149:3; cf. 34:19). That is why in the penitential Psalms it is difficult to determine whether the speaker is suffering, on the one hand, from natural disease, economic want, or political persecution; or, on the other, from mental torment of guilt. ... The reason may well be that unexplainable suffering is held to be the result of sin, and the sufferer's efforts are therefore directed toward the discovery of the specific offence that gave rise to the plight. The result is predictable: wrongdoing creates guilt and fear of punishment, and, conversely, suffering reinforces the presence of guilt feelings because it is interpreted as punishment for sin.[44]

Even though a sinner may at first realize his own sin by external consequential suffering, this external prompting will sooner or later involve a subjective and inward recognition that is accompanied by guilty feelings—that is, conscience. Therefore, it seems plausible that in some contexts the verb אָשֵׁם refers specifically to feeling guilty.[45] After all, external consequential suffering in most cases does not bring about *necessarily* and *by itself* a true recognition of sin, because it may be earlier than or independent of the developing of a subjective awareness of guilt. And conversely, there can be no real recognition of sin without feeling some remorse and something of the legal force of conscience. Thus, even if—as Sklar thinks—people who were unaware that they had sinned became aware of sin because "their suffering prompted them to seek out what they had done wrong,"[46] the suffering that prompts

---

remorse be verbalized; the sin must be articulated and responsibility assumed" (*A Severe Mercy*, 65). If אָשֵׁם is understood as remorse for voluntary sin and is followed by confession, the nature of that realization seems to derive from a conscience that feels guilty. Thus, understanding אָשֵׁם as remorse points more closely to the meaning of "feeling guilt." Moreover, it seems that Boda overstates his evaluation when he says, "Milgrom is merely arguing from an expectation he has about the Hebrew language rather than from evidence" (*A Severe Mercy*, 63).

44. Milgrom, *Leviticus 1-16*, 342-43.

45. See Jacob Milgrom, *Leviticus 23-27*, Anchor Yale Bible Commentaries (Yale University Press, 2001), 2446-52.

46. Sklar, *Sin, Impurity, Sacrifice, Atonement*, 40.

the seeking out always involves the whole personality, including conscience. The inward consciousness of sin that is involved when David faces a famine in 2 Samuel 21:1 is attested to by the fact that his chief preoccupation is to understand what was wrong *in relation to God*. His motive was not simply to have the famine removed. David knew in his conscience that the God who searches the heart and the kidneys also visits the world through his providential judgments, and he wondered if the famine was perhaps one of these judgments. The prompting of conscience caused him to seek the Lord's face, and the word of the Lord confirmed the anxiety of his conscience.[47]

Having considered the most important Old Testament linguistic evidence corresponding explicitly to the religious and moral awareness indicated by the more familiar terms συνείδησις and *conscientia*, the following sections will consider the more implicit manifestations of conscience as a subjective emotional experience.

SHAME MANIFESTING CONSCIENCE

In speaking of shame, the Bible indicates conscience's presence implicitly. When Adam and Eve disobey God's "commandment of life,"[48] three things happen: they feel ashamed (cf. Gen 2:25; see 3:7, 10); they are afraid (Gen 3:10); and because they are afraid, they hide from the presence of the Lord (Gen 3:8). As noted earlier, although conscience was given to humanity when the man and the woman were created, it began to manifest itself consequentially in a negative way after the fall. In what follows, conscience will be considered as it is experienced in shame, fear, and hiding, with reference in each case first to Genesis and then to other texts in Scripture.

The first affective and afflictive manifestation of conscience referred to in Genesis is shame.[49] Scripture does not dissect the relation between conscience and shame analytically in a philosophical, cultural, psychological,

---

47. Referring to 2 Samuel 21, Gerhard von Rad explains that "awareness of the act-consequences relationship was one of the most basic perceptions" in Israel, rooted "deeply in the consciousness that great disorders such as national disasters immediately raise the retrospective question of a corresponding guilt." At the beginning there is the shattering disaster, and this "is followed by a reaction on the part of the conscience which interprets the event." *Wisdom in Israel* (SCM Press, 1972), 196, 213.

48. See "The Belgic Confession: Article XIV," in *The Evangelical Protestant Creeds*, vol. 3 of *The Creeds of Christendom*, ed. Philip Schaff (Baker Books, 1993), 398.

49. The biblical root is בוש, which means "to be ashamed."

or physiological manner; instead, it shows their connection primarily theologically, namely in relation to God.[50] As the heart beats and the kidneys are searched, human conscience is awakened and people feel ashamed. And all of this happens primarily *coram Deo*, since human conscience is always placed first and foremost in relation to God. Even though conscience and shame can be considered from the perspective of individual experience *in* human beings or of sociocultural experience *among* human beings, in Scripture shame is understood chiefly in relation to God[51] so that the theological perspective grounds and is determinative of the individual and the sociocultural perspectives. In other words, theologically, the vertical dimension of humanity's relationship with God comes before the horizontal dimension of humanity's relationship with the human self and with human society.[52]

Genesis 2:25 says that "the man and his wife were both naked and were not ashamed." If—as defined by Philip Nel—"in a religious sense *bwš* refers to the painful experience of guilt because of sinful conduct,"[53] then it must be the case that before the fall Adam and Eve were conscious of being positively pure, in the sense that they had no perception of culpability and therefore of shame. According to the narrative, the source of this inward sense of innocence was the harmony between humanity and God, and it was that

---

50. Of course, this does not mean that in the Bible we do not find material that can be used in philosophical, cultural, psychological, or physiological investigations. The Bible can be legitimately considered from the perspectives of many disciplines. However its chief trajectory is theological, spiritual, and religious.

51. According to Dan Lé, even though "shame is an emotional phenomenon whereas sin can be [only] a forensic problem, the relational aspect of both shame and sin makes it possible for the two notions to be complementary parts of each other." *The Naked Christ: An Atonement Model for a Body Obsessed Culture* (Wipf & Stock, 2012), 75.

52. In relationship to the former, Webster observes, "The refusal to orient ethics around subjectivity is particularly important in a theology of conscience. Only by expounding conscience as one feature within a larger moral landscape, characterized by God's saving presence and action and the truthful human response which that presence and action evoke, are we able to extricate ourselves from one of the most potent of modern myths, namely, the idea of the virtual infinity or indefiniteness of the moral situation. We need somehow to shake our ideas of conscience free from the authoritative notion that the moral situation is an empty space, extending limitlessly outwards from my moral awareness." Referring to the latter, he writes: "Christian theology ... will describe [the moral field] not through socio-pragmatic ethnography but through dogmatics. ... Christian dogmatics, however, precisely because it talks of God, and of all other matters in the light of God, will not rest content with descriptions of contingent moral culture. Its concern will be with those cultural fields as fields of divine action" ("God and Conscience," 238, 245).

53. Philip J. Nel, "בוש," in *New International Dictionary of Old Testament Theology and Exegesis* 1:624.

harmony that made the relation between Adam and Eve harmonious in its nakedness. As soon as the commandment of life was transgressed, nudity became a problem: "Then the eyes of both were opened, and they knew that they were naked. And they sewed fig leaves together and made themselves loincloths" (Gen 3:7).[54] The shame of nudity derived from the loss of original innocence before the Lord. Nahum M. Sarna clarifies: "So long as the harmony with God remained undisturbed, the pristine innocence and dignity of sexuality was not despoiled."[55]

There is considerable agreement that the attempt to cover their nudity derives from Adam and Eve's awakening to a subjective consciousness of guilt.[56] For example, Bruce Waltke and Cathi Fredricks observe that it is "with an awareness of guilt and a loss of innocence [that] the couple now feels shame in their naked state."[57] A sense of guilt is the origin of a sense of shame, and without guilt, Adam and Eve would have not felt any shame. Stressing the subjective experience of shame rather than the objective guilt before God, Bonhoeffer writes, "Man feels remorse when he has been at fault, and he feels shame when he lacks something. *Shame is more original than remorse.*"[58] A number of theologians have followed Bonhoeffer's lead and separated even more sharply guilt and shame, integrating his scant and unsystematic observations on shame into the honor-shame grid of cultural and psychological analysis.[59] For instance, T. Mark McConnell thinks that in Genesis 3 "guilt is not named, referred to, or implied," and that "Adam and Eve tellingly did not feel guilt or remorse"; he insists that "shame must be seen as a more

---

54. The idea of the "eyes [being] opened" as a manifestation of conscience will be considered below in exploring fallen conscience.

55. Nahum M. Sarna, *The JPS Torah Commentary: Genesis* (Jewish Publication Society, 1989), 23.

56. Adam and Eve were already objectively guilty before God in a forensic sense.

57. Bruce K. Waltke and Cathi J. Fredricks, *Genesis: A Commentary* (Zondervan, 2001), 92. In a footnote, these authors note that "one image of God's redemption is his covering for human sin (3:21; Exodus 25:17)." This observation is theologically important because it shows that shame needs to be understood first of all as godward in its orientation, namely as concerned with divine glory and humanity's share in that glory and only secondarily in a subjective or social manner. See also William N. Wilder, "Illumination and Investiture: The Royal Significance of the Tree of Wisdom in Genesis 3," *Westminster Theological Journal* 68, no. 1 (2006), 51–69.

58. Dietrich Bonhoeffer, *Ethics* (Macmillan, 1955), 20 (emphasis added).

59. For a bibliography on honor-shame, see "Update Bibliography on Honor-Shame," HonorShame, accessed November 17, 2024, https://honorshame.com/update-bibliography-on-honor-shame/.

significant problem than guilt," as if the two were not related.[60] Stephen Pattison states, "For most theologians, shame has not been a significant phenomenon," so much so that even "Bonhoeffer's comments upon shame are tantalisingly brief."[61] Moreover, according to Pattison, Christianity in general "has failed to recognise the ways in which its own ideology and practices may have contributed to the production and exploitation of dysfunctional shame."[62] However, precisely this kind of reasoning seems to be similar to that of Adam and Eve, for, as Horton observes, "Thinking that their problem was merely shame rather than guilt, [they] covered themselves with loincloths. ... Religion is one of the chief ways we cover up our shame without actually dealing with the guilt that gives rise to it."[63]

Proposing that shame should be understood primarily as a manifestation of conscience in relation to God, I do not intend to deny or minimize the horrible reality of the psychological and sociocultural consequences of shame. Indeed, in Genesis we see that it is not only God's holiness and justice that engenders subjective shame. Adam does not recognize his guilt before God and does not confess his sin, but he explicitly shames and humiliates the woman by placing on her shoulders his own responsibility; furthermore, implicitly he tries to shame God by blaming him for giving the woman to be with him (see Gen 3:12). On her part, Eve seeks to shift the blame onto the serpent, showing that shame and hostility mar the relationship between humans and other creatures (see Gen 3:13). Thus, the infection that contaminates the vertical relationship between God and humans also pollutes the horizontal relationships among human beings and between human beings and other creatures. Although shame must remain anchored to the primary theological reality of guilt and demerit before God, that does not mean that it becomes insignificant in itself when considered individually or socially. Rather, a theocentric understanding of shame shows its devastating and humiliating power within and among people as well as in their relationship

---

60. T. Mark McConnell, "From 'I Have Done Wrong' to 'I Am Wrong': (Re)Constructing Atonement as a Response to Shame," in *Locating Atonement: Explorations in Constructive Dogmatics*, ed. Oliver D. Crisp and Fred Sanders (Zondervan, 2015), 178, 182, 185. For a similar view, see Robin Stockitt, *Restoring the Shamed: Towards a Theology of Shame* (Cascade Books, 2012), 19.

61. Stephen Pattison, *Shame: Theory, Therapy, Theology* (Cambridge University Press, 2000), 187, 190.

62. Pattison, *Shame: Theory, Therapy, Theology*, 192.

63. Horton, *The Christian Faith*, 413, 429.

to the rest of creation, and it thereby summons humanity before the presence of God to receive the grace that overcomes shame.[64]

Giving priority to a theocentric explanation of shame, Calvin holds together conscience, guilt, and shame as follows:

> [Adam and Eve] are not yet summoned to the tribunal of God; there is no one who accuses them; is not then the sense of shame, which rises spontaneously, a sure token of guilt? The eloquence, therefore, of the whole world will avail nothing to deliver those from condemnation, whose own conscience has become the judge to compel them to confess their fault.[65]

Similarly, Meredith G. Kline considers shame as an immediate manifestation of conscience:

> Even before the judicial disclosures made in formal pronouncements of the Lord, a process of self-exposure and self-judgment on the part of Adam and Eve had already occurred. Theirs was the God-like vocation to discern between good and evil and no sooner had they sinned by judging God to be evil and the devil to be good that involuntarily, and more accurately, their own consciences delivered a verdict of evil against themselves. It took the form of a sense of shame over their physical nakedness (Gen. 3:7a).[66]

---

64. In comparing the Jewish-Christian *guilt-culture* with the Greco-Roman *shame-culture*, Thiselton strikes a good balance: "It is important to hold together the aspect of social status and the honor-shame contrast stressed in literature on the social history or sociology ... with the theological aspect of the achievement-acceptance contrast emphasized most characteristically in literature of a more Lutheran tradition," (*The First Epistle to the Corinthians*, 187).

65. John Calvin, *Commentary on the First Book of Moses Called Genesis*, vol. 1 of *Calvin's Commentaries* (Baker Books, 1996), 157. See also Bavinck, *Reformed Dogmatics*, 3:197.

66. Kline, *Kingdom Prologue*, 129. Keeping guilt and shame connected as manifestations of conscience helps to explain them within the bounds of Trinitarian and covenantal theology: the gospel is about the Father sending the Son and the Father and the Son sending the Spirit to provide a remedy both to guilt through justification in the Son and to shame through the Spirit of adoption. Edward T. Welch addresses the pastoral challenges posed by the serious and at times inhuman consequences of shame: "Adam and Eve hid from each other and from God. Shame is experienced horizontally, before other people, and vertically, before God. But a curious amnesia takes place as soon as the man and woman leave the borders of Eden. We continue to feel shame before other people, but we are blind to the fact that shame is also, and primarily, before God." *Shame Interrupted: How God Lifts the Pain of Worthlessness and Rejection* (New Growth Press, 2012), 47–48.

The primacy of the godward orientation of shame is particularly prominent in the Prophets.[67] According to prophetic preaching, those who trust in the vain idols made by human hands—either in Israel or among the nations—will be put to shame because of God's judgment, like Adam and Eve in their idolatry (Isa 1:29; 30:5; 42:17; 44:9; 45:16; Jer 10:14; 50:2; 51:17, 47; Ezek 16:52; 36:32; Dan 9:6–8; Hos 10:6; Mic 3:7).[68]

In the book of Psalms, the phenomenon of shame with reference to God is predominantly related to the absence of faith and trust in the Lord. Unlike Adam and Eve in the garden, those who trust in the Lord and his word are not put to shame before God's justice (Pss 22:5; 25:2–3, 20; 31:1, 17; 71:1). However, the godward orientation of shame is also directly related to the law and justice. The suppliant prays, "Oh that my ways may be steadfast in keeping your statutes! Then I shall not be put to shame" (Ps 119:5–6a). A comment by Goldingay explains that the godward orientation of shame caused by disobedience intertwines with the subjective and sociocultural experience of it:

> Shaming is part of the negative counterpart of good fortune ... the two helping to nuance their respective significances. On the one hand, good fortune is not merely a matter of blessings such as prosperity and good health, but of honor in the community, which respects a person of integrity. On the other hand, a devastating consequence of refusing to walk in Yhwh's ways is losing one's honor before the community. All these interlink. Obedience generates prosperity and thus honor; disobedience generates trouble and thus shame.[69]

---

67. In *The Construction of Shame in the Hebrew Bible* (Sheffield Academic, 2002). Johanna Stiebert dwells on the weaknesses of reading the Prophets through the lens of cultural honor-shame approaches and rejects the split between guilt and shame. See also Jacqueline E. Lapsley, "Shame and Self-Knowledge: The Positive Role of Shame in Ezekiel's View of the Moral Self," in *The Book of Ezekiel: Theological and Anthropological Perspectives*, ed. Margaret S. Odell and John T. Strong (Society of Biblical Literature, 2000), 143–73.

68. In the third Servant Song, the servant proclaims, "I know that I shall not be put to shame" (Isa 50:7). Because of the servant's full obedience (see Isa 53:9b, 11b), the righteous servant maintained his innocence and therefore could neither be objectively ashamed nor feel ashamed before God, *in spite of the sociocultural shame that he encountered*. From a christological perspective, the servant is the last Adam, who—unlike the first Adam—is neither objectively ashamed nor feels ashamed because he did not violate God's justice and always obeyed him. However, it should be remembered that at the time of his death, the righteous servant bore, both objectively and subjectively, *our* shame (see Isa 53:10–11; Heb 12:2; 13:13).

69. Goldingay, *Psalms*, 3:383–84.

Proverbs speaks of shame as marring the conduct of those who think and act contrary to the dictates of the wisdom with which God endowed the whole of humanity. Fools not only bring shame on themselves but on those related to them (Prov 10:5; 12:4; 17:2; 19:26; 29:15). Even though Proverbs focuses at times more on the sociocultural perspective than on the divine-human relationship, the background against which shame is viewed is always the divine wisdom that summons people to live in fear of the Lord. Therefore, the shame experienced on the horizontal level among people ultimately derives from a violation of God's universal moral order due to the lack of fear of the Lord. Michael Fox notes, "The participle *mebiš* [one who acts shamefully] is always used [in Proverbs] of a person in a subordinate relation to another," a person who "causes disappointment to one who had reason to expect better."[70] Because of the demands of justice, in Proverbs those who act shamefully bring upon themselves wrath from their superiors because they are God's representatives (see Prov 14:35).

In conclusion, being closely associated with the reality of guilt before God, the sense of shame is to be understood primarily in relation to God as a manifestation of conscience.

FEAR MANIFESTING CONSCIENCE

Along with shame, Adam experienced fear of God as the judge—the one whose covenant had been defiantly broken.[71] That which aroused fear in Adam (and Eve) was God's voice/sound as he made himself known to them in the garden. Given that voice/sound (קוֹל) is usually used in conjunction with sonorous and grandiose theophanies (cf. Deut 4:12; 5:22–23; 1 Kgs 19:12; Ezek 1:24, 25, 28; Ps 29), Kline writes, "There is every reason ... to perceive God's movement through the garden in Genesis 3 as an advent in terrible judicial majesty of his Glory theophany and to hear 'the voice' that heralded this advent as the characteristic theophanic thunder."[72] Because of

---

70. Michael V. Fox, *Proverbs 10–31: A New Translation with Introduction and Commentary*, Anchor Yale Bible Commentaries (Yale University Press, 2009), 514.

71. Although there are various experiences that can cause fear, it is also an instinctive and emotional response produced by the consciousness of guilt, and that is why moral philosophers define fear—as well as shame—as a "moral emotion." The importance of moral emotions in relation to conscience will be addressed later in the discussion of conscience in relation to other human capacities.

72. Kline, *Images of the Spirit*, 102.

this, The Belgic Confession (1561) speaks of "the conscience of fear, terror and dread ... of our first father, Adam, who, trembling, attempted to cover himself with fig-leaves."[73] Horton also understands fear as a manifestation of conscience: "Adam answered God, 'and I was afraid, because I was naked, and I hid myself.' ... This will now be the tragic response of the human conscience in the presence of God."[74] Fear is a second aspect of conscience's response in the presence of God.

According to David VanDrunen, the fear of God is related to conscience because in Scripture it is seen in covenantal and relational terms, in light of the vocation that humanity has received from the triune creator, who is the Lord of the covenant. This means that the voice of obligation "forces [human beings] to remember the covenant in which [they are] bound to God."[75] And since the fall, this voice of obligation finds expression in the form of fear. In VanDrunen's words: "The 'fear of God' refers to a respect for moral basic obligations ... rooted ultimately in a sense of accountability to someone greater than oneself. ... *Fear* [is] precisely [a] response before God."[76]

Fear as a perception of accountability before God is important in wisdom literature.[77] In Proverbs—as in Genesis 1-3—God is seen as the sovereign creator of the universe and especially of humanity (Prov 3:19-20; 8:22-31; 14:31; 17:5). Consequently, by the very nature of reality, human wisdom is supposed to be in harmony with and conform to the wisdom of the Creator. When this does not occur, the threat of judicial retribution arises—another significant topic in Proverbs and in Genesis 1-3. In his wisdom, God created a morally ordered universe, and when this order is disrupted through a rejection of

---

73. "The Belgic Confession: Article XXIII," in *The Creeds of Christendom*, 3:410.

74. Horton, *The Christian Faith*, 410.

75. John B. Webster, *Confronted by Grace: Meditation of a Theologian* (Lexham Press, 2015), 8.

76. David VanDrunen, *Divine Covenants and Moral Order: A Biblical Theology of Natural Law* (Eerdmans, 2014), 158. VanDrunen's arguments at this point resonate with those of David Novak in *Covenantal Rights: A Study in Jewish Political Theory* (Princeton University Press, 2000) and *Natural Law in Judaism* (Cambridge University Press, 1998).

77. Michael V. Fox explains fear as a spontaneous phenomenon: "Fear of the Lord is essentially an emotion or attitude, ... [and] in its elementary form, it requires little learning or understanding." *Proverbs 1-9: A New Translation with Introduction and Commentary*, Anchor Yale Bible Commentaries (Yale University Press, 2010), 112. However, Fox carefully makes room for a range of different manifestations of fear: "One person may worry about consequences, another may be uneasy about divine disapproval without thinking about retribution, and yet another may be in trepidation before the otherness of the holy. At the very start, a God-fearing child may simply worry that God will punish him for misdeeds," (Fox, *Proverbs 1-9*, 70).

wisdom, the destiny of the fool and the wicked is divine retribution (Prov 2:21-22).[78] Because a religious and moral order was built by God's wisdom into the very fabric of creation, according to Webster, "Creation is an 'ethical' not a 'physical' act."[79] This implies both that wisdom is divinely created and universally consistent and that—even without the aid of special revelation—it is possible for creatures, however dimly, to perceive and recognize that wisdom. This is supported by the fact that the wisdom genre was quite common across the ancient Near East, reflecting a kind of multicultural, shared experience; this is attested to by the fact that Proverbs probably incorporates non-Israelite authors (see Prov 30:1; 31:1).[80]

Since Proverbs presents fear as an instinctive human response in relation to right and wrong, some scholars (as will be seen below) understand the fear of God as a manifestation of conscience. Indeed, although the fear of the Lord is something that can be taught (Ps 34:11) and that can be related to knowledge and understanding (Prov 2:5), in its basic expressions, it should be seen as connected with the manifestation of conscience. According to the pedagogy of Proverbs, as the child grows, fear, understanding, and the knowledge of God and his ways should grow as well. Though fear, understanding, and knowledge remain distinct, they blend together to bring about a growth in wisdom. Thinking about their relationship in Proverbs 2:5, Fox writes:

> *Hokmah* is linked with, but not identical to, fear and knowledge of God. If these virtues were one and the same, the entire passage would be a tautology: if you take in *hokmah* you will get *hokmah*, which will give you *hokmah*. The author has a clear idea of the components of wisdom and how they tie together. Fear of God motivates the search

---

78. On the doctrines of God as sovereign creator and a righteous judge in Proverbs, see Craig G. Bartholomew, "A God for Life, and Not Just for Christmas! The Revelation of God in the Old Testament Wisdom Literature," in *The Trustworthiness of God: Perspectives on the Nature of Scripture*, ed. Paul Helm and Carl Trueman (Apollos, 2002), 39-57.

79. Webster, "Trinity and Creation," 92.

80. For von Rad there is a mystery inherent in the created world: "In the opinions of the teachers, Yahweh had at his service a quite different means, besides priests and prophets, whereby he could reach men, namely the voice of primeval order, a voice which came from creation [as] means of revelation," (*Wisdom in Israel*, 163). See also Fox, *Proverbs 1-9*, 3; VanDrunen, *Divine Covenants and Moral Order*, 369-70, 396.

for wisdom, which develops into a more sophisticated fear of God, one in which a moral conscience is fused with knowledge of his will.[81]

Thus, the pupil progresses "from unreflective fear to a cognitive awareness of what fear of God really is, and this is equivalent to knowledge of God. This is fear of God *as conscience*."[82]

HIDDENNESS MANIFESTING CONSCIENCE

The third reaction of Adam and Eve after the fall was to hide themselves from the presence of the Lord (Gen 3:8). Hiding followed shame and fear as if that hiding was a way out for them. One response of human beings to sin in Eden was to recoil from God's presence: Adam and Eve concealed themselves in fear because of their awareness of guilt (see Gen 3:10).

In general, commentators agree that a feeling of guilt caused this movement into hiding. Kline's comments are eloquent and moving:

> Adapting the mode of his self-revelation to the judicial purpose of his coming the Lord approached the judgment-site in the awesome glory of his theophanic Presence. ... It is this kind of fearful advent that is reported in Genesis 3:8. ... Their hiding from God betrayed their guilty awareness of having broken the covenant with him. ... Their hiding from God under the covering of the trees, like their hiding from each other under the covering of leaves, pointed to a sense of shameful nakedness, in this case a spiritual nakedness which they felt before God's eyes. This nakedness resulted from the loss of the covering of righteousness, the garment of the beauty of holiness. They had lost the ethical glory of God-likeness which is the prerequisite to stand as priest before the face of God and reflect the Glory of God.[83]

---

81. Fox, *Proverbs 1-9*, 113.

82. Fox, *Proverbs 1-9*, 70 (emphasis added). Commenting on the midwives who saved the Israelite male children from Pharaoh, Nahum M. Sarna writes, "Faced with a conflict between the laws of God and those of the pharaoh, the midwives followed the dictates of conscience. ... They were actuated by 'fear of God,' a phrase frequently associated with moral and ethical behavior. 'Fear of God' connotes a conception of God as One who makes moral demands on humankind; it functions as the ultimate restraint on evil and the supreme stimulus for good." *The JPS Torah Commentary: Exodus* (Jewish Publication Society, 1991), 7.

83. Kline, *Kingdom Prologue*, 128-130. For a more detailed treatment of Genesis 3:8 by Kline, see *Images of the Spirit*, 97-131; see also Sarna, *Genesis*, 26.

The prophets also speak of this hiding in fear and desperation: "Enter into the rock and hide in the dust from before the terror of the Lord, and from the splendor of his majesty" (Isa 2:10). As a consequence, the people "shall enter the caves of the rocks and the holes of the ground, from before the terror of the Lord, and from the splendor of his majesty, when he rises to terrify the earth" (Isa 2:19). Confronted with God's righteous judgment, idolaters "shall say to the mountains, 'Cover us,' and to the hills, 'Fall on us'" (Hos 10:8; see also Jer 4:29).

The gospel of Luke tells us that while the Lord Jesus was walking to the place of his execution, bearing the cross, he was meditating on these very words of Hosea. Jesus appropriates the vocabulary of the prophets, exhorting the people to weep for themselves (Luke 23:26-29). As the Lord warns Jerusalem, he describes the desire of idolaters to hide from God's presence in the last days, quoting the ancient prophet: "Then they will begin to say to the mountains, 'Fall on us,' and to the hills, 'Cover us'" (Luke 23:30). This petition reappears in Revelation 6:15-16: "Then the kings of the earth and the great ones and the generals and the rich and the powerful, and everyone, slave and free, hid themselves in the caves and among the rocks of the mountains, calling to the mountains and rocks, 'Fall on us and hide us from the face of him who is seated on the throne, and from the wrath of the Lamb.'" Gregory Beale sees behind the text in Revelation and behind the oracles of the prophets an allusion to Genesis 3:8, and he comes to the following conclusion:

> Behind Rev. 6:16 and even the Hosea and Jeremiah references stands an allusion to the incident in Gen. 3:8 in which Adam and Eve "hid from the presence of the Lord." ... John understands Genesis as a typological prophesy on the basis of his presupposition that God has determined that sinful history must end in the same way that it began.[84]

Referring to the same passage, Genesis 3:8, Bavinck connects shame, fear, and hiddenness as different manifestations of conscience:

> The fact that in Adam and Eve a sense of shame over their nakedness had an ethical cause is further evident in that the sense of guilt in their case also manifested itself in still another way: in fear before God. ...

---

84. Gregory K. Beale, *The Book of Revelation* (Eerdmans, 1999), 400.

While as a result of their transgression they felt unfree in each other's presence, they were much more ashamed vis-à-vis the One who had given them the commandment. Their *conscience* had awakened — the realization that they had sinned and deserved punishment. And that conscience gives them no peace; it drives them away from God, not toward him. It makes them fear, flee, and hide themselves from his presence.[85]

For Bavinck, the emotional responses of shame, guilt, and fear cause a recoiling from God's presence, a desire to turn away from him.

SUMMARY

This chapter has devoted attention to the manifestation of conscience in the experiences of human creatures. It considered, first, that the phenomenon of conscience is referred to explicitly in the Old Testament through the language of the heart, the kidneys, the hands, and the feeling of guilt. Secondly, it observed that the Old Testament refers to the conscience implicitly, by describing the subjective experiences of shame, fear, and the desire to hide.

In the next chapter, we will return to the idea of conscience being *created* in particular. Drawing on the manifestations of conscience explored in this first chapter, its *function* as created will be explored.

---

85. Bavinck, *Reformed Dogmatics*, 3:198. Going back to Bavinck's assertion that there was no conscience before the fall, it should be noted that his reference to conscience as "awakened" seems to contradict that statement; see *Reformed Ethics*, 1:205. Pannenberg reflects in related fashion on sin causing "alienation" from God and considers this in a way that connects it to the present focus on the presence of conscience and its manifestation in the urge to hide (*Anthropology in Theological Perspective*, 283–85).

2

THE FUNCTION OF CONSCIENCE

In the previous chapter, it was demonstrated that conscience is present in the Old Testament. Now we will consider the *function* of conscience as a created reality. Though again, we encounter the problem that much of the available exegetical material is related to humanity after the fall. This raises the questions of *whether* this is the case and *how* it can be shown: was the conscience of human beings functioning in the state of innocence, and what scriptural grounds can serve as resources to demonstrate that it was so? In seeking to answer these questions, the following chapter considers the function of created conscience across three tasks: witnessing, summoning, and legislating.

A WITNESSING CONSCIENCE

According to Scripture, the first function of conscience is to bear witness to God and to his truth as sovereign creator. Calvin—who, as many other theologians of the past, "refers to the conscience virtually every doctrine he discusses, and yet ... he has no sustained discussion of the conscience per se"[1]—echoes Quintilian in affirming that "conscience is a thousand witnesses."[2] While Calvin asserts that conscience witnesses to what "is good and worthy of being desired,"[3] he stresses more—both in the *Institutes* and his commentaries and sermons—the judicial and condemning aspect of this witness, as will be seen later. This is understandable given our ignorance of humanity's experience in innocence and the paucity of details about this state in the Bible. However, while avoiding speculation, it can be said that the Old Testament shows that God created humanity with a good conscience, capable—*even before the fall*—of functioning in a positive manner as

---

1. Zachman, *The Assurance of Faith*, 98.
2. Calvin, *Institutes*, 3.19.15.
3. John Calvin, *Commentaries on the Epistle of Paul the Apostle to the Romans*, vol. 19 in *Calvin's Commentaries* (Baker Books, 1996), 98.

a spontaneous witness both antecedent (prospective) and consequent (retrospective), expressing itself with delight and in harmony with God.

In this respect, Webster remarks that even after the fall "conscience is indicative moral reason *before* it is legislative; it is the amazed acknowledgment of moral and theological truth *before* it is an awareness of obligation."[4] The apostle Paul seems to affirm that conscience bears a *positive* witness to truth in relation to the law as well as to simplicity and godly sincerity in conduct (see Rom 2:15; 9:1; 2 Cor 1:12). If this is so *after* the fall, is it plausible that in the beginning conscience was the amazed acknowledgment of moral and theological truth too? These observations compel further analysis of conscience as a positive witness in light of the doctrine of creation and not only as a negative witness in the context of the doctrine of the fall.

At the end of the days of creation, before entering into the royal resting of his Sabbath/enthronement as creator/king,[5] "God saw everything that he had made, and behold, it was very good" (Gen 1:31). According to the narrative, there is an element of delight and even of enthusiasm[6] as God contemplates his handiwork not only ontologically but first and foremost ethically. Kline writes:

> The work process of the six days is marked by the judicial refrain of divine approbation: "God saw that it was good." This succession of judgments expressing the builder's pleasure in the work of each day led to the final verdict of delighted satisfaction: "God saw everything that he had made and behold it was very good" (Gen. 1:31a; Exod. 39:43). ... The Creator's Sabbath rest is much more a matter of taking satisfaction and delight in his consummated building.[7]

God's approval was not just to inform Adam's and Eve's mind but to involve them ethically and even aesthetically in his divine delight.[8] Even if this human participation in the divine act is not archetypal and identical but

---

4. Webster, "God and Conscience," 254–55 (emphasis added).
5. See Kline, *Kingdom Prologue*, 34–40.
6. Gordon J. Wenham, *Genesis 1–15*, Word Biblical Commentary (Thomas Nelson, 1987), 34.
7. Kline, *Kingdom Prologue*, 34. See also Calvin, *Calvin's Commentaries*, 1:100.
8. This observation is important in relation to what will be investigated later when discussing the regeneration of conscience as the renewal of the *sensus divinitatis* and the restoration of spiritual delight.

ectypal and analogical, human beings before the fall partook in God's passion for his glory as it is displayed and known in creation, reflecting some of his perfections. It seems therefore plausible to affirm that if conscience still retains a measure of the positive perception of moral and ontological perfection after the fall, it was much more so before the fall.

The plausibility of this claim is reinforced by considering that the first Adam participated in God's approbation in the exercise of his conscience, pronouncing—as it were—his "Amen" to the goodness, the beauty, and the pleasantness of creation to the glory of the sovereign creator. Adam did so with his whole being—body, mind, and will—including his affections and conscience, as humanity *tasted* in the beginning that the Lord is good (see Ps 34:8).[9] As Adam participated in the seventh day, he witnessed and gave assent to God's approving evaluation of his divine work with the whole of his humanity, including his uncontaminated and uncorrupted religious and moral self-awareness.

This dynamic is pictured at work in Psalm 92, "a song for the Sabbath." It is possible to read this psalm backward, imagining what kind of experience Adam and Eve had on the seventh day. The psalm starts where Genesis 1 ends (cf. Gen 1:31 with Ps 92:1). Although a number of interpreters have understood this psalm primarily as eschatological, Goldingay observes that the targum to the Psalms "infers that it was composed by the first human being; the implication would be that the acts the psalm celebrates are the acts of creation."[10] Sarna similarly highlights the centrality of the creation motif here: "The Sabbath is the symbol of creation and of cessation from creation. It expresses human imitation of 'the primordial gesture of the Lord' when he transformed chaos into cosmos [and] it would be highly unreasonable to assume that Ps 92 ... is not ... to be interpreted as praise of God in his capacity of Creator of the world."[11] Because the original Sabbath pointed to the perfected eternal rest of blessing promised by God already before the fall, Delitzsch blends the creational and eschatological perspectives: "[The

---

9. Again, this passage and the verb "to taste" will become important in the later discussion on the regeneration of conscience as the restoration of spiritual delight.

10. Goldingay, *Psalms*, 3:53. See also Adele Berlin and Marc Zvi Brettler, eds., *The Jewish Study Bible* (Oxford University Press, 2004), 1386.

11. Nahum M. Sarna, "The Psalm for the Sabbath Day (Ps 92)," *Journal of Biblical Literature* 81, no. 2 (1962): 159, 164.

Psalm] praises God, the Creator of the world, as the Ruler of the world, whose rule is pure loving-kindness and faithfulness, and calms itself, in the face of the flourishing condition of the evil-doers, with the prospect of the final issue, which will brilliantly vindicate the righteousness of God."[12] Thus, to participate in the seventh day was for Adam a rejoicing in the protological work of God while anticipating the promised eschatological entering into God's rest. On that day Adam and Eve experienced something of the eschatological destiny of human life for—in the words of Vos—"there is to be to the world-process a finale, as there was an overture, and these two belong inseparably together"; indeed, to give up "the one means to give up the other, and to give up either means to abandon the fundamental scheme of Biblical history."[13]

Psalm 92 begins by showing us firstly that human beings witnessed to and confessed the glory of God. Adam gave witness to God's sovereignty, confessing that God is the Lord, the Most High who is on high forever (92:1, 8). Secondly, it indicates that in the garden humanity gave witness to and confessed the perfection of God's attributes: his reliable faithfulness and covenantal loyalty (92:2); his omnipotence displayed in the works of his hands (92:4-5a); the wisdom of his counsel (92:5b); his providence (92:7-14); and his righteousness (92:15).

Psalm 92 indicates, thirdly, that Adam's witness and confession is not a cerebral and detached recognition of God and his works, but—employing again Webster's expression—it is an *amazed* acknowledgment of God and the reality he created. Instead of guilt, shame, fear, and hiddenness, Adam experienced amazement; Psalm 92 is, after all, a song! Adam's witness was expressed in celebration (92:1, 3, 4b) as well as in mental reflection (92:5-6) that perceived and affirmed the טוב (goodness/beautifulness/pleasantness) of God's approbation and rest (92:1a). Delitzsch writes: "It is good, i.e. not merely good in the eyes of God, but also good for man, beneficial to the heart, pleasant and blessed."[14] Humanity's experience of witness is crowned with gladness and rejoicing (92:4).

---

12. Carl Friedrich Keil and Franz Delitzsch, *The Psalms*, Commentary on the Old Testament (Eerdmans, 1986), 5:3.66–67.

13. Vos, *Biblical Theology*, 140.

14. Keil and Delitzsch, *The Psalms*, 3:67.

This retrospective hermeneutic can be applied as well to a New Testament passage in order to substantiate that created conscience was functioning before the fall. The gospel of Luke shows that the last Adam also participated in God's ethical approval: Jesus, contemplating what pleased the Father, "rejoiced greatly in the Holy Spirit, and said, 'I praise You, O Father, Lord of heaven and earth, that You have hidden these things from the wise and intelligent and have revealed them to infants. Yes, Father, for this way was well-pleasing in Your sight' " (Luke 10:21 NASB). This particular passage is relevant for the notion of created conscience because *Jesus was without sin, unaffected by the fall, and yet his conscience was active and functioning*.[15] In the gospel of John, Jesus poses the following question: "Which one of you convicts me of sin?" (John 8:46). Challenging his opponents to prove both objectively and subjectively his sin and guilt, the Lord appeals explicitly to the witness of the conscience of all and implicitly, therefore, to his own conscience. This rhetorical question shows that, although he was without sin and guilt and thus in the same state as the first human being before the fall, the conscience of Jesus is nevertheless active and at work. Commenting on this passage in John, Leon Morris states, "It betokens a clear and serene conscience. Only one who was in the closest and most intimate communion with the Father could have spoken such words. It is impossible to envisage any other figure in history to make such a claim."[16] The pure conscience ascribed both implicitly and explicitly to Jesus in his history as one whose humanity was not corrupted by the fall further suggests that the original Adam also enjoyed a clear conscience, witnessing to his innocence.

A SUMMONING CONSCIENCE

Bearing witness to God, to his claims, and to his ethical evaluation of reality, conscience summons human beings to be what God made them to be and, specifically, to live in a way that honors the sacred bond of the covenant.

In speaking of conscience in the context of the doctrine of creation, the positive function of conscience should remain dominant. In the previous chapter on the manifestation of conscience, the expressions of this

---

15. Bavinck admits somewhat reluctantly that Jesus had a conscience: "Only a regenerated person (and, if one wishes, Adam and Jesus) can have an objectively good conscience," (*Reformed Ethics*, 1:207).

16. Leon Morris, *The Gospel According to John* (Eerdmans, 1971), 465.

phenomenon were primarily found within the context of the doctrine of the fall, since the special revelation of Scripture exists because of the fall in order to reveal the gospel. It is understandable that readers of the Bible might inadvertently assume that conscience has nothing to do with humanity's experience before the fall. However, even apart from the reality of sin, conscience calls and summons human beings and makes them aware of the religious and ethical *telos* of their life.

In the beginning, humanity could not be self-aware without being at the same time conscious of God. Cornelius Van Til explains:

> Man had originally not merely a capacity for receiving the truth; he was in actual possession of the truth. ... Man could not be aware of himself without also being aware of objects about him and without also being aware of his responsibility to manage himself and all things for the glory of God. ... Man's first sense of self-awareness implied the awareness of the presence of God as the one from whom he had a great task to accomplish.[17]

In the book of Psalms, we find evidence of this summons to a great task that pervades all creation. Psalm 148, for example, shows that all creatures are called to answer the creative word of God, responding with praise to the sovereign creator. Expressing a grand cosmic vision, this psalm calls the heavenly realm—angels, sun, moon, stars, and waters above—to praise the Lord, "for he commanded and they were created" (Ps 148:1-5). Then the earthly realm receives the same summons: sea monsters and all the deeps, hail, snow, smoke, stormy wind, mountains, hills, trees, all beasts, birds, kings, young men and women, elders, and all things in the creation here below are summoned to serve the Lord for "his majesty is above earth and heaven" (Ps 148:6-13). Since in this psalm the chief theme is the bidding of the whole creation to praise God, the perception of this summons is experienced in relation to God as creator and, therefore, independently of the reality of sin (see Ps 103:20-22).

A further example is Psalm 29, which declares that creation is given a sevenfold summons by the קוֹל יְהוָה (Ps 29:3, 4, 5, 7, 8, 9), so that even the heavenly sons of God may "ascribe to the Lord the glory due his name" (Ps 29:2).

---

17. Cornelius Van Til, *Christian Apologetics* (P&R Publishing, 1976), 55-56.

Everything in creation receives its real meaning in relation to God, having been created and summoned to glorify him. It is interesting to note that it was precisely the same summoning קוֹל יְהוָה that Adam and Eve heard in the garden after they transgressed the commandment of life (Gen 3:8, 10). On the seventh day, conscience responded positively to that voice, tasting that everything was very טוֹב; but after the fall, conscience's response was negative, causing Adam and Eve to feel guilty, ashamed, fearful, and to hide from the presence of the Lord. Therefore, it seems likely that the same voice of the Lord that calls humanity to be accountable after the fall was already calling humanity—and, indeed, all creation—to be accountable before the fall, as suggested in Psalm 29.

The reference to the קוֹל יְהוָה in both Psalm 29 and in Genesis 3 raises the question of whether Adam, when summoned by God while still in a state of innocence, experienced something of the same shame, fear, and the desire to hide that he felt after the fall. After all, were not Adam and Eve in their unfallen state also summoned before the presence of the majestic and awesome sovereign creator of the universe?

It seems evident that before the fall Adam neither perceived nor manifested any desire to hide himself from the presence of God. Even after God summoned Adam, giving him the commandment of life accompanied by the threat of death (Gen 2:16-17), he appeared calm before the Lord. Indeed, Adam seemed completely open and totally available when God brought to him every beast of the field and every bird so that he could give them a name (Gen 2:19-20a). Later, when God caused a deep sleep to fall upon Adam, there was no sign of resistance or recoiling (Gen 2:21). Finally, when God brought the woman to Adam, his response was one of commitment, confession, and doxology (Gen 2:22-23). As for shame, Adam and Eve were unashamed, as their nudity shows straightforwardly.

It is more difficult to speak about fear, a term applied both to the attitude of unbelievers and to the reverential sentiment that characterizes those who walk with God.[18] The question here is whether the filial fear of the Lord can be applied to humanity in their state of innocence. It seems at first that before the fall Adam and Eve could not experience fear, "for fear has to do

---

18. VanDrunen observes that in Scripture "fear of God" is applied to unbelievers and "fear of the Lord" to believers (*Divine Covenants and Moral Order*, 160-61).

with punishment" (1 John 4:18), and no sense of punishment was present then. However, it appears more arduous to determine whether Adam and Eve perceived a measure of the religious fear of the believing heart—that filial, reverential, and humble fear known to the children of God. Levenson thinks that fear in a negative sense is always mixed with trust and love of God:

> There surely is a tinge of fear in the negative sense, even in the reverence, the awe, or the sense of being overwhelmed that one has in the presence of a superior. And if the description of God in the Bible is at all accurate, there would be something gravely wrong with someone in whom the thought of God and the sense of his immediate presence did not evoke those very feelings.[19]

Levenson's assessment appears true in the experience of human beings in their fallen state. But is it possible to speak of fear in a *positive* sense before the fall?[20] It seems helpful to try to answer this question by considering Pannenberg's statement on alienation, which was previously (and briefly) related to the hiding conscience: "The subjective experience of alienation depends on what it is that individuals do or do not identify with. Every act of identification is an act of love ... where love is at work, alienation disappears."[21] If transgression and the resultant guilty conscience are what cause shame, fear, and the desire to hide, then where that cause disappears, it would seem also that the consequences are removed. In sum, it seems possible that Adam and Eve in their innocence not only did not desire to hide or feel any shame but did not experience any kind of fear—whether negative or positive—for if "perfect love casts out fear" (1 John 4:18) after the fall, then it did so all the more in Eden.[22]

---

19. Jon D. Levenson, *The Love of God: Divine Gift, Human Gratitude, and Mutual Faithfulness in Judaism* (Princeton University Press, 2016), 30.

20. The need for a love for God that is devoid of fear is felt by those Talmudic rabbis who perceive a tension between love and fear, as they "tend to think of the fear of God as the fear of *punishment* and thus something to be contrasted with the love of God," (Levenson, *The Love of God*, 31).

21. Pannenberg, *Anthropology in Theological Perspective*, 284.

22. The biblical eschatological hope comforts us in that it envisions a future in which the flock of God "shall fear no more" (Jer 23:4; see also Isa 25:8; Rev 21:4). Benjamin B. Warfield writes, "The religion of sinless man will therefore exhibit no other traits but trust and love. In sinful man, the same knowledge of God must produce, rather, a reaction of fear and hate—until the

A LEGISLATING CONSCIENCE

The witnessing and summoning conscience also enables humanity to be aware of religious and ethical judgments. Speaking in the context of the doctrine of creation, Kline writes:

> Likeness to God is signified by both image of God and son of God. Man's likeness to God is a demand to be like God; *the indicative here has the force of an imperative*. Formed in the image of God, man is informed by *a sense of deity* by which he knows what God is like, not merely that God is (Rom. 1:19ff.). And knowledge of what one's Father-God is, is knowledge of what, in creaturely semblance, one must be himself. *With the sense of deity comes conscience, the sense of deity in the imperative mode*. The basic and general covenantal norm of the imitation of God was thus written on the tables of man's heart (Rom. 1:32; 2:14ff.).[23]

Because of the *imago Dei*, a positive imperative function of conscience has been intrinsic to humanity's sense of deity since the beginning of creation. Bavinck believes that conscience stands above other human capacities[24] due to its ability to call humanity to be accountable before God as the sovereign legislator:

> Conscience is not my fabrication ... but points to an authority above me that has been given to me as a law of my personality. ... God himself is the last factor of the conscience. *This law of the personality points back to him as the Legislator.*[25]

This legislative function of conscience raises again the question of whether conscience has a positive function or even existed before the fall. Bavinck does not believe it did: "The working of conscience always remains

---

grace of God intervenes with a message of mercy." "Calvin's Doctrine of the Knowledge of God," in *Calvin and Augustine*, ed. Samuel G. Craig (P&R Publishing, 1980), 38.

23. Kline, *Kingdom Prologue*, 62 (emphasis added). Calvin too conceptualized that the *sensus divinitatis* brings with itself the *sensus divini iudicii* (*Institutes*, 1.3.1; 3.19.15).

24. Alexis Torrance claims that early patristic theology shows a similar high view of conscience. "Conscience in the Early Church Fathers," in Alvaré and Hammond, *Christianity and the Laws of Conscience*, 95–98, 101–3.

25. Bavinck, "Conscience," 125. This quote seems to suggest that conscience is a created reality, and it shows how difficult it is for Bavinck to be consistent with his own statements, since elsewhere he claims that before the fall there was no conscience.

the same. It is always condemning in nature, it consists of the awareness of having acted wrongly."[26] Understandably, if a theology of conscience is located within the boundaries of the doctrines of sin and salvation, the tendency will be to consider it an accusing conscience. However, interpreting conscience in light of the doctrine of creation compels us to affirm that before the fall and apart from sin, it was already functioning *positively* as an imperative conscience. Indeed, on the seventh day, Adam shared with delight in the *judicial* approval of God's handiwork, being summoned to do so by God.

An example demonstrating this positive legislative aspect of conscience prior to the fall relates to the covenant of marriage (see Gen 2:23; Prov 2:17; Ezek 16:8; Mal 2:14). It appears that Adam self-consciously patterns his relationship with Eve according to the pattern of his relation to God. In the case of this first marriage, the indicative legislative witness outside Adam was coupled with an inward legislative summons normative for human conduct.

In his work on *Marriage as a Covenant*, Gordon Hugenberger affirms the paradigmatic nature of Adam and Eve's marriage. According to Hugenberger, marriage as covenant is not merely a synonym of "relationship." As in the case of the sacred bond between the creator and humanity, marriage is "an elected, as opposed to natural, relationship of obligation established under divine sanction," and this implies: "1) a relationship 2) with a non-relative 3) which involves obligations and 4) is established through an oath."[27] When God brought the woman to the man, Adam said, "This at last is bone of my bones and flesh of my flesh; she shall be called Woman, because she was taken out of Man" (Gen 2:23). Hugenberger highlights Adam's awareness of his obligations at this point:

> We observed that the paradigmatic marriage of Adam and Eve was accompanied by *verba solemnia*, spoken by Adam before God. ... As we argued, the fact that the "bone of my bones" formula is well-attested elsewhere within the Old Testament helps to identify these words as covenant-forming *verba solemnia*, rather than merely an ejaculatory

---

26. Bavinck, "Conscience," 118.
27. Gordon P. Hugenberger, *Marriage as a Covenant: Biblical Law and Ethics as Developed from Malachi* (Brill, 1994), 215. Referring to God's covenantal dealings with Israel, Geoffrey W. Grogan similarly observes that "Israel's relation to Yahweh was not based on natural kinship as in some ancient ethnic mythologies, but on a covenant he initiated." "The Old Testament Concept of Solidarity in Hebrews," *Tyndale Bulletin* 49 (1998): 162.

comment of delight. With variations this formula is found in Gen. 29:14; Judg. 9:2–3; 2 Sam. 5:2 (and the parallel in 1 Chron. 11:1); and 2 Sam. 19:13f. [ET 12f.]. Although in each case some notion of kinship is in view, the formula produces an effect well beyond the bare recognition of a familial relationship to include a commitment of loyalty and an appeal for reciprocal allegiance (i.e., as expected for *verba solemnia*, it effects a covenant commitment). As observed ... in the ancient world the solemn acknowledgment of a relationship was frequently the very means of creating it. These parallels as well as Adam's words spoken in the presence of the deity in Gen. 2:23 appear to offer unmistakable examples.[28]

Thus, the covenant-forming formula of Genesis 2:23 does not merely show Adam's approval with what he recognizes as fitting for him. According to Hugenberger, "These words appear to have been intended as a solemn affirmation of his marital commitment, an elliptical way of saying something like, 'I hereby invite you, God, to hold me accountable to treat this woman as part of my own body.'"[29] It therefore seems reasonable to note a correspondence between God's summoning and holding accountable humanity and Adam's inward sense of his legislative accountability before God and the woman.

The paradigmatic character of the marriage in the garden before the Lord causes even the narrator of Genesis to recognize a legislative obligation for all the descendants of the first couple: "Therefore a man shall leave his father and his mother and hold fast to his wife, and they shall become one flesh" (Gen 2:24). Sarna further explains this:

> Hebrew *'al ken* is not part of the narration, but it introduces an etiological observation on the part of the Narrator; that is, the origin of an existing custom or institution is assigned to some specific event in the past. In this case, some interrelated and fundamental aspects of the marital relationship are traced to God's original creative act and seen as part of the divinely ordained natural order.[30]

---

28. Hugenberger, *Marriage as a Covenant*, 230–31.
29. Hugenberger, *Marriage as a Covenant*, 165.
30. Sarna, *Genesis*, 23.

This example demonstrates that the legislative function of conscience operates in relation to and as a reflection of God's law from creation onward.[31]

SUMMARY

This chapter has considered the function of conscience within the context of the doctrine of creation. Having been created by God *ex nihilo*, conscience is at work before the fall, witnessing to, summoning, and legislating for the human being on behalf of God. Pointing humanity indisputably back to God, the function of conscience raises the question about the reasons why conscience works in such a manner. The next chapter will reflect in more detail upon the *nature* of conscience.

---

31. See Berkouwer, *Man: the Image of God*, 175.

3

THE NATURE OF CONSCIENCE

This chapter will attempt to conceptualize and systematize the previous findings within the larger fields of theological anthropology and theology proper to show that conscience is best understood in light of the reality of the triune creator. Starting from a reflection on human vocation in creation, conscience will be explored in terms of covenantal vocation and understood as covenantal awareness. The triune creator is the Lord of the covenant—the one who, in calling creation into being through his word, has simultaneously created a sacred bond with it, so that the whole cosmos has been founded on a covenantal order. Thereafter, the nature and work of the triune creator will be explored. A reflection on God's inner being as it is made known to us in his outer works of creation and redemption will provide an understanding of the phenomenon of conscience as a covenantal awareness of God and of his righteousness, showing that the ultimate explanation of the nature of conscience is God's own triune nature.

CONSCIENCE AND COVENANTAL VOCATION

In offering an explanation of the nature of conscience primarily in terms of a covenantal vocation and only secondarily in relation to the morality of human actions—whether good or bad—this chapter breaks new ground, and it therefore proceeds with a measure of hesitancy and in a provisional manner. Before considering conscience explicitly in relation to covenantal vocation, we will begin by investigating the notion of covenant in general, asking whether God already acted covenantally in creation. Then we will explore the reality of covenantal vocation and consider the way in which covenantal vocation helps to understand the nature of conscience.

Although Reformed theologians have developed the concept of covenantal vocation in depth, we will start with the work of N. T. Wright. Although Wright is not a Reformed theologian, his affirmation of the notion of covenantal vocation from outside the bounds of Reformed theology reinforces the case for the classic Reformed doctrine of the so-called covenant of works.[1]

Wright affirms that "the creator God is the covenant God, and vice versa."[2] However, a little later, Wright qualifies his previous statement by saying that "the creator God is *also* the redeeming, covenant God, and vice versa."[3] These slightly different statements raise a question: is God already in creation and from the very beginning a covenantal creator, or does God become a covenant God only later—as covenantal redeemer?

Wright answers the question by insisting that God's covenantal speaking activity is already at work in creation when he addresses the first Adam according to a "covenant of vocation."[4] Wright thus seems to move very close to the classical concept of a "covenant of works" as developed in Reformed theology. Proposing that humanity has been engaged since the beginning in a covenant of vocation, Wright makes the following claim:

> The vocation in question is that of being a genuine human being, with genuinely human tasks to perform as part of the Creator's purpose for his world. The main task of this vocation is "image-bearing," reflecting the Creator's wise stewardship into the world and reflecting the

---

1. Scholars are sometimes reticent about (or simply deny) the concept of a covenantal vocation/covenant of works in creation as distinct from a subsequent covenant of grace; see Mark Boda, *The Heartbeat of Old Testament Theology: Three Creedal Expressions* (Baker Academic, 2017), 61, 100; Scott J. Hafemann, "The Covenant Relationship," in *Central Themes in Biblical Theology: Mapping Unity in Diversity*, ed. Scott J. Hafemann and Paul R. House (Baker Academic, 2007), 20–42; Paul R. Williamson, *Sealed with an Oath: Covenant in God's Unfolding Purpose* (InterVarsity Press, 2007), 52–58, 69–76. However, Scott W. Hahn observes that even though "the notion of a covenant [of works] in creation remains a minority report ... nonetheless, the idea still enjoys considerable support." *Kinship by Covenant: A Canonical Approach to the Fulfillment of God's Saving Promises* (Yale University Press, 2009), 388. Besides the works of M. Horton and D. VanDrunen, for other contemporary affirmations of the covenant of works, see Jeong Koo Jeon, *Biblical Theology: Covenants and the Kingdom of God in Redemptive History* (Wipf & Stock, 2017); Harrison Perkins, *Catholicity and the Covenant of Works: James Ussher and the Reformed Tradition* (Oxford University Press, 2020); John V. Fesko, *The Covenant of Works: The Origins, Development, and Reception of the Doctrine* (Oxford University Press, 2020); and Guy Prentiss Waters, J. Nicholas Reid, John R. Muether, eds., *Covenant Theology: Biblical, Theological, and Historical Perspectives* (Crossway, 2020).

2. Nicholas T. Wright, *Paul in Fresh Perspective* (Fortress Press, 2005), 24.

3. Wright, *Paul in Fresh Perspective*, 27 (emphasis added).

4. It is very important to note that according to Wright, "covenant is the hidden presupposition of Jewish literature even when the word hardly occurs" (*Paul in Fresh Perspective*, 26). It seems, therefore, that this general presupposition should apply also to Genesis 1–3.

praises of all creation back to its maker. Those who do so are the "royal priesthood," the "kingdom of priests," the people who are called to stand at the dangerous but exhilarating point where heaven and earth meet. In saying this I am echoing what many theologians (including John Calvin, the founder of all "Reformed" theologies) have said before me. This is not surprising, because it is all there in the Bible.[5]

Apparently, for Wright, the creator God is the covenant God and vice versa, for God's word and acts are intrinsically covenantal, in the sense that when God speaks and acts his words and actions give birth to and establish a covenant, a sacred bond, with the recipients of those words and actions. And this is so not only in redemption but also in creation.[6]

By virtue of God's creative speech-act,[7] in creation humanity was bonded to God in a covenant, being called by the covenant Lord to be the covenant servant. Instead of approaching anthropology from a metaphysical and

---

5. Nicholas T. Wright, *The Day the Revolution Began: Reconsidering the Meaning of Jesus's Crucifixion* (HarperOne, 2016), 76. Even though he does not mention any scholar or give any bibliographical indication, Wright seems to approve of a number of Reformed theologians who "have used the phrase 'covenant of works' in a way significantly different from the view [he is] opposing" (Wright, *The Day the Revolution Began*, 75). As will be shown shortly, Wright seems to understand the covenant of vocation in a similar way to a number of Reformed theologians, such as F. Turretin, G. Vos, M. Kline, and M. Horton.

6. It should be stressed that even though Wright's notion of a covenant of vocation comes very close to and can even be identified with the concept of a covenant of works, his writings do not distinguish such a covenant from a covenant of grace, and thus he does not provide the larger context within which to frame the fulfillment of the first covenant by Jesus Christ. The covenant theology of Judaism proposes a distinction similar to that of Reformed theology, distinguishing between a treaty covenant (covenant of works) and a grant covenant (covenant of grace); see Moshe Weinfeld, "The Covenant of Grant in the Old Testament and in the Ancient Near East," *Journal of the American Oriental Society* 90 (1970): 184-203; Levenson, *The Love of God*, 1-58.

7. Applying speech-act theory to theological discourse, some scholars have investigated the relation between God's words and actions in order to show that God acts by speaking. Thus, when God uttered his creative word, he did not simply call creation into being but related to it "in a *covenantal* manner, that is, according to the same pattern he will repeat constantly in his ongoing relationship with human creatures, and that will become the fundamental characteristic of his redemptive relationship with humanity," (Ward, *Words of Life*, 27). On the usefulness of speech-act theory in theology, see Ward, *Word and Supplement*, 75-136; Nicholas Wolterstorff, *Divine Discourse: Philosophical Reflections on the Claim that God Speaks* (Cambridge University Press, 1995). Commenting upon Goethe's criticism of the common translation of John 1:1 and his alternative proposal of "in the beginning was the act," Martin Hengel makes the following assertion: "Faust with his false alternative does not understand that word and act become one in the divine word in creation and revelation, as influenced by Genesis 1:1ff. in Psalms 33." "The Prologue of the Gospel of John as the Gateway to Christological Truth," in *The Gospel of John and Christian Theology*, ed. Richard Bauckham and Carl Mosser (Eerdmans, 2008), 274.

ontological perspective, Scripture is concerned to stress God's covenantal vocation "in order to place the whole man before his total life's *calling*."[8] Far from reducing the original covenantal vocation to a mere works-contract that requires simply conformity to an external moral code,[9] classical covenantal theology focuses on the vocation given to the whole human being in creation. Thus, the expressions "covenant of works" and "covenant of vocation" should be taken as synonymous, and the perfect obedience required by the covenant is not required in relation to arbitrary and abstract moral principles[10] but in relation to God's comprehensive call to humanity to worship and serve him as the only true and living God.[11]

Francis Turretin, far from upholding a reductive notion of a works-contract, observes that the duty—that is, the vocation of the first Adam—consisted both in a larger and moral dimension and in a stricter and symbolic aspect, and, most importantly, the latter was subordinate to the former:

> The duty was partly general, partly special (according to the twofold law given to him: the moral or natural and the symbolic). The general was the knowledge and worship of God, justice towards his neighbor and every kind of holiness; the special was abstinence from the forbidden fruit (in which obedience to the whole law was contained as in a compendium and specimen). The former was founded on the law of nature not written in a book, but engraven and stamped upon the heart. ... The latter was founded upon the symbolic and positive law. The former was principal and primary; the latter, however, only secondary. For although he was bound to obey each special precept

---

8. Berkouwer, *Man: The Image of God*, 207 (emphasis added).
9. Wright, *The Day the Revolution Began*, 75.
10. In this regard, Horton observes, "The law is not to be understood as simply an external list of rules imposed on those who are already constituted as human persons on some other (autonomous) basis, but as that righteousness that defines both God and God's works. As with God himself, the law does not simply stand over against the creature as a heteronomous authority, but belongs to the creature's own identity. The law of God and the image of God are therefore two sides of the same coin," (*Lord and Servant*, 101-2).
11. In a manner similar to that of Wright, Horton stresses that for Calvin "the 'image' has ... to do with the vocation given to humanity." *Calvin on the Christian Life: Glorifying and Enjoying God Forever* (Crossway, 2014), 64. Cf. Calvin, *Institutes*, 3.10.6. Similarly, Richard Lints claims, "In their calling to 'fill' and 'govern,' humankind reflected [the image of] God." *Identity and Idolatry: The Image of God and Its Inversion* (InterVarsity Press, 2015), 76.

or that symbolic law given to him, still most especially was obedience to the natural law required of him.[12]

Likewise, Kline proposes a comprehensive explanation of human vocation:

> There were mandates that defined man's *role* in the advancement of the kingdom of God and there were ordinances that established the institutional structures of man's historical existence. These covenant stipulations were concerned with both the vertical and horizontal dimensions of covenant life. They dealt with man's cultural *task*, his *commission* with respect to his horizontal relationship to the world that was his environment and to all his fellow creatures. They dealt also with man's cultic *role*, his duties in his directly vertical relationship to his Creator-Lord. *Man's theocratic commission involved a dual priest-king office.*[13]

These representative Reformed theologians assert—in a manner remarkably similar to that of N. T. Wright—that, in Adam, human beings are called by the covenant Lord to fulfill a covenantal vocation in creation as sons and servants, reflecting and filling the earth with the splendor of God's glory as prophets, priests, and kings.[14]

Implied in the covenantal vocation there is the notion of merit and demerit. In fact, the vocation was explicitly accompanied by a promise: the

---

12. Turretin, *Institutes of Elenctic Theology*, 1:577. See also Bavinck, *Reformed Dogmatics*, 2:574.

13. Kline, *Kingdom Prologue*, 66 (emphasis added). In commenting upon Genesis 2:16–17, Kline later observes that "if we call this the probationary stipulation, our intention is not to suggest that man's covenantal obligations and testing were reduced to this one requirement, but simply to indicate that this stipulation had a special function to perform in bringing the probation into concentrated focus for a radical decision" (*Kingdom Prologue*, 104).

14. Ricoeur explains conscience by the term "summoned subject," which refers to "a self in relation and, in this way, a self in the position of respondent," specifically a self responsive to a vocation. His reflection points back to the summoning function of conscience within the context of the structure common to all the Scriptures, namely "their dialogic structure that confronts the words and acts of God with the response human beings give to them"; as examples of the summoned self, he mentions the vocation of priests, judges, and especially prophets. According to Ricoeur, a theology of conscience should arise from within this common structure of vocation/response ("The Summoned Subject," 262–63). Similarly, Webster asserts that although conscience "occurs as a mode of my reflection ... that reflection is not self-generated, arbitrary and finally responsible to nothing other than itself"; he then adds: "It is an answer, a hearing, and thus a responsibility to truth. In conscience I attend to the call" ("God and Conscience," 258).

promise of a perfect, indestructible, and everlasting life of communion with God in a creation filled through Adam's obedience with the glory of the creator and with all good—on earth as in heaven. That was the ultimate goal that would have been achieved by humanity keeping the divine law, namely by complying with the call received from the Lord of the covenant. In the words of Vos, Adam "is immediately directed not to his own bliss but to the honor of the Creator, and *assigned a task* so that, by completing it, he might enter the full joy of his covenant God."[15] Similarly, Wright observes:

> Within this narrative [of Genesis], creation itself is understood as a kind of Temple, a heaven-and-earth duality, where humans function as the "image-bearers" in the cosmic Temple, part of earth yet reflecting the life of love of heaven. This is how creation was designed to function and flourish: under the stewardship of the image-bearers. Humans are called not just to keep certain moral standards in the present and to enjoy God's presence here and hereafter, but to celebrate, worship, procreate, and take responsibility within the rich, vivid developing life of creation. According to Genesis, that is what humans were made for.[16]

Human creatures were made to live their lives in obedience. "Do this and live, fulfill your vocation, accomplish your task!" were the imperative words of the creator and Lord of the covenant. It is not that God was obligated to bestow a perfect life of love on humanity in response to their obedience. Rather, God freely and generously determined to impart his promised blessing as a reward to the image-bearers for their fulfilling the covenant.

Going back to Turretin's definition of vocation, the first Adam transgressed not only the special precept of the symbolic law given to him but also the more comprehensive calling to know and worship God, love his neighbor justly, and fulfill every kind of holiness implicit in the natural covenant vocation. And this is why he merited the threatened curse rather than the

---

15. Geerhardus Vos, "The Doctrine of the Covenant in Reformed Theology," in *Redemptive History and Biblical Theology: The Shorter Writings of Geerhardus Vos*, ed. Richard B. Gaffin Jr., (P&R Publishing, 2001), 245 (emphasis added).

16. Wright, *The Day the Revolution Began*, 76–77. For a thorough investigation of the pristine garden as temple, see Kline, *Kingdom Prologue*, 14–90; Gregory K. Beale, *The Temple and the Church's Mission: A Biblical Theology of the Dwelling Place of God* (InterVarsity Press, 2004), 23–121.

promised blessing. Disturbed by a moralizing of the problem of sin and by a paganizing view of God, Wright in general concurs with Turretin's understanding of the fall:

> The diagnosis of the human plight is then not simply that humans have broken God's moral law, offending and insulting the creator, whose image they bear—though that is true as well. This lawbreaking is a symptom of a much more serious disease. Morality is important, but it isn't the whole story. Called to responsibility and authority within and over the creation, humans have turned their vocation upside down, giving worship and allegiance to forces and powers within creation itself. The name for this is idolatry. The result is slavery and finally death. It isn't just that humans do wrong things and so incur punishment. This is one element of the larger problem, which isn't much about a punishment ... it is, rather, about direct consequences. When we worship and serve forces within the creation, ... we hand over our power to other forces only too happy to usurp our position.[17]

Because the call to loyalty implicit in the covenant of vocation was not heeded, God judged humanity—in and by his righteousness and not arbitrarily—giving it up to the consequences of its idolatry and disloyalty. The covenant called Adam to merit the blessing, but his betraying of that calling was counted against him as a demerit. And that is the judgment or the punishment, to use Wright's expression.[18]

---

17. Wright, *The Day the Revolution Began*, 77. On idolatry as the "sin of sins," see Gregory K. Beale, *We Become What We Worship: A Biblical Theology of Idolatry* (InterVarsity Press, 2008); Richard Lints, *Identity and Idolatry*. Calvin's assessment of the human's heart is well-known: "Man's nature, so to speak, is a perpetual factory of idols" (*Institutes*, 1.11.8).

18. Referring to the last quote by Wright, in his argument he is concerned not to reduce the reality of sin to a mere violation of a moral code and God to a replica of a paganized version of the deity. However, setting lawbreaking and idolatry against each other appears to be a false dichotomy. Moral lawbreaking—offending and insulting the creator—is implicit in idolatry, and idolatry is implicit in moral lawbreaking; they are two sides of the same coin. For example, in the two accounts of the covenant ceremony in Joshua 8:30–35 and chapter 24, in the first episode Joshua calls Israel to covenantal fidelity in relation to the law. Obeying the law—especially the "first table"—is to resist and renounce idolatry and vice versa. And this is so for the very reason adduced by Wright: moral lawbreaking is not just the violation of a positive command (such as that of Gen 2:16–17) apart from the covenant. The act of lawbreaking was an act of turning upside down the covenant of vocation, symbolized by the positive command that brought into concentrated focus the substance of the whole vocation. For the same reason, the dichotomy between punishment and direct consequences is fallacious, for the two are different aspects

The reality of conscience sits within this covenantal ontology and anthropology. It should be understood comprehensively in relation to the intended accomplishing of humanity's vocation to fill the earth with the glory of God's image[19] and not just to some isolated or external moral norms. Having been created in that image, humans were intrinsically conscious of a religious and moral vocation from the beginning. The external and objective witness of creation as the theater of the glory of the creator, coupled with the symbolic summons of the positive and probationary command relative to the tree of the knowledge of good and evil, joined with the internal and subjective witness of human conscience in order to make humanity aware of its vocation as covenant servant.[20] Accordingly, within the covenantal order of reality, *conscience should be understood as covenantal perception or awareness of God in relation to this vocation*.[21] For Berkouwer, conscience "does not at all refer to some separate [autonomous] organ of moral norms, but rather to *a consciousness of being in a good relationship with God*."[22] Conscience is therefore to be conceived as the spontaneous, intuitive, inner, and subjective awareness of being called by God, the Lord of the covenant, to fulfill human vocation within the created realm as image-bearers.

---

of the same reality and the diagnosis of the human plight concerns one and the same problem, namely God's cosmic lawsuit. See Andrew T. Lincoln, *Truth on Trial: The Lawsuit Motif in the Fourth Gospel* (Hendrikson, 2000), 185–93.

19. On the theme of a human's vocation as filling the earth with the image of God's glory, see Gregory K. Beale, *A New Testament Biblical Theology: The Unfolding of the Old Testament in the New* (Baker Academic, 2011), 29–46.

20. While in classical and Hellenistic Greek culture "neither in a philosophical nor a moral sense has conscience a great deal to do with the deity," so that it "is not in any sense a special mode or source of revelation," in the Old Testament, "the reflection of the I about itself is thus obedient listening to God ... the I is a single person confronting the God who speaks." Christian Maurer, "σύνοιδα, συνείδησις," in *Theological Dictionary of the New Testament*, ed. Gerhard Kittel and Gerhard Friedrich (Eerdmans, 1971), 7:902, 908.

21. This understanding of conscience helps to reduce the tension between "divine command theory" and "natural law theory" in ethics. These two approaches should not be taken in absolute terms as radically opposed one to the other but as compatible and inseparable. God's explicit commands work alongside conscience as an innate awareness of natural law. On the concurrence of God's commands and conscience, see Paul Helm, *John Calvin's Ideas* (Oxford University Press, 2004), 347–54.

22. Berkouwer, *Man: The Image of God*, 173 (emphasis added). Similarly, Webster affirms that "law is not arbitrary command, but the imperative presence of God, quickening creatures to responsible life in accordance with the nature given to them by the creator; *law is not simply statute, but the form of fellowship*" ("Rector et iudex super omnia genera doctrinarium?," 171 emphasis added).

Understood in both religious and ethical terms, then, conscience gives witness to God's law and is intended not merely as a moral code condensed into one positive command but as a summons that, with legislative power, calls humanity to serve God's purposes in the world in general.[23] So understood, God's law is not merely external commands or a legal model, as if it was not written on the human heart and as if humans could decide—independently and apart from their own nature—what is good and evil. Covenantal awareness does not allow for human creatures to assume for themselves an identity different from the one given to them according to God's image. And covenantal consciousness—even apart from sin—is meant to prompt people to perceive that by nature they are called to live by loving God and other creatures.[24] Horton makes the relationship between conscience and God's covenant vocation explicit:

> Intrinsic to humanness, particularly the *imago*, is a covenantal office or commission into which every person is born; it is therefore, as an equally universal phenomenon, the basis for God's righteous judgment of humankind even apart from special revelation (Romans 1 and 2). This is to say that "law"—in particular, the divine covenant-law—is natural, a *verbum internum* (internal word) that rings in yet is not identical to the conscience. The covenant of creation renders every person a dignified and therefore accountable image-bearer of God.

---

23. Since the plot of the biblical narrative moves forward by recapitulating earlier events and patterns, the history of Israel recapitulates the history of Adam. Accordingly, in the Old Testament, Israel's consciousness (just as that of Adam) was related not primarily to the law in itself but more comprehensively to the unique covenant relation with Yahweh to which the law gave extrinsic expression. For example, in Psalm 50 the term "covenant" appears twice (Ps 50:5, 16). The covenant is referred to only secondarily in terms of law when part of the Decalogue is cited before the conclusion (Ps 50:16–20). The first mention of the covenant is in terms of fellowship through the so-called covenant formula, which puts weight not so much on norm and precept but on relationship: "I am God, your God" (Ps 50:7). On the covenant formula in general, see Rolf Rendtorff, *The Covenant Formula: An Exegetical and Theological Investigation* (T&T Clark, 1998).

24. Webster shares this comprehensive view, writing that Christian theology talks "of the human person as one whose humanity is to be found in fellowship with God, and therefore defined, not in terms of reason, will or consciousness anterior to God, *but in terms of the good purposes of God, to which active allegiance is given in worship, confession and service*" ("God and Conscience," 234, emphasis added).

Even the fall did not eradicate the original revelation of God's righteous law to the conscience.[25]

However, it is not the nature of the covenant that by itself determines the nature of conscience. Rather, it is the nature of the Lord that explains the nature of conscience, and that is why theology must not restrict the understanding of conscience to the sphere of the moral or of the anthropological. It is who God is that ultimately determines our understanding of the phenomenon of conscience as a covenantal awareness of God and of his righteous demands implicit in the covenantal vocation. This requires the rooting of the phenomenon of conscience in the ground of theology proper, in order to show that what explains the nature of conscience is ultimately God himself. And it is to this task that the next section turns, albeit with a degree of measured care.

CONSCIENCE AND THE TRIUNE GOD

The second subdivision of this chapter will attempt to investigate conscience specifically in relation to God—that is, as arising from and corresponding to his inner life. If "all being and occurrence that is not God is to its very depths *ex nihilo*"[26] it might be said that conscience—and all God's external works—in some manner "arise[s] from and correspond[s] to his inner life [for] from himself God gives himself."[27] Because of this arising and corresponding, conscience can only be properly understood by looking at the one from whom it came for, as Gilles Emery notes, "We cannot study creation until we have considered God's immanent actions."[28] In some measure, the created order exhibits the glory and perfection of the inner life of the triune God, and as a consequence, the *ex nihilo* origin of all things is significant not only in cosmological terms but especially in anthropological terms, for the reality of the *imago Dei* defines the identity of human creatures. It could be said that the

---

25. Horton, *Lord and Servant*, 94.

26. Webster, "Love Is Also a Lover," 100.

27. Webster, "Life in and of Himself," 23. From the perspective of biblical theology, Lints writes, "That which is straightforwardly on the surface of the text [is] that the image reflects the original. Humankind *in some manner* reflects the Creator" (*Identity and Idolatry*, 57, emphasis added).

28. Gilles Emery, *The Trinitarian Theology of Saint Thomas Aquinas* (Oxford University Press, 2004), 42.

identity of human beings is ontologically derivative of the essential inner identity of the triune God. Now, if conscience is part of God's external work in creation, arising from and corresponding in some manner to his inner life, in what sense and in what manner does it correspond to that inner life? Or, putting the question differently, why and how is the reality of conscience a reflection of God's own life?

Webster states that "theological contemplation of the scriptural mystery of creation necessarily requires speculative attention to the being and acts of the Triune God." He continues: "Properly conducted, speculative divinity simply draws attention to God *in se* as the founding condition of God *pro nobis*." Moreover, Webster believes that salvation history cannot be grasped without reference to its grounding in the perfect life of God himself, ergo he roots covenantal history as a whole[29] in the life of the triune God: "The speculative is not an alternative to the drama of covenant history; it is an indication of what takes place in the covenant, and of how *the covenant reaches back into the infinite glory of the one who needs no creature and who creates out of inherent goodness*."[30] Therefore, conscience, with its covenantal awareness, is also to be understood as reaching back into the life of the triune God.

The claim that conscience renders one aware of oneself in relation to God and his vocation presupposes that the natural and fundamental tendency of conscience is to move human creatures outside themselves, directing them toward others and toward God. In other words, conscience is the awareness of alterity and its concomitant call to reciprocity; theologically, and primarily, it is to be understood as human responsiveness to God and his vocation.[31]

---

29. In general, it appears that in his writings Webster refers to covenant history when thinking of the broad history of God relating to creatures, making no distinctions among covenants. Michael Allen, "Covenant in Recent Theology," in Waters, Reid, and Muether, *Covenant Theology: Biblical, Theological, and Historical Perspectives*, 432–37.

30. John B. Webster, "Creation Out of Nothing," in *Christian Dogmatics: Reformed Theology for the Church Catholic*, ed. Michael Allen and Scott R. Swain (Baker Academic, 2016), 135–37 (emphasis added).

31. Ricoeur explains conscience as "the place of an original form of the dialectic between selfhood and otherness." For Ricoeur, the identity of human beings may be considered in terms of parity and continuity or in terms of singularity and discontinuity. Concentrating on the personal singularity and the unique quality of the individual, in Ricoeur's dialogical model conscience is the responsive posture before the request or injunction of the other. Ricoeur understands conscience not as activity but as passivity, and he explains the phenomenon primarily not by the metaphor of the accusing tribunal but by that of the calling voice: "Being-enjoined would then constitute the moment of otherness proper to the phenomenon of conscience, in accordance with the metaphor of the voice. Listening to the voice of conscience would signify

In this sense, the reality of conscience reaches back to the reality of God's Trinitarian communion and of his inexhaustibly active life. In some manner, conscience points back to the reality of the processions that ground the relations of Father, Son, and Spirit.[32]

Expounding the Trinitarian theology of Thomas Aquinas, Emery writes:

> So one single reality [the triune God] is envisaged from many different angles. First of all, it can be considered under the aspect of the *action* in which one person communicates the divine substance to another. This is a matter of generation and spiration. This *action* is signified in a dynamic way, "like the surging of one person toward another." ... This same reality can also be considered under the aspect of the process of the "outcoming" person: this is then the *procession*, signified as the "pathway" leading to the constitution of that person; the Son "is begotten," the Holy Spirit "proceeds." The very same reality can be further considered in the light of the property or characteristic which the persons possess in virtue of the processions: this is then a matter of the *relation* which distinctly characterizes each person. ... Finally, the same reality can be considered under the aspect of that which possesses this relation, based on the procession: this is the *person*, signified in the manner of the reality which exists or subsists.[33]

However, actions, processions, relations, and persons do not exhaust the reality of Trinitarian life. Reasoning backward from God's outer works, more can be said about the communion of the persons and the above ways of envisaging the reality of God's Trinitarian life. In this regard, it is important to consider the *reciprocity* of the divine persons in the sense of "the

---

being-enjoined by the Other." For Ricoeur, in the calling of conscience it is another who speaks in the heart of the self: "The passivity of being-enjoined consists in the situation of listening in which the ethical subject is placed in relation to the voice addressed to it in the second person." *Oneself as Another* (University of Chicago Press, 1992), 341, 351, 352.

32. Looking at conscience through the lens of soteriology as created, fallen, redeemed, and perfected, it is possible to apply to conscience what Webster affirms about soteriology in general: "Soteriology therefore has its place within the theology of the *mysterium trinitatis*, that is, God's inherent and communicated richness of life as Father, Son and Holy Spirit." John B. Webster, "It Was the Will of the Lord to Bruise Him," in *God and the Works of God*, 148.

33. Emery, *Trinitarian Theology*, 75.

reciprocal presence of the divine persons" to each other.[34] It might be tentatively suggested that this conscious reciprocal presence of the divine persons is the spring from which conscience was created, because—in the words of Webster—"the inner order in which God lives [is that] to which the external economy of God's works is anchored."[35] The Father, the Son, and the Spirit live *consciously* in and with one another in a reciprocal immanence that gives rise to an interaction of communication and activity. This is the doctrine of perichoresis, which "means the communal immanence, or the reciprocated interiority of the three persons."[36] Commenting on Aquinas's language of this reciprocal interiority, Emery writes:

> In presenting the "in being" of the persons, [Thomas] uses ... the expressions *union* or *intrinsic conjunction, interiority, intimacy, existing in, being in that which is the most intimate and most secret* (this is how the Son is in the Father), *reciprocal communality of "in being," communal union*, etc. In every case, the communal presence of the persons excludes their confusion, because it is based in their real distinction. It rules out the "isolation" of one person, since it implies a communal relationship of persons. The divine persons are not "solitaries"; they are "inseparables."[37]

The reciprocal communality and intimacy of the divine persons entails a conscious awareness of the other persons and of their being in relationship to each other. It is important to insist that this conscious awareness is reciprocal, in the sense that the modes of communal presence "are not

---

34. Emery, *Trinitarian Theology*, 298. Owen concurs: "Such is the distinction of the persons in the unity of the divine essence, as they act in natural and essential acts *reciprocally* one towards another,—namely, in understanding, love, and the like; they know and mutually love each other" (*The Works of John Owen*, 18:87).

35. Webster, "It Was the Will," 153.

36. Emery, *The Trinitarian Theology*, 299.

37. Emery, *The Trinitarian Theology*, 302. Speaking of this mutual reciprocity, Thiselton writes, "Twenty centuries of reflection have hardly made it easier for us today *both* to assert the primacy of God as source and goal *and* to maintain the mutuality and reciprocity which characterize God's own self-differentiation as an aspect of his gracious respect for the otherness of the 'other' whom the One loves as the self" (*The First Epistle to the Corinthians*, 1,238).

interchangeable, but distinct within their reciprocity."[38] Consequently, "each person [is] present to the others in a distinct mode."[39]

It is this conscious reciprocal awareness and interaction that helps us to consider the reality of human conscience. Conscience can be tentatively conceived of as arising and corresponding to God's inner life because it is a reflection—a sort of replication—of the conscious relationships between the persons of the Godhead. In creating conscience, God established a covenantal relationship between himself and humanity of which human creatures are inherently aware. As in the case of the triune God himself, the conscience of human creatures *analogously* rules out any form of absolute isolation and solitariness given their covenantal bond with the creator.[40] Horton writes:

> Human existence is "very good" insofar as humans answer back according to the purpose of their existence. *Human personhood is analogous to divine personhood in its ecstatic character.*[41]

---

38. Emery, *The Trinitarian Theology*, 305.

39. Emery, *The Trinitarian Theology*, 307. The retrieval of classical Trinitarian theism—such as that of Aquinas and Owen—allows for an exploration of the richness of the reciprocal conscious awareness of the divine persons without presupposing in the essential life of the Triune God three separate and individual centers of consciousness, volition, and agency. In fact, the presupposition of classical theism is that God's unity of essence is the ground of perichoresis; see Lewis Ayres, *Nicaea and Its Legacy: An Approach to Fourth-Century Trinitarian Theology* (Oxford University Press, 2004), 288–301, 344–63; Horton, *The Christian Faith*, 294–303; Fred Sanders, "The Trinity," in *The Oxford Handbook of Systematic Theology*, ed. John Webster, Kathryn Tanner, and Iain Torrance (Oxford University Press, 2007), 35–53. For a critical assessment of the "social Trinitarianism" of theologians such as J. Moltmann, C. Gunton, L. Boff, J. Zizioulas, C. Plantinga Jr., and others, see Karen Kilby, "Perichoresis and Projection: Problems with Social Doctrines of the Trinity," *New Blackfriars* 81.956 (2000): 432–45. For a more positive evaluation, see Gijsbert van den Brink, "Social Trinitarianism: A Discussion of Some Recent Theological Criticisms," *International Journal of Systematic Theology* 16, no. 3 (2014): 331–50. For some anthropological repercussions of relational theism, see Harriet A. Harris, "Should We Say that Personhood Is Relational?," *Scottish Journal of Theology* 41, no. 2 (1998): 214–34. Craig A. Carter—a former student of John Webster—develops an extended critique of relational theism in *Contemplating God with the Great Tradition: Recovering Trinitarian Classical Theism* (Baker Academic, 2021). See also D. Stephen Long, *The Perfectly Simple Triune God: Aquinas and His Legacy* (Fortress Press, 2016), 307–62; Paul D. Molnar, *Divine Freedom and the Doctrine of the Immanent Trinity: In Dialogue with Karl Barth and Contemporary Theology* (Bloomsbury, 2017), 404–27; Stephen R. Holmes, *The Quest for the Trinity: The Doctrine of God in Scripture, History and Modernity* (InterVarsity Press, 2012), 1–32.

40. For some reflection on the usefulness of perichoresis as an analogy in relation to the *imago Dei*, see Randall E. Otto, "The Use and Abuse of *Perichoresis* in Recent Theology," *Scottish Journal of Theology* 54 (2001): 377–79, 384.

41. Horton, *Lord and Servant*, 98 (emphasis added).

Thus, it might be proposed that the conscience is the ecstatic capacity of human persons for conscious reciprocal awareness, primarily in relation to God, as it witnesses to God's alterity. In fact, it has been noted above that the human conscience in relation to God has a summoning function.

This observation raises a further question: does the conscious inner reciprocity of the persons of Father, Son, and Spirit indicate any presence of a reciprocal and *binding* summons among the divine persons? If conscience involves a witness to God's alterity and a legislative summons, is there among the persons of the Godhead something similar at work? Put in different terms, why and in what manner does the witnessing, and especially the summoning and legislating activities of human conscience, reach back into the immanent life of God? If it is the case that "the works manifest the nature of the one who acts,"[42] then there must be a way in which conscience—in its summoning and legislating activities—points back to God's essential life.

Since the use of analogy at this point is even more complex than in the case of the previous considerations, a few words of qualification seem appropriate. First, it should be reiterated that a reflection on conscience and God's immanent justice must proceed tentatively and cautiously. In previous works about the function and nature of conscience, little has been said to root this human phenomenon in the reality of God's essential righteousness in an analogical way.[43] Secondly, in order not to import anything inappropriate into a description of the inner life of God, theological discourse should adhere to the authorized, analogical language of Scripture, as noted at various points in the introduction. Horton recently stressed that this is necessary because otherwise "the only knowledge of God that could be gleaned apart from God's own gracious initiative would be confused and utterly equivocal apart from God's initiative in self-communication."[44] Moreover, in avoiding the illusion of univocal knowledge, the analogical language of Scripture aims at a sufficiently true and appropriate—even though not exhaustive—investigation of God and of everything else as related to God. Indeed, what we have is, in Horton's words, an "epistemology of pilgrims: no final truth-as-vision here

---

42. Emery, *The Trinitarian Theology*, 309.
43. None of the sources I consulted gave any evidence of taking this step of inquiry.
44. Horton, *Covenant and Eschatology*, 8.

and now, but truthful divine accommodation for the purposes at hand, which the church's theology and proclamation exist to serve."[45]

With these qualifications in mind, the following statement can be considered: as justice is predicated of humanity so (analogously) it is predicated of God. Even though God communicated this attribute to human creatures, righteousness is not found in them in the perfection that it is found in God nor is rectitude known by humans as God knows it. However, in a manner analogical to human creatures who "are a law to themselves" (Rom 2:14), it might be suggested that God too is a law unto himself, for there is perfect harmony between his being and his own eternal justice.[46] As law fits human identity, so it belongs especially to God's identity, particularly if it is remembered that "law is not simply statute, but the form of fellowship."[47] Thus, it might be said that the form of fellowship of the divine persons is perfectly righteous. Given that the nature of the one who acts as creator is perfectly righteous, that righteousness shapes, regulates, and overflows into the communion and the acts of the persons of the Father, Son, and Spirit in their reciprocal intimacy. Webster's comments in this regard are worthy of attention:

> [God's] fullness of life in relation is the order of righteousness of God's being. God's righteousness in himself, his *iustitia interna*, is his perfect correspondence with the law of his being, the integrity of his will and his existence, the completeness and bliss of his self-relation. ... The triune God is in himself righteousness. His righteousness is, as we have already noted, the peace and order of his perfect self-relation as Father, Son and Spirit. In this perfect communion God corresponds with himself, that is, perfectly fulfils his own will to be the one he is, and so perfectly enacts the law of his being. His righteousness is the unbroken and fully realized harmony of God's life and his will, in the

---

45. Horton, *Covenant and Eschatology*, 9. For a deeper reflection on the difference between *theologia archetypa* and *theologia ectypa*, see 184–91. On the "preservative" function of analogy, see Michael S. Horton, *Covenant and Salvation: Union with Christ* (Westminster John Knox, 2007), 204–9.

46. Calvin understands Romans 2:14 in the same sense: "We do not imagine God to be lawless. He is a law to himself; because, as Plato says, men laboring under the influence of concupiscence need law; but the will of God is not only free from all vice, but is the supreme standard of perfection, the law of all laws." *Institutes*, 3.23.2 (from the translation by Henry Beveridge [Hendrickson, 2007]).

47. Webster, "*Rector et iudex super omnia genera doctrinarium?*," 171.

eternal moments of paternity, filiation and spiration which constitute his being.[48]

This reflection has its counterpart in Bavinck's claim that conscience is the law of human personality and that "this law of the personality points back to [God] as the Legislator."[49] It might be affirmed that God is "legislator" not only in relation to human creatures but in regard to himself. Therefore, just as in the blessed life of the Godhead *ad intra* righteousness determines and controls the fully realized harmony of the reciprocal intimacy of the divine persons, so conscience was created as the law of human creatures in order that they might live according to their nature as covenant servants not in isolation but freely as summoned subjects in conscious communion with God. It is in regard to this communion that conscience functions as witnessing, summoning, and legislating according to God's own righteousness so that his *ad intra* justice is manifested *ad extra* in the creation of conscience.[50]

Moreover, the notion of conscience as covenantal awareness might further be considered as reaching back into God's inner life in relation to the Reformed doctrine of the covenant of redemption.[51] Is there anything in God's eternal decree to save that resembles the covenantal awareness of those who have been created in God's image? Although speaking of God's eternal decree is speaking already about God *pro nobis*, the language of decree and covenant of redemption remains anchored to the eternal reciprocity, mutuality, and unity of God *in se*. Therefore, thinking about this reciprocity and the mutuality of the divine will in eternity, it might be affirmed that speaking of the notion of the covenant of redemption is still speaking of God *in se* and not only of God in relation to creatures.[52] That is why it seems permissible to

---

48. Webster, "Rector et iudex super omnia genera doctrinarium?," 160, 170.

49. Bavinck, "Conscience," 125.

50. It seems that Bavinck's persuasion that the "presence of conscience requires sin as its basis" leads him to believe that "God does not have a conscience," for he is the lawgiver and not a subject (*Reformed Ethics*, 1:204). However, thinking about God (and conscience) only in terms of law-giver seems to restrict the reflection on God's righteousness to his *iustitia externa* alone, losing sight of his *iustitia interna*. If the divine persons are conscious of their perfect communion in righteousness and mutually aware of each other in justice, the general picture may change.

51. The notion of a covenant of redemption is hotly debated. For an overview of and response to negative evaluations, see J. Mark Beach, "The Doctrine of the *Pactum Salutis* in the Covenant Theology of Herman Witsius," *Mid-America Journal of Theology* 13 (2002): 101-42.

52. See Michael Allen and Scott R. Swain, "Obedience of the Eternal Son," *International Journal of Systematic Theology* 15, no. 2 (2013): 114-34; Scott R. Swain, "The Covenant of Redemption," in

investigate with caution some form of correspondence between the reality of the covenant of redemption in eternity and the phenomenon of covenantal conscience.

John Fesko defines the so-called *pactum salutis* as follows:

> The covenant of redemption is the pre-temporal, intra-trinitarian agreement among Father, Son, and Holy Spirit to plan and execute the redemption of the elect. The covenant entails the appointment of the Son as surety of the covenant of grace who accomplishes the redemption of the elect through His incarnation, perfect obedience, suffering, resurrection, and ascension. The covenant of redemption is also the root of the Spirit's role to anoint and equip the Son for His mission as surety and to apply His finished work to the elect.[53]

What is important in the construction of a theology of conscience is that the decree of God's will to save is realized *per modum foederis*—that is, by way of the covenant. The concept of covenant is used to make understandable the counsel of the divine will, and it serves the purpose of stressing the unity and mutuality of that will. Speaking of the origin of the priesthood of Christ in the intra-Trinitarian *consilium Dei*, Owen recognizes the limitations of such language but suggests that it nonetheless conveys divine truth to human capacity and experience:

> In the framing and producing the things which concern mankind, there were *peculiar, internal, personal transactions* between the Father, the Son, and Spirit. The scheme of speech here used is in *genere deliberativo*,—by way of consultation. But whereas this cannot directly and properly be ascribed unto God, an anthropopathy must be allowed in the words. The mutual distinct actings and concurrence of the several

---

Allen and Swain, *Christian Dogmatics*, 107-25.

53. John V. Fesko, *The Trinity and the Covenant of Redemption* (Christian Focus Publications, 2016), 131-32. To this thicker Trinitarian definition of the covenant of redemption that includes the Spirit, compare the more common christological definition in terms of an agreement only between Father and Son given by Richard A. Muller in *Dictionary of Latin and Greek Theological Terms Drawn Principally from Protestant Scholastic Theology* (Baker Books, 1985), 217.

persons in the Trinity are expressed by way of deliberation, and that because we can no otherwise determine or act.[54]

What is of importance here is that covenantal language shows that there is a reciprocal awareness among the divine persons related to the *ad intra* eternal decree to redeem. In Scripture, that divine reciprocal awareness of the divine persons is described analogically in terms of covenant,[55] and the extension of the processions through the missions of the persons is explained as covenantal.[56]

Thus, it might be suggested that the covenantal reciprocity that made the Son eternally aware of the Father's vocation to him as mediator according to the redemptive decree and that made the Spirit eternally aware of the Father's and the Son's vocation to him as executor of the saving decree is also, in the created realm, determinative of the nature of conscience. Conscience arises from and corresponds to God's inner life in that it makes human creatures aware of God and his claims in the form of covenantal vocation. As the Father, the Son, and the Spirit are eternally and reciprocally aware of each

---

54. Owen, *The Works of John Owen*, 18:58. Speaking in broad terms of the analogical and metaphorical language of Scripture, Owen remarks, "For such allusions are exceedingly suited to let in a sense into our minds of those things which we cannot distinctly comprehend. And there is an infinite condescension of divine wisdom in this way of instruction, representing unto us the power of things spiritual in what we naturally discern." "Meditations and Discourses on the Glory of Christ, in His Person, Office, and Grace," in *The Works of John Owen* (Banner of Truth, 1966), 1:351-52. For a contemporary evaluation of Owen's understanding of the covenant of redemption, see T. Robert Baylor, "He Humbled Himself: Trinity, Covenant, and the Gracious Condescension of the Son in John Owen," in *Trinity without Hierarchy: Reclaiming Nicene Orthodoxy in Evangelical Theology*, ed. Michael Bird and Scott Harrower (Kregel Publications, 2019), 165-94.

55. Considering the plausibility of referring to a covenant in the Trinity *in se*, Louis Berkhof offers the following comment: "Covenants among men had been made long before God established His covenant with Noah and with Abraham, and this prepared men to understand the significance of a covenant in a world divided by sin, and helped them to understand the divine revelation, when it presented man's relation to God as a covenant relation. This does not mean, however, that the covenant idea originated with man and was then borrowed by God as an appropriate form for the description of the mutual relationship between Himself and man. Quite the opposite is true; the archetype of all covenant life is found in the Trinitarian being of God, and what is seen among men is but a faint copy (ectype) of this." *Systematic Theology* (Banner of Truth, 1958), 263.

56. Space does not allow for an exegetical defense of the notion of the covenant of redemption, for more, see Swain, "The Covenant of Redemption," 107-25; Webster, "It Was the Will," 143-57 (even though Webster does not speak explicitly in terms of the covenant of redemption, he grounds the covenant of grace in the eternal counsel of the Triune God); and especially, Fesko, *The Trinity and the Covenant of Redemption*.

other in a covenantal manner in relation to the external work of redemption, so conscience makes human creatures aware in a covenantal manner of the claims of the other, namely of God and of his covenantal vocation. Even though the degree of dissimilarity is great, it seems at least plausible that in this sense conscience reflects analogically the covenantal reciprocal consciousness of the divine persons in relation to the common divine will to save.

Regarding God's eternal purpose to save, Webster observes that the "special character of Jesus's saving history may be stated by speaking of it as a *commissioned* history, the discharge of an office," so that in relation to the covenant of redemption, Christ's obedience as human being is "a temporal repetition of the Son's active consent to the will of the Father" in eternity.[57] As the Father's eternal purpose to create, redeem, and perfect in the Son encounters the conscious consent of the Son and of the Spirit,[58] so analogously the commission of the triune God to human creatures had to encounter the conscious consent of the servant of the covenant. Therefore, the covenantal form of fellowship that determines and regulates the inner reciprocity of the divine persons according to righteousness is what analogically determines and controls the reciprocity between the triune God and those who have been created in his image.

SUMMARY

In exploring the nature of conscience, this chapter proposed that it is determined by the realities of God's triunity, of his inherent righteousness, and of the covenantal interaction of the distinct divine persons in respect to

---

57. Webster, "It Was the Will," 157. N. T. Wright considers the Son's active consent to the will of the Father in eternity in terms of choice. In a Trinitarian interpretation of Philippians 2:5–11 proposed in *The Climax of the Covenant: Christ and the Law in Pauline Theology* (T&T Clark, 1991), Wright makes the following claim: "Until recently it was an automatic assumption that in this passage above all others Paul attributed to the one whom we know as Jesus of Nazareth, the Lord Christ, an existence prior to his human birth. Moreover, during this existence this figure made *a conscious choice*, described in the two verbs ['to consider' or 'to regard' in v. 6 and 'to make empty' or 'to make of no effect' in v. 7]. This traditional view has found it easy to read v. 6 as the Pauline equivalent of, say, John 1:1–14, and to align it with such other passages as 2 Corinthians 8:9, in which a similar *choice* appears to be attributed to the pre-existent Christ" (91, emphasis added).

58. Fesko writes: "A thicker account of the biblical data requires that one coordinate and include the Spirit's role within the *pactum* itself. In this respect, just as the Son acknowledges that the Father sent Him into the world, which implies His agreement to be sent, so the fact that the Spirit is sent implies His agreement and consent to the same" (*The Trinity and the Covenant*, 135). See also Andreas J. Köstenberger and Scott R. Swain, *Father, Son and Spirit: The Trinity and John's Gospel* (Apollos, 2008), 111–48.

the divine will in regard to salvation. Conscience causes human creatures to relate covenantally to God, making them aware of the divine will of the Lord. And this is so because, in Owen's words, "by this divine communication [creation], God did not intend only to glorify himself in the essential properties of his nature, but his existence also in three persons, of Father, Son, and Spirit."[59]

---

59. Owen, *The Works of John Owen*, 1:361.

Part 2

FALLEN CONSCIENCE

The second part of this book turns to consider conscience as fallen. Following the suggestion of Webster noted earlier, this exploration of fallen conscience will consider three features of fruitful theological engagement: first, it will seek "to offer an interpretation of the bodies of thought and practice with which it engages (including its own) which is properly attentive to their complexity and variety"; second, it will attempt "to offer a *theological* reading of its cultural and intellectual situation, so as to avoid the resignation which comes from thinking that context is fate"; and third, this "engagement with worlds of meaning outside the Christian faith [will be] subordinate to and guided by biblical and dogmatic description ... because the defense of the Christian confession is inseparable from, and largely accomplished by, its portrayal, not by the elaboration of external condition for its possibility."[1]

For these reasons, chapter 4 will consider fallen conscience in light of the *imago Dei*, highlighting the weaknesses of a structural or substantive understanding of conscience. In doing so, it will propose that fallen conscience operates as a basic awareness of God that is capable of perceiving his covenantal vocation. This conception of conscience will open the door for exploring the role of conscience in concurrence with other human capacities, resulting in a more comprehensive and better-integrated view of the experiential phenomenon of conscience.[2] There will follow an investigation of the contributions of Aquinas and Calvin, along with those of some contemporary philosophers and ethical theorists, which will allow for a broad portrayal of

---

1. Webster, "The Human Person," 220-21.
2. In examining conscience in its interaction with other human capabilities, more will be said about idioms and metaphors that in the Old Testament refer specifically to the manifestation of conscience, adding further weight to the case developed in the previous part on created conscience.

the experience of conscience to be offered—one that will demonstrate the remarkable contemporary relevance of Calvin's notion of *sensus*. In this way, the requirement that the construction of a theological anthropology (and consequently a theology of conscience) necessitates an understanding of human identity "sufficiently sturdy and expansive to resist being collapsed into the psychological or ethical dramas of selfhood"[3] will be satisfied. Finally, at the end of chapter 4, attention will be devoted to a concentrated analysis of conscience as nonphysical perceptual awareness.

Chapter 5 will then explore *how* conscience is fallen, proposing that conscience is fallen for three reasons: because it has been corrupted from a state of integrity, because human beings lack transparency in self-knowledge, and because humanity is incapable of innocent and thorough self-scrutiny. This chapter then will explore the notion of complete corruption in relation to conscience and, especially through a detailed exegesis of Romans 1, how the noetic effects of sin affect human conscience. In the final section, chapter 5 will address the problem of self-deception, concentrating on the fallenness of conscience as evaluative.

---

3. John B. Webster, "Eschatology and Anthropology," in *Word and Church*, 265.

4

FALLEN CONSCIENCE AS NONPHYSICAL PERCEPTUAL AWARENESS

This chapter offers a first approach to the phenomenon of fallen conscience within the view of conscience as created that was developed in the previous three chapters. The purpose of this chapter is to set forth a conception of conscience as *nonphysical perceptual awareness* through a series of steps. The first section will elaborate on conscience operating as a basic awareness. In the second section, conscience will be considered as cooperating with other human capacities. In the third section, attention will be given to the Scholastic notion of *synderesis* and Calvin's notion of *sensus*, leading to the final section in which fallen conscience will be conceived of specifically as nonphysical perceptual awareness.[1]

FALLEN CONSCIENCE OPERATING AS A BASIC AWARENESS

In writing on conscience, Bavinck affirms the primacy and independence of conscience in relation to other human capacities. He upholds the idea that conscience stands above other capacities, such as thinking, willing, and feeling, writing that conscience "has authority over them, and supplies each with its standard." He insists that while thinking, willing, and feeling are within

---

1. In this regard, and to anticipate a little the following discussion, John A. McGuckin argues for a "mystical approach" to conscience in the steps of Paul. In his view, conscience is "a matter of sensing": "Already for some of the more philosophically advanced Greek Christians of the second century onward, *syneidesis* in the human being was pre-eminently understood as the 'awareness,' or consciousness of God and divine things." "Conscience in Early Christian Thought," in Hammond and Alvaré, *Christianity and the Laws of Conscience*, 61, 64, 63.

our power, at least in part, "conscience does not allow itself to be dominated, and, occasionally given to slumber, it awakens with all the more power." This occurs because conscience is the law of our own personality, for it "points back to [God] as the Legislator."[2] Therefore human beings think, feel, and will under the superior authority and oversight of conscience,[3] and its authority points to the ultimate authority of God himself in relation to humanity.[4]

It should be noted that in the context of Bavinck's covenant theology, humanity is not independent of God, and therefore, any notion of conscience's authority must be qualified. Rather than claiming that humanity's most important or essential faculty is conscience within the context of a purely structural understanding of the *imago Dei*—as if conscience somehow defined the *imago Dei*—for Bavinck, conscience shows that it is the relation to God that is essential in the definition of the human person.[5] If a theology of conscience is constructed upon concepts such as human nature or human essence alone, humanity's covenantal bond with God runs the risk of being left out of the picture and human conscience (or other capacities such as reason or even the soul in its totality) may become autonomous. Bavinck asserts that it is "in the doctrine of the covenant of works ... that the locus of the image of God [and therefore conscience as a created reality] can be

---

2. Bavinck, "Conscience," 124-25. Jewett writes: "Although it is the person himself who knows his own deeds in the conscience, such knowledge is involuntary to the extent that the conscience becomes an autonomous agent whose witness has independent value over against the person. ... Although [conscience] may be thought of as belonging to the person, and although the verbal form of the word expresses clearly that the 'I' is the subject of such knowledge, nonetheless Paul ascribes to it an autonomy which is inviolable even by the person himself" (*Paul's Anthropological Terms*, 446, 459).

3. It appears that a shift occurred in Bavinck's thinking. In this article from 1881, he explicitly distinguishes conscience from thinking, feeling, and willing: "The conscience does not stand alongside our thought, feeling, or will, and even less is it included within one of these three." "Conscience," 124. However, in his lectures on theological ethics delivered in Kampen from 1883 through 1902, he seems to include conscience within the intellect: "Conscience belongs to the knowing dimension of human life, to the sphere of the intellect. ... Conscience is not, however, a distinct capacity alongside others, but 'the intellect itself ordered to specific actions'" (*Reformed Ethics*, 1:193, 195). I prefer to follow the earlier understanding of Bavinck, according to which conscience "is not an *awareness* that is merely moral but also religious" ("Conscience," 124, emphasis added).

4. Calvin asserts that conscience "is a certain mean between God and man," for ultimately "conscience refers to God" (*Institutes*, 3.19.15-16).

5. For a similar view, see Berkouwer, *Man: The Image of God*, 35. For a contemporary assessment of the limitations of the so-called structural conception of human nature, see Cortez, *Theological Anthropology*, 18-21.

treated to the full extent."[6] In this locus alone can justice be done to the understanding of human being as covenantal creature.

These observations depend upon the overarching view that it is the whole person, together with all her properties, who should holistically be conceived of as the image of God. Within this conceptual framework, the authority of conscience over other human competencies does not point to a supposed human essence or faculty that in itself functions as an autonomous religious or moral organ. It is not conscience in itself that is the law of human personality. Rather, witnessing, summoning, and legislating at once, conscience points to God as the Lord of the covenant; its authority is a reflection of God's authority and derives from its relation to God himself as covenant Lord.[7] As Dowey observes, the ultimacy of conscience does not reveal the absoluteness of conscience as compared to other capacities but rather "the absoluteness of what God reveals in it."[8]

As it will be shortly explored in detail, because of its interrelation with other human capacities, conscience does not operate alone but in conjunction with them. The operations of the various capacities cannot be dissected into a clear-cut anatomy. The different powers of the mind are experienced as coexistent, constantly intertwining and intermingling, so that it is practically impossible to set precise limits on the activities of the various capacities to show when a bodily sensation ends, when an emotion begins to work,

---

6. Bavinck, *Reformed Dogmatics*, 2:550. Lints writes, "We should remember that the Old Testament had little interest in articulating an autonomous or universal notion of humanness, but instead was intent on situating humankind in covenant relationship to God" (*Identity and Idolatry*, 74).

7. A covenantal framework allows for the integration of the structural/substantive, functional/representative, and relational/interpersonal perspectives on the *imago Dei* without one perspective standing above the others; see Cortez, *Theological Anthropology*, 16–40. A holistic and integrated understanding of the *imago* fits also a christological model of the *imago Dei*, according to which human nature is created with the capacities and powers necessary and sufficient to be in hypostatic union with a divine person. God created human beings with the properties and powers such that they might be prophets, priests, and kings within the created order to fill it with the image of God's glory. And these properties and powers are exactly those that are needed to conform to, and be in personal union with, God the Son, so that once incarnate he could be the true prophet, priest, and king as the last Adam; see Oliver Crisp, "A Christological Model of the *Imago Dei*," in Farris and Taliaferro, *The Ashgate Research Companion to Theological Anthropology*, 224–28.

8. Dowey, *The Knowledge of God*, 59. Stressing the covenantal motif, Lints writes, "The 'image' language in Genesis 1–9 occurs in the context of a longer covenantal argument about Israel's relationship with YHWH as Creator, and thus an account of the *imago Dei* should not be turned into a generic account of natural attributes" (*Identity and Idolatry*, 35).

when moral emotions are integrated with the activities of conscience, when reasoning steps in or when it is aided by the memory or the imagination, or when language gives expression to all that a person experiences inwardly, for most of the time, all of these phenomena are experienced spontaneously and simultaneously.[9]

Concerning this human complexity, Berkouwer writes that in Scripture, "no part of man is emphasized as independent of other parts; not because the various parts are not important, but because the Word of God is concerned precisely with the whole man in his relation to God."[10] All human faculties and capacities should be seen as interrelated, interdependent, and working in unison in a holistic way, even though they retain their own function in respect to each other. It is similar to a symphony, where each musical instrument plays its own sound yet contributes with the others to one composition, even though at times a violin, a piano, an oboe, or a trumpet may take the lead for a while. Similarly, the various human capacities act together concurrently and continually, producing innumerable subjective experiences, such as perceptions, apprehensions, intuitions, moods, inclinations, and deliberations, as well as consciousness about the self, about other creatures, and about God. Berkouwer writes:

> Such words [as heart, flesh, kidneys, spirit] have as their purpose not the shedding of light on the compositional structure of man, but rather to deal with the whole man in all his complex of functions; not to deal with a part of man in distinction from other parts, but to deal with man in his total existence, which lies open before the examining eye of God.[11]

---

9. The concept of synesthesia might be of help here. This condition is marked by a measure of sensory merging, such as "seeing" sounds. The phenomenon is not restricted to the five senses but has a cognitive dimension as well. See Julia Simner, *Synaesthesia: A Very Short Introduction* (Oxford University Press, 2019), 1–19; Anthony C. Thiselton, *The Last Things: A New Approach* (SPCK, 2012), 211–12.

10. Berkouwer, *Man: The Image of God*, 200.

11. Berkouwer, *Man: The Image of God*, 202. Berkouwer's point is that Scripture's anthropological terminology always refers to the whole human being without applying anachronistically later ontological, functional, and relational distinctions. Noticing that the word "heart" generally denotes the whole inner man "*and all the faculties of it*," Owen quickly adds, "not absolutely, but as they are all one principle of moral operations, *as they concur* in our doing good or evil" (*The Works of John Owen*, 6:170, emphasis added).

As was hinted at in the introduction to the present chapter and mentioned when reflecting on created conscience and the covenant of vocation, the reflection above on a holistic view of capacities allows for a primary definition of conscience as *a subjective and immediate experience of a covenantal awareness of God in relation to his vocation to humanity*. At a bare minimum it might be said that this perceptual awareness is the beginning of our making sense of our identity in relation to God.[12]

Contemporary philosopher Jason Howard explains that conscience can be called a faculty in two senses:

> It can be understood in a "thin" sense meaning that conscience is an innate capacity of sorts. ... However, it can also be understood in a "thick" sense, which is the usage that I am concerned with and one to which my criticisms will be mostly directed. To speak of conscience as a faculty in this "thick" sense is to see it as an independent entity in its own right. Rather than see conscience as referring to certain inherent cognitive capacities or an innate disposition, ... the "thick" view denotes conscience as an actual entity of sorts that resides within each of us, the identity of which is distinguished by its unwavering and unimpeachable concern for moral conduct.[13]

Howard proceeds to define conscience as a "basic competency of human agency," or "as a particular expression of [a] *basic awareness* of our own capacity for imputability."[14] Thus understood, conscience is a faculty only in a thin or raw sense, namely as a prerequisite capacity that manifests itself at a basic level in experiences of spontaneous awareness, apart from learning information and skills (even though learning information and skills serve the formation and development of conscience). Rather than being conceived as a faculty in a strong sense, conscience seems to be better understood (as Howard does) as an experience of which we become spontaneously and involuntarily aware and which gives meaning to our existence. He writes:

---

12. For some theological considerations on perceptual awareness, see Joanna Collicutt, "Discernment and the Psychology of Perception," in *The Open Secret: A New Vision for Natural Theology*, by Alister E. McGrath (Blackwell, 2008), 80-111.

13. Jason J. Howard, *Conscience in Moral Life: Rethinking How Our Convictions Structure Self and Society* (Rowan & Littlefield, 2014), 18. For a "thick" view of human faculties, see Dominik Perler, ed., *The Faculties: A History* (Oxford University Press, 2015), 97-149.

14. Howard, *Conscience in Moral Life*, 88, 65 (emphasis added).

The experience of conscience highlights a particular mode of moral agency, a complex occurrence in which our moral commitments seem to speak through us. ... Once we see conscience as a type of experience—that there is something it is like to experience conscience just as there is something it is like to see green or feel angry—one of the first distinguishing features that comes to light is that of the agent's passivity; conscience speaks to a series of experiences that we undergo or *suffer through*.[15]

Howard believes that it was especially during the Enlightenment that the notion of conscience as an inherent and independent faculty came to be crystallized in philosophy as well as in theology.[16] The result has been that, taken out of the larger setting of the revelation of the gospel (namely, the self-disclosure of the Trinity as the Father sending the Son to provide salvation and as the Father and the Son sending the Spirit to make salvation efficacious), conscience has been conceived of as virtually untouched by the fall, as if it were in the same condition as when it was given to Adam in his state of innocence. In this case, conscience, as the unaided and supreme faculty, becomes an autonomous rule for humanity independent of God, in spite of the reality of sin and apart from the triune work of redemption.[17]

As an alternative to such a thick, structural explanation of conscience as a faculty, it is here proposed that conscience is a faculty in a thin sense and that it is operative as a basic awareness—as a *sensus*, to use Calvin's expression—even in its fallen condition. In this respect, Howard relates this basic and unlearned awareness of conscience to other human cognitive capacities:

> Conscience is most adequately understood as a basic competency of human agency that arises out of the effort to constructively incorporate the moral emotions ... into a coherent sense of moral

---

15. Howard, *Conscience in Moral Life*, 51.

16. Howard, *Conscience in Moral Life*, 11-30. As an example, he refers to the sermons of Joseph Butler who was particularly influential in promoting an understanding of conscience as a superior faculty. Butler, *Fifteen Sermons and Other Writings on Ethics*, ed. David McNaughton (Oxford University Press, 2017), 19-34. For an overview of conscience in modern philosophy and for an evaluation of Butler on conscience, see Stoker, *Conscience: Phenomena and Theories*, 43-64, 122.

17. In this respect, Webster writes, "Anthropology is no longer part of an assemblage of doctrines which seek to articulate the history of salvation [and] its content is also decisively altered as interiority comes to be co-terminous with moral selfhood" ("God and Conscience," 255).

accountability for individual agents. ... If it turns out that emotions do not develop in interaction with our cognitive capacities, have no intentional focus and are impossible to regulate or positively incorporate into a larger sense of personal identity, then my interpretation is mistaken.[18]

Howard's observation that conscience interacts with moral emotions and with our cognitive capacities introduces the theme of fallen conscience cooperating with other human capacities, to which the next section turns.

FALLEN CONSCIENCE COOPERATING WITH OTHER HUMAN CAPACITIES

To exemplify the way in which conscience is interrelated with and interdependent upon other human powers, this section will consider the concurrence of conscience and emotions, conscience and the body, conscience and thinking, conscience and willing, and finally, conscience and language.[19] At this juncture, idioms and metaphors of the Old Testament that refer tacitly to the manifestation of conscience will be reflected on, though some consideration also will be given to the writings of the New Testament. Moreover, certain contemporary expressions and concepts commonly employed in debates in moral psychology, philosophy of the mind, and ethical theory will be examined within the overarching theological perspective.

CONSCIENCE AND EMOTIONS

That there is a correlation between conscience and emotions[20] is so evident that Pannenberg—although recognizing that conscience should neither be identified with, nor exclusively related to, feelings—stresses that "conscience

---

18. Howard, *Conscience in Moral Life*, 51, 56.

19. For a similar understanding of conscience as interrelated to other human capacities, see Torrance, "Conscience in the Early Church Fathers," in Alvaré and Hammond, *Christianity and the Laws of Conscience*, 95-98.

20. In light of the many shades of meaning of the word "emotion," as well as the ambiguity that such variety engenders, the term will be used interchangeably with "affection," "feeling," and less frequently, "passion." On the ambiguity of such terms and the difficulty of choosing just one of them, see John B. Webster, "*Dolent Gaudentque*: Sorrow in the Christian Life," in *Virtue and Intellect*, vol. 2 of *God Without Measure: Working Papers in Christian Theology* (T&T Clark, 2016), 73.

belongs to the realm of feelings."²¹ Similarly, noticing that in the New Testament the concurrence of conscience and the emotions is very clear, Pierce asserts that "the fundamental connotation of the συνείδησις group of words is that man is by nature so constituted that, if he overstep the moral limits of his nature he will normally *feel* pain."²² In concurrence with emotions, conscience is an awareness that directs a person to the otherness and supremacy of God.²³ In particular, when persons experience the moral emotions of guilt, fear, and shame, conscience works to integrate these emotions positively, incorporating them into a larger sense of personal identity in relation to God.²⁴

The following observations about moral emotions presuppose a *theological* interpretation of these feelings, for they are not merely subjective or private. On the contrary, emotions—whether experienced alongside or apart from conscience—always point to realities other than the self. Webster's observation here is both deep and precise: "Emotion has an object. It is a state and activity of a person *in relation* to circumstances, occurrences and agents other than the self. As such, it is an 'undergoing' or 'suffering': *a movement*

---

21. Pannenberg, *Anthropology in Theological Perspective*, 308. Even though he recognizes that conscience necessarily requires some sort of knowledge, Stoker favors emotionalism in identifying primordial conscience with the moral emotion of guilt experienced by a bad conscience (*Conscience: Phenomena and Theories*, 66–73, 187–88, 211–30). By contrast, Bavinck's later approach is more intellectual: "Nor does [conscience] belong to the realm of feelings" (*Reformed Ethics*, 1:193). Webster warns against the temptation to make the complexity of the phenomenon of conscience manageable by some kind of essentialist theory: "Essentialism afflicts those accounts which try to resolve the historical variety [in interpretation] by establishing a criterion of a 'pure' phenomenon of conscience (usually on the basis of an anthropology)" ("God and Conscience," 249).

22. Pierce, *Conscience in the New Testament*, 50 (emphasis added).

23. Drawing from social cognition research, Zahl stresses the *relational* function of emotions that aims at maintaining and promoting harmonious relationships, making possible a reading of "attachment theory" in relation to conscience through a covenantal and Trinitarian lens (*The Holy Spirit and Christian Experience*, 216–21).

24. For an exploration of the spirituality, morality, and intelligibility of the emotions, see Robert C. Roberts, *Emotions: An Essay in Aid of Moral Psychology* (Cambridge University Press, 2003); Roberts, *Spiritual Emotions: A Psychology of Christian Virtues* (Eerdmans, 2007); Roberts, *Emotions in the Moral Life* (Cambridge University Press, 2013); Anthony J. Steinbock, *Moral Emotions: Reclaiming the Evidence of the Heart* (Northwestern University Press, 2014); Martha C. Nussbaum, *Upheavals of Thought: The Intelligence of Emotions* (Cambridge University Press, 2001); Carla Bagnoli, ed., *Morality and the Emotions* (Oxford University Press, 2011); Robert Audi, *Moral Perception* (Princeton University Press, 2013).

of the inner self in response to being moved from outside, a reaction."[25] Howard too recognizes the social—or theologically, the relational and covenantal—character of emotions:

> Whatever emotions are, they generally develop in their sophistication in their reciprocal interaction with other capacities, such as language, cognition, imagination and socialization, both multiplying and anchoring our needs through interaction with others. ... Guilt and shame refer to a "radical heterogeneity" [because the] very fact that we have moral emotions means we are involved inextricably in a world of others.[26]

These general remarks about the importance of moral emotions lead now to a deeper analysis of guilt, fear, and shame, in particular as related to, and manifesting in a special manner, the operations of conscience.[27] Looking at additional biblical material will further validate the witness of the whole of Scripture, especially the Old Testament, to the reality of conscience. In Scripture, it is quite clear that guilt, fear, and shame are evidence of a person's response to being moved from outside—a reaction caused by a perception of God and of the requirements implicit in the covenant of vocation.

First, we consider further conscience in relation to guilt. In Leviticus, for example, it appears that the whole cultic system was a special revelation that had among its goals the appeasing and reassuring of the sinner's conscience. Milgrom writes:

> In these chapters, the sacrifices are listed from the point of view of the donor: chaps. 1–3, the spontaneously motivated sacrifices (burnt, cereal, and well-being) and chaps 4–5, the sacrifices required for expiation (purification and reparation). Their common denominator is that *they arise in answer to an unpredictable religious or emotional need,*

---

25. Webster, "Dolent Gaudentque," 73 (emphasis added). Audi conceives of emotions as "responses to experience, whether of the outer or inner world, or to the real or merely imagined" (*Moral Perception*, 125).

26. Howard, *Conscience in Moral Life*, 68.

27. There are other moral emotions such as anger or sorrow (cf. Mark 3:5). However, since conscience interacts in a special manner with guilt, fear, and shame, they are more significant for the present work.

and are thereby set off from sacrifices of the public feasts and fasts that are fixed by the calendar (chaps 9, 16, 23; cf. Num 28-29).[28]

The sacrifices, the offerings, and the priestly intercession had to be continually offered in order to give fallen human beings at least some feeling of acceptability as they drew near to God, for, in the words of Pierce, "conscience is the real obstacle to worship."[29]

Guilt is a moral emotion that implies an evaluation of the self that influences one's relation to other people. Of course, emotions—even moral emotions—are not sufficient in and of themselves to form a religious and moral assessment of the self; it is the spontaneous perception of conscience that supplements them with the experience of a theological and moral awareness that is cognitive in nature, even though (as will be more fully explained later) it may not yet be accompanied by inferential reasoning or formulated explicitly through language. Scholars usually refer to the self-assessment involved in guilt to some kind of "act-assessment" associated with specific thoughts, sentiments, desires, or actions.[30] This connection is evident in Hebrews where the feeling of guilt is associated with a consciousness of sins (note the plural), which indicates that guilt is experienced by the individual consciousness in relation to definite transgressions. And because of this "consciousness of sins" (Heb 10:2), conscience becomes "guilty" (Heb 10:22 NIV).

Guilt is discerned also in the experience of Cain, who responds to God's disapprobation with intense emotional pain that finds expression even in his physical appearance: "[Cain] was much distressed and his face fell" (Gen 4:5 NJPS). Sarna writes, "Cain's mood is depression, not anger. Hebrew *harah l-* expresses despondency or distress, as opposed to *harah 'af*, which means 'to be angry.' " This interpretation is confirmed by the fact that Cain's face fell: "This too is a figure of sadness and depression, not only in Hebrew but in several other ancient Near East texts as well."[31] Cain's sense of guilt took

---

28. Milgrom, *Leviticus 1-16*, 134 (emphasis added).
29. Pierce, *Conscience in the New Testament*, 101.
30. Steinbock writes, "In guilt I am given to myself before another as accused through an experienced transgression and as responsive to another. ... Colloquially speaking, when I experience guilt, I experience guilt about *something*. ... Generally, this something can be a deed done or undone, a thought had or not had" (*Moral Emotions*, 101, 103); see also June P. Tangney and Ronda L. Dearing, *Shame and Guilt* (Guilford Press, 2002), 24.
31. Sarna, *Genesis*, 33.

the form of distress and depression while his conscience was working as an awareness of God and what was pleasing to God. As explained above in the discussion on covenantal vocation, Cain's conscience was operating not only in relation to some positive and specific commandment but primarily and comprehensively as covenantal consciousness.[32]

A similar reaction to guilt is that of King Josiah. After the book of the covenant of vocation for Israel was found (2 Kgs 22:8), the teaching of the law was read to the king. When Josiah heard the words of the book, "he tore his clothes" (2 Kgs 22:11). The king then sent someone to inquire of the Lord on his behalf, having become conscious of the Lord's wrath because the covenant people did not "obey ... the words of this book, to do according to all that is written" (2 Kgs 22:13; see also Exod 24:7; Deut 28:58; Josh 1:8). At the end, the prophetic oracle spoke to the king with these words: "Because your heart *was penitent*, and you humbled yourself before the LORD, when you heard how I spoke against this place and against its inhabitants, that they should become a desolation and a curse, and you have torn your clothes and wept before me, I also have heard you, declares the LORD" (2 Kgs 22:19, emphasis added). The verb translated as "be penitent" literally means to become soft, to soften, to mollify, and figuratively, to become faint-hearted or to be despondent (see Lev 26:36; Job 23:16; Deut 20:3; Isa 7:4; Jer 51:46). Emotionally, Josiah's heart experienced a similar kind of distress and despondency as felt by Cain, even though he humbled himself, unlike Cain. However, for both, the broad principle outlined by Roberts applies: "In general, the paradigm cases of *feeling guilt* are those in which we stand face to face with the one we have wronged,

---

32. What provoked this feeling of guilt was the failure to abide by the covenant of vocation—in other words, failure to worship God in faith and according to his will (see Gen 4:7). This shows that the original covenant with humanity was much broader than just one or a few specific commandments. In this regard, at the beginning of his exposition of the Decalogue, Calvin stresses the role of conscience as it is informed both by inward or natural law and by written law (*Institutes*, 2.8.1). Calvin remarks that the written law is the teaching of God *as creator*: "Now, what is to be learned from the law can be readily understood: that God, *as he is our Creator*, has towards us by right the place of Father and Lord; for this reason we owe to him glory, reverence, love and fear" (*Institutes*, 2.8.2, emphasis added). Lints also highlights this relation between worship and creation: "Genesis 1 is a prologue to a story of how and why Israel were to worship their God in contrast to the worship of the gods of the nations surrounding them. The bonus on worshipping God is grounded in part by the claim that humanity has been created as the image of God. This argues for seeing the covenantal arrangement between Israel and their God as a covenant of worship" (*Identity and Idolatry*, 45).

stared at, as it were, by our victim, in his status of victim-accuser. *Guilt is enhanced by a sense of the accuser's presence.*"[33]

Turning, second, to conscience in relation to fear, it is important to note that—unlike the feeling of guilt—fear does not always possess a religious or moral connotation: individuals may be fearful even when they are not called to give an account of themselves before God or when they are not under any kind of religious judgment or moral evaluation by others. A person may be afraid not because of anything sinful but because of human weakness and frailty, as in the case of a frightened student who must sit through a very difficult exam or a scared young lady who is having a baby.

However, at times, fear is experienced explicitly in religious or ethical terms. The pagan king Abimelech and his people provide a good example. When the king is confronted with Abraham's devious and unjust behavior (Gen 20:1-2), he affirms his innocence before the Lord (Gen 20:3-5) and receives the assurance of God's acquittal and the promise of preservation (Gen 20:6-7). Later, he summons Abraham to ask him: "What have you done to us? And how have I sinned against you, that you have brought on me and my kingdom a great sin? You have done to me things that ought not to be done" (Gen 20:9). Even though he was not in a redemptive covenantal bond with God as Abraham was, Abimelech demonstrates that, by nature, he had a measure of awareness of right and wrong. More importantly, contrary to Abraham's supposition (Gen 20:11), in the place where Abimelech ruled there was fear of God; indeed, all his servants "were very much afraid" (Gen 20:8) after they received the witness of their lord Abimelech. It is important to observe the intertwining of the external and objective witness delivered by God to the king with the internal and subjective response of the people who were afraid. Sarna interprets their fear as awareness of God's justice:

> In a situation where no legal sanction or reward is enforceable, the ultimate restraint on evil, as well as the supreme incentive for good, is the *consciousness* of the existence of a higher power who demands certain standards of conduct. ... The phrase "fear of God" is used overwhelmingly in connection with situations that involve norms of moral

---

33. Roberts, *Spiritual Emotions*, 101 (emphasis added).

or ethical conduct. Its application is universal, transcending religious or national divisions.[34]

According to Sarna, this consciousness of the existence of a higher power works in concurrence with the emotion of fear, which, in this case, is specifically religious.

Looking to the New Testament, Paul—in defending his ministry before some members of the Corinthian church—makes the following statement: "Therefore, knowing the fear of the Lord, we persuade others. But what we are is known to God, and I hope it is known also to your conscience" (2 Cor 5:11). At the beginning of 2 Corinthians, the apostle makes an appeal to conscience: "For our boast is this, the testimony of our conscience, that we behaved in the world with simplicity and godly sincerity, not by earthly wisdom but by the grace of God, and supremely so toward you" (2 Cor 1:12). However, Paul was not only concerned with the testimony of his own conscience; he cared about the consciences of other people, as his practice was to commend himself in integrity "to everyone's conscience" (2 Cor 4:2). Although God knew who and what Paul was, the apostle had to persuade the Corinthians of the genuineness of his apostolic authority and the integrity of his ministry. In 2 Corinthians 5:11, a new element is coupled with or added to the testimony of conscience: Paul's knowledge of the fear of the Lord. The kind of knowing Paul is thinking about here is "from experience,"[35] a perception and an intuition that is not obtained by logical reasoning, even though the intellect cooperates with conscience's spiritual and moral perceptions and apprehensions. According to Philip E. Hughes, this knowledge is "a deep consciousness of the awe which should be inspired in the heart of every servant who will be required to give an account of his stewardship to his master."[36] Paul's conscience was operating in concurrence with his deep experience of fear in relation to the Lord as a perception of God's righteous standards.

Finally, as far as conscience in relation to shame, when compared to guilt and fear, shame is a feeling associated with an evaluation of the whole person.

---

34. Sarna, *Genesis*, 143 (emphasis added).

35. George H. Guthrie, *2 Corinthians*, Baker Exegetical Commentary on the New Testament (Baker Academic, 2015), 296.

36. Philip E. Hughes, *The Second Epistle to the Corinthians*, The New International Commentary on the New Testament (Eerdmans, 1962), 186.

In its religious or moral dimension,[37] shame does not simply have to do with some concupiscence or with an offensive word or with a base action. Rather, as Steinbock notes, shame "calls *me* into question [and] concerns who we are *as persons*."[38] During the discussion on created conscience, it was noted that the experience of shame was followed by a desire to hide. Instead of the willing, free, and open covenantal response, "Here I am" (see Gen 22:1; 31:11; 46:2; Exod 3:4; 1 Sam 3:4; Isa 6:8; Luke 1:38; Heb 10:7),[39] Adam and Eve hid *themselves* from the presence of the Lord. Because of shame, they tried to hide their whole person and not just the specific transgression for which they felt guilty.

The confession of Ezra shows the relation between shame provoked by the conscience and a comprehensive evaluation of the whole person. When he learns of the covenantal unfaithfulness of the Israelites, Ezra feels completely desolate and gives expression to his consternation by tearing his clothes and pulling his hair (Ezra 9:1-3). At the evening sacrifice, surrounded by those who trembled at God's word, Ezra fell upon his knees, saying, "O my God, I am ashamed and blush to lift *my face* to you, my God, for our iniquities have risen higher than our heads, and our guilt has mounted up to the heavens" (Ezra 9:6, emphasis added). Ezra feels personally ashamed or dishonored before God. The cause of such emotions is a deep, individual awareness of sin and guilt that in turn produces the inability to lift *one's face* in the presence of God—as in the case of Cain's fallen face noted above. According to Johnson, the fact that the term "face" is used always in the plural in the Hebrew is significant, and on many occasions, it is simply "a periphrasis for the personal pronoun."[40] It might be claimed, then, that the face often denotes all of one's characteristics and the presence of the individual person in totality (see Gen 43:3, 5; 2 Sam 14:24; Jer 23:39). So, the fallen, shamed, or humiliated face becomes another expression denoting the manifestation of conscience. The shame and humiliation Ezra felt expressed an inclusive and

---

37. Of course, the subjective experience of shame or its social dimension does not always arise because of any kind of personal transgression, for example, when an individual is mistakenly assumed to be at fault or when innocent people are mistreated and victimized. That dimension of shame is not what is in view in this book but only shame related to conscience and covenantal vocation.

38. Steinbock, *Moral Emotions*, 76, 77 (emphasis added).

39. On the covenantal response, "Here I am," see Horton, *Lord and Servant*, 117-19.

40. Johnson, *The Vitality of the Individual*, 43.

spontaneous evaluation of his own self, not just in relation to some specific transgressions; it is an evaluation that speaks of his sense of unworthiness as a person in general (see Neh 1:6–7; Dan 9:4–19).

CONSCIENCE AND THE BODY

Scripture (especially the Old Testament) not only identifies various internal dispositions with various parts of the body, as was previously discussed in relation to the heart, the kidneys, and the hands or the face. Conscience in its interacting with emotions can affect the whole body.

In Psalm 6, for example—another penitential psalm that should consequently be read as related to conscience (cf. Ps 38)—the psalmist makes the following invocation: "O LORD, rebuke me not in your anger, nor discipline me in your wrath. Be gracious to me, O LORD, for I am languishing; heal me, O LORD, *for my bones are troubled*" (Ps 6:1–2, emphasis added). Being conscious of sin, the supplicant does not describe his inner condition as referring to his most sensitive inward organs, such as the heart or the kidneys, nor does he mention the most visible bodily parts, such as the hands or the face. On this occasion, he affirms that it is his bones—the strong armor of his organism— that are shaken to the core because of his perception of guilt before the Lord.

Another example is that of the idolatrous king Belshazzar in Daniel 5. As the king was drinking wine and praising gods of gold and silver, bronze, iron, wood, and stone with his lords, his wives, and his concubines (Dan 5:3–4), something frightful happened: "Immediately the fingers of a human hand appeared and wrote on the plaster of the wall of the king's palace, opposite the lampstand. And the king saw the hand as it wrote" (Dan 5:5). This objective and external witness was followed by a subjective and internal response: "Then the king's color changed, and his thoughts alarmed him; his limbs gave way, and his knees knocked together" (Dan 5:6). So inwardly distressed, wounded, and terrified was the king that he lost his composure and "called loudly to bring in the enchanters, the Chaldeans, and the astrologers" (Dan 5:7). Edward Young cautiously suggests that the king's alarmed thoughts were "probably called forth by a guilty conscience."[41] Carl Keil is more direct in relating the king's reaction to the operations of conscience: "The alarm was heightened by a bad conscience, which roused itself and filled

---

41. Edward J. Young, *A Commentary on Daniel* (Banner of Truth, 1949), 120.

him with dark foreboding."[42] Even though Calvin does not explicitly mention conscience in his commentary on this passage, his comment clearly refers to its manifestations:

> Here Daniel shews [sic] how the king's mind was struck with fear, lest any one should think his fright without foundation. But he expresses, by many circumstances, how disturbed the king was, and thus the sufficiency of the reason would easily appear. It was needful for him to be so struck, that all might understand how God was seated on his throne, and summoned him as a criminal. ... We see King Belshazzar not only admonished by *an outward sign* of his approaching death, but *inwardly stirred up* to acknowledge himself to be dealing with God.[43]

The case of King Belshazzar clearly evidences the interaction between the operations of conscience and bodily sensations, but it also introduces the consideration of the concurrence of conscience and reason because, as the passage indicates, "his thoughts alarmed him."

CONSCIENCE AND THINKING

In the Bible there is a correspondence between self-awareness in relation to God and thinking, though not in the form of inferential reasoning but rather as a spontaneous reflection arising out of experience. There is a difference between spontaneous reflection and attentive reasoning understood as "a mental event or process that requires a set of premises and a conclusion."[44] In Scripture, knowing and thinking relates to conscience not as an inferential or deductive process of the mind that is deliberately concentrated on some propositional premise in order to reach a conclusion. Stated differently, religious and moral awareness is primarily noninferential and based on perceptions and intuitions that nevertheless deliver genuine knowledge.[45] In this way, conscience as a basic awareness is engaged in the spontaneous

---

42. Carl F. Keil, *Biblical Commentary to the Book of Daniel*, vol. 9 of *Commentary on the Old Testament*, (Eerdmans, 1986), 182.

43. John Calvin, *Commentary on the Book of Daniel*, vol. 7 of *Calvin's Commentaries* (Baker Books, 1996), 316, 318 (emphasis added).

44. Audi, *Moral Perception*, 52.

45. On the distinction between the different functions of perceptual and inferential knowledge, see Audi, *Moral Perception*, 61–62. For a definition of intuitions as apprehensions, see Audi, *Moral Perception*, 83–102.

recognition of perceptions, intuitions, and apprehensions that relate to God and his covenantal vocation to humanity in interaction with spontaneous reflective reasoning.[46]

One text that displays this feature of conscience is Genesis 3:7-10, in which Adam and Eve enter into a new mode of discernment that precedes and causes their shame, fear, and hiddenness: "Then *the eyes of both were opened, and they knew* [יֵדְעוּ] that they were naked" (Gen 3:7, emphasis added). It seems that the opening of their eyes produced an unprompted knowing of their nakedness. Their perceptual knowing followed by an intuitive judgment[47] was *new* because it was experienced for the first time in a *negative* manner and not because conscience did not exist before the fall. It is important to stress this point to show that conscience is still operative in a state of sin and death, although operating differently than before the fall. Immediately after their idolatry, Adam and Eve experienced a new mode of perception that caused a new kind of intuition, showing that the Creator had furnished their conscience not only with the ability to recognize and approve the good but to perceive and disapprove evil. As soon as humanity violated the sacred bond of the covenantal vocation, brought into focus by the commandment of life, human creatures experienced a condemning conscience, and they had the cognitive perception of having transgressed and done evil. Sarna explains "the new insight they gain" in terms of "consciousness" is evident in their perception of their lack of that glorious covering with which God had clothed

---

46. Recalling what was said about the conscious reciprocity of the divine persons, it might be helpful to consider Sarna's comment on the meaning of the verb "to know" in the Old Testament: "'Knowing' in the Bible is not essentially intellectual activity, not simply objective contemplation of reality. Rather, it is experiential, emotional, and, above all, relational. ... For that reason, the Hebrew stem *y-d-ʻ* can encompass a range of meanings that includes involvement, interaction, loyalty, and obligation. It can be used of the most intimate and most hallowed relationship between man and wife and between man and God" (*Genesis*, 31). Similarly, Anna N. Williams writes, "To know God certainly entails mastery of information, but it also entails personal contact. Knowledge of God is personal knowledge in the fullest sense, in that it encompasses both knowledge-about and acquaintance-with, that is, both mastery of information related to the person and immediate personal contact with the same. ... Acquaintance-with, the intimate contact of one person with another, inevitably fosters knowledge-about, a grasp of facts concerning the person." *The Divine Sense: The Intellect in Patristic Theology* (Cambridge University Press, 2007), 164, 177.

47. On the importance of perceptual knowledge and moral intuition for ethics, see Audi, *Moral Perception*, 143-69.

them in the beginning.[48] In this way, humanity's awareness—conscience—enabled them to make a cognitive self-evaluation before God (see Ps 51:3).

This function of conscience relates to another important idiom in the Old Testament— דַּעַת אֱלֹהִים ("knowledge of God"). According to Fox, *da'at* is the broadest of the wisdom words "as it includes minimal acts of awareness and innate intellectual capacities apart from learned information and skills" but extends its meaning to "elevated sagacity."[49] Commenting on Proverbs 2:5—where the expressions "fear of the Lord" and "knowledge of God" are found in parallel—Fox intertwines the operations of conscience and understanding, claiming that the fear of God "becomes conscience, an inner sense of right and wrong."[50] Observing that this kind of knowledge of God is not inferential-theological or moral reasoning, Fox explains it in terms of consciousness or awareness relating to conscience as fear of the Lord:

> The fear of the Lord and the knowledge of God have much the same qualities and functions, but there is a difference. Fear of the Lord is essentially an emotion or attitude. Hence it can commence before the attainment of knowledge. A child may have fear of God before he acquires knowledge of him. ... Fear of God does have content and can be learned, but in its elementary form, it requires little learning or understanding. Knowledge of God is in essence an awareness or cognition, though it is inextricably bound to the fear of God and righteous action.[51]

Once more, these observations show how integrated and intertwined the cognitive operations are of the emotions, thinking, and conscience.

In the New Testament, the concurrence of conscience and thinking appears in Romans 2:14-15. It should be noted that in Romans 1 to 2 Paul is

---

48. Sarna, *Genesis*, 25.

49. Fox, *Proverbs 1-9*, 31.

50. Fox, *Proverbs 1-9*, 111. Having broadly defined conscience as a primal or basic awareness in terms of religious and moral perception, it is noteworthy to observe that von Rad believes that wisdom literature "tend[s] ... towards *theological perceptions* which are of more fundamental and more general significance for men" (*Wisdom in Israel*, 70, emphasis added).

51. Fox, *Proverbs 1-9*, 112. In the New Testament the idiom "knowledge of God" presupposes its Old Testament equivalent and according to Spicq this form of cognition that is inextricably bound to the operations of conscience is what explains the concept of conscience in the whole New Testament ("La conscience dans le Nouveau Testament," 77-79).

considering the dual natural witness to God's truth in relation to the gentiles: the *external* witness of the created order (Rom 1:18-20) corresponds to the *internal* witness of human beings (Rom 2:14-15; see also 1:32).[52] This double witness has one and the same purpose: to leave gentiles without excuse before God's righteous judgment (Rom 1:20; 2:16). Indeed, the general conclusion of the whole discussion points in that same direction (Rom 3:19-20). Paul is also interested to show that the condition of the gentiles matches that of the Jews. Since "God shows no partiality" (Rom 2:11), Paul writes, "All who have sinned without the law will also perish without the law, and all who have sinned under the law will be judged by the law" (Rom 2:12). Paul's argument implies that if God judges Jews according to the law, this does not mean that there is no law by which God will judge gentiles as well. That, in turn, raises the question of how God can hold gentiles accountable to the law, since gentiles "do not have the law" (Rom 2:14). In response, Paul introduces the idea of the conscience or the heart on which the law is written, as is verified by the joint activity of both conscience and thinking.[53] Bavinck writes:

> With those actions, which prove the existence of a law in their heart, their moral awareness, their conscience, agrees. … According to Paul, then, the conscience is not the law itself; nor does the conscience contain this law, for the law was written in the heart. But together with the actions the conscience testifies in the heart concerning the

---

52. A number of scholars, such as Augustine, K. Barth, C. E. B. Cranfield, and N. T. Wright think that in Romans 2:14-15 Paul is referring only to gentiles who became Christians; see Simon J. Gathercole, "A Law unto Themselves: The Gentiles in Romans 2:14-15 Revisited," *Journal for the Study of the New Testament* 85 (2002): 27-49. This work takes the opposite view, supported by scholars such as Luther and Calvin and more recently by Berkouwer and VanDrunen, that Romans 2:14-15 is referring to unregenerate gentiles; see Richard N. Longenecker, *The Epistle to the Romans*, New International Greek Testament Commentary (Eerdmans, 2016), 273; VanDrunen, *Divine Covenants and Moral Order*, 231-51. For the sake of argument, even if in Romans 2:14-15 Paul is speaking of believing gentiles, this by itself would not negate the reality of the phenomenon of conscience in nonbelieving gentiles.

53. The Old Testament doctrine of creation and of the so-called covenant of creation or of works is foundational for Paul's understanding of conscience. At this point, suffice it to say that here the link between conscience and God's law points to the fact that the background to Paul's discussion of conscience is chiefly the Old Testament. The reality of conscience answers the problem raised by N. T. Wright concerning "Gentiles [being] 'under' a law they never possessed" (*The Climax of the Covenant*, 143).

existence of that law, a testimony that at the same time pronounces a verdict in the thoughts as to whether the law has been violated.[54]

In light of Bavinck's comments, it seems plausible to conclude that these thoughts give evidence of the witnessing, summoning, and legislating operations of conscience that stimulate the thinking, and in turn, conscience gives evidence of the fact that the law of God is written on people's hearts. Indeed, in Romans 2:14-15 there are three witnesses at work: conscience, thinking, and the heart. It seems that Paul is using the metaphor of the heart to indicate the whole inner person—the inner human being is aware of the law.[55] How? In the human heart—in the inner person as a whole—conscience and thinking work together, each serving to keep people's hearts aware of their relation to God and his law. Therefore, although each retains a certain freedom, conscience and thinking concur with the heart to keep people accountable to God's law.[56]

To conclude this survey of the relation between conscience and thinking, a few words will be said on memory and imagination.[57] Through the activity of memory conscience may operate in the present with reference to the past. For example, in Psalm 25 the psalmist prays: "Remember your mercy, O LORD, and your steadfast love, for they have been from of old. Remember not the sins of my youth or my transgressions; according to your steadfast love remember me, for the sake of your goodness, O LORD!" (Ps 25:6-7). The psalmist is heavily burdened under the weight of his felt guilt, "for it is great" (Ps 25:11), and his present experience of conscience is also affected by the sins of his past in his youth. Thus, in his present felt need of forgiveness, the

---

54. Bavinck, "Conscience," 117.

55. Referring to Romans 2:14-15, Owen writes, "The law of God was at first inbred and natural unto man; it was concreated with his faculties, and was their rectitude, both in being and operation, in reference to his end of living unto God and glorifying of him" (*The Works of John Owen*, 6:165).

56. Noticing the singular reference to conscience in Romans 2:15b and the plural reference to thoughts in Romans 2:15c, Jewett affirms that thoughts are separated from conscience: "Paul distinguishes quite sharply between the mind and the conscience at this point. ... He also assumes that the conscience acts independently from the heart" (*Paul's Anthropological Terms*, 444). On the threefold witness of heart, conscience, and thoughts, see Gathercole, "A Law unto Themselves," 40-46.

57. On the moral nature of the cognitive contributions of memory and imagination, see Audi, *Moral Perception*, 42-49, 157-61.

suppliant goes back with his mind to the folly of his youth, casting himself utterly on the steadfast love of the Lord, asking him to remember not his sins—past and present—but his mercies (see Gen 41:9; 1 Kgs 17:18; Pss 38:1; 51:5; 79:8; Isa 43:18; Ezek 16:63).

Conscience also interacts with imagination: in relation to the past, as when a person regrets not having taken a better course in respect of a wrong one; in relation to the present, as when someone imagines different scenarios before making an urgent decision in order to pursue good and avoid evil; and in relation to the future, as when one imagines what may or may not happen and reaches moral conclusions in the present in light of the imagined circumstances that may become reality. In what appears to be the only prayer in Proverbs, Agur envisions his future within a theological framework: "Two things I ask of you; deny them not to me before I die: Remove far from me falsehood and lying; give me neither poverty nor riches; feed me with the food that is needful for me, *lest I be full* and deny you and say, "Who is the LORD?" or *lest I be poor* and steal and profane the name of my God" (Prov 30:7-9, emphasis added). After the first petition in which he asks God for the moral nerve to adhere to truth, Agur prays secondly not to be led into temptation, and as he prays, he imagines two possible causes of testing: poverty and riches. The concern of Agur's conscience is not primarily related to being afraid of becoming poor or to the culpability and consequences of theft; rather, he imagines his future in religious and moral terms in relation to God's fame and reputation, namely in relation to God's glory.[58]

CONSCIENCE AND THE WILL

Conscience is also active with the will or volition, as a few examples will sufficiently demonstrate.

In Psalm 17:3 there is an evident correlation between conscience and will: "You have tried my heart, you have visited me by night, you have tested me, and you will find nothing; I have purposed that my mouth will not transgress." The important verb in this verse is זַמֹּתִי, usually translated "to purpose" or "to

---

58. Expounding on Genesis 32, Sarna believes that "long suppressed memories from [Jacob's] ignoble past intrude his consciousness," and he further explains Jacob's great fear and anxiety when he is about to meet Esau face to face as the intermingling of conscience, memory, and imagination: "Jacob's troubled conscience and the memory of Esau's terrible resolve (27:41) lead him to imagine the worst" (*Genesis*, 223, 224).

intend," a verb that indicates the inclination of the will (see Gen 11:6). Here, the supplicant describes the struggle of conscience caused by his awareness of being visited and tested by God. At the conclusion of this testing, he comes to a resolution, to a determination: he wills or purposes that his mouth will not transgress.

Another instance of the relation between conscience and will is found in 2 Samuel 24:10 when David numbers the people: "David's heart struck him after he had numbered the people. And David said to the Lord, 'I have sinned greatly in what I have done. But now, O Lord, please take away the iniquity of your servant, for I have done very foolishly.'" This passage was quoted earlier with a focus on the ethical judgment formed by the conscience. However, if David's reaction is analyzed more carefully in its totality, it is also possible to discern here the interrelatedness of a number of human capacities. Not only does the heart being struck refer to a manifestation of a conscience operating alongside the emotions, but David's afflictive awareness is followed by thoughts accusing and excusing one another. And these thoughts find expression through language in a prayer of confession. Finally, and crucially at this point, the prayer of confession is a demonstration of the intention of David's will: if previously David's will to sin overrode the dictates of conscience, now the same will desires that the Lord will take away his iniquity and not reject him. Just as the will can affect conscience in a negative manner, so too conscience can affect the will in a positive manner.

One last example may suffice to show the interaction between conscience and volition, from Proverbs 30:32. This verse reads: "If you have been foolish, exalting yourself, or if you have been devising [זָמֹם] evil, put your hand on your mouth." As compared with the two previous instances, in which conscience anticipates and gives rise to a specific volition, in this case the retrospective judgment of the conscience follows the devising or purposing of the vainglorious self. To the presence of proud scheming, the conscience reacts by ordering the individual back to the humility of silence.

CONSCIENCE AND LANGUAGE

Finally, there is a concurrence between the self-awareness of conscience and language. Through language human creatures give conscious expression to the spontaneous and subconscious workings of emotions, of bodily sensations and perceptions, of volition, of thinking, and of conscience. None of these instinctive and involuntary capacities is learned, and as people experience the various operations of their biological and innate dispositions, language gives them conscious manifestation.[59] It may be said that language enables the individual conscience to give focused expression to the raw material that is provided by bodily sensations and by moral emotions, which operate alongside understanding and result in or follow volitional deliberations.

One example of the interaction of conscience and language is found in the second line of Psalm 4:4, which Alter translates: "Speak in your heart on your beds, and be still."[60] In this instance, conscience is operative alongside language: human beings are exhorted to be conscientious in speaking in their own hearts as they live before God. Another occurrence of the same phenomenon, at Psalm 27:8, is again made clear by Alter's translation: "Of You, my heart said: 'Seek My face.'"[61] Goldingay writes, "[The] implication is apparently that the suppliant's heart speaks on Yhwh's behalf as the suppliant senses an internal voice speaking for Yhwh."[62] Therefore, the heart works in a dialogical manner, namely as a dialogue within the inner self stimulated by the cooperation of conscience and language concerning the relation to God and his righteousness (see Rom 2:15).[63]

In the Old Testament, the verb הָגָה indicates an action that is audible. Its range of meaning is wide, stretching from the inarticulate sounds of animals or individuals (see Isa 31:4; 38:14; 59:11; Jer 48:31) to the clearer and more coherent forms of human speech (see Pss 37:30; 71:24; Prov 8:7). At times this

---

59. Ray Jackendoff investigates the operations of the body, and the importance of moral emotions, of volitional and reciprocal acts, and of evaluation processes that result in the formation of distinct values: affective value, quality value, utility value, resource value, prowess value, esteem value, personal normative value, and a more general normative value concerning right and wrong. In all these cases of mental and psychological (and it might be added "religious") phenomena, Jackendoff considers the same principle to hold true, namely that language is a conscious manifestation of the innate and subconscious activity of mental structures intrinsic to human nature; see *Language, Consciousness, Culture: Essays on Mental Structure* (MIT Press, 2007).

60. Alter, *The Book of Psalms*, 11.

61. Alter, *The Book of Psalms*, 93.

62. Goldingay, *Psalms*, vol. 1, *Psalms 1–41*, 396.

63. Speaking of the perception of truth in wisdom literature, von Rad believes that in the human mind the "process of becoming aware of the perception and of giving linguistic expression to it in word and form are one and the same act" (*Wisdom in Israel*, 30). Similarly, Fox writes, "The heart works its power in tandem with the tongue. The heart is the source of life, and it sends up the thoughts that the tongue utters" (*Proverbs 1–9*, 186).

verb is used to describe the practice of meditation, as in Psalm 1:2, which Alter translates: "But the LORD's teaching is his desire, and His teaching he *murmurs* day and night" (emphasis added; see also Josh 1:8; Ps 37:30; 63:6). Alter comments, "The verb *hagah* means to make a low muttering sound, which is what one does with a text in a culture where there is no silent reading. By extension, predominantly in post-biblical Hebrew, it has the sense of 'to meditate.' "[64] Since the conscience participates in the spiritual act of reading, meditating, and repeating the word of God in interaction with other human powers, its operations intertwine spontaneously with those of language, which gives expression to conscience's awareness and perceptions in soliloquies, dialogues, and in "contemplative paraphrase[s]."[65]

In sum, conscience is part of the internal organization of human nature, and its activity is spontaneous, involuntary, and not completely explicable. Human creatures experience conscience as a subjective and immediate covenantal awareness of God in relation to his vocation to humanity. The experience of conscience is not isolated from other human capacities, as if conscience could work independently of them; rather, it is so constituted that it cannot operate but in concurrence with them. Thus, there is no human capacity that in isolation can be considered in a special way to actualize the *imago Dei*. Nevertheless, as conscience operates in conjunction with other human powers—influencing and being influenced by them—it remains "a certain mean between God and man,"[66] and as the law of personality, in a certain sense, it stands above and has a measure of authority over other capacities because it was bestowed upon humanity with the specific purpose of calling human creatures to take heed of their true identity as covenant servants.

---

64. Alter, *The Book of Psalms*, 3. In fact, it is the *tongue* that *meditates* on God's righteousness (Ps 35:28).

65. For "contemplative paraphrase," see John B. Webster, "Biblical Reasoning," in *The Domain of the Word: Scripture and Theological Reasoning* (T&T Clark, 2012), 130.

66. On the Reformed notion of conscience as a mediator between God and humanity, see Irena Backus, "Calvin's Concept of Natural Law and Roman Law," *Calvin Theological Journal* 38 (2003): 7–26.

FALLEN CONSCIENCE: THE SCHOLASTIC SYNDERESIS AND CALVIN'S SENSUS

At this point, it is helpful to dwell briefly on the medieval notion of *synderesis*,[67] to relate the Scholastic reflection on conscience to the theology of conscience that is being developed here.[68]

Medieval theologians devoted much attention to and engaged in rigorous scrutiny of the phenomenon of conscience.[69] Their investigation distinguished between *synderesis* and *conscientia*.[70] In general, according to the Scholastics, *synderesis* is the "innate habit [disposition] of the understanding which grasps basic principles of moral law apart from the activity of formal moral training."[71]

One important reason for why this innate habit was distinguished from *conscientia* was an apparent inconsistency in Jerome's commentary on Ezekiel 1:7.[72] He first asserts that the "spark of conscience [*synderesis*] was not even extinguished in the breast of Cain after he was turned out of Paradise, and by which we discern that we sin," and then later, he seems to contradict himself, stating, "We also see that this conscience is cast down in some people, who have neither shame nor insight regarding their offences and loses its place."[73] Medieval theologians thought that, in order to untangle this knot, it was necessary to distinguish between *synderesis* and *conscientia*: "*synderesis* being the 'spark of conscience' rather than conscience proper."[74] While *synderesis* was conceived of as the innate knowledge of fundamental principles

---

67. On the uncertain exegetical origins of the term *synderesis*, see Potts, *Conscience in Medieval Philosophy*, 1-11.

68. Perhaps significantly, neither Paul nor Augustine distinguished between *synderesis* and *conscientia*.

69. The story of the elaboration of the medieval concept of conscience is told by Odon Lottin, "Syndérèse et conscience aux XIIe et XIIIe siècles," in *Psychologie et morale aux XIIe et XIIIe siècles: table chronologique des écrits et leur influence littéraire* (J. Duculot, 1948), 2:101-349.

70. In making such a distinction, these scholars proceeded slowly but steadily to reach greater clarity and to arrive at a consensus concerning a number of questions: whether *synderesis* and *conscientia* are a *habitus* (disposition), an *actus* (actualization), or a *potentia* (potentiality); whether they reside in the reason, in the affections, or in the will; whether they are innate or acquired; whether they possess compelling force; and whether they are infallible.

71. Muller, *Dictionary of Latin and Greek Theological Terms*, 294.

72. See Douglas Kries, "Origen, Plato, and Conscience (*Synderesis*) in Jerome's Ezekiel Commentary," *Traditio* 57 (2002): 67-83.

73. Quoted in Potts, *Conscience in Medieval Philosophy*, 79-80.

74. Potts, *Conscience in Medieval Philosophy*, 10.

of moral law, conscience was identified with human acts of applying those basic ethical notions to particular actions.[75]

Integrating, ordering, and consolidating the received tradition, Aquinas addresses the three fundamental questions of the medieval debate on *synderesis*: "Is it a potentiality or a disposition? Then, can it do wrong? And, to conclude, is it extinguishable in some people?"[76] The answer to the first question is that *synderesis* is a natural disposition of human reason. This means it is innate and rational and that it belongs to the sphere of practical reason, which, on the basis of the first moral principles provided by *synderesis*, is further concerned with reflection on human actions and thus distinguished from speculative reason, which aims at contemplating truth. Therefore, human beings inherently possess the basic principles of right action, and these tacit presuppositions belong to *synderesis*, which is the innate understanding of the first principles of natural law that are known to us independently of the training of the intellect.[77] Aquinas answers the second question by affirming that *synderesis* is infallible in its immediate knowledge of practical first principles—not so much because psychologically these universal principles are perceptively and intuitively obvious to everyone, but rather from a logical perspective they must be necessarily true, otherwise nothing could be known with certainty. Being innately aware of practical reason, these general principles of *synderesis* may never be in error because mistakes only happen in judging or in the process of reasoning. In other words, in relation to these first principles, *synderesis* remains impeccable. Error can occur only in the application of general principles to specific cases and circumstances because of wrong inferences or because of false premises.[78] Lastly, Aquinas responds negatively to the question of whether *synderesis* can be extinguished, and he claims this for the same reason that he posits that it cannot do wrong: as a natural disposition which pertains to practical reason and according to which human beings have an immediate and stable knowledge of practical first principles, it cannot be extinguished, even though sin

---

75. This is basically Bavinck's understanding at the time of his lectures on Reformed Ethics (*Reformed Ethics*, 1:193–206).

76. Potts, *Conscience in Medieval Philosophy*, 45.

77. Jan Krokos, *Conscience as Cognition: Phenomenological Complementing of Aquinas's Theory of Conscience* (Peter Lang, 2013), 73–87; Potts, *Conscience in Medieval Philosophy*, 45–48.

78. Krokos, *Conscience as Cognition*, 87–90; Potts, *Conscience in Medieval Philosophy*, 48–49.

makes people utterly insensitive to it so that its operations are impeded. Even in the damned, *synderesis* is not extinguished but rather continues to be felt in its condemnation of the irreducible resistance of the will to what is good and right.[79]

As for *conscientia*, Aquinas asserts that it is not a disposition but an act by which practical reason applies the basic knowledge of moral principles that are supplied by *synderesis*. Aquinas uses Aristotelian inferential logic to show how *conscientia* applies the information provided by *synderesis*: *conscientia* reaches a conclusion by inferring from the major innate premises furnished by *synderesis* and from the minor premises added by practical reason. Possessing innate first moral principles known apart from inferential reasoning, practical reason considers and reflects further upon those principles so that *conscientia* may reach a conclusion by applying the major and minor premises.[80] Aquinas provides the following example: "If 'Nothing forbidden by the law of God ought to be done' is put forward by the judgement of *synderesis*, and 'Sexual intercourse with this woman is forbidden by the law of God' is added from what is known to higher reason, then an application of *conscientia* is made in concluding: 'This sexual intercourse is to be refrained from.'"[81] However, as noted before, in its conclusions *conscientia* may err because of false premises of reason (though not, of course, the first and basic principles supplied by *synderesis*) or wrong deductions of *conscientia* itself.[82]

Despite a measure of continuity between medieval Scholasticism and Reformation theology with respect to conscience and natural law,[83] Calvin is not in favor of the distinction between *synderesis* and *conscientia*,[84] and he

---

79. Krokos, *Conscience as Cognition*, 90-94; Potts, *Conscience in Medieval Philosophy*, 49-50.
80. Krokos, *Conscience as Cognition*, 95-106; Potts, *Conscience in Medieval Philosophy*, 50-52.
81. Quoted in Potts, *Conscience in Medieval Philosophy*, 132-33.
82. Krokos, *Conscience as Cognition*, 107-10; Potts, *Conscience in Medieval Philosophy*, 54-55.
83. See David VanDrunen, "Medieval Natural Law and the Reformation: A Comparison of Aquinas and Calvin," *American Catholic Philosophical Quarterly*, 80.1 (2006): 77-98; VanDrunen, "Conscience and Natural Law in Scripture," in Alvaré and Hammond, *Christianity and the Laws of Conscience*, 39-56; Paul Helm, "Nature and Grace," in *Aquinas among the Protestants*, ed. Manfred Svensson and David VanDrunen (John Wiley & Sons, 2018), 229-47; Daniel Westberg, "The Influence of Aquinas on Protestant Ethics," in Svensson and VanDrunen, *Aquinas among the Protestants*, 267-86.
84. In general, Reformed Scholastics maintained a Thomistic understanding of conscience over against Calvin; see Beeke and Jones, *A Puritan Theology*, 911-13; David S. Sytsma, "The Logic of the Heart: Analyzing the Affections in Early Reformed Orthodoxy," in *Church and School in Early Modern Protestantism: Studies in Honor of Richard Muller on the Maturation of a Theological Tradition*,

abandons the concept of *synderesis* for two main reasons. The first reason relates to philology and exegesis, for in the language of Scripture he found, on the one hand, words designating the experience of thinking attributed to the intellect and, on the other hand, words designating the experience of conscience in relation to perceiving and applying divine law.[85] For Calvin, what the Scholastics designated as *synderesis*—namely, the innate grasping of basic principles of moral law—was simply understood as the law written in the heart, which in turn related to the activity of *conscientia*, operating as a *sensus* and producing an awareness of God, his will, and his judgments. The second reason why Calvin did not uphold the notion of an infallible *synderesis* relates to the theological anthropology that he constructed upon the foundation of Scripture alone. His view of fallen humanity (and therefore of both *synderesis* and *conscientia*) convinced him that there was nothing left untouched in humanity by the fall, and consequently, the possession of infallible and impeccable first moral principles in human beings was impossible.[86] Probably because of these two related reasons, Calvin set aside the notion of *synderesis*, concentrating instead on the single reality of the experience of conscience.[87]

---

ed. Jordan J. Ballor, David S. Sytsma, and Jason Zuidema (Brill, 2013), 471–88. Paul Helm thinks that even though conscience was relevant in Calvin's theology, conscience became of distinct and developing importance in the Reformed tradition due to William Perkins's and William Ames's syllogistic understanding of conscience, which was the spark that ignited Protestant casuistry. *Human Nature from Calvin to Edwards* (Reformation Heritage Books, 2018), 111–21.

85. Calvin writes, "I wish that Christian writers had always exercised such restraint as not to take it into their heads needlessly to use terms foreign to Scripture that would produce great offence and very little fruit" (*Institutes* 3.15.2). Calvin's choice to set aside *synderesis* as referring to conscience (or to some aspects of it) is buttressed by the fact that *synderesis* is probably a corruption of the original New Testament word due to an error in transcription by copyists who were possibly using ruined manuscripts; see Tobias Hoffmann, "Conscience and *Synderesis*," in *The Oxford Handbook of Aquinas*, ed. Brian Davies and Eleonore Stump (Oxford University Press, 2012), 255. According to Hoffmann, Aquinas's "main concern is not exegetical but philosophical." "Conscience and *Synderesis*," in Davies and Stump, *The Oxford Handbook of Aquinas*, 256. This may explain why he does not adhere to the scriptural language and conceptuality alone.

86. See Berkouwer, *Man: The Image of God*, 170–72.

87. Matt Jenson points out the similar stance of Luther: "Luther rejects a faculty anthropology in favour of a holistic focus on the whole person (*totus homo*). Two central reasons assert themselves for Luther's radical divergence from scholastic anthropology on this point. The first is a concern to return to scriptural ways of speaking. ... [T]he second reason for Luther's abandonment of the faculty anthropology [is] the corruption which is original sin extends to the whole person. ... Particularly of note here is Luther's rejection around the time of his lectures on Romans of any soteriological component to the much-vaunted mediaeval concept of *synderesis*." *The Gravity of Sin: Augustine, Luther and Barth on "homo incurvatus in se"* (T&T Clark,

There is more to be said about Calvin's second reason. As it will be explored shortly, instead of conceiving of conscience in intellectual terms, Calvin regards it as *sensus*.[88] By contrast, Aquinas asserts that humanity participates in the universal divine government—that is, in God's eternal law—precisely *through the intellect*.[89] Concerning this primacy of the intellect, Aquinas writes:

> [The rational creature] has a share of the Eternal Reason, whereby it has a natural inclination to its proper act and end: and this participation of the eternal law in the rational creature is called the natural law. ... The light of natural reason, whereby we discern what is good and what is evil, which is the function of the natural law, is nothing else than an imprint on us of the Divine light. It is therefore evident that the natural law is nothing else than the rational creature's participation of the eternal law.[90]

It is at this particular juncture that Calvin parts ways with the Scholastics with respect to *synderesis*, conceiving of the reality of *conscientia* in a different manner due to his more drastic understanding of the noetic effects of the fall. Irena Backus makes the following observations on the differences between Aquinas and Calvin, adding weight to what was affirmed above:

> To Aquinas the term *natural law* applies in its strict sense not to the natural tendencies and inclinations of man on which his reason reflects but to the precepts that his reason enunciates as a result of this reflection. This metaphysical definition of natural law, which

---

2006), 66, 68; see also Michael G. Baylor, *Action and Person: Conscience in Late Scholasticism and the Young Luther* (Brill, 1977), 156–208.

88. It is interesting to note (only in passing) that Roman Catholic theologian Joseph Ratzinger - in retrieving the Augustinian notion of conscience as *memoria sui* - drops *synderesis* as one of the two components of conscience and adopts *anamnesis* instead, explaining the nature of conscience in terms of "an interior sense." *On Conscience* (San Francisco: Ignatius Press, 2007), 31–32. Cf. Vincent Twomey, *Pope Benedict XVI: The Conscience of Our Age* (San Francisco: Ignatius Press, 2007); Peter J. Casarella, "Culture and Conscience in the Thought of Jospeh Ratzinger, Pope Benedict XVI," in Alvaré and Hammond, *Christianity and the Laws of Conscience*, 265–284.

89. This explains the fact that, according to Hoffmann's observation, Aquinas "occasionally replaces the word *synderesis* by the term understanding (*intellectus*)" ("Conscience and *Synderesis*," 256). On Aquinas's intellectual interpretation of conscience, see Cajetan Cuddy, "St. Thomas Aquinas on Conscience," in Alvaré and Hammond, *Christianity and the Laws of Conscience*, 118–29.

90. Thomas Aquinas, *The Summa Theologica*, trans. the Fathers of the English Dominican Province (Benziger Bros., 1947–1948), I-II, q. 91, art. 2.

allows human reason a certain amount of autonomy in the moral realm, is absent from Calvin's work. Needless to say, it implies that Aquinas cannot define conscience as simply the mediator between God and man. *Conscientia* in his system is the human act of applying moral principles to particular actions and is to be distinguished from *synderesis*, which is the habitual knowledge of primary moral principles.[91]

While for Aquinas intellect and reasoning are prior to the operation of conscience, for Calvin conscience as *sensus* is more immediate and spontaneous in its activities; conscience is not a finishing knowledge but a beginning awareness, while reason follows along as a subsequent kind of knowing. However, conscience does not become epistemologically superior over reason, but working in conjunction with the intellect as well as with other human capacities, it functions according to the end for which it was created—namely, as a basic perception and intuition in the form of a subjective and immediate awareness of God and of humanity's covenantal vocation. Believing that "Calvin, in distinction to Aquinas … attributes greater priority to the post-lapsarian conscience than to the pre-lapsarian reason as the defining characteristic of his doctrine of natural law,"[92] Stephen Grabill detects the following theological reason behind this move:

> Calvin's accent on conscience suggests that he may have sought to modify the realist natural-law tradition to bring it more fully into line with Reformation teaching on the epistemological consequences of sin. … Conscience enables him to overcome the fundamental epistemological problem attending all forms of natural revelation, namely, that humans misperceive natural revelation because of sin and thus

---

91. Backus, "Calvin's Concept of Natural Law and Roman Law," 11-12. That "certain amount of autonomy" in the moral realm appears to be the reason why philosophers of very different orientations still find the notion of *synderesis* useful in contemporary moral philosophy, completely apart from any reference to the drama of redemption narrated in Scripture. For analytic philosophy, see Potts, *Conscience in Medieval Philosophy*, 11, 70-71; for phenomenology, see Howard, *Conscience in Moral Life*, 19-22; for virtue ethics, see Douglas C. Langdon, *Conscience and Other Virtues* (Pennsylvania State University Press, 2001), 21-69. For some further reflections on the incompatibility between the Protestant view of the noetic effects of sin and a theological interpretation of virtue ethics, see Simeon Zahl, "Non-Competitive Agency and Luther's Experiential Argument against Virtue," *Modern Theology* 35, no.2 (2019): 199-222; see also Zahl, *The Holy Spirit and Christian Experience*, 114-16, 152-53.

92. Grabill, *Rediscovering the Natural Law*, 90.

suppress, distort, and abuse the knowledge God has placed at their disposal, because conscience, far more than merely distinguishing between right and wrong, carries *an immediate awareness* of divine judgment for wrongdoing that compels people to acknowledge their guilt.[93]

Calvin's idea of reason, according to Dowey, "does not imply an ability a priori to deduce a natural ethic based solely on axioms of reason, apart from experience."[94] Rather than affirming the primacy of prelapsarian reason, Calvin identifies conscience as a "*sensus divini iudicii.*"[95] He writes:

> We must take our definition from the etymology of the word. When men grasp the conception of things with the mind and the understanding they are said "to know," from which the word "knowledge" is derived. In like manner, when men have an *awareness* of divine judgment [*sensum divini iudicii*] adjoined to them as a witness which does not hide their sins but arraigns them as guilty before the judgement seat—this *awareness* is called "conscience" [*sensus ille vocatur conscientia*]. *It is a certain mean between God and man*, for it does not allow man to suppress within himself what he knows, but pursues him to the point of making him acknowledge his guilt. ... Therefore, this *feeling* [*sensus*], which draws men to God's judgment, is like a keeper assigned to man, that watches and observes all his secrets so that nothing may remain buried in darkness. Hence, that ancient proverb: conscience is a thousand witnesses.[96]

For Calvin, the phenomenon of conscience is experienced as a *sensus*, a sort of intuitive perception or an instinctive apprehension not preceded by practical reasoning.

Sensus is the noun form of the verb *sentire*, which, according to Lewis, fundamentally describes "something like 'to experience, learn by experience, undergo, know at first hand.' "[97] In his study on the word "sense," Lewis

---

93. Grabill, *Rediscovering the Natural Law*, 92–93 (emphasis added).
94. Dowey, *The Knowledge of God*, 25.
95. Calvin, *Institutes*, 3.19.15.
96. Calvin, *Institutes*, 4.10.3 (emphasis added).
97. Lewis, *Studies in Words*, 134.

writes, "*Sensus* is first-hand experience, immediate awareness of one's own mental and emotional content." Consequently, it is possible to translate the word in some contexts with "experience" while in others with "awareness or (sometimes) consciousness" so that it refers to apprehensions that are undergone inwardly: "our experience, emotions, thoughts, apprehensions, and opinions. The *communis sensus* of mankind is what all men have 'been through' (e.g. pain and pleasure), or feel emotionally (fears and hopes), or think (that half a loaf's better than no bread) or have some apprehension of (the comic, the praiseworthy), or agree to be true (that two and two make four)."[98] Similarly, for Calvin the two nouns *conscientia* and *sensus* are very close in meaning, and he uses the latter to explain the nature of the former.[99]

It appears that Aquinas—the theoretician and systematizer of natural law—gives precedence to human inferential rationality in his understanding of conscience.[100] For him, *conscientia* is part of the demanding interplay of practical reason with *synderesis* that implies a progression from premises to inferences.[101] Calvin, by contrast, understands conscience in affective terms, as a subjective awareness and a spontaneous perception that makes religious

---

98. Lewis, *Studies in Words*, 141-42, 148. On the words "conscience" and "conscious," Lewis explains that the verb *conscio* and the noun *conscientia* are used in reference to a basic "knowledge, awareness, apprehension—even something like mind or thought" (which Lewis calls "the weakened branch") or to the sharing of those experiences with others, namely other people or in reflexive form with oneself (which Lewis calls "the together branch") (*Studies in Words*, 181-82).

99. For Calvin, this divine sense of the inner person is a cognitive capacity, though not yet in the form of logical and syllogistic practical reason; see Zachman, *The Assurance of Faith*, 99-100.

100. In spite of his intellectualistic interpretation of conscience, Aquinas does not exclude the appetitive power of the affections—that is, the doctrine of the "spiritual senses" (as will be seen in chapter 7 on redeemed conscience). In his own way, Aquinas elaborates a convergence or integration between the cognitive power of reason and the appetitive power of the affections in the form of a reciprocal influence. On this topic, see the investigation by Marco D'Avenia of the Thomistic notion of affective knowledge known as "connatural knowledge." *La conoscenza per connaturalità in S. Tommaso d'Aquino* (Edizioni Studio Domenicano, 1992).

101. According to Merold Westphal, Aquinas is not sensitive enough to the noetic effects of sin: "Compared to Augustine, Luther, and Calvin ... Aquinas does epistemology as if in the Garden of Eden." *Overcoming Onto-Theology: Toward a Postmodern Christian Faith* (Fordham University Press, 2001), 105. According to Hoffmann, "Aquinas's emphasis on reason points in the direction of secular accounts" of conscience ("Conscience and *Synderesis*," 262).

and moral knowledge more readily and easily available to all people.[102] It is this view of conscience as *sensus* that governs the current work.[103]

FALLEN CONSCIENCE AS NONPHYSICAL PERCEPTUAL AWARENESS

The preceding analysis has argued that conscience does not operate predominantly as inferential reasoning but as a primal or innate human capacity to perceive[104] the reality of God's existence, his personal presence, and the righteous requirements of his will. Because God is spirit, it follows that the capacity to perceive him must be primarily a nonphysical kind. As human beings have been created with a set of capacities to relate to the rest of creation, so too they have been created with a set of capacities to be in relation with the Creator. This capacity for nonphysical perception is therefore to be distinguished from the capacity to gain knowledge of God from the external world (see Rom 1:20), which is dependent on previous perception through the five senses that causes the human heart to ask questions and to think about the existence and the nature of God.

This is not to say that conscience can operate apart from physical perception; though distinct, the former is correlated to and inseparable from the latter, as there is a sort of simultaneous collaboration between the inner world of the mind and the outer world of the cosmos.[105] Indeed, conscience—created or fallen—is experienced within the order of nature and cannot operate as if isolated from the perception of the external world.[106] The inter-

---

102. Calvin maintains that "all people are given a knowledge of the natural law, and all people are given both the ability and the responsibility to test the correspondence between human laws and natural law" (Zachman, *The Assurance of Faith*, 116).

103. For a useful investigation of a more affective understanding of *synderesis* and *conscientia* in Scholasticism and especially in Bonaventure, see Robert Glenn Davis, *The Weight of Love: Affect, Ecstasy, and Union in the Theology of Bonaventure* (Fordham University Press, 2017), 45–87.

104. Von Rad notices the presence of this basic *perceptual* capacity as it is given expression in the poetry of the Old Testament: "In that period, a wide range of *basic perceptions about life and the world* could be expressed only in poetic form, and thus poetic expression was something which was necessary for life and knowledge. This poetic function of fixing *perceptions* was occasionally characterized by the solemnity of an oath, just as even today a poetic word can exercise a magical power" (*Wisdom in Israel*, 50, emphasis added).

105. Turretin affirms that "there is a natural theology, partly innate (derived from the book of conscience by means of common notions) and partly acquired (drawn from the book of creatures discursively)" (*Institutes of Elenctic Theology*, 1:6); see also Bavinck, *Reformed Dogmatics*, 2:54.

106. See Collicut, "Discernment and the Psychology of Perception," 98.

nal world of the mind and the external world of the cosmos are the sole environment in which human creatures live and move and have their being, and they do so before the omnipresent triune God.[107] Considering the sources of the knowledge of God as creator in Calvin, Dowey writes:

> By creation we do not mean only the external world, or "nature," as something upon which man looks from inside out to garner knowledge of God. Man himself, including his inner mental life, his subjectivity, is part of creation. Calvin's conception of the revelation in creation corresponds to the doubleness, the subjectivity and objectivity, which is one of the elemental characteristics of mental life. In fact, it is the subjective element of the revelation in creation that receives his first attention in the *Institutes*, though the objective receives more detailed attention. *God reveals himself to man internally by a direct perception of which Calvin distinguishes two elements: the sense of divinity, and the conscience.*[108]

Besides attributing equal importance to the objective and subjective dimensions of revelation, another great merit of Dowey's analysis is that he does not consider the *sensus divinitatis* independently of conscience.[109] Similarly, even though he does not explicitly mention conscience or the

---

107. God's spirituality and omnipresence affect the *sensus* of fallen human beings. These divine attributes in particular show that the failure to perceive God is not to be confused with his absence. Bavinck—alluding to the testimony of the *sensus*—simply states that God himself makes his own presence "felt in our heart and conscience" (Bavinck, *Reformed Dogmatics*, 2:169). Without downplaying the Trinitarian revelation of the gospel in its christological and pneumatological orientation, Puritan divine Stephen Charnock similarly insists on the "influential" omnipresence of God's essence, which is "universal with all creatures." Charnock alludes to the witness of the *sensus* when he says that the "presence of God is evident to our sense, a presence we feel; his essential presence is evident in our reason." In fact, human creatures "are *capacitated* for [his] presence" so that "there is an objective presence of God with rational creatures, because he offers himself to them to be known." *Discourses upon the Existence and Attributes of God* (Baker Books, 1979), 1:369-70 (emphasis added).

108. Dowey, *The Knowledge of God*, 50 (emphasis added).

109. Dowey conceives of the *sensus iudicii* as the other side of the same coin, namely of the one "subjective revelation in creation" (*The Knowledge of God in Calvin's Theology*, 56). Helm too isolates a single subjective disposition for knowledge of God, which he defines broadly as *sensus divinitatis*. According to Helm, the one *sensus divinitatis* is to be understood as consisting of two aspects: 1) the metaphysical-cognitive component (which for Calvin is the *sensus divinitatis* proper) and 2) the moral-cognitive component (which for Calvin is conscience or *sensus divini iudicii*). Helm identifies the moral-cognitive component with conscience (*John Calvin's Ideas*, 224-29, 231, 237); see also Zachman, *The Assurance of Faith*, 102-4, 112-13. This distinction between the metaphysical-cognitive component and the moral-cognitive component might be

notion of the *sensus divinitatis*, Vos's comments on John 1:4 accentuate the importance of the subjective capacity for perception of the reality of God:

> In the natural religion ... the Logos-revelation is actually mediated through the subjective life which man in dependence of the Logos possesses. The life here naturally produces the light. ... The life which man receives carries in itself and of itself kindles in him, the light of the knowledge of God.[110]

Thus, subjective/internal perception and objective/external realities are not disconnected but part of one and the same created reality.[111]

Using his characteristic plain form of speech (rather than formal and analytical language), Calvin explains why and how the *sensus divinitatis* and *sensus iudicii* intertwine: "Now, the knowledge of God, as I understand it, is that by which we not only conceive that there is a God but also grasp what befits us and is proper to his glory, in fine, what is to our advantage to know him."[112]

Although he does not explicitly mention the *sensus* here, Calvin affirms that it takes two forms: first, a perception/cognition of the reality of God as creator, and second, a perception/cognition of obligation toward this creator. What is significant is that this dual *sensus* is a perceptual and nonphysical awareness; the *sensus* is formed in its two related components spontaneously, and as such, it results not only, or even primarily, from a process of formal reasoning.[113]

The *sensus divinitatis* works in tandem with the *sensus iudicii* so that they complement each other. However, the *sensus iudicii* is derivative, while the

---

discerned in the two tablets of the Decalogue, which adds a divine confirmation to the *sensus* of conscience (see Mark 12:28-34).

110. Vos, *Redemptive History and Biblical Theology*, 76 (emphasis added).

111. Douglas F. Kelly maintains that the testimony of God—not just of moral order—is present within the conscience of humankind: "Human religion flows, as we have just seen, from God's clear revelation *of Himself* in the created order, perverted though it is by the rebellious mind and fallen mankind. But there is a second context (closely related to creation, and indeed, part of it) from which mankind derives *a sense of the divine*, and is thus fully responsible for it: the human conscience." *The God Who Is: The Holy Trinity*, in vol. 1 of *Systematic Theology: Grounded in Holy Scripture and Understood in the Light of the Church* (Christian Focus Publications, 2008), 144 (emphasis added).

112. Calvin, *Institutes*, 1.2.1.

113. In thinking about the *sensus* in moral terms, Helm is explicit in affirming that it "is a judgement of a highly un-self-conscious and automatic kind" (*John Calvin's Ideas*, 227).

former is more original.[114] Indeed, there cannot be a sense of divine judgment without a more basic sense of the divine in the same way that there cannot be knowledge of the justice of a person without a previous knowledge of the person who is just. Thus understood, the *sensus* might be considered as a natural capacity for reciprocal mutual awareness, an inborn disposition for immediate perception of the other (in this case the other is God, the creator).[115]

In this regard, according to William Alston, what distinguishes "perception from abstract thought is that the object is *directly presented* or *immediately present* to the subject."[116] Using sense perception to explain the concept of immediacy, Alston writes:

> To be sure, there is a sense in which I perceive T through having a visual experience, and that point puts us in a position to recognize a still more direct mode of awareness. Consider one's awareness of one's conscious states: one's feeling, sensations, thoughts, and imaginings. Here there is no state of consciousness distinct from the object of awareness through which one is aware of that object. When I am aware of feeling excited, there is not a conscious state of being aware of my feeling that is distinguishable from the feeling—the way there is a conscious visual experience of the computer which is distinguishable from the computer. Our own states of consciousness are *given* to us with maximum immediacy, not given to us *through* anything.[117]

Alston, therefore, discriminates between two modes of perceiving. There is a *mediated immediacy*, or direct perception, in which "one is aware of X through a state of consciousness that is distinguishable from X, and can be made an object of absolutely immediate awareness, but is not perceived," and a *mediate perception* in which "one is aware of X through the awareness of

---

114. Helm writes, "So the cognitive content of the *sensus* is not merely that God exists, but that God the Creator exists. This awareness, that oneself and all that one sees is the creation of God, in turn triggers beliefs and feelings of awe, respect, gratitude, and obligation to the benefactor of the whole" (*John Calvin's Ideas*, 227).

115. For a reflection on the relational character of this intuitive knowledge in patristic theology, see Williams, *The Divine Sense*, 234-36.

116. William P. Alston, *Perceiving God: The Epistemology of Religious Experience* (Cornell University Press, 1991), 20-21.

117. Alston, *Perceiving God*, 21.

another object of perception."[118] Accordingly, the *sensus* (both *divinitatis* and *iudicii*) can be conceived of as a phenomenon of mediated immediacy, as a direct perception[119] that is cognitive in nature (even though it is not complete and distinct).[120] In this way it corresponds to the traditional Reformed notion of *cognitio insita*, an intuitive and immediate apprehension of the divine not based on ratiocinative processes.[121]

However, Helm expresses a slightly different explanation:

> Much less is Calvin saying that all men have a direct experience of God. The sentences that we are discussing do not amount to an appeal to religious experience either as a mystical "encounter" with the divine or as some other kind of direct awareness of God. The idea of an experience of God does not enter into any of the terminology that Calvin uses to characterize the SD [*sensus divinitatis*]. Rather, by the SD all men conceive (or perceive) *that there is a God*; that is, there is a recognition by all men of the fact that there is a God. This basic knowledge of God is propositional in content rather than a person to person awareness of God.[122]

---

118. Alston, *Perceiving God*, 22.

119. Even though speaking of mediate immediacy as "a state of consciousness," it appears that for Alston conscience is not to be explained in terms of mediated immediacy: "Turning now to *indirect perception of God* [there is] much talk of experiencing God in the beauties of nature, of hearing God's voice in the Bible or in sermons *or in the dictates of conscience*, of being aware of God's providential activity in the events of our lives, of seeing God's hand at work in salvation history, and so on" (*Perceiving God*, 25, emphasis added). However, according to the argument presented thus far, conscience is conceived as a state of consciousness and not as another object like nature, the Bible, or a sermon, and therefore it is understood as mediated immediacy in the same way in which Alston speaks of one's awareness of one's feeling, sensations, thoughts, and imaginings.

120. Thinking about the tendency to construe religious experience as noncognitive in nature, Michael Sudduth makes the following observation: "On a realist conception of perceptual experience, it is God himself who is directly known in the perceptual experience of God, in much the same way that physical objects are directly known by way of sensory perceptual experience." "The Contribution of Religious Experience to Dogmatic Theology," in *Analytic Theology: New Essays in the Philosophy of Theology*, ed. Oliver D. Crisp and Michael C. Rea (Oxford University Press, 2009), 231.

121. On the Reformed concept of *cognitio insita*, see Muller, *Dictionary of Latin and Greek Theological Terms*, 70–71.

122. Helm, *John Calvin's Ideas*, 225. Dowey affirms instead "the irrelevance of the bare proposition 'God exists' " for Calvin because of "the existentiality of all our knowledge of God" (*The Knowledge of God*, 153).

Helm's explanation of the *sensus* and his denial of the possibility of a direct experience or awareness of God must be given some consideration. Since Helm is discussing the *sensus* in the context of creation and prior to the fall, it is doubtful that it can be maintained that what he calls "the pristine" *sensus* would have not allowed human beings—in their state of innocence and original integrity in the garden—a direct awareness of God's presence of the sort that might be labeled a religious experience. On the contrary, the pristine *sensus* of Adam and Eve granted them a direct awareness and knowledge of God, not just a proposition about God. God furnished human creatures with the capacity to be aware that there is a God in order to make *himself* immediately present to them.[123] Because of this, the *sensus* even allowed for an immediate and personal encounter with God as creator apart from special preredemptive revelations.[124]

Helm himself acknowledges that the natural capacity of the pristine *sensus* is more than merely recognizing the proposition that there is a God: "So the cognitive content of the *sensus* is not merely that God exists, but that God the Creator exists. This awareness, that oneself and all that one sees is the creation of God, in turn triggers beliefs and feelings of awe, respect, gratitude, and obligation *to* the benefactor of the whole."[125] It seems, then, that the *sensus* is not merely propositional but that it produces spontaneously

---

123. Horton states, "God is never the revealed object without being the revealing subject. ... Revelation cannot simply be revelation *about* God. ... In revelation God is present in personal address, which creates a crisis and calls for a decision" (*The Christian Faith*, 116–17). Although Horton is considering the object and subject of redemptive revelation, the argument here is that the same applies to preredemptive and general revelation. Collicut writes, "However revelation is to be understood, it involves human cognition and perception, which recognize it for what it actually is" ("Discernment and the Psychology of Perception," 107). In this respect, John B. Webster claims that "self-manifestation is ingredient to the being of God: as Father, Son and Spirit, God is antecedently one who wills, effects and brings to fruition the knowledge of himself on the part of his creatures" ("Hermeneutic in Modern Theology: Some Doctrinal Reflections," in *Word and Church*, 65).

124. For Vos, "God reveals *Himself* to the inner sense of man through the religious consciousness and the moral conscience" (*Biblical Theology*, 19, emphasis added). From Vos's perspective on the covenantal and therefore relational and personal nature of revelation, what is missing in Helm's explanation of the *sensus* is what the Dutch theologian describes as its "dramatic" element. Because the Bible "is not a dogmatic handbook but a historical book full of dramatic interest," the Semitic concept of knowledge is to be understood in terms of person-to-person awareness: "God's self-revelation to us was not made for a primarily intellectual purpose. ... Because God desires to be *known* after this fashion [in love], He has caused His revelation to take place in the milieu of the historical life of a people. The circle of revelation is not a school, but a 'covenant'" (*Biblical Theology*, 17, 8).

125. Helm, *John Calvin's Ideas*, 227 (emphasis added).

and freely a person-to-person awareness of God himself, so much so that the *sensus* causes a realization of awe, respect, gratitude, and obligation *to* (the preposition used by Helm) God. For Helm, the *sensus* delivers a proposition or a belief present to consciousness, but it also, subsequently, provides an awareness of being in the very presence of God the creator, even though fallen creatures may not understand or explain their experience in terms of being in the presence of God.

Helm is right when he says that the *sensus* "is not a case of immediate experience of God, as the experience of a patch of blue may be immediate,"[126] especially for fallen human beings. However, the difference between the experience of God and the experience of a patch of blue is not so absolutely dissimilar that it completely precludes any measure of immediacy in our nonphysical perceptions.[127] The propositional knowledge that there is a God who is present to us does not exclude the fact that God himself—through the perceptions formed by the *sensus*—is present to us.[128] Therefore, it seems that Helm contradicts himself when he compares the nonphysical perceptual awareness of the *sensus* to the *immediacy* of sense perception: "This judgement [of the *sensus*] is accompanied by a feeling of obviousness or naturalness *in the way in which* it is natural for us to believe that there has been a past, or that there are minds other than our own minds, or that 2 + 2 = 4."[129] But precisely on this reckoning, it seems reductive to claim that the nonphysical

---

126. Helm, *John Calvin's Ideas*, 226.

127. To the categories of mediated immediacy and mediate perception, Alston helpfully adds that of *absolute immediacy*, which is what seems to trouble Helm: "Extreme mystical experience in which all distinctions are transcended in an undifferentiated unity is properly thought of as absolute immediacy. If no distinctions can be made within the seamless unity, then there is no possibility of distinguishing the experience involved from the object of awareness. Indeed, the immediacy here is more absolute than in one's awareness of one's conscious states." *Perceiving God*, 23. This distinction makes clear that the immediacy that Alston is thinking about is relative and not total or unconditioned and as such not one that erases the distinction between archetypal divine knowledge and human knowledge.

128. Speaking of the very presence of God, John Owen writes, "Under the ashes of our collapsed nature there are yet remaining certain *sparks of celestial fire*, consisting in inbred notices of good and evil, of rewards and punishment, *of the presence and all-seeing eye of God*, of help and assistance to be had from him, with a dread of his excellencies where any thing is apprehended unworthy of him or provoking unto him" ("A Discourse on the Holy Spirit," in *The Works of John Owen*, 3:345, emphasis added).

129. Helm, *John Calvin's Ideas*, 227 (emphasis added). In another book, Helm compares quite explicitly general sense perception with divine general (or natural) revelation; see Paul Helm, *The Divine Revelation: The Basic Issues* (Regent College Publishing, 2004), 13-32.

perception of the *sensus* is a mere proposition or belief, thus excluding the possibility that this *sensus* has been created for the very purpose of bringing us into the presence of God himself.[130]

Therefore, the *sensus* goes beyond the mere proposition that there is a God, revealing immediately (that is, intuitively and spontaneously) some knowledge of God himself, which is a direct religious experience of God.[131] It should be stressed again that this directness or immediacy is not to be understood absolutely, for it remains mediated by character and it does not exclude or render unnecessary the objective witness of the external world and special revelation for salvation. Nor does it imply perfection or completeness, as if the content of the knowledge obtained through the *sensus* coincides fully and precisely with the identity of the one who reveals himself as creator. Such a perfect and complete knowledge is only possible for the Trinity where the capacity for perfect mutual awareness and living reciprocal presence is experienced and enjoyed by the divine persons. To a limited extent, though, through the *sensus* human creatures experience the triune divine life in that they possess a subjective capacity to be consciously aware of God, a capacity that calls for constantly responding, understanding, listening, and reflecting.

SUMMARY

This chapter has argued that the distinct role of conscience as a mediator between God and humanity derives not from the fact that it is a special faculty above others by virtue of its structural location or superior position. Rather, having been designed to function—in collaboration with other human competencies—as the particular capacity for a basic awareness and immediate perception of God, conscience continues to operate in fallen human creatures. Even in sin, as has been demonstrated above, human nature—unified and integrated as a whole—remains aware of God and his covenantal vocation

---

130. In another essay on the knowledge of God and of ourselves, Helm writes of people being "immediately aware" of God. Later, commenting on the fact that the knowledge of God is meant to affect us and stressing that Calvin points out that even some philosophers (particularly Plato) noticed this connection, he writes, "Here is another case where the knowledge of God affects the state of the knower by a kind of immediate reflex." Helm, *Calvin at the Centre* (Oxford University Press, 2010), 8–9, 10.

131. Commenting on Genesis 3:7, Sarna observes that (fallen) conscience perceives not so much a proposition but a presence: "Now, prompted by a guilty conscience, the disobedient couple suddenly becomes aware of the Divine Presence. God reemerges and moves to the center of the stage" (*Genesis*, 26).

not through conscience in and of itself but through conscience giving its own specific contribution in concurrence with the role played by emotions, bodily sensations, thinking, will, and language. Moreover, following Calvin over Aquinas, conscience's primary mode of operation is to be understood as *sensus*, namely as a nonphysical perceptual basic awareness rather than a practical inferential reasoning deriving from impeccable first principles. Finally, some notions were discussed in contemporary moral psychology, ethical theory, and philosophy of mind in order to show the relevance of the concept of *sensus* understood primarily in Trinitarian terms and only secondarily anthropologically. To conclude this part on fallen conscience, it now remains to explore how conscience is fallen.

5
—
HOW CONSCIENCE IS FALLEN

If fallen conscience, as nonphysical perceptual awareness, allows people to have a primal awareness of God and a moral consciousness in their fallen state, one theological problem is to explain *how* conscience is fallen—that is, in what ways fallenness manifests itself specifically in relation to conscience and its operations. Up to this point, it might appear—to express the concern of Merold Westphal—as if in this theology of conscience, "creation does a full day's work, while the fall is only asked to put in a cameo appearance."[1] Indeed, from what has been said thus far, it may even be feared that the general portrayal of fallen conscience shows that conscience is doing fine in spite of the reality of sin.[2] Echoing Westphal's concern, Webster makes the following penetrating observation regarding the reality of the fallenness of conscience:

> The human moral agent acts and reflects within the drama of salvation, a drama in which we—including our consciences—are put to death and made alive. Conscience is caught up by the struggle of God against sin: conscience, too, is overthrown. And so, for Christian theology, it can never be the location of a serene process of self-review which, even in self-reproof, is not exposed to any kind of *final* judgment. It cannot be simply internal moral auditing which never calls into question the project of me being me, but simply corrects, modifies or chastises without ever putting to death. Anxieties along these

---

1. Merold Westphal, "Taking St. Paul Seriously: Sin as an Epistemological Category," in *Christian Philosophy*, ed. Thomas P. Flint (Notre Dame University Press, 1990), 215.

2. According to Torrance, in general the fallenness of conscience is rarely considered in modern views of conscience; see "Conscience in the Early Church Fathers," in *Christianity and the Laws of Conscience*, 104-7. For a meticulous analysis of the ways in which conscience manifests its fallenness in relation to law and gospel, see Thomas Goodwin, *The Works of Thomas Goodwin* (Tanski Publications, 1996), 6:231-319.

lines always underlie rejections of construals of conscience as a phenomenon of natural existence whose operations are reliable and of whose probity we can be justly confident. If such a natural account is to be rejected, it is because of the theological miscalculation involved: about human depravity, about the lack of transparency in human self-knowledge, about our incapacity for innocent and scrupulous enquiry into ourselves.[3]

Following Webster's suggestive remarks in his final sentence, this chapter seeks to answer the question of how conscience is fallen by setting out three main claims: conscience is fallen in that it has been depraved from a state of integrity; conscience is fallen in that it has become ineffective in promoting transparency in self-knowledge; and conscience is fallen in that humanity is incapable of innocent and scrupulous self-scrutiny.

CONSCIENCE IS FALLEN IN THAT IT HAS BEEN DEPRAVED

To affirm the total depravity of conscience does not mean to affirm that this complete perversion has destroyed entirely the capacity of conscience to function. Notwithstanding the fall into sin, the *sensus divinitatis* (in its twofold correlated mode of operation) continues to bear its witness, summoning human creatures before the Creator and legislating for them according to his will. This persistency of conscience begs the following question: in what sense, then, is conscience fallen? This section will seek to answer this question in relation to the traditional Reformed understanding of the noetic effects of sin as they affected conscience.

The fact that conscience is fallen should be kept distinct from the fact that it is finite. The problem is not finitude. As a created reality, finite conscience was freely exposed to the final judgment of God and ready to embrace it. In the beginning, finite conscience knew the blessed absence of any disharmony in relation to the Creator, and therefore there was no reason for hiddenness, for shame, or even for any kind of fear. However, with the fall, things changed, and the *imago Dei* was so completely corrupted that human creatures became alienated from God and the whole of their humanity was

---

3. Webster, "God and Conscience," 257.

devastatingly affected. Nevertheless, in affirming the notion of complete corruption, Reformed theology does not intend to assert that human beings are as evil as they could possibly be but rather that no human power, disposition, capacity, or aptitude was spared from the distortion caused by the fall. All the endowments bestowed by the Creator—the emotions, body, intellect, will, language, and conscience operating together with them—ceased to function as they were originally conceived of and intended, namely in order to glorify and enjoy God and to love and serve other creatures. This loss does not imply that human powers and aptitudes ceased to exist or to function but rather that they have been corrupted from their original integrity—having their orientation twisted toward the love of self, they became inefficient and futile in relation to God and their original end.

It is possible to gain insight into how sin has corrupted human capacities by considering Ephesians 4:17-19, which according to Steven Baugh "is a portrait of total depravity, which refers to the infection of sin that has permeated the whole person."[4] The text reads:

> Now this I say and testify in the Lord, that you must no longer walk as the Gentiles do, in the *futility of their minds*. They are *darkened in their understanding, alienated from the life of God* because of the *ignorance that is in them*, due to their *hardness of heart*. They have become *callous* and have *given themselves up* to sensuality, greedy to practice every kind of impurity.

This passage provides seven features that characterize sinful humanity: (1) futility of mind, (2) darkness in thinking, (3) alienation from the life of God, (4) ignorance within, (5) hardness of heart, (6) callousness and, consequently, (7) idolatrous and immoral conduct. These describe how sin has affected human capacities and existence in relation to God. Even though it does not mention conscience, this passage opens a way of thinking about how the fall perverted conscience in particular. For example, in describing sinfulness in terms of callousness, Scripture is saying that the human capacity of being *sympathetic* (in the literal sense of being able to sympathize with— that is, to share the same feeling and to suffer in common with someone

---

4. Steven M. Baugh, *Ephesians*, Evangelical Exegetical Commentary (Lexham Press, 2016), 364, emphasis added.

else) in relation to God was seriously impaired.⁵ The *sensus*, or the natural capacity for reciprocity with and awareness of alterity, has been ruined by the fall. Baugh identifies a connection between the idea of callousness and conscience, suggesting that in Ephesians 4:18 the word callousness "refers to people with 'seared' consciences (1 Tim 4:2) who have no human *sympathy* or regard for anything but their own greed and passions."⁶ Peter O'Brien also makes this connection:

> The thought of hardening their hearts continues in the statement that they have "lost all sensitivity," a vivid classical term which literally could refer to skin that had become callous and no longer felt pain. Here it means to *"lose the capacity to feel shame* or embarrassment," ... *their lack of moral feeling and discernment.*⁷

Commenting on the usage of "to sear" (καυστηριάζω) to describe fallen conscience in 1 Timothy 4:2, Pierce observes that "it and the other words of the same family are, it is true, all found in connection with *branding*: but they are also found in medical and veterinary writers in connection presumably with therapeutic cauterization."⁸ Even though most contemporary commentators, such as Gordon Fee, understand the verb as referring to an external description, such that the apostates in 1 Timothy 4:1 are seen as "branded by Satan [and] belonging to him,"⁹ it seems more plausible that Paul is pointing

---

5. Antonia Cancrini explains that the verb "to sympathize" is analogous in its formation to various verbal forms resulting from the union of the prepositional prefix "with" and verbs indicating some form of knowledge (pointing to the experience of conscience): "[To sympathize] is born out of the need to express an emotion of particular commonality that binds some and that—precisely for this—necessarily excludes others" (*Syneidesis*, 24, translation mine). The previous consideration about the concurrence of emotions and conscience helps to establish the relevance of the concept of sympathizing; see Eric Schliesser, ed., *Sympathy: A History* (Oxford University Press, 2015).

6. Baugh, *Ephesians*, 362–63 (emphasis added).

7. Peter T. O'Brien, *The Letter to the Ephesians*, Pillar New Testament Commentary (Eerdmans, 1999), 322 (emphasis added). John Calvin is explicit in his sermons on Ephesians that Paul is speaking of people who "throw their consciences into such a sleep that they no longer feel any remorse or grief" and who "show themselves to be without scruple of conscience." *Sermons on the Epistle to the Ephesians* (Banner of Truth, 1973), 417.

8. Pierce, *Conscience in the New Testament*, 91.

9. Gordon D. Fee, *1 and 2 Timothy, Titus*, Understanding the Bible Commentary Series (Hendrickson, 1984), 99. Other scholars interpret the verb as a penal branding—a mark showing the apostates to be transgressors, emphasizing again the external use. On the various interpretations, see George W. Knight III, *The Pastoral Epistles* (Eerdmans, 1992), 189.

to the subjective condition of their consciences. The structure of the phrase "consciences are seared" appears to point in that direction, since the focus of the statement is on the inner characterization of the apostates' consciences and not some outward sign or symptom.[10] In light of the material presented thus far stressing the inwardness of the phenomenon of conscience, the proposal of Pierce that the "natural interpretation of such metaphorical use is *made callous*"[11] appears likely, and therefore the "searing" probably refers not to an external mark but to an inward condition. As George Knight III observes, the concluding participial phrase in 1 Timothy 4:2 "gives the *inner* basis for the conduct just described."[12] So, it appears that a cauterized or callous conscience is the cause of the departure from the faith mentioned in the previous verse (see also 1 Tim 1:19). Considering the course of action described in 1 Timothy 4:1-2, Pierce observes that the "author takes it for granted that such a career [of apostates] could not be embarked upon unless those who did so were already completely under the anaesthetic, or, rather, had *with a hot iron* completely destroyed the 'nerve-endings.' "[13] Pierce insists on affirming the *complete* corruption or defilement of conscience. However, in the case of the mind (see Titus 1:15), the completeness of corruption or of cauterization does not imply that the conscience or the mind have absolutely ceased to function in relation to God. On the contrary, the previous investigation of the *sensus* demonstrates that is not the case. According to Pierce, conscience becomes callous and loses its sensitivity to the extent that "it ceases to be effective in its proper office" in relation to God.[14]

Thus, the fallenness of conscience consists primarily in its being oriented away from God and inclined instead toward religious insensitivity and moral callousness. Conscience has ceased to be competent and reliable in relation to the purpose for which it was given, even though humanity is

---

10. The verb καυστηριάζω is defined as "burn with a hot iron so as to deaden to feeling" in the dictionary at the back of Barbara Aland et. al, eds., *The Greek New Testament*, 4th rev. ed. (Deutsche Bibelgesellschaft, 2001), 98. Other dictionaries—such as the *Theological Dictionary of the New Testament* or the *Exegetical Dictionary on the New Testament*—do not mention this possible association of the verb with therapeutic cauterization.

11. Pierce, *Conscience in the New Testament*, 91.

12. Knight, *The Pastoral Epistles*, 189 (emphasis added).

13. Pierce, *Conscience in the New Testament*, 92.

14. Pierce, *Conscience in the New Testament*, 93. On this theme in early patristic theology, see Torrance, "Conscience in the Early Church Fathers," 104-7.

still inclined naturally to religion. Its originally open and welcoming orientation toward God has been twisted and inverted so that its present orientation is introverted—directed toward the self and consequently toward idolatry. And because of this, conscience cannot be construed as a phenomenon of natural existence whose operations are reliable and of whose probity we can be confident.[15]

CONSCIENCE IS FALLEN IN THAT IT HINDERS TRANSPARENCY IN SELF-KNOWLEDGE

The loss of transparency in self-knowledge is a direct consequence of the forfeiture of the original knowledge of God, along with which true knowledge of oneself is given. The two are indissolubly bound: in gaining the one we also gain the other, and in losing the former we lose the latter.[16] Having lost true knowledge of God, human beings have lost true knowledge of themselves as image-bearers, yet sinful humanity does not experience this loss reluctantly, as if it were imposed against their will and desire. Rather, the loss of knowledge of God and of ourselves derives from the disruption caused by the bondage of the will to sinful desires, which manifests itself in the suppression of the truth (see Rom 1:18). The fall led to conscience—as well as anthropology and human identity in general—being conceived and interpreted solely within a horizontal perspective and in human terms, independently of God. And since true human self-knowledge is related to true knowledge of God, in this situation even the best and most sincere human efforts to know oneself lack real transparency, as we are unable to attain the truth. The more human creatures persist in knowing themselves and their

---

15. If what has been said concerning conscience in wisdom literature is correct, and if wisdom, fear of the Lord, knowledge of God, and language are understood as being related to conscience, the following observations by von Rad are very pertinent: "She [wisdom] does not only rule, she also speaks. ... *The voice of primeval order* does not address man in such a way that he has at his disposal, whenever he might require it, an ever-flowing well of truth. She can also withdraw herself from a man who does not heed her. ... *The loss of this organizing voice* will have catastrophic consequences. Horror, terror, distress will come upon men. They will be thrown back upon themselves and will have to live by their own initiative, that is, they will destroy themselves" (*Wisdom in Israel*, 161, emphasis added).

16. See Calvin, *Institutes*, 1.1.1. On the knowledge of God and of ourselves in Calvin, see Helm, *Calvin at the Centre*, 8–12. For a thorough investigation of the ancient precept "know thyself" in the philosophy of classical antiquity and in the theology of patristic Christianity and the early Middle Ages, see Pierre Courcelle, *Connais-toi toi-même: De Socrate à Saint Bernard* (Études augustiniennes, 1974–1975).

humanity independently of knowledge of the living God of the Trinity, the greater the lack of transparency in self-knowledge.

This lack of transparency in self-knowledge does not depend exclusively on fallen conscience's tendency toward insensitivity and callousness, considered independently from other human capacities and dispositions, as if conscience was an autonomous or superior organ. The interacting of fallen conscience with other fallen human capacities is attested to in Romans 1:18-32, which provides another compelling portrait of total depravity. This text shows that an insufficient capacity for clear self-perception and a consequently blurred self-knowledge derive from the dysfunction of diverse human capacities in their concurrent tasks in relation to the knowledge of God.

The first allusion to conscience is in verse 19: "That which is known about God is evident *within them*; for God made it evident to them" (NASB, emphasis added). According to this translation, the knowledge of God that is possible for human beings to know is not merely potential but real and actual, strengthening to the utmost the declaration that "they are without excuse" (Rom 1:20 NASB).[17] Specifically, that which is known about God manifests itself *within* humans. Although the majority of contemporary commentators assign to the proposition ἐν the corporate meaning of "in their midst,"[18] or "among them,"[19] or "to" them,[20] there is an important case for understanding it in the literal sense of "in them," as older commentators usually did.[21] Cranfield makes two objections to the interpretation that refers to the preposition "in" as a subjective and inner knowledge of God. The first is that the only revelation that Paul has in mind is the objective external revelation

---

17. Commenting upon the possibility that the expression might suggest "a rather full knowledge of God"—and adding in a footnote that that is how it is used in the LXX and in Acts— Longenecker quotes approvingly Calvin's statement that it is a knowledge "too forceful to allow men to escape from it" (*The Epistle to the Romans*, 205-6). Even though some scholars prefer the meaning of "what can be known" or "what is knowable" (as does Longenecker himself) to avoid the possible tautology implied in translating "what is known of God is manifest" or because Paul is referring only to certain basic matters that can be known about God, this grammatical preference should not weaken the emphasis on the truthfulness and certainty of this knowledge.

18. Cranfield, *A Critical and Exegetical Commentary*, 1:113-14.

19. Douglas Moo, *The Epistle to the Romans*, The New International Commentary on the New Testament (Eerdmans, 1996), 103.

20. Longenecker, *The Epistle to the Romans*, 206.

21. See Calvin, *Calvin's Commentaries*, 19:69-70; William Sanday and Arthur C. Headlam, *A Critical and Exegetical Commentary on the Epistle to the Romans* (T&T Clark, 1902), 42. For reference to other older commentators, see Ernst Käsemann, *Commentary on Romans* (Eerdmans, 1980), 38.

of the Creator in his creation: "The phrase should not be taken to imply a belief that fallen man is capable in himself of a knowledge, in the sense of a subjective knowledge, of God."[22] The second objection has to do with the noetic effects of sin:

> An assertion that God is manifest within them in the sense that the revelation has been inwardly apprehended by them would be incompatible with what is said in v. 21; and it is unlikely ... that Paul meant to refer here exclusively to the existence and functioning of men's inward capacities (as, for instance, their consciences, as is often suggested) as manifestation of God.[23]

However, while proposing that this knowledge of God should be understood as manifested in the midst of human beings by the objective external revelation of creation, Cranfield feels that he cannot completely omit from his exegesis the subjective dimension:

> The meaning is rather that [that which is knowable of God] is manifest in their midst. In their midst and all around them and also in their own creaturely existence (*including of course what is inward as well as what is external*) God is objectively manifest: His whole creation declares Him.[24]

Even when it is asserted that Paul's primary emphasis is on objective external revelation in creation, it is impossible for Cranfield to exclude absolutely the consideration of that which is inward in humanity, as if that were not part of creation or as if subjectivity did not deliver any (general) revelation about basic but nevertheless significant truths concerning God.[25] It appears that appeal to the immediate context of Romans 1:19 is not sufficient

---

22. Cranfield, *A Critical and Exegetical Commentary*, 1:113; see also 134.

23. Cranfield, *A Critical and Exegetical Commentary*, 1:114. It should be stressed that it is not our inner constitution in itself that is a manifestation of God (even though as part of creation it points us to God), but rather it is God who makes himself present to humanity by manifesting himself to our *sensus*, which in some way responds to the omnipresence of God.

24. Cranfield, *A Critical and Exegetical Commentary*, 1:114 (emphasis added).

25. Even if the preposition is rendered "in their midst," or "among them," or simply "to" them, the corporate sense in and of itself does not warrant the exclusion of an inward locative understanding of the preposition. According to Murray J. Harris, the ambiguity of a prepositional phrase should not restrict the meaning of the preposition as to exclude other nuances: "The exegete is hesitant to exclude either sense, since both are appropriate, but only a paraphrase

to rule out a reference to an inward witness, and considering what Paul says elsewhere about conscience and his attention to the inner person, subjectivity cannot be excluded from the knowledge of God communicated by the whole of creation. Therefore, on the basis of Romans 1:19, it seems impossible to propose that creation tells only objectively or propositionally that there is a God, ruling out any inward or conscious perception of God himself through the *sensus*.[26] As was explained above, nonphysical perception and sense perception, though distinct, are correlated and inseparable. A purely objective and external general (or natural) revelation would be useless without the inward capacity for response of the *sensus* cooperating with the other human powers.[27]

It is useful here to quote Calvin's comment on Paul's affirmation in Acts 17:27 that God is "not far from each one of us":

> To the end he may the more touch the forwardness of men, he saith that God is not to be sought through many crooks, neither need we make any long journey to find him; because every man shall find him in himself, if so be that he will take any heed. By which experience we are convicted that our dullness is not without fault. ... For though no corner of the world be void of the testimony of God's glory, yet we need not go without ourselves to lay hold upon him. For he doth affect and move every one of us inwardly with his power in such sort, that our blockishness is like to a monster, in that feeling him we feel him not.[28]

---

such as 'in your hearts and in your midst' can incorporate both options." *Preposition and Theology in the Greek New Testament* (Zondervan, 2012), 122.

26. Calvin writes, "There is within the human mind, and indeed by natural instinct [*naturali instinctu*], an awareness of divinity [*divinitatis sensum*]" (*Institutes*, 1.3.1).

27. In his recent Gifford Lectures, N. T. Wright explores how a revival of Epicureanism in the modern era provoked the eclipse of natural theology. Claiming that natural theology became theology without history (particularly without Jesus in his first-century context) and that biblical studies became history without God, Wright proposes what he calls *an epistemology of love*: "The rationalist Enlightenment, screening out the god-dimension of reality, screened out love at the same time *and for the same reason*: it claimed instead the 'objective' knowledge of the physical world, obtained and exploited through science and technology, and wrote off the 'subjective' elements as mere opinion or, worse, mere projection. ... We need, to put it simplistically, both the subjective and the objective pole. ... 'Love' simultaneously *affirms and celebrates the otherness* of the beloved (be it a person, a tree, a star) and wants it to be itself, not to be a mere projection of one's own hopes or desires, and also *takes appropriate delight* in this knowing, leaping beyond mere cool appraisal to a sense of homecoming, of belonging-with." *History and Eschatology: Jesus and the Promise of Natural Theology* (SPCK, 2019), 38.

28. Calvin, *Calvin's Commentaries*, 19:167.

These remarks further explain how conscience and the other human powers are fallen. First, Calvin once more emphasizes the inward and subjective quality of the (natural and general) knowledge of God, and that is why he speaks of it in terms of an "experience." The experience of the knowledge of God is not a mere proposition or belief that God the creator exists; it is an experiential knowing, in the sense conveyed by the Latin verb *experior*—to know by practical testing or to learn by proving personally. The reality of sin and of fallenness cannot detract from or minimize the actuality of the natural and general revelation of God in creation, yet at the same time, Calvin concludes sadly but elegantly, "In feeling him we feel him not." The theological problem—for both Paul and Calvin—is not the weakness or insufficiency of the knowledge of himself that God reveals through creation and concurrently within human beings but rather the greatness and powerfulness of sin, which causes a lack of transparency in self-knowledge (and knowledge of God) so that what is said regarding God can also be said regarding humanity: "In knowing the human person we know her not."

In Romans 1:20–21, the relationship between conscience and other human capacities is further clarified, shedding more light on how conscience is fallen. Having affirmed that the whole creation (the macrocosm as well as the microcosm) communicates some genuine (objective as well as subjective) knowledge of God, Paul explains how human beings respond to this general (or natural) revelation: "For since the creation of the world His invisible attributes, His eternal power and divine nature, have been clearly seen, being understood through what has been made" (Rom 1:20 NASB). The objective and external witness of the book of nature generates a subjective and internal response on the part of human beings because they perceive the reality of God and his perfections and they become conscious of God's presence. There is, then, an interaction between sense perception and nonphysical perception, as Longenecker recognizes: "Thus it seems that both the ideas of (1) external observation of data and (2) inner apprehension or understanding of that data are present in this statement."[29]

Notably, in Romans 1:20 Paul is not limiting his statement to intellectual elites; he refers to pagans in general without any limitation. In response to the question, "How universal is this perception?" Moo answers, "The flow of

---

29. Longenecker, *The Epistle to the Romans*, 208.

Paul's argument makes any limitation impossible. Those who perceive the attributes of God in creation must be the same as those who suppress the truth in unrighteousness and are therefore liable to the wrath of God. Paul makes clear that this includes all people."[30] As opposed to classical antiquity, according to which the human mind can ascend through Herculean philosophical exertions to ultimate reality (reasoning from what is known to what is unknown),[31] Scripture reverses the order: it is not the human intellect that reasons its way upward to ultimate truth, but it is God who has implanted himself into the very life of creation knowledge from the beginning.[32]

In the next verse, Romans 1:21, it is possible to see how the knowledge of God conveyed by the combined witness of the inward *sensus* and the outward world becomes insufficient in view of the fall, thus inhibiting transparent self-knowledge. To repeat Calvin's elegant but sad expression, the reality of our experience is that "feeling him we feel him not." The problem does not derive from the fact that it is only in a *"limited* sense [that human beings] have known Him all their lives."[33] The issue at stake is not a supposed limitation in transparency of the reality and efficacy of the knowledge of God (and of oneself) in creation. Instead, the real issue is the tragic transformation experienced by human creatures because of sin, as Romans 1:22 will explain. The theological concern is that if the accent is put on the limitation and insufficiency of natural revelation, the emphasis will be removed from the catastrophic power of sin and its devastating consequences upon one's knowledge of God and of oneself in relation to God.

It should be kept in mind that while the general revelation deriving from the *sensus* had an efficacious role in the divine economy of creation, it does not in the economy of redemption because of sin. The observations of Vos clarify the continuities as well as the discontinuities in this connection between nature and grace:

---

30. Moo, *The Epistle to the Romans*, 105.

31. See Stephen R. L. Clark, "The Classical Origins of Natural Theology," in *The Oxford Handbook of Natural Theology*, ed. Russell Re Manning (Oxford University Press, 2013), 9–22.

32. Longenecker, *The Epistle to the Romans*, 208–12; 221–22; Christopher Rowland, "Natural Theology and the Christian Bible," in Manning, *The Oxford Handbook of Natural Theology*, 23–37; William D. Wood, "Reason's Rapport: Pascalian Reflections on the Persuasiveness of Natural Theology," *Faith and Philosophy* 21/4 (2004): 519–32.

33. Cranfield, *A Critical and Exegetical Commentary*, 1:117 (emphasis added); see also Moo, *The Epistle to the Romans*, 106–7; Helm, *The Divine Revelation*, 30–32.

The most important function of Special Revelation, however, under the regime of sin, does not lie in the correction and renewal of the faculty of perception of natural verities; it consists in the introduction of an altogether new world of truth, that relating to the redemption of man. ... It should be emphasized, however, that in this world of redemption the substance of things is absolutely new. It is inaccessible to the natural mind as such. To be sure, God does not create the world of redemption without regard to the antecedent world of nature, nor does He begin His redemptive revelation *de novo*, as though nothing had preceded. The knowledge from nature, even though corrupted, is presupposed. Only, this does not involve that there is a natural transition from the state of nature to the state of redemption. Nature cannot unlock the door of redemption.[34]

Addressing here the chief function of special revelation in light of the spiritual need of sinful humanity, Vos indirectly attends to the question of how it is possible that "feeling him we feel him not." Commenting on Romans 1:21, Cranfield points out that in the Septuagint one particular usage of the verb "to become futile" (or "to be given to futility") "is in connection with idolatry, idols being referred to as ... mere useless nothings."[35] So, it is probable that Paul's assertion that human beings "became futile in their thinking" should be interpreted in the light of idolatry. According to Beale, the real problem of humanity is not the limitation of the general and natural revelation of God but rather that we bear the image of that which we worship: "The principle ... for us is: *we resemble what we revere, either for ruin or restoration.*"[36] Throughout his treatment of idolatry, Beale gives substance to Calvin's statement that "our blockishness *is like* to a monster."[37] Again, the emphasis falls not primarily on the supposedly limited power of general and natural revelation, but on the enormous power of sin to hinder true knowledge of God and ourselves as image-bearers. Referencing Isaiah 6:9-13, Beale identifies what he calls the "sensory-organ-malfunction language ... repeated throughout

---

34. Vos, *Biblical Theology*, 20, 21.
35. Cranfield, *A Critical and Exegetical Commentary*, 1:117.
36. Beale, *We Become What We Worship*, 49.
37. Calvin, *Calvin's Commentaries*, 19:167 (emphasis added).

Isaiah."[38] In Isaiah this sensory-organ-malfunction language is a way to indicate the spiritual malfunction of the nonphysical perceptual human capacity corrupted by idolatry. The ears that cannot hear and the eyes that cannot see are an illustration of the heart that is incapable of understanding God and oneself in relation to him. Developing a possible parallelism between Jeremiah 2:5 and Romans 1:21b, and referring in general to the Old Testament background of Romans 1:21–25, Beale reaches the following conclusion:

> We have ... two allusions to Jeremiah 2 in Romans 1, which ... indicate that Israel became like the idols that they worshipped, and that Paul appears to have followed that line of thought. He appears to see Israelite idolaters as representative of all human idolaters, probably because of his presupposition that Israel was intended to be a kind of representative corporate Adam. It is possible that Paul's shortening of the Jeremiah 2:5 wording to "and they became empty" and omitting the directly preceding clause ("and they followed after emptiness") is Paul's way of highlighting the notion of people becoming as corruptible as their corruptible idols.[39]

It seems that instead of being troubled by the concept and the supposed limitations of general revelation, Paul is more concerned to show that the noetic effects of sin are so deep and deadly that human creatures become "futile" (Rom 1:21) like the idols they worship, as expressed in Psalms: "They have mouths, but do not speak; eyes, but do not see. They have ears, but do not hear; noses, but do not smell. They have hands, but do not feel; feet, but do not walk; and they do not make a sound in their throat" (115:5–7).

Speaking of the corruption of the nonphysical perceptual human powers, Paul adds "and their foolish hearts were darkened" (Rom 1:21). It is difficult here to make a definite choice between understanding "heart" as referring to "the intellectual element of their inner lives which here is particularly in mind"[40] or understanding it more broadly, in line with the view that "in the NT, 'heart' is broad in its meaning, denoting the thinking, feeling, willing

---

38. Beale, *We Become What We Worship*, 41, 42.
39. Beale, *We Become What We Worship*, 211.
40. Cranfield, *A Critical and Exegetical Commentary*, 1:118.

ego of man, with particular regard to his responsibility to God."[41] However, both interpretations might be relevant for fallen conscience. If emphasis is put on the intellectual corruption of the capacity for inferential reasoning, it might be said that even though fallen conscience still continues to witness, summon, and legislate (see Rom 2:14-15), the thinking capacity of human creatures does not support and even contradicts conscience's perceptions and awareness at those moments when, even in its fallenness, it is in some measure religiously or morally awakened; meanwhile, if emphasis is put on the inner person in totality, it might be said in general that conscience—along with the thinking, feeling, willing ego of human beings—ultimately ceases to be effective in relation to the end for which God bestowed it upon humanity. As a consequence, Paul writes, "claiming to be wise, they became fools," and having lost a true knowledge of their own identity (*imago Dei*), they "exchanged the glory of the immortal God for images resembling mortal man and birds and animals and creeping things" (Rom 1:22-23).

After concentrating on the deadly and immoral religious and ethical consequences of idolatry (Rom 1:24-27), Paul returns to the theme of the knowledge of God and, indirectly, of ourselves. In Romans 1:28, the refusal "to acknowledge God" seems to be of an existential and experiential character rather than being speculative or theoretical.[42] If so, this kind of knowledge is the kind described by the notion of *sensus*—that is, consciousness of and sympathy for God (see Ps 46:10)—rather than knowledge that is obtained by means of logical reasoning. Because of this deliberate refusal, human creatures fell under the captivity of a "debased mind." Yet this raises further questions: What is the referent of the word "mind," and what does it mean to describe the mind as "debased"?

Even though the standard translations of νοῦς—intellect, intelligence, mind, or thinking—are correct, the development of the Greek language as well as the history of ancient Greek and Hellenistic philosophy show that the term was applied in many different ways so that the exact meaning could vary significantly. According to Alexander Sand, "The Hebrew language knew of no adequate equivalent to Gr. νοῦς. Consequently, the noun

---

41. Moo, *The Epistle to the Romans*, 107.

42. See Cranfield, *A Critical and Exegetical Commentary*, 1:128; Moo, *The Epistle to the Romans*, 117.

also plays no special role in the NT and it appears only 24 times. The meaning is not univocal."[43]

In line with the constructive theology of conscience being developed here, it seems useful to understand the "debased mind" of Romans 1:28 in light of what Paul says about the mind and its relation to God's law in Romans 7:21-25.[44] Even if at first it might appear that there is an incongruity between the "debased mind" of Romans 1:28 and the mind that takes "delight in the law of God" in Romans 7:22-23, in both the case of the regenerate believer and that of the unregenerate unbeliever the debasedness is relative and not absolute and the delight is relative and not absolute. Moreover, while in chapter 1 Paul is concerned to show the worst possible immoral gentile, in chapter 7—as noted by Dennis Johnson—he is concerned to show "the best of all possible situations within the sphere of 'the flesh,' unaided human nature":

> Here we see, not the idolatrous sensual Gentile sinner, bent on pleasing himself and hating God, but rather the situation of the Jew who knows the law, confesses its goodness, and even experiences distress that his behavior falls short of the righteousness required in the law.[45]

Commenting on Romans 7:23, Moo also sees a reference to unaided, if fallen, human nature:

---

43. Alexander Sand, "νοῦς, νοός," in Balz and Schneider, *Exegetical Dictionary of the New Testament* 2:478. Herman Ridderbos thinks that in "English there is really no equivalent for *nous*." *Paul: An Outline of His Theology* (Eerdmans, 1975), 117.

44. Leaving aside the dispute about the identity of the "I" speaking in Romans 7:7-25, it should at least be noted that what Paul says here could be applied at times to the experience of the regenerate Christian while at other times it seems a more fitting description of the condition of unbelievers; see Dennis E. Johnson, "The Function of Romans 7:13-25 in Paul's Argument for the Law's Impotence and the Spirit's Power, and Its Bearing on the Identity of the Schizophrenic 'I,'" in *Resurrection and Eschatology: Theology in Service of the Church*, ed. Lane G. Tipton and Jeffrey C. Waddington (P&R Publishing, 2008), 3-14. What is important in the context of the current chapter on *fallen* conscience is that in applying Romans 7:7-25 either to believers or to unbelievers the reality is that in both cases the conscience (and other human capacities and dispositions) is fallen. Nevertheless, in both interpretations the conscious mind affirms and upholds the moral law written in the heart.

45. Johnson, "The Function of Romans 7:13-25," 58-59. Considering the different emphases and goal of Romans 1:18-32 and Romans 7:7-25 and reading Romans 1:18-32 with Romans 2:14-15 in view, it should be noted that what Johnson says about the Jew who knows the law is applicable to unaided human nature in general. For more, see Johnson, "The Function of Romans 7:13-25," 52-54.

> Paul implies that the mind is an ally of God's law. ... Granted that the mind of people apart from Christ is tragically and fatally flawed, it does not follow that the mind cannot understand and respond to God at all. ... Especially if, as we have argued, Paul is speaking of his own experience under the law as typical of others, this capability cannot be denied (cf. 1:32; 2:14-15).[46]

It seems, therefore, that there is a parallel between Paul's defense of the goodness of natural revelation in Romans 1:19-21 and his maintaining the usefulness of God's law in Romans 7:7-25. In both cases, Paul is neither detracting from natural revelation or from the law nor reducing their natural goodness and usefulness; rather his chief aim is to magnify the utterly powerful sinfulness of sin that—in spite of the goodness and usefulness of natural revelation and the law—renders knowledge of God and of oneself lacking in transparency.[47]

It appears that there might be some sort of coexistence between a debased mind and the mind that takes delight in the law of God. Here the mind should, again, be understood primarily in terms of the perceptual capacity of the *sensus* and only secondarily and derivatively as the speculative processes of human reason. According to Herman Ridderbos, in the context of Romans 1 and 7, the mind is not merely a theoretical (and untainted) capacity:

> The *nous* here [Romans 1:20] is ... *the capacity, the susceptibility of man to take in the revelation of God that comes to him from without.* ... Romans 7:23 is also typical of this meaning. ... Because not only the individual decisions are thought of here, but the continuous moral posture of man, *nous* can mean more generally: disposition, mind.[48]

---

46. Moo, *The Epistle to the Romans*, 465.

47. It should be remembered that general revelation delivered through the *sensus* retains a measure of power only in the divine economy of creation. And the same must be said about the law or the covenant of works: nature cannot unlock the door of grace. The general point of Wright's narrative analysis of Romans 8:3-4 is that the Torah has an extremely positive role, which is not diminished by the negative things said about it; see *The Climax of the Covenant*, 204-16. That applies also to the natural revelation of Romans 1:19-21 and to the law written in the heart of Romans 2:14-15. In an acutely perceptive sentence, Wright says, "The 'problem of Romans 7' is emphatically *not* that of 'man under the law' ... but of 'the law under man,' or, more specifically, under flesh" (*The Climax of the Covenant*, 209).

48. Ridderbos, *Paul*, 118 (emphasis added).

At a bare minimum, understanding "mind" as a predisposition to receptivity provides a basis for interaction between the capacity for thinking and conscience.[49] Such an expansive understanding of "mind" might indicate a direct presence and engagement of conscience in the susceptibility of human creatures to take in the objective revelation of God in a subjective modality. Indeed, in Romans 7:22 the verb συνήδομαι (Lat. *condēlector*) means "rejoice together with" or even "sympathize with"[50] and therefore additionally suggests (if indirectly) the operations of conscience. Nevertheless, in spite of the reality of the activity of this mind (along with that of conscience), in its debased state it cannot bring humanity to a clear knowledge of God and oneself.

Lastly, there is in Romans 1:32 a concluding and more straightforward reference to conscience: "They know God's righteous decree that those who practice such things deserve to die." The kind of knowledge of which Paul is speaking here is not merely or even primarily a notional proposition arrived at by way of inference. What fallen human beings perceive (even though only partially, imperfectly, distortedly, and most of the time without even realizing it) is God himself as covenant Lord. What Paul in Romans 1:32 calls "God's righteous decree" is referred to as "the righteous requirement of the law" in Romans 8:4.[51] This language is covenantal, and it evokes two related theological themes. The first is, of course, the reality of God exhibiting himself as covenant Lord of the universe; the second is that of obedience unto life. These two themes intertwine with the Adam-Christology of Romans (see especially Rom 5:12–21). Moo observes that besides Romans 8:4, with its reference in the singular to the righteous requirement of the law, "Paul uses the plural [precepts] in 2:26 to denote those things commanded in the Mosaic

---

49. Examining conscience in early patristic theology, Torrance points out that in reference to Romans 7:22-23 John of Damascus identifies the "law of the mind" with conscience; see "Conscience in the Early Church Fathers," in Alvaré and Hammond, *Christianity and the Laws of Conscience*, 100.

50. Moo, *The Epistle to the Romans*, 461. The form of this verb is analogous in its formation to those forms resulting from the union of the prepositional prefix "with" and verbs indicating some form of shared experience. Thus, it may point to the phenomenon of conscience because it refers to a perceptual capacity for complacency or shared agreement. Horst Balz ascribes to the verb the meaning of "I joyfully agree with" ("συνήδομαι," in Balz and Schneider, *Exegetical Dictionary of the New Testament*, 3:306).

51. The only difference in Greek is that in 1:32 the genitive refers to God while in 8:4 it refers to the law.

law and the singular in 5:16, 18 of a 'righteous act' performed by Christ."[52] The language and concepts used by Paul in Romans refer to the classical distinction between the covenant of works and the covenant of grace, and in this regard, it is of particular interest to notice another important connection to "the very commandment that promised life" (Rom 7:10).

This terminology of Romans 7:10 brings the reader back to Genesis and God's commandment to humanity in the garden. As N. T. Wright notes, the presupposition in this verse is "a sort of *heilsgeschichtlich* scheme in which there is a divine purpose, that of giving life, which stands behind the role of the law."[53] In the words of Moo, "The parallels between Adam and Israel in Jewish literature, as well as 5:13-14, would suggest that the experience of Israel with the law depicted here is parallel to and, to some extent, recapitulates the experience of Adam with the commandment of God in the Garden."[54] This understanding renders clear why article 14 of the Belgic Confession speaks of the sin and idolatry of humanity as follows: "For *the commandment of life*, which he [Adam] had received, he transgressed; and by sin he separated himself from God, who was his true life."[55] Thus, in the case of Romans 1:32, the knowledge of which Paul is speaking is to be identified not narrowly as the theoretical rationality of practical reason but more broadly as the disposition that makes human beings aware of God and sensitive in regard to his will (see Rom 2:14-15).

In conclusion, conscience hinders or prevents transparency in self-knowledge not only in that its corruption has resulted in a natural inclination toward insensitivity and moral callousness in relation to God, but also because it has become so weakened that it does not have the capacity to oppose the dysfunction of the mind that has become futile and debased in subjugation to the idolatrous desires of the will. In their fallen state human creatures identify themselves not with the image of God but with the image of the idols they serve. Even though the heart, the mind, and the conscience still retain some common notions of God and of humanity in relation to God, that knowledge is deficient in transparency and is utterly confused

---

52. Moo, *The Epistle to the Romans*, 121.
53. Wright, *The Climax of the Covenant*, 207.
54. Moo, *The Epistle to the Romans*, 438-39.
55. *The Creeds of Christendom*, 3:398 (emphasis added).

and blurred. This confirms the truth of Jeremiah's old oracle: "The heart is deceitful above all things, and desperately sick; who can understand [know] it? 'I the LORD search the heart and test the mind' " (Jer 17:9).

CONSCIENCE IS FALLEN IN THAT HUMANITY IS INCAPABLE OF INNOCENT SELF-SCRUTINY

So far, conscience is fallen in that, generally speaking, it has been corrupted from a state of integrity, and in its fallenness it hinders transparency in self-knowledge. In this section, we turn to one of the principal effects of fallen conscience that Webster mentions in his assessment: humanity is incapable of innocent self-scrutiny. Webster's analysis introduces into the account of the fall a phenomenon that is not usually considered significant in conventional theological interpretations of the doctrine of sin, namely the subject of self-deception.[56] As conscience becomes prone to insensitivity and callousness and the mind suppresses the knowledge of God and the truth about oneself, the consequence is idolatrous self-deception.

The statement that fallen conscience is incapable of innocent self-scrutiny is not to be taken as a mere creaturely limitation, for humanity's predicament is not finitude. Human limitation is not intrinsically incommensurable with proper and true knowledge. The incapacity for innocent self-scrutiny is not to be understood as a passive deficiency or as an innocuous privation but as an active stance, a deliberate aversion.[57]

---

56. Both the Old and the New Testaments contain raw material relevant for a theological treatment of self-deception (Gen 6:5; 8:21; Prov 28:26; Isa 44:20; Jer 17:9-10; 23:26; 37:9; 42:20; 49:16; Obad 3; 1 Cor 3:18; 15:33; Gal 6:3, 7; Jas 1:16, 26; Heb 3:13; 1 John 1:8). Self-deception was always of great interest in the pastoral theology of ancient, medieval, and Reformation and post-Reformation periods. However, in modern and contemporary practical theology this interest has drastically diminished. Ancient and modern philosophy investigated the problem, and contemporary philosophy of mind in particular has been actively engaged in analytically dissecting this phenomenon. Theology, stimulated by this philosophical effort, is beginning to develop anew its own pastoral perspective on self-deception. As an introduction to the debates within contemporary philosophy of mind, see the essay (and the bibliography) by Kent Bach, "Self-Deception," in *The Oxford Handbook of Philosophy of Mind*, ed. Brian P. McLaughlin, Ansgar Beckermann, Sven Walter (Oxford University Press, 2009), 781-95.

57. For a theological perspective on self-deception, see Kevin J. Vanhoozer, "Ezekiel 14: 'I, The Lord, Have Deceived That Prophet,' " in *Theological Commentary: Evangelical Perspectives*, ed. R. Michael Allen (T&T Clark, 2011), 94-95; Joseph K. Pak, "Self-Deception in Current Philosophical Discussions and Its Importance in Theology," *International Journal of Philosophy and Theology* 4, no. 1 (2016): 13-21; Gregg A. Ten Elshof, *I Told Me So: Self-Deception and the Christian Life* (Eerdmans, 2009); Jonathan P. Badgett, "Undermining Moral Self-Deception with the Help of Puritan Pastoral Theology," *Journal of Spiritual Formation and Soul Care* 11, no. 1 (2018): 23-38; and the

Considering the insidious and dangerous reality of self-deception, it seems fitting at this point to devote some attention to the constructive and meaningful work on Pascal by William Wood. Wood contends that a thick doctrine of the fall should not simply concentrate on the bondage of the will and on the darkness of the understanding on the basis that "an adequate account of sin will also be an account of self-deception, and of how the sinner deceives himself about his own value and the value of his project."[58] Wood insists that a theological analysis of the noetic effects of sin should include an investigation of the "evaluative" effects of the fall besides the effects on the mind and on the will.[59] Rooting the evaluative fall in the Augustinian notion of disordered love that produces an aversion to truth and an attraction to falsehood, Wood writes:

> The cognitive consequences of the Fall result from disordered love. Since we are fallen, we are not able to love and evaluate goods properly. We resist the truth about ourselves and God because we do not love them as we should. Thus, *the Fall has cognitive consequences because it is first and foremost an evaluative fall*. Most studies treat Pascal's account of the Fall in straightforward conventional terms as a fall of the reason or the will. In my view, we may arrive at a better understanding of Pascal's account of the Fall by looking beyond the Fall of the reason and the will—understood narrowly as the faculties of calculating and choosing—to an even deeper fall, *a fall in our ability to perceive and respond to value*.[60]

The language of "perceiving and responding" highlights once more the notion of the *sensus* and addresses specifically the issue of how conscience is fallen: even though it remains aware of God and truth, its perceptions do not have the strength to allow human creatures to respond to God properly. Each of these claims is worth pursuing in turn.

---

remarkable work by William Wood, *Blaise Pascal on Duplicity, Sin and the Fall: The Secret Instinct* (Oxford University Press, 2013).

58. Wood, *Blaise Pascal*, 11.
59. Wood, *Blaise Pascal*, 19–50.
60. Wood, *Blaise Pascal*, 30 (emphasis added).

First, and following Pascal, Wood contends that human beings have a "secret instinct" leftover from the state of innocence that is still able to make people aware of God:

> It is the heart that furnishes us with the knowledge of first principles that cannot be demonstrated. It operates by means of its own kind of perception, characterized by the verb *sentir* and its derivations (usually translated as "to feel," but used by Pascal to signify any immediate apprehension). ... The heart is also the faculty that allows us to perceive God.[61]

Crucially, he associates this instinct—this tacit and spontaneous knowledge—with the operations of conscience:

> Pascal's account of moral judgment depends on a unique faculty, the heart. The heart has a characteristic operation, feeling or intuiting (*sentiment*), and a characteristic form of reasoning, *finesse*. ... The Pascalian heart is a cognitive faculty that unifies key operations of the will and the intellect. It is a faculty of tacit, intuitive knowledge, including moral knowledge—it might be glossed as, among other things, the seat of conscience. ... One may think of a moral sentiment as something like a spontaneous deliverance of the conscience.[62]

Second, Wood provides a plausible explanation of how conscience is nonetheless fallen. In line with the desire above to emphasize the interplay of the various human capacities within the individual as a unified agent, Wood concentrates on the relation in the fallen human being between the conscience and the imagination, in which the latter naturally seduces and misleads the human mind. He writes, even though the heart "produces immediate moral *sentiments* [and] those *sentiments* are both true and compelling," fallen humanity "rejects the *sentiments* of the heart—the seat of conscience—and instead acts on the basis of the false, self-serving *fantaisies*

---

61. Wood, *Blaise Pascal*, 130-31. In continuity with what was explored above on Calvin's notion of *sensus*, it is interesting to note that Wood explains the knowledge of first principles in terms of perception and immediate apprehension, as does Calvin.

62. Wood, *Blaise Pascal*, 129, 134.

of the imagination."⁶³ It is here that self-deception occurs: "To take the imagination for the heart is to self-deceptively believe that one's own self-serving fantasies reveal the felt sense of conscience."⁶⁴ Again, because of disordered love and an attraction toward what is not God, human imagination is not just innocuously deficient or innocently confused. Rather, as Wood observes, "taking the imagination for the heart—mistaking *fantaisie* for *sentiment*—is usually a willful misconstrual."⁶⁵ In a step-by-step description of self-deception as morally culpable self-persuasion, Wood describes how the various mental abilities concur together and simultaneously in the process of self-deception.⁶⁶ And he reaches the following conclusion:

> What we do, mainly, is sin—and then try to persuade ourselves that we are innocent. Sin and self-deception go hand in hand precisely because we are fallen. That is, we are *fallen*, but we are not demonic. While it is true in a way to say that the sinner rejects God, it is not the whole truth. We do not—cannot—reject God explicitly, in full awareness. We do not consciously hate goodness and truth *as such*. Rather, we lie to ourselves about what really is good and true. Only then we can we preserve the fiction that we love the truth and goodness, although we repeatedly turn away from them. Yet, even our lies witness to our love for truth. We care about the truth just enough to pretend to love it, and no more. Someone utterly unmoved by the truth cannot be bothered to pretend. We pretend because we are fallen—and therefore both great and wretched at the same time. The Fall has

---

63. Wood, *Blaise Pascal*, 139. For a survey of the capacity for imagination in its twofold form of sensory imagination (x forms an image of y) and cognitive imagination (x imagines that p) see Colin McGinn, "Imagination," in McLaughlin, Beckermann, and Walter, *The Oxford Handbook of Philosophy of Mind*, 595–606.

64. Wood, *Blaise Pascal*, 141.

65. Wood, *Blaise Pascal*, 143. The corruption of the imagination and of its relation to the other human capacities is implied in biblical anthropology (Ps 73:7; Prov 18:11; Matt 9:4; 12:25; Acts 17:29; 1 Cor 8:2; Heb 4:12). In the Old Testament, the language of image and imagining intermingle and the same Hebrew root can refer both to the idol itself and to human imaginations, showing that idolatry and image worship is a product of the self-deceiving human imagination (Lev 26:1; Num 33:52; Ezek 8:12; Ps 73:7; Prov 18:11). In the New Testament, the verb νομίζω is often used in relation to the formation of erroneous imaginings and wrong assumptions (Matt 20:10; Luke 2:44; Acts 8:20; 17:29; 1 Tim 6:5).

66. Wood, *Blaise Pascal*, 179–211. Besides the language of image/imagination, another important Old Testament idiom pointing to the phenomenon of self-deception is "one's own eyes" (Num 15:39; Judg 17:6; 21:25; Ps 36:2; Prov 12:15; 16:2; 26:16; 30:12; Isa 5:21).

left us with a secret instinct that draws us toward God and truth, in addition to the secret instinct that drives us away.[67]

Wood's understanding of the secret instinct in terms of conscience resonates well with the notion of conscience presented here. Indeed, many of Wood's observations on the secret instinct in Pascal echo Calvin's notion of *sensus*, both in light of the doctrine of creation and the fall.

SUMMARY

There are three important things that should be highlighted about fallen conscience from this chapter. First, because of the diversion from God and the introversion toward the self-initiated by the fall, conscience became inclined to callousness in relation to God, thereby losing its capacity to evaluate truth and real good.[68] Second, because of the perversion of our constitutive relationality due to the fall, fallen conscience became powerless to resist and correct the dysfunction of a mind that became futile because of the idolatrous desires of the will, with the effect that, paradoxically, although human creatures feel God's presence they do not feel him. Lastly, and perhaps most importantly, human beings suppress the "secret instinct that draws [them] toward God and truth,"[69] in that they practice a strategy of self-deception through which they persuade themselves by their imaginations of the goodness of that which is not God—that which is not true, righteous, or beautiful.

---

67. Wood, *Blaise Pascal*, 210.

68. Wood's notion of an "evaluative fall" will be determinative for understanding the approach taken in the next chapter to investigate redeemed conscience. Without repeating what was proposed above regarding the perceptual capacity of the *sensus*, the notion of a capacity for religious and moral appreciation makes sense in relation to Wood's claim that "we have lost the ability *to evaluate* goods properly" (*Blaise Pascal*, 34, emphasis added).

69. Wood, *Blaise Pascal*, 210.

Part 3

REDEEMED CONSCIENCE

The third part of this theology of conscience will consider the redemption of conscience as one particular aspect of the inversion of the cognitive consequences of the fall, for as sin resulted in an inversion of the holy image of God, so salvation results in a reversal of the corrupted image of idols that human beings have become.[1] The examination of fallen conscience undertaken in the previous chapter considered the noetic effects of the fall with regard to the power of the conscience to "evaluate" (as well as in terms of the bondage of the will and of the darkness of the mind). This loss of the capacity of the *sensus* to evaluate leads to the perversion of the desires of the will, which has direct affective—that is, "evaluative"—consequences. Hence, an exploration of redeemed conscience should attend not only to the renewal of the ability to recognize and understand truth and goodness propositionally but to the restoration of the capacity to desire them and to delight in their value.

Consequently, the following analysis begins with a chapter on the *preparation* of fallen conscience for redemption, focusing first on the action of the Holy Spirit in the conviction of natural and fallen conscience through the Word and then on the further illumination of conscience through additional gospel light.

---

1. As was explained in the previous exegesis of Romans 1, Gregory K. Beale affirms that the experience of Israel recapitulates the ironic reversal experienced by the first Adam, whose image after the fall becomes characterized by the serpent's attributes. In considering this reversal of the *imago*, Beale describes its concomitant consequences in terms of "spiritual anesthesia," referring implicitly to the reality of the *sensus*: "Like Israel, when you worship something of this earth, you become like it—spiritually lifeless and insensitive to God as a piece of wood, rock, and stone. ... You need to be shocked out of the anesthesia by God's word. Thus, we must come to God's word continually to be continually shocked out of our spiritual anesthesia." *Redemptive Reversals and the Ironic Overturning of Human Wisdom* (Crossway, 2019), 74–75.

In the following chapter, consideration will be given to the way in which following this preparation there must be an actual *regeneration* of conscience, so that it might begin to experience a spiritual transformation. It will be argued that if conscience is understood primarily in terms of *sensus* and of nonphysical perception, the experience of salvation for humanity should begin with a renewal of the aesthetic—that is, related to the *sensus*—capacity for spiritual sensibility.[2]

Chapter 8 will focus on the *justification* of conscience. The investigation of this topic will be examined under two major headings. The first is *the experience of subjective justification*. The exploration of this experiential aspect of justification is important as it will show the palpable inward effects of justification and its relation to adoption and progressive sanctification. The goal is to show how the subjective reception of justification constitutes the fountain that purifies the conscience.[3]

The subjective realization of justification is combined, secondly, with *the cherishing of adoption*. It will be stressed that conscience is redeemed in knowing God experientially as a merciful father. To quote the title of a famous sermon by Thomas Chalmers, "the expulsive power of a new affection"[4] in the conscience casts away the sad and wretched awareness of estrangement from God and of his righteous judgment that afflicts conscience.

Finally, chapter 9 will focus on the sanctification of conscience, which will be developed under three headings relating to three progressive reversals: the soothing of guilt; the appeasing of shame; and the relaxing of fear and the abandoning of hiddenness.

---

2. To anticipate the argument to be developed later, Zahl claims that in experiencing redemption "there is no love of God or of neighbour that is not fundamentally *an experience of delight*" (*The Holy Spirit and Christian Experience*, 183, emphasis added).

3. Active or objective justification is to be related to the *forum divinum* and as referring to the objective work of Christ and its effect, while passive or subjective justification is to be seen as happening *in foro conscientiae*, referring to the inner and subjective realization by the believer of the gift of Christ's imputed righteousness. Bavinck maintains that the distinction between "active" and "passive" is to be applied to the doctrines of regeneration, justification, and sanctification; see *Reformed Dogmatics* 4:77, 87–95, 200–204, 218–29, 248–56. In the following discussion this distinction between "active" and "passive" is presupposed also in relation to the preparatory work of conviction and illumination, as the objective redeeming work that originates *extra nos* always aims at eliciting—in one way or another—its subjective reception *in nobis*, for the *extra nos* would be meaningless if disconnected from the *in nobis*. See John V. Fesko, "Reformed Orthodoxy on Imputation: Active and Passive Justification," *Perichoresis* 14, no. 3 (2016): 61–80.

4. Thomas Chalmers, *The Expulsive Power of a New Affection*, ed. Rev. William Hannah (Thomas Constable and Co., 1855).

6

THE PREPARATION OF CONSCIENCE

The investigation into the beginning of the redemption of conscience will proceed in two sections: the first relates to the conviction of conscience and the second to its illumination through additional gospel light. This subdivision already indicates that because of the fallenness of conscience two things are necessary to begin the renewal of the human *sensus*: the application of the law to conscience and the vivification of its capacity for spiritual perception through the gospel.

THE CONVICTION OF CONSCIENCE

An examination of redeemed conscience requires an explanation of the relation between fallen conscience and redeemed conscience. Although there is continuity between them, conscience's redemption is also a matter of discontinuity. This is so because salvation requires more than the mere light of natural conscience; along with the whole theater of creation, conscience provides only a perception of God as creator but does not convey any knowledge of a prodigal God who acts generously like a loving father reconciling himself to rebellious children (cf. Luke 15:11-32).

It should be noted immediately that both the conviction and the illumination of conscience occur by the Spirit through the Word. Moreover, it might be said that conviction is one particular aspect of illumination, and indeed Muller observes that Reformed theology includes in one and the same concept of illumination both an *illuminatio legalis* and an *illuminatio evangelica*, "by which the Holy Spirit instructs the sinner in and through the ministry of the Word, both *to convict the individual of sin by means of the law* and *to convey to him a knowledge of salvation by means of the gospel*."[1] Within the work of

---

1. Muller, *Dictionary of Latin and Greek Theological Terms*, 142-43 (emphasis added); See also Owen, *The Works of John Owen*, 3:315-16.

illumination, therefore, the Spirit communicates through the law a special sense of need to the conscience and through the gospel a new knowledge to the mind.[2]

In considering that the Holy Spirit confirms old/natural knowledge by the law and imparts new/supernatural knowledge by the gospel (see the terminology of Rom 7:6), the spontaneous and understandable tendency of theological language is to restrict the reality of illumination to the latter—that is, the cognitive enlightening of the mind. Muller explains this as *illuminatio legalis* is commonly referred to only as "conviction" and usually applied simply and directly to conscience. For instance, speaking of certain operations on the human heart by the Holy Spirit that are preparatory to regeneration, Owen keeps the conviction of conscience and the illumination of the understanding distinct: "They [the effects of the Spirit's work] are reducible unto three heads: 1. *Illumination*; 2. *Conviction*; 3. *Reformation*. The first of these respects the mind only; the second, the mind, the conscience, and affections; and the third, the life and conversation."[3] In this case, the distinction made by Owen derives from the fact that for him illumination relates more specifically to the newness of the message of the gospel (a newness relating to the supernatural character of its revelation focused on the person and mission of the Son of God) rather than to the oldness of the precepts of the law (an oldness deriving from the natural character of its revelation as imprinted in the human heart in creation).[4] For Owen, illumination is "a light *superadded to the innate conceptions of men's minds, and beyond what of themselves they can extend unto,—because it is concerning such things as the heart of man could never of itself conceive*, but the very knowledge of them is communicated by their revelation."[5] Owen's choice of the two different expressions, "conviction" and "illumination," presupposes the distinct emphasis of the

---

[2]. On the Spirit's "affective pedagogy" through law and gospel see Zahl, *The Holy Spirit and Christian Experience*, 164–77.

[3]. Owen is not making a temporal distinction here, only a conceptual one. His only observation about what might be called a *chronology* of salvation is that the three effects mentioned together "ordinarily do precede the work of regeneration, or real conversion to God" (*The Works of John Owen*, 3:231).

[4]. As will be observed later, for Owen the notion of illumination is quite flexible and on other occasions he applies it to conscience. Likewise, at times he speaks of conviction as especially relative to the mind.

[5]. Owen, *The Works of John Owen*, 3:231–32 (emphasis added).

latter on the newness of the spiritual mysteries revealed in the gospel and consequently implies that—in God's ordinary modus operandi through the means of grace—the former, conviction, is merely related to and aims at evangelical illumination.[6]

This conventional distinction between conviction and illumination is useful for what follows because it indicates that conscience—besides being convicted of what it already, in some ongoing and limited sense and in spite of the fall, knows by nature (namely, the covenant of works)—receives in redemption additional gospel light, or a new awareness beyond what it can perceive and agree with naturally (namely, the covenant of grace). And because of its relation to this evangelical illumination, the convicting application of the law needs similarly to be conceived of as spiritual, supernatural, and special, not so much to go beyond and above the natural operations of conscience[7] but because of the need to address the fallenness of the sinner and the sinner's need for grace, pardon, and justification.

In conviction the Holy Spirit actively applies the law to human conscience in a special manner from outside specifically *as word of God*. This convicting application of the law by the Spirit is not the natural moral testimony rendered by fallen conscience as *sensus*. The two witnesses may at times and in a certain measure coincide, but their range, intensity, purpose, and effect will vary. The application of the law by word and Spirit will have a specifically religious or (better) *covenantal* nature, not just a general ethical character. The event of redemption requires that conscience must be influenced from outside in an evangelical manner—that is, in a way that is produced and shaped by the gospel. This implies that the *illuminatio legalis* by the Spirit is always related to and in service of the supplemental *illuminatio evangelica*. Saving or redeeming conviction is different from the operations of natural conscience in that it is wholly a divine work, a spiritual work that only the Spirit can accomplish by relating it to the message concerning the person and mission of Jesus Christ.

---

6. For some reflections on Owen's understanding of illumination, see John B. Webster, "Illumination," in *The Domain of the Word: Scripture and Theological Reasoning* (T&T Clark, 2012), 50–64.

7. For Owen what is superadded is new "gospel" knowledge by the Spirit through the Word and not a new capacity or disposition; see "The Doctrine of Justification by Faith," in *The Works of John Owen* (Banner of Truth, 1967), 5:44–47.

As explained earlier, the nature and function of conscience are determined by the covenant of vocation, and its purpose is to make humanity capable of responding to *that* covenant, which is a covenant of works that gives testimony to God as creator and to the law of creation inherent in the created order. Although conscience by nature provides this testimony to God and to his law, because of the fallenness of the human being, it is the Spirit who must now make real the word, namely the law.[8] In this respect, a classic text is John 16:8-11:

> And when he [the Spirit] comes, he will convict [ἐλέγχω] the world concerning sin and righteousness and judgment: concerning sin, because they do not believe in me; concerning righteousness, because I go to the Father, and you will see me no longer; concerning judgment, because the ruler of this world is judged.

Commentators on this verse are divided between those who stress an objective view in terms of a heavenly lawsuit in which the world is publicly declared guilty and *convicted*, and those who emphasize a subjective view according to which sinners in the world are *convinced* in a personal manner.[9] Considering the range of the usage of the Greek verb ἐλέγχω,[10] it seems that the objective witness of the Spirit does not exclude the subjective effect of such a witness. After all, a general and objective witness makes sense only in relation to the goal of a personal convicting and subjective reception, at least after the fall. Conviction cannot arise without that which is really objective: the subjective witness of conscience has the specific function of appropriating the objective testimony of God's revelation, both general and special.

---

8. Owen distinguishes between a spiritual conviction and both "moral reformation" on one hand and "moral suasion" on the other. In the former case, "moral reformation" is distinct because by the operations of natural conscience even pagans or atheists may appreciate and practice moral virtue; in the latter case, "moral suasion" is distinct because even though a sinner may experience to a certain degree a truly spiritual persuasion, his conviction may not result in a response characterized by evangelical faith grounded in spiritual conviction; see *The Works of John Owen*, 3:217-24, 301-15.

9. For the former interpretation, see, for example, Nicholas T. Wright, *John for Everyone: Part 2, Chapters 11-21* (SPCK, 2002), 81-83; for the latter sense of convincing personally, or "to bring home to the conscience," see William Hendriksen, *A Commentary on the Gospel of John: Commentary on Chapters 7-21* (Banner of Truth, 1959), 324-27.

10. For an analysis of the possibilities, see Donald A. Carson, *The Gospel According to John* (Eerdmans, 1991), 534-38.

So, it is probably better to see the objective convicting and the subjective convincing as two aspects of the same activity of the Spirit in John 16:8.[11]

This preparatory conviction is preliminary to the new birth spoken of in John 3:5-6. Reflecting on that passage, Owen affirms that there is a work of the Spirit through the word that prepares for the work of regeneration, directed specifically at the conscience:

> Two things [this preparatory work] effects upon the conscience: (1.) It renders it more *ready*, *quick*, and *sharp* in the reproving and condemning of all sin than it was before. To condemn sin, according unto its light and guidance, is natural unto and indispensable for the conscience of man; but its readiness and ability to exercise this condemning power may, by custom and course of sinning in the world, be variously weakened and impeded. ... (2.) Conscience is assisted and directed hereby to condemn *many things in sin* which before it approved of.[12]

Thus, the Spirit's work in conviction affects the conscience *directly*. Commenting on John 4:10, Calvin refers to the same activity of the Spirit, explaining the expression "living water" as a metaphor for saving knowledge: "But that knowledge begins with a sense of our poverty. For to desire a remedy one must first be conscious of one's ills."[13] Although here Calvin does not mention conscience explicitly, it is possible to make the following observations. The experiential knowledge of salvation begins with an inner perception, or interior awareness, of one's own poverty before God. In light of Calvin's understanding of the *sensus*, it is noteworthy that he speaks of cognition in terms of "sense"—that is, as a spontaneous awareness and an

---

11. This recommendation applies also to the proposal of Herman N. Ridderbos who considers the referents of the work of the Spirit to be the disciples; see *The Gospel of John: A Theological Commentary* (Eerdmans, 1997), 531-32. Even as the Spirit portrays the true nature of the world for the benefit of the disciples, the Spirit's activity has both objective and subjective aspects that presuppose, imply, and keep each other together.

12. Owen, *The Works of John Owen*, 3:239. Owen subsequently analyzes the mind, the will, and the affections, but forgets conscience almost completely. However, much of what Owen says about the "affections" (passions, emotions) would also apply to the conscience.

13. In Latin, Calvin writes, "*Ea autem cognitio ab inopiae nostrae sensu incipit. Nam ut ad remedium quis adspiret, eum prius necesse est malis suis affici.*" *Joannis Calvini Opera quae supersunt omnia* (A. Shwetschke and Son, 1863-1900), ed. Wilhelm Maum, Edward Cunitz, and Edward Reuss, 47:80. The quote is taken from *Calvin's New Testament Commentaries*, ed. David W. Torrance and Thomas F. Torrance (Eerdmans, 1959-1972), 4:91.

intuitive perception and not as the cogitations of practical reason that arrive at conclusions by analytical thinking. Consequently, before someone willingly seeks a remedy, he must first be moved to do so by the Spirit, being brought from a position of passivity (as shown by the passive form of the verb *adfĭcĭo*) to one of activity.

More specifically, the impression of the law in its narrow aspect (namely, of the law strictly *as law*[14] and not as the general history of redemptive revelation through Moses and the prophets[15]) on conscience in the opening stage of salvation is not an effect produced by the testimony of the law alone, even though that witness is itself perfectly clear and encounters a natural response in the human heart even in its fallen condition. It is, rather, the Spirit that generates *a new awareness* in the conscience by the law. This is a special new perception in the sense that it revives, strengthens, deepens, and expands the summoning and legislative force of the witness of fallen conscience, thus preparing it for the disclosure of the gospel. Commenting on John 7:37, Calvin writes:

> For it is true that we are poor and destitute of every blessing, but it is far from being true that all are aroused by a conviction of their poverty to seek relief. Hence it arises that many persons do not stir a foot, but wretchedly wither and decay, and there are even many who are not affected by a perception of their emptiness, until the Spirit of God, by his own fire, kindle hunger and thirst in their hearts.[16]

However, this is only the starting point of the Spirit's salvific work. Writing on Calvin's understanding of conscience, Zachman states:

---

14. Reformed theology maintains that the preparation of conscience by the Spirit is accomplished by "the first use of the law"; see Calvin, *Institutes*, 2.7.6-9.

15. For Calvin there is a difference between a "broad" and a "narrow" understanding of the law. In its broad dimension, the law of Moses is an anticipation of the fuller revelation of the gospel in the New Testament and of one and the same covenant of grace; see *Institutes*, 2.7.9-11; *Calvin's Commentaries*, 19:383-85. Taken in its narrow sense, however, the law of Moses corresponds to the so-called covenant of works or of creation and to its reprise in the Decalogue whose substance is written in conscience; see *Institutes*, 2.7.6-9. On this topic, see Zachman, *The Assurance of Faith*, 141-45.

16. John Calvin, *Commentary on the Gospel According to John*, vol. 17 of *Calvin's Commentaries*, (Baker Books, 1996), 306-7.

The testimony of the law, which awakens and reinforces the condemning testimony of the conscience, is necessary but not sufficient to bring about the awareness of our poverty. It is the proper work of the Holy Spirit to awaken *this sense* of our inner poverty, thereby preparing us to receive the grace of Christ.[17]

These observations pave the way for the next topic of consideration: the need for illumination of conscience through additional gospel light, because conscience is by itself incapable of delivering any sort of witness concerning the gospel, which is a *verbum alienum*, a special revelation and a supernatural message, proclaiming a covenant wholly of grace.

THE ILLUMINATION OF CONSCIENCE

While the Spirit communicates primarily to conscience through conviction by the law, illumination is usually related to the understanding, envisioned in a rather narrow sense as reason. For Webster, in general, "illumination refers to the ways in which the operation of creaturely intelligence is caused, preserved and directed by divine light, whose radiance makes creatures to know."[18] If, as Webster believes, "the workings of the Spirit in illumination, as in all things, are mysterious, exceeding creaturely capacity,"[19] so that "to understand illumination, therefore, theological reason needs illumination,"[20] things become even more complicated.

There are at least two things that need to be considered about the illumination of the conscience: first, an explanation of how conscience is illuminated; and second, an explanation of how it is through gospel light that conscience is illuminated.

Ordinarily, while the Spirit is convicting conscience in a special manner (*illuminatio legalis*), human reason is enlightened as well (*illuminatio evangelica*).[21] This happens more or less simultaneously as the Spirit often intertwines law and gospel, because the former is the presupposition of the latter

---

17. Zachman, *The Assurance of Faith*, 154 (emphasis added).
18. Webster, "Illumination," 50; see also Carl R. Trueman, "Illumination," in *Dictionary for Theological Interpretation of the Bible*, ed. Kevin J. Vanhoozer et al. (Baker Books, 2005), 316.
19. Webster, "Illumination," 51.
20. Webster, "Illumination," 52.
21. On exceptions, see Owen, *The Works of John Owen*, 3:231-15, 224-26, 231. In his treatment of calling, regeneration, faith, and conversion, Bavinck intersperses his exposition with a number

in the sense that the latter is the response to the predicament caused by the former.[22] Indeed, the redemption of conscience is accomplished by the Spirit's power through the gospel in relation to the condemnation of the law—that is, by the proclamation of the message concerning the person of Jesus Christ and his mission as the last Adam (see John 1:14-18; Rom 1:1-4; 8:3; 10:17; Gal 3:8-14; 4:4-5).

In conviction, as the Spirit applies the condemnation of the law *directly* to conscience, he finds in conscience—as it were—a natural ally, for conscience spontaneously responds to the law of covenantal vocation with its sense of God's presence and righteous judgment. In this way, the Spirit adds his own testimony to the natural, yet fallen, witness of conscience.[23] However, in regard to the gospel, neither human conscience nor human reason has any natural sense or awareness. Consequently, before being affected by a subjective and perceptual cognition concerning the gospel, conscience needs an objective disclosure and representation concerning the message about the person and work of Jesus Christ.[24] That revelation reaches conscience *indirectly* through the previous evangelical illumination of creaturely intelligence by which the gospel is objectively portrayed before the eyes of human beings (Gal 3:1b), in preaching and in the sacraments, so that they may perceive and be made aware of its reality. The objective work accomplished by Christ is a *verbum externum* that needs first to be subjectively known and appropriated so that, becoming a *verbum internum*, conscience might then be made aware of it and respond to it.[25]

---

of observations related to the experience of pagans and covenant children, especially babies who die in infancy; *Reformed Dogmatics*, 4:33-175.

22. Horton elucidates the connection between law and gospel, saying, "the law in its wrath even serves as a merciful accomplice to the gospel" (*Covenant and Salvation*, 151).

23. In expounding Calvin's doctrine of conscience and echoing Emil Brunner's concept of *Anknüpfungspunkt*, Zachman refers to conscience as "a necessary and indelible point of contact (*Anknüpfungspunkt*) for the Word of God, awakening the knowledge of sin and awareness of judgment in even the most hardened sinners" (*The Assurance of Faith*, 149; see also 130, 154, 159). See Emil Brunner and Karl Barth, *Natural Theology: Comprising "Nature and Grace" by Professor Dr. Emil Brunner and the Reply "No!" by Dr. Karl Barth* (Wipf & Stock, n.d.). On Emil Brunner's concept of *Anknüpfungspunkt*, see Alister E. McGrath, *Christian Theology: An Introduction* (Blackwell, 1994), 161-63; McGrath, *Emil Brunner: A Reappraisal* (John Wiley & Sons, 2014).

24. Owen, *The Works of John Owen*, 3:247.

25. Even what is commonly defined as "*outward* calling" must reach human creatures *inwardly* and in this sense the word becomes—at least in a measure—a *verbum internum*. It seems that this is the reason why Reformed theology distinguishes between effectual and ineffectual "special calling"; see Muller, *Dictionary of Latin and Greek Theological Terms*, 329. It should

In the earlier consideration of the interaction between conscience and the affections, it was observed that emotions are always *moved or affected by an object*. Webster writes: "[Emotion] is a state and activity of a person in relation to circumstances, occurrences and agents other than the self. As such, it is an 'undergoing' or 'suffering': a movement of the inner self in response to being moved from outside, a reaction."[26] In the experience of illumination, that which moves the conscience and the affections is the word of God, made first verbally, and secondly mentally, objective by the proclamation of the good news by the Holy Spirit (see Matt 10:20; 1 Pet 1:12). Therefore, conscience is illuminated by the Spirit, for in making the gospel the object of the mind, the imagination, and the memory, the Spirit's witness causes conscience to perceive the new reality of the gospel. This summons the conscience to respond to the one who is revealing himself in a new evangelical manner not only as the Lord creator (*illuminatio legalis*/covenant of works) but also as the gracious Father (*illuminatio evangelica*/covenant of grace).

As noted above, Reformed theology understands illumination as one activity of the Spirit, distinguishing it in the two related aspects of conviction by the law and enlightenment by the gospel (see Gal 2:19–21). Even when individuals do not respond with faith to the proclamation of the revelation of Jesus Christ, in Scripture the condemnation of the law remains indissolubly attached to the promise of the grace offered in the gospel and thus to the person and work of Jesus Christ (see John 3:18–19; 12:47–48; 16:8–11). Explaining conscience as created and fallen, and therefore in need of redemption, a gospel-shaped theology of conscience talks of created conscience as *nonautonomous*, of fallen conscience as *accused*, and of redeemed conscience as *acquitted*. In this gospel-shaped context, the illumination of conscience preparatory to its salvation is not natural and moral but spiritual and evangelical so that while convicted conscience is naturally alarmed by the dark prospect of condemnation, enlightened conscience is surprisingly amazed by the bright promise of reconciliation. For this reason, the apostle Paul compares the work of the *creator Spiritus* in giving life to the original creation to his work in giving new life to the new creation: "For God, who said, 'Let light

---

be observed again that the active and objective *extra nos* is always in service of and aims at stimulating the passive and subjective response *in nobis*.

26. Webster, "*Dolent Gaudentque*," 73.

shine out of darkness,' has shone in our hearts to give the light of the knowledge of the glory of God in the face of Jesus Christ" (2 Cor 4:6). Theissen's comment brings out the full force of the comparison:

> What interests us is the process of illumination that is described in these parallel statements. ... Paul portrays the process as renewal of the process of creation. The God who once created light (Gen. 1:3) causes it to become bright again within. The God who formed man according to his image (*eikon*) reveals himself in the image of Christ. The Creator God makes a new creature: a *kaine ktisis* (2 Cor. 5:17; Gal. 6:15) and a second Adam (1 Cor. 15:44-45). We always observe the same process: the concepts connected with primeval times—"light," "image," "creation," and "Adam"—are actualized anew. The primeval event is surpassed by a new act of creation. What once was determinative for the whole creation becomes the goal and model of a new process. This process can be described psychodynamically by stating that regression to primeval images stands in the service of a progression toward new goals.[27]

As Theissen notes, what is ultimately at stake in illumination is the radical recasting of the whole inward person, including conscience.

SUMMARY

This chapter investigated the preparation of conscience by considering the convicting application of the law to conscience and its illumination through additional gospel light. In the following chapters, the next steps in the redemption of the conscience will be considered in turn: the regeneration, the justification, and the sanctification of conscience.

---

27. Theissen, *Psychological Aspects of Pauline Theology*, 151.

7

THE REGENERATION OF CONSCIENCE

After the experience of illumination, the human conscience needs to be regenerated—that is, given a new life. Regeneration is distinct from both conviction by the law (*illuminatio legalis*) and enlightenment by the gospel (*illuminatio evangelica*), even though it is the same Spirit working in them all through the same word. The difference is a matter of efficacy. Both types of supernatural illumination come from *extra nos* and certainly influence the conscience, the mind, the affections, and the will. But illumination does not always lead to regeneration. Commenting on John 16:8, Calvin writes:

> Christ does not speak of secret revelations, but of the power of the Spirit, which appears in the outward doctrine of the Gospel, and in the voice of men. ... Under the term *world* are, I think, included not only those who would be truly converted to Christ, but hypocrites and reprobates. For there are two ways in which *the Spirit convinces* men by the preaching of the Gospel. Some are moved in good earnest, so as to bow down willingly. ... Others, though they are convinced of guilt and cannot escape, yet do not sincerely yield, or submit themselves to the authority and jurisdiction of the Holy Spirit.[1]

---

1. Calvin, *Calvin's Commentaries*, 18:138. Calvin's well-known distinction between "outward" preaching and "inward" calling does not imply that in the outward presentation of law and gospel individuals (who are not elect) are not *inwardly* affected. That would be impossible because of the constitution of human nature and because in the outward preaching it is the Spirit himself who is speaking. Calvin writes: "There is the general call, by which God invites all equally to himself through the outward preaching of the word." However, he continues: "The other kind of call is special, which he designs for the most part to give to the believers alone, while by the inward illumination of his Spirit he causes the preached Word to dwell in their hearts. *Yet sometimes he also causes those whom he illumines only for a time to partake of it.*" (*Institutes*, 3.24.8, emphasis added); cf. Richard A. Muller, *Post-Reformation Reformed Dogmatics: The Rise and Development of Reformed Orthodoxy, ca. 1520-1725* (Baker Academic, 2003), 2:83-84.

Similarly, while affirming that conscience is enlightened by the Spirit such that "the illumination here intended [in Hebrews 6:4–6] is attended with efficacy, so as that it doth effectually press in the conscience and whole soul unto an abstinence from sin and the performance of all known duties," Owen states that the efficacy of illumination is not always absolute but can remain relative: on occasion there "is a saving, sanctifying light and knowledge which this spiritual illumination riseth not up unto; for though it transiently affects the mind with some glances of the beauty, glory, and excellency of spiritual things, yet it doth not give that direct, steady, intuitive insight into them which is obtained by grace."[2] Therefore, conviction and illumination are not enough; to be redeemed, conscience needs to be regenerated and made alive.

As hinted at above, salvation entails not only a renewed ability for thinking God's thoughts after him and a transformed inclination of the will, but also *a renewed evaluative capacity*. It is this last component of the personal experience of salvation that will be addressed in this chapter, in the belief that the noetic effects of sin upon the conscience are best conceived of as an incapacity to perceive and taste properly divine truth. If the *"will can choose only that in which our nature delights,"*[3] the redemption of humanity must include a vivification of human sensibility. Therefore, this chapter will propose that the regeneration of conscience consists in a renewal of the original *sensus* and a restoration of spiritual delight.

THE REGENERATION OF CONSCIENCE AS THE RENEWAL OF THE *SENSUS DIVINITATIS*

In understanding the regeneration of the conscience as the renewal of the *sensus divinitatis*, the focus, in the words of Michael Allen, is on "the history of sin's undoing and redemption's remaking of wise *perception*."[4] In terms of the theological moral psychology presented in this book, the reality of

---

2. John Owen, "The Nature of Apostasy from the Profession of the Gospel and the Punishment of Apostates Declared," in *The Works of John Owen* (Banner of Truth Trust, 1966), 7:21. Once more, the flexibility of the notion of illumination and its applicability to both conscience and reason should be noticed.

3. Horton, *The Christian Faith*, 564 (emphasis added).

4. Allen, "Reason," in Allen and Nelson, *A Companion to the Theology of John Webster*, 137 (emphasis added).

perception to which Allen refers has a direct connection to the conscience as *sensus* and as a nonphysical capacity for (covenantal) awareness.

Webster affirms the continuity between creation and new creation, noting that regeneration consists in the restoration of created nature:

> [T]he work of the Spirit in the *opus gratiae* of regeneration accords with his work in the *opus naturae* of creation. ... [T]he mode of the Spirit's regenerative work on and in the redeemed repeats, confirms and completes his mode of operation on and in all creatures, especially rational creatures. More specifically, the Holy Spirit is the giver and preserver of life. ... By the Spirit, the new creation which was set in motion by the incarnation is filled out, establishing and preserving a creaturely coordinate to the Son's saving work. There is really this coordinate; and it is really creaturely. *Regeneration is the reinstitution of created nature, and the restoration of all those powers and activities in which it consists.*[5]

The regeneration of created human nature does not imply any adjunct to the powers and activities which that nature *already* possesses. After all, though fallen, conscience is a created reality, and it is a created reality that the word comes to redeem. From a traditional Reformed theological perspective, the regeneration of conscience is a reordering and a reorienting of a capacity that has been part and parcel of human nature since the beginning and not the impartation of a special quality or the infusion of a superior disposition[6] or a new addition to nature in order to make it what it was not. Instead, it is "the liberation of nature—adding nothing new, while making all things new."[7]

To clarify this point, it is helpful to reflect by way of contrast on the example provided by Thomas Goodwin. Reasoning in terms of what is known as "common grace" and the manifestation of God's providential goodness to all

---

5. Webster, "Illumination," 54, 56 (emphasis added).

6. On the problematic notion of infusion in relation to regeneration and justification in Protestant theology, see Bruce L. McCormack, "What's at Stake in Current Debates over Justification," in *Justification: What's at Stake in the Current Debates*, ed. Mark Husbands and Daniel J. Treier (InterVarsity Press, 2004), 81–117; see also Michael S. Horton, *Justification* (Zondervan, 2018) 1:93–129, 244–53.

7. Horton, *Covenant and Salvation*, 211. Bavinck writes that in "not a single respect does it introduce any new substance into existing creation," while for the people who are regenerated the "continuity of the self, their entire human nature with all its capacities and powers, is maintained" (*Reformed Dogmatics*, 4:92).

creatures in spite of human sin, Goodwin understands conscience as being given *de novo* after the fall:

> Common notions of God and goodness, are indeed the imperfect shadow of that former image created in true holiness ... *yet they are no way the relics or remainders of it, but indeed are new donatives*, over and above that birthright of nothing but sin, and natural faculties, the necessary subject thereof, which Adam, and the curse for his sin, left unto us. ... *This light of conscience is not the remainder of the former image*, and so no part or spark of the former holiness, but a light *de novo*, brought in by God and Christ, as, in common, a mediator for all mankind.[8]

It seems that, for Goodwin, conscience is a new creation of God in the sense that—bypassing natural and fallen human faculties—God acts immediately to create it in human beings post-fall.[9]

As for regeneration, Goodwin's reasoning is similar. Instead of referring to the restoration or healing by word and Spirit of created human capacities, regeneration is considered as the infusion of an additional ability:

> Herein lies to me the necessity of such an inward principle of spiritual life to be infused (besides what life of understanding or willing the soul hath of itself, as also besides God's assisting motions and strengthenings), that if any soul be ever brought to put forth any act of spiritual supernatural life, that soul must be constituted or made first a supernatural agent or worker: it must be put into that order or rank of agents or workers, and thereby so be fitted to move from, and within itself, as a supernatural living agent or worker, that so all such acts of life as proceed from it may come to be denominated, or called his own.[10]

---

8. Goodwin, *The Works of Thomas Goodwin*, 6:252–53, 255 (emphasis added).

9. See Goodwin, *The Works of Thomas Goodwin*, 10:100–103. On such a view, it is difficult to understand how Goodwin can explain the fallenness of conscience (as he often rightly does in volumes 6 and 10 of his *Works*) if conscience is not the remainder of the former image but a light *de novo*. If common notions of God and good—the conscience—are new donatives given because of the fall, then they should not in any way be affected by sin. And if common notions of God and good as new donatives are indeed affected by the fall (as Goodwin believes), their being donated anew is meaningless and useless.

10. Goodwin, *The Works of Thomas Goodwin*, 6:209–11 (emphasis added). In saying that this infusion results in the constitution of a supernatural *agent* or *worker*, Goodwin—at least on

Goodwin implies that the new principle infused in regeneration is not to be identified with the renewed or resurrected old capacities of the *imago* but is instead a new sense altogether—that is, something that has not been part of human nature before.[11]

By contrast, insisting on the continuing nature of the relationship between the human being with their capacities and the word and the Spirit that are operative throughout the individual experience of salvation, another puritan theologian—Stephen Charnock—maintains the congruity between nature and grace:

> [Regeneration] is not a removal or taking away of the old substance or faculties of the soul. Some thought that the substance of Adam's soul was corrupted when he sinned, therefore suppose the substance of his soul to be altered when he is renewed. Sin took not away the essence but the rectitude; the new creation, therefore, gives not a new faculty but a new quality.[12]

---

certain occasions—seems to lose sight of the crucial distinction between the *extra nos* and the *in nobis*, consequently separating and isolating the objective work of Christ from the subjective work of the Spirit, insisting so much on an ontological transformation that this transformation practically becomes disconnected from the covenantal and forensic nature or framework of the gospel. For him (at least here), the newly created supernatural *agent* or *worker* has been made able through a *de novo* subjective ontological transformation to fulfill *on his own* the covenant of works apart from Christ the mediator of the covenant of grace, thus disconnecting regeneration from justification. On this topic of the relation between the objective and subjective sides of redemption, see Willem van't Spijker, "Extra Nos and In Nobis by Calvin in a Pneumatological Light," *Calvin and the Holy Spirit: Papers and Responses Presented at the Sixth Colloquium on Calvin and Calvin Studies*, ed. Peter De Klerk (Calvin Studies Society, 1989), 39-62; McCormack, "What's at Stake in Current Debates," 81-117; Horton, *Justification*, 1:173-82.

11. To be fair to Goodwin, in his treatment of conscience in his discussion on regeneration, he often refers to word and Spirit; but it seems that in speaking of regeneration in terms of a necessary infusion of a new spiritual capacity, his implication is that this infusion is actualized independently of word and Spirit, as if this previous transformative infusion is the determinative factor before and apart from the subsequent special call of the Spirit through the word and, paradoxically, apart from the person and work of the mediator. In a book published in 1903, Bavinck seeks to mitigate Kuyper's belief in "immediate" or "unmediated" regeneration (a view close to that of Goodwin), according to which grace is first worked in the sinner directly, without any use of means and, therefore, *without his knowledge and independently of his consciousness*. According to Kuyper, God subsequently works a second grace in regenerate persons, who can then respond with knowledge and understanding; see Abraham Kuyper, *The Work of the Holy Spirit* (Eerdmans, 1946), 283-353. In spite of his irenic spirit, Bavinck nevertheless affirmed that the Spirit's role in regeneration was not to be divorced from the preaching of the word and its effect upon created human capacities; see *Saved by Grace: The Holy Spirit's Work in Calling and Regeneration* (Reformation Heritage Books, 2008).

12. Stephen Charnock, *The New Birth* (Banner of Truth, 1986), 91; see also Bavinck, *Reformed Dogmatics*, 4:94.

On this account, the regeneration of conscience is the effect of a communicative act of God by which the Spirit brings new life to those fallen human capacities and dispositions given in creation.[13]

Princeton theologian B. B. Warfield notes that the new birth of regeneration is coincident with what old divines referred to as "effectual calling," in order to stress that the initiator and perfecter of salvation is God and not the human person.[14] "This new birth," writes Warfield, "pushes itself *into man's own consciousness* through the call of the Word, responded to under the persuasive movements of the Spirit; *his conscious possession of it* is thus mediated by the Word."[15] Considering further this great objective communicative act of the Spirit, Warfield investigates the modality in which it generates subjective effects, thereby relating the passive reception of regeneration to its active effects. Beginning with the doctrine of creation and observing that no person exists, or has ever existed, or will ever exist without being conscious of God (*sensus divinitatis*), he stresses that even fallen human creatures did not cease to be conscious of God, having what was called earlier "the secret instinct of conscience."[16] Moving forward to redemption, he claims that it is this original consciousness of dependent trust that is regenerated by the Spirit:

> There is not required a creation of something entirely new, but only a restoration of an old relation and renewal therewith of an old disposition. Accordingly, although faith in the renewed man bears a different character from faith in unfallen man, inasmuch it is trust in God not merely for general goodness but for the specific blessing of

---

13. On God's communicative action resulting in salvation, see Vanhoozer, "Effectual Call or Causal Effect? Summons, Sovereignty, and Supervenient Grace," in *First Theology: God, Scripture and Hermeneutics*, 96–124. Vanhoozer's analysis of effectual calling by word and Spirit resonates well with the witnessing and summoning function of conscience and fits the covenantal and responsive nature of conscience that is being proposed in this book.

14. Distinguishing between general and special calling, Calvin affirms that the latter "bears with it the Spirit of regeneration" (*Institutes*, 3.24.8). In his comment on James 1:18, Calvin explains that God regenerates sinners by working through the ministers of the gospel, adding that the word "*begotten* means that we become new men, so that we put off our former nature when we are effectually called by God ... by the *word of truth.*" *Commentary on Hebrews, 1 Peter, 1 John, James, 2 Peter, Jude*, vol. 22 of *Calvin's Commentaries* (Baker Books, 1996), 293; see also Bavinck, *Reformed Dogmatics*, 4:77.

15. Benjamin B. Warfield, "On the Biblical Notion of 'Renewal,'" in *Biblical and Theological Studies* (P&R Publishing, 1968), 369–70 (emphasis added). See also Owen, *The Works of John Owen*, 3:225.

16. See Wood, *Blaise Pascal*, 130–31.

salvation—that is to say that is soteriological—*it yet remains essentially the same thing as in unfallen man*. ... And, therefore, though in renewed man it is a gift of God's grace, it does not come to him as something alien to his nature. It is beyond the powers of his nature as sinful man; but it is something which belongs to human nature as such. ... In this sense faith remains natural even in the renewed sinner.[17]

If regeneration is the restoration of the original consciousness, as Warfield argues, it is not difficult to understand why analytical philosopher Alvin Plantinga suggests that redemption, considered in its subjective effects of regeneration and sanctification, is a radical repairing of the *sensus divinitatis* that has been damaged by the ravages of sin:

> Just what are the *cognitive* benefits of regeneration? First, there is a repair of the *sensus divinitatis*, so that once again we can see God and be put in mind of him in the sorts of situations in which that belief-producing process is designed to work.[18]

The regeneration of conscience includes, therefore, the renewal of the *sensus divinitatis*. Yet following Calvin in his understanding of conscience as *sensus* suggests that its transformation is to be explained also in *affective* terms and not only in *rational* terms. Therefore, the next section will propose that the regeneration of conscience consists specifically in the restoration of spiritual *delight*.

---

17. Warfield, "On Faith in its Psychological Aspects," in *Biblical and Theological Studies*, 401; see also Bavinck, *Reformed Dogmatics*, 4:100.

18. Alvin Plantinga, *Warranted Christian Belief* (Oxford University Press, 2000), 280-81. Plantinga reaches this conclusion because in his affirmation of the Aquinas/Calvin model he stresses the fundamental role of the *sensus divinitatis* as a capacity for knowledge; see *Warranted Christian Belief*, 168-84. Plantinga's analysis of the *sensus* as a disposition or capacity for knowledge comes very close to what is being affirmed in this book, even though he does not explicitly relate the *sensus* to conscience as, for instance, Helm does; see Helm, *John Calvin's Ideas*, 224-29, 231, 237. On Plantinga's notion of the repairing of the *sensus divinitatis*, see William J. Abraham, "Analytical Philosophers of Religion," in *The Spiritual Senses: Perceiving God in Western Christianity*, ed. Paul Gravilyuk and Sarah Coakley (Cambridge University Press, 2012), 275-90.

THE REGENERATION OF CONSCIENCE CONSISTS IN THE RESTORATION OF SPIRITUAL DELIGHT

In regeneration, conscience as *sensus* is renewed, and this divine work reactivates the human capacity for truthful perception. Regeneration, therefore, engenders not only new thoughts and desires but also a reorienting of the evaluative powers of the human creature.

The examination of the experience of regeneration is usually considered primarily with reference to the darkness of the mind in relation to truth and/or the bondage of the will in relation to good. Although he mentions the conscience and the affections, Owen focuses on the will among other human powers, almost to the point that it appears to be the major and decisive target of the Spirit's work through the word.[19] Owen writes:

> It may be observed, that we have placed all the effects of this work [of regeneration] in the *mind, conscience, affections,* and *conversation.* Hence, it follows, notwithstanding all that is or may be spoken of it, that the *will* is neither really changed nor internally renewed by it. Now the will is the ruling, governing faculty of the soul, as the mind is the guiding and leading. Whilst this abides unchanged, unrenewed, the power and reign of sin continue in the soul, though not undisturbed yet unruined.[20]

At first glance, it seems that for Owen even though the mind, conscience, affections, and conduct can be deeply influenced by word and Spirit, it is only the change of the will that causes a real conversion in human persons. This is so because for Owen it "is principally with respect unto the *will and its depravation* by nature that we are said to be *dead in sin.*"[21] This conclusion results from Owen's attempt to explain with as much meticulousness as possible the inward efficacy of grace, as he is convinced that this "will better appear *if we consider the faculties of the soul distinctly,* and what is the especial work

---

19. At other times, Owen concentrates his reflection on the mind, so much so that he scarcely mentions the will, the conscience, or the affections. See, for example, Owen, "The Causes, Ways, and Means of Understanding the Mind of God as Revealed in His Word, with Assurance Therein," in *The Works of John Owen* (Banner of Truth, 1966), 4:117-234.

20. Owen, *The Works of John Owen*, 3:238.

21. Owen, *The Works of John Owen*, 3:334.

of the Holy Spirit upon them."[22] It is in his effort to distinguish precisely the different dimensions of the work of the Spirit and the "thick view" of human faculties that results from it that Owen assumes—at least in his treatise on the work of the Spirit in regeneration—a sort of hierarchical supremacy of the will over and above the mind and the affections.

However, even though Owen posits this primary role for the human will (or at other times, for the mind), he nevertheless relates the conversion of the will specifically to the renewal of the affections, surprisingly making the restoration of the latter the origin of the transformation of the former. In this way, he reverses the hierarchical order to the point that the affective character of conscience becomes the determinative factor in the change of the orientation of the will. Indeed, speaking of the regenerating activity of the Spirit, Owen explains that the renewal of the mind and the will is indissolubly connected with the restoration of the affections:

> In like manner a prevailing *love* is implanted upon the affections by the Spirit of grace, causing the soul with delight and complacency to cleave to God and his ways. ... Wherefore, in the circumcision of our hearts, wherein the flesh, with the lusts, affections, and deeds thereof, is crucified by the Spirit, he takes from them their enmity, carnal prejudices, and depraved inclinations, really though not absolutely and perfectly; and instead of them he fills us with *holy spiritual love, joy, fear, and delight*, not changing the being of our affections, but sanctifying and guiding them by the principle of saving light and knowledge before described.[23]

For Owen, as for Calvin and Plantinga, the repairing of the original *sensus* includes *simultaneously* a cognitive and an affective renewal. It is not the will alone, or the mind, or the affections, or even the conscience that has a unique and decisive place in regeneration, but it is all of them taken together, in their interaction and concurrence, each one of them delivering in its own way a

---

22. Owen, *The Works of John Owen*, 3:330 (emphasis added).
23. Owen, *The Works of John Owen*, 3:335. In a later work, Owen expresses the opinion that "affections are in the soul as the helm in the ship." "The Grace and Duty of Being Spiritually Minded," in *The Works of John Owen* (Banner of Truth Trust, 1965), 7:397. For the pivotal role of the affections in regeneration, see Owen's extended discussion in *The Works of John Owen*, 7:394–445; see also David M. King, "The Affective Spirituality of John Owen," *The Evangelical Quarterly* 68, no. 3 (1996): 223–33.

different contribution. Again, in the words of Horton, the Spirit's regenerative work through the word consists in "the liberation of nature—adding nothing new, while making *all things new*."[24]

It should be noted that the renewed sense of delight that results from the Spirit's work of regeneration is not just spiritual or religious in general but specifically evangelical in character—that is, a delight in God for the sake of Christ and his work—for the mission of the Spirit of truth is specifically that of glorying the Son in the life of those whom the Father gave him before the foundation of the world.[25] Plantinga refers to the soteriological dimension of this renewed sense of delight in a profound way:

> The work of the Holy Spirit ... gives us a much clearer view of the beauty, splendor, loveliness, attractiveness, glory of God. It enables us *to see something of the spectacular depth of love revealed in the incarnation and atonement.* Correlatively, it also gives me a much clearer view of the heinousness of sin, and of the degree and extent to which I am enmeshed in it.[26]

Of course, conscience and affections are not exactly the same thing, and it would be a mistake to collapse the one into the other and confuse them or, worse, to concentrate only on the former as if the latter were of secondary importance. Yet a careful distinction between affections and conscience should not prevent a harmonious understanding of their specific cognitive operations, for so similar is their nature and so ingrained is their interaction

---

24. Horton, *Covenant and Salvation*, 211 (emphasis added).

25. Wood writes, "Divine grace operates on the soul by overwhelming it with aesthetic delight, which causes it to love spiritual goods over carnal goods. ... God's grace is experienced as pleasure. ... [The sinner's] pleasure allows him to see the world differently" (*Blaise Pascal*, 213-14). See also Calvin, *Institutes* 1.7.5; Warfield, *Calvin and Augustine*, 77-79, 89-90; Zahl, *The Holy Spirit and Christian Experience*, 184-208.

26. Plantinga, *Warranted Christian Belief*, 280-81 (emphasis added). His numerous references to Calvin, the Belgic Confession, and the Heidelberg Catechism attest to Plantinga's Dutch Reformed upbringing. It may be, then, that Plantinga is unconsciously echoing the Canons of Dort; in their explanation of regeneration the canons affirm that "it is evidently a supernatural work, most powerful, *and at the same time most delightful*, astonishing, mysterious, and ineffable," which "*does not treat men as senseless* stocks and blocks, nor take away their will and its properties, neither does violence thereto; but spiritually quickens, heals, corrects, and *at the same time sweetly and powerfully* bends it." *The Canons of the Synod of Dort* (1619), 3-4.7, 16, in Schaff, *The Creeds of Christendom*, 3:590-91 (emphasis added).

that they share three common characteristics: *sensitivity, passivity,* and *movement.* Each of these characteristics can briefly be developed further.

First, the emotions and the conscience, far from being inimical to the logical activity of reason, possess an intrinsic intelligence that not only contributes toward, but fundamentally makes possible, conceptual thinking. The sensitive and cognitive contribution of the affections and conscience usually precedes, and always supports and refines, abstract thinking. The affective experience of the emotions and the conscience allows the recognition of outward reality while generating an inward consciousness of the self that brings the individual into a relation with that outward reality—God included. Theologically interpreted, conscience is a subjective and spontaneous response that aims at integrating religious and moral emotions positively, incorporating them into a larger sense (*sensus*) or awareness of personal identity in relation to the objective reality of God, while the affections constitute, as it were, the subjective raw material that needs to be assimilated and adjusted for this purpose to be realized.

Second, being responsive by nature, passivity is the primary mode in which conscience and emotions function. In being redeemed, the individual experiences the affective and cognitive regeneration of conscience and emotions passively. Just as in natural birth human beings do not choose to be born, so in the new birth by the Spirit through the word the individual is brought to the beginnings of a new and conscious life in Christ by God himself (see John 1:13), slowly starting to become relationally more and more self-conscious in regard to God. Webster explains well the passive sensitivity of conscience by pointing out that even though conscience "occurs as a mode of my reflection ... *that reflection is not self-generated,* arbitrary and finally responsible to nothing other than itself."[27] Conscience is an inward motion of the self in response to being moved from outside. The action of the self in becoming conscious is preceded by the presence of someone else or something else. The individual comes to self-consciousness when touched by the presence of alterity, a presence that is already there.

Third, because of their sensibility and passivity, both affections and conscience take the form of a subjective movement of response to this real and experienced external presence. That response presupposes and implies that

---

27. Webster, "God and Conscience," 258 (emphasis added).

the human person is somewhat influenced and changed by the awareness of that presence. In other words, being affected by the presence of someone else or something else triggers a living recognition of the reality of someone or something that is other than and distinct from the self.

On this basis, the regeneration of conscience as *sensus* can be understood to consist in the restoration of the capacity to respond to God's revealed presence by law and gospel with a renewed sense of spiritual delight. The Spirit works though the word in a powerful manner, instigating a sweet delight in the inner person and prompting—in harmony with the affective nature of conscience—a new and joyful response to the revelation of God's presence through this convicting and enlightening activity, which reveals God not only as righteous Lord but also, in Christ, as merciful Father.

This understanding of regeneration as the restoration of a sense of spiritual delight in the affections and in the conscience is found in Scripture and implicitly in various expressions in the teaching of the church.[28] In Scripture, all five senses are used to express the ways in which human beings perceive God: seeing (Eph 1:18); hearing (Mark 4:9); tasting (Heb 6:4–5); touching (1 John 1:1); and smelling (2 Cor 2:14). Although Scripture does not present a developed doctrine of the spiritual senses, some contemporary theologians have proposed that the five physical senses correspond analogically (and not merely metaphorically) to the five spiritual senses.[29] The distinction between a simple metaphorical and a more substantial analogical understanding of the spiritual senses is one of the central issues in the current debate. In considering briefly this debate, it should be noted that while in the past theologians intertwined with remarkable flexibility both metaphorical and analogical language, Mark McInroy observes that "modern scholarship has excluded one interpretive option by reference to its counterpart," favoring only a metaphorical understanding of the sensory language *or* eliminating the metaphorical and giving priority solely to an analogical interpretation.[30] Recovering a certain flexibility, the language of the Bible should

---

28. Theological interest in the theme of "spiritual perception" has been recently revived by a number of scholars as is evident from the dense volume *The Spiritual Senses* and The Spiritual Perception Project, accessed June 1st, 2021, https://spiritualperceptionproject.wordpress.com.

29. On this topic, see Karl Rahner's examination of the spiritual senses in Origen, detailed in Mark J. McInroy, "Origen of Alexandria," and McInroy, "Karl Rahner and Hans Urs von Balthasar," in Gavrilyuk and Coakley, *The Spiritual Senses*, 20–35; 258–68.

30. McInroy, "Origen of Alexandria," 35.

be considered at the same time metaphorical *and* analogical: metaphorical, in that neither in creation nor in redemption is there any special faculty or superior disposition for perceiving God that is added to human nature; and analogical, in the sense that the activities of the heart, reason, affections, will, and conscience operate according to a modality similar to the physical senses and in harmony with them. Besides avoiding reductionism, this integration of the metaphorical and analogical language allows for the reality of somatic affections to explain through sensory vocabulary the complexity of the inward reality of religious and moral affections.[31]

Psalm 34:8 has stimulated particular reflection on this point: "Oh, taste and see that the LORD is good!" (see also 1 Peter 2:3). The superscription of the acrostic Psalm 34 refers to the incident narrated in 1 Samuel 21:13 in which David, surrounded by the Philistines, changed his *taste*, or as translated by Alter, "altered his good sense."[32] Relating the superscription to verse 8, where the same root is used, Alter makes the following observation: "The sensory concreteness of the verb is somewhat startling, perhaps intended to suggest the powerful immediacy of experiencing God's benevolence. It also puns on the same root—t-'-m—used as a noun in the superscription with the meaning of 'good sense.'"[33] Stressing the importance of this sensory concreteness, Rachel Fulton considers how the language of taste has been appropriated by the monastic tradition. She indicates that Bernard of Clairvaux connects taste to the perceptions of conscience and, implicitly, to the experience of regeneration:

---

31. In spite of his particular conception of conscience as distinct from *synderesis*, Aquinas's understanding of the spiritual senses as incorporated in ordinary mental acts is not so distant from that of Calvin or Owen; see Richard Cross, "Thomas Aquinas," in Gavrilyuk and Coakley, *The Spiritual Senses*, 174-89. Marco Salvioli reads the sparse comments of Aquinas on the spiritual senses as in greater continuity with the previous theological tradition than does Cross, whose insistence that according to Aquinas faith is rooted in reason leads him to weaken the continuity between Aquinas and the patristic doctrine of the spiritual senses and downplay Aquinas's appreciation for the affective and experiential nature of the Christian life *in via*. "Il fascino discreto di un tema marginale: I sensi spirituali in Tommaso d'Aquino," in *I sensi spirituali: Tra anima e corpo*, ed. Antonio Montanari (Edizioni Glossa, 2012), 211-34. D'Avenia demonstrates that Aquinas's notion of "affective knowledge" has great relevance in relation to the Christian life *in via* (*La conoscenza per connaturalità in S. Tommaso d'Aquino*, 141-204).

32. Alter, *The Book of Psalms*, 117.

33. Alter, *The Book of Psalms*, 118. For the metaphor and analogy of delight, pleasure, and satisfaction in the book of Psalms, see, for instance, Psalms 1:2; 19:10b; 16:11; 36:8-9; 37:4; 65:5; 90:4; 119:103; 143:8.

Indeed, in at least one instance, Bernard takes tasting itself to be a prerequisite for spiritual sight. As he told the clerics of Paris to whom he was preaching conversion, "Doubtless the Lord is sweetness (*suavitas*), but unless you have tasted, you will not see (*nisi gustaveris, non videbis*). For it is said: "Taste and see that the Lord is sweet." This is hidden manna, it is the new name which no one knows except him who receives it. Not learning, but anointing teaches it; not knowledge (*scientia*), but conscience (*conscientia*) grasps it.[34]

Even though he does not understand conscience as *sensus*, Aquinas explicitly relates the interaction of rational and affective knowledge to the spiritual sense:

> *Knowledge of truth is twofold. One is purely speculative. ... The other knowledge of truth is affective*, and this is directly hindered by pride, because the proud, through delighting in their own excellence, disdain the excellence of truth; thus Gregory says (Moral. xxiii, 17) that "the proud, although certain hidden truths be conveyed to their understanding, cannot realize their sweetness [*experiri dulcedinem*]: and if they know of them they cannot relish [*sapiunt*] them."[35]

Furthermore, Aquinas relates the two kinds of cognitive capacities to the reality of the Trinitarian economy, observing that while the mission of the Son as Word aims at the objective informing of the intellect, the mission of the Spirit as Love aims at the subjective "kindling of the affection [*inflammatio affectus*]."[36] Aquinas attributes a cognitive capacity not only to the intellect but to the inclinations or affections, and while the affections do not add any

---

34. Rachel Fulton, "Taste and See That the Lord Is Sweet (Ps. 33:9): The Flavor of God in the Monastic West," *The Journal of Religion* 86, no. 2 (April 2006), 192.

35. Aquinas, *Summa Theologica*, II-II, q. 162, art. 3 (emphasis added). Another text is more explicit and even mentions Psalm 34:8: "Now it is lawful to test the divine goodness or will, for it is written (Ps. 33:9): 'O taste and see that the Lord is sweet.' ... There is a twofold knowledge of God's goodness or will. One is speculative and as to this it is not lawful to doubt or to prove whether God's will be good, or whether God is sweet. The other knowledge of God's will or goodness is affective or experimental and thereby *a man experiences in himself the taste of God's sweetness*, and complacency in God's will" (*Summa Theologica*, II-II, q. 97, art. 2, emphasis added and translation revised).

36. Aquinas, *Summa Theologica*, I, q. 43, art. 5.

new content to knowledge, they supply a subjective sensory perception that informs and enriches the objective understanding of reason.[37]

Reformed theology has also stressed the importance of affective cognition. For Calvin, this regeneration of spiritual delight in God, through Christ and by the Spirit, coincides with the gift of faith, as subjectively "faith involves delight, joy, relief in adhering to the object of faith."[38] Speaking of faith as the way in which we receive the grace of Christ and by which we know God as our redeemer, Calvin—referencing specific examples from Scripture of people who believed—equates faith with the sense of taste: "It is certain that they were instructed in principles such as might give them some taste, however small, of Christ [*gustum aliquem Christi*]."[39] Commenting on Hebrews 6:4-5, and observing that there is no reason why God should "not grant to the reprobate also *some taste* of his grace, why he should not irradiate their minds with some sparks of his light, why he should not give them *some perception* of his goodness," Calvin lingers on the expression "a tasting of the good word of God," by which is meant:

> That the will of God is therein revealed, not in any sort of way, but *in such a way as sweetly to delight us*; in short, by this title is pointed out the difference between the Law and the Gospel; for that has nothing but severity and condemnation, but this is *a sweet testimony* of God's love and fatherly kindness towards us.[40]

---

[37]. In his work on affective knowledge in Aquinas, Marco d'Avenia proposes a definition of knowledge applicable to both earthly and heavenly things: "First of all, knowledge is given by connaturality where an inclination is inserted within knowledge ... and so it is not a simple knowledge of the tangible singular, but of the tangible singular inasmuch as it is appetible. The inclination is therefore a source of knowledge, not in the sense that it directly knows anything, but in so far as it offers a new scope to knowledge: the appetibility of the tangible, which the mere intellect is not able to reach on its own. Relying on an affective reaction, this knowledge can only reveal an immediate appetibility and therefore does not justify it through a demonstrative process. ... What definition can then be given of knowledge by connaturality? *It is a non-rational cognitive judgment that determines the goodness of a concrete object, by virtue of the convergence of the apprehension of the object and of the appetitive inclination towards it*" (*La conoscenza per connaturalità in S. Tommaso d'Aquino*, 176-77, translation mine).

[38]. Helm, *Calvin at the Centre*, 69. See also Warfield, *Calvin and Augustine*, 77-79, 89-90; Dowey, *The Knowledge of God*, 106-23, 173-84.

[39]. Calvin, *Institutes*, 3.2.32.

[40]. Calvin, *Calvin's Commentaries*, 22:137-38 (emphasis added). On Calvin's emphasis on sweetness (*suavitas*), see the excellent article by John Hesselink, "Calvin, Theologian of Sweetness," *Calvin Theological Journal* 37, no. 2 (November 2002), 318-32.

Princeton theologian Archibald Alexander makes a similar connection between aesthetic pleasure and spiritual delight, mentioning conscience explicitly:

> It appears that conscience, or the moral sense, is not a simple but a compound faculty, including both an intellectual act or judgment, and a peculiar feeling or emotion. The name moral sense was probably adopted to express this feeling, or internal emotion. It will serve perhaps to illustrate this subject, if we bring into view another faculty, *between which and the moral sense there is a remarkable analogy.* I refer to what is commonly called Taste, or the faculty by which men are in some degree capable of perceiving and relishing the beauties of nature and art. ... There is in the human mind a capacity of discerning what is termed beauty, in the work of nature and art. This judgment is accompanied by a pleasurable emotion, and to this capacity or susceptibility we give the name Taste. There is also a power of discerning moral qualities, which conception is also attended with a vivid emotion; and to this power or faculty we give the name Conscience, or the moral faculty. Both these are so far original parts of our constitution, that if there did not exist in every mind *a sense* of beauty and its contrary, and *a sense* of right and wrong, such ideas could be generated, or communicated by no process of education.[41]

It is remarkable that—besides observing the concurrence of conscience with the intellect and the feelings—Alexander conceives of conscience as sense. Moreover, he relates spiritual delight explicitly to conscience, adding support to an understanding of regeneration that includes the reality of the affective renewal of the *sensus*. In other words, in regeneration conscience is restored—by word and Spirit—in respect of its God-given evaluative capacity to perceive and delight (albeit not perfectly) in God.

---

41. Archibald Alexander, *Outlines of Moral Science* (Charles Scribner, 1854), 43, 46-47 (emphasis added). Conscience as a capacity for spiritual sense is also observed by Stoker: "This power in our experience of conscience is invisible to our eyes, inaudible to our ears, and untouchable to our hands! Nevertheless this power is definitely there" (*Conscience: Phenomena and Theories*, 164).

SUMMARY

Drawing these ideas together, the regeneration of conscience consists in a renovation of the original *sensus* bestowed to humanity in creation, and in particular, it entails the restoration of the capacity for spiritual delight.[42] In other words, besides the illumination of the intellect, regeneration includes the repair of the affective capacity of the conscience so that the will may start to desire to say "Amen" to God. The work of the Spirit is made efficacious in regeneration through the word with the result that the same human affective and cognitive capacities by which persons perceive, respond to, and interact with the otherness of the created realm begin once again to be able to perceive, respond to, and interact appropriately—even though not perfectly—with the otherness of the triune God. Along with setting aside the problematic notion of "infusion," this section has shown that the idea of the renewal of spiritual delight is not a new proposal but one that has accompanied in various expressions the experiential theology of the Christian church through the centuries.[43]

In redeeming the conscience, the process does not end with regeneration but continues in justification, which will now be explored.

---

42. Zahl ends his treatise on Christian experience with: "The ultimate orientation of any pneumatology worthy of the name must always be to the living Spirit of God, who moves in power, and *whose method is delight*" (*The Holy Spirit and Christian Experience*, 242, emphasis added).

43. As will be shown in what follows, the identification of conscience with the *sensus*—both *divinitatis* and *iudicii*—and the attempt to interpret it as fundamental for the spiritual sense should not be taken as granting to conscience and consciousness an independent authority. The phenomenon of conscience—as a *natural* phenomenon—should not be invested of an authority in religious and moral matters that belongs only to the word of God. That is why the religious experiences of conscience should be unequivocally framed within the soteriological context of the gospel. For an analysis of human religious consciousness and of the distinction between mysticism and gospel—that is, "evangelical" spirituality—see Warfield, "Mysticism and Christianity," in *Biblical and Theological Studies*, 445-62; Donald A. Carson, "When Is Spirituality Spiritual?" in *The Gagging of God: Christianity Confronts Pluralism* (Apollos: 1996), 555-69.

8
THE JUSTIFICATION OF CONSCIENCE

The Spirit who began a good work in conscience through the word continues to be active through the same word in making real justification for the human conscience. This theme will be examined under two major headings.

The first is *the realization of subjective justification*, which is in reference to the personal experience of the reality of justification.[1] Reformed theologians such as Bavinck have been at pains to show the problematic character of the currently resurgent concept of infusion, arguing that justification is not to be understood as a "making righteous."[2] In reaffirming today the forensic nature of justification, Muller states that it consists in "a legal declaration made, figuratively speaking, *in foro divino*, in the divine assize, *and not an infusion of righteousness into the sinner*."[3] However, these same theologians have been equally at pains to show that the prominence accorded to the objective aspect of justification does not imply a consequent neglect on their part of the subjective or experiential side.

The realization of subjective justification in the sinner is accompanied, secondly, by *the cherishing of adoption*. Here, it will be stressed that conscience is redeemed in experientially knowing God as a merciful father. In light of the earlier explanation of the regeneration of conscience in terms of the

---

1. Bavinck observes that, at first, the Reformers were concerned to expound the doctrine of justification in experimental terms, summing up everything in a single experience and in a single derivative concept. However, later Reformed theologians were compelled to consider justification in diverse ways: in its relation to God's eternal decree, to Christ's resurrection, to the preaching of the gospel, and to personal faith. That deeper conceptual analysis led them to differentiate between active and passive justification; see *Reformed Dogmatics*, 4:202.

2. For the classic formulation of this notion by the Council of Trent, see Bavinck, *Reformed Dogmatics*, 4:186–89.

3. Muller, *Dictionary of Latin and Greek Theological Terms*, 162 (emphasis added).

restoration of spiritual delight, it will be shown that the benefits of justification and adoption are experienced by conscience in an affective way.

THE JUSTIFICATION OF CONSCIENCE AS SUBJECTIVE JUSTIFICATION

Berkouwer observes that one of the complaints "which assails us constantly is that sanctification is being cut loose, or abstracted, from justification,"[4] as if justification were exclusively objective and completely disconnected from any kind of subjective experience. In order to address that complaint, it is useful to think about three things: first, the relation between justification and sanctification; second, the distinction between objective and subjective justification; and lastly, the prominence of conscience in the experience of subjective justification.

First, in considering the relation between justification and sanctification, it should be noted that the chief interest of the Bible in discussing righteousness and justice belongs to the condition of humanity before the loving demands of God's righteous will.[5] In stressing the forensic and declarative act of justification, and in highlighting that it is not a regenerative process, Reformed theologians do not neglect the personal reception of justification, which is indeed experiential and related to sanctification. They carefully try to avoid creating some kind of dichotomy between justification and sanctification, as if the forensic reality did not have any relation to the transformative work of the Spirit of Christ. For example, writing about the reality of the "double grace" of justification and sanctification, Calvin considers justification in Christ crucial in relation to spiritual transformation: "For unless you first of all grasp what your relationship to God is, and the nature of his judgment concerning you, you have neither a foundation on which to establish your salvation nor one on which to build your piety toward God."[6]

---

4. Gerrit C. Berkouwer, *Faith and Sanctification* (Eerdmans, 1952), 20.

5. Accordingly, in stressing that the "dogmatic location of justification is a comprehensive Trinitarian soteriology" and recognizing "the need to place the theology of justification within a larger Trinitarian structure," Webster observes that to be a creature is to stand beneath the divine requirement and to "live before the righteous God is to be summoned to life in righteous fellowship" ("*Rector et iudex super omnia genera doctrinarium?*," 164–65, 171).

6. Calvin, *Institutes*, 3.11.1; see also *Institutes*, 3.14.21. Calvin concludes his comment on Romans 5:18 with: "Then life proceeds from justification" (*Calvin's Commentaries*, 19:212). On the other hand, it appears that in general medieval theologians "like Thomas made no distinction between justification and sanctification" (McCormack, "What's at Stake in Current Debates over

Similarly, Bavinck explains the nature of this relation by observing that the "acts of God performed in justification and sanctification are inseparably connected," so much so that because of this unity justification "brings life in its train ([Rom] 5:18)"; thus, those who have been brought into a restored covenantal relation with God "begin immediately to live."[7]

Second, and relating to this discussion on justification and sanctification, there exists a distinction between objective (active) and subjective (passive) justification.[8] From our limited human perspective, it is in the transition from objective to subjective justification that God begins to make individual sinners already partakers of the eschatological life of the new creation (see Rom 5:18, 21; 2 Cor 5:17; Gal 6:15). Bavinck describes this transition as God effectually "pronouncing his acquittal *in our conscience*."[9] The result is that the reality of the forensic objective work of Christ *extra nos* starts—in virtue of its own power made effectual by the Spirit—to generate a subjective response *in nobis* (in the conscience). "God's declaration of righteousness," explains Bavinck, "is not a mere sentence God pronounces to himself."[10] Conscience is akin to a conduit, giving unity and continuity to God's acting to meet the human predicament objectively, *in foro divino*, and subjectively,

---

Justification," 91); see also J. Todd Billings, "John Calvin's Soteriology: On the Multifaceted 'Sum' of the Gospel," *International Journal of Systematic Theology* 11, no. 4 (2009): 428-47.

7. Bavinck, *Reformed Dogmatics*, 4:249-50. According to Zahl, this is so because "the work of the Spirit in justification and the work of the Spirit in regeneration ultimately constitute a single work" (*The Holy Spirit and Christian Experience*, 129-30).

8. The difficulty in explaining how the reality of forensic righteousness *extra nos* is experienced *in nobis* can be seen, for example, in Owen's expositions of the doctrines of regeneration, sanctification, and justification. Considering regeneration in light of the state of death caused by sin, Owen has only a passing reference to justification: "legal, with reference unto the sentence of the law"; and then he adds that we are not delivered from the state of death "by regeneration, but by justification." In the rest of his treatise Owen does not address the relation between justification and regeneration ("A Discourse on the Holy Spirit," 3:283, emphasis original). Although in the volume on justification Owen touches briefly on the matter of subjective justification and conscience, he is concerned to point out that "evangelical" justification is not to be confused with inherent righteousness (sanctification), and he stresses the distinction between justification and sanctification but without considering if and how the two are experientially related (*The Works of John Owen*, 5:139, 155-62).

9. Bavinck, *Reformed Dogmatics*, 4:248 (emphasis added).

10. Bavinck, *Reformed Dogmatics*, 4:176-77. For further reflection on justification as something pertaining to our subjective religious experience, see Bruce L. McCormack, "*Iustitia aliena*: Karl Barth in Conversation with the Evangelical Doctrine of Imputed Righteousness," in *Justification in Perspective: Historical Developments and Contemporary Challenges*, ed. Bruce L. McCormack (Baker Academic, 2006), 167-96. On the difficult relation between Protestant theology and subjective religious experiences, see Zahl, *The Holy Spirit and Christian Experience*, 10-47.

in foro conscientiae. What are real events *coram Deo* are directly experienced through human conscience *coram mundo*,[11] providing a way to discern a general and broad experiential dimension in justification.

Bavinck stresses the central role given by Scripture to this subjective realization of justification:

> As Savior, Christ not only aims at objective satisfaction but also at the subjective redemption of his own from sin. Now this redemption is fully achieved, not by an objective justification in the divine decree or in the resurrection of Christ, but only when, both in terms of reality and of the consciousness of that reality, human beings are freed from sin and hence regenerated and justified. It is of *this* justification that Scripture continually speaks.[12]

According to Bavinck, the active and objective aspect of justification (that also characterizes election, resurrection, Christian preaching, and the effectual call) does not contradict the passive and subjective reception of Christ's *iustitia aliena*. The extrinsic and intrinsic sides of justification should be kept united, as the redeeming work of the Father in the Son and by the Spirit cannot be dissected to the point that it loses its fundamental coherence. The Father's acquittal accomplished in the Son and applied by the Spirit is a single and integrated Trinitarian work, so that what takes place *in Christ* according to the Father's will cannot be separated from what takes place *in us* according to the Spirit's activity, even in the case of forensic justification,[13] since

---

11. On the compatibility between the *coram Deo* perspective and the *coram mundo* perspective, see Zahl, *The Holy Spirit and Christian Experience*, 130-31. The point of contact invoked repeatedly by Zahl, providing for the place of an affective impact where the objective/ontological and the subjective/experiential meet, might plausibly be constituted by a covenantal understanding of conscience; see also Zahl, *The Holy Spirit and Christian Experience*, 108, 114, 117, 122, 188. After all, as Calvin pointed out very clearly and cogently, conscience is a kind of mediator, "a certain mean between God and man" (*Institutes*, 3.19.15-16).

12. Bavinck, *Reformed Dogmatics*, 4:218-19. Berkouwer believes that the "doctrine of justification cannot be grasped apart from [subjectivism]," and he adds, "We need not to be afraid that by reflecting on the relation of this divine salvation to human subjectivity we are harboring an objection to the sovereignty of grace. *Salvation has everything to do with human life down to its most subjective facets*" (*Faith and Justification*, 17-18, 32, emphasis added). See also Zahl, *The Holy Spirit and Christian Experience*, 70.

13. For further reflection on the unity and inseparability of the Triune divine operations in salvation in general and sanctification in particular, see Zahl, *The Holy Spirit and Christian Experience*, 62-63, 132-36.

a Trinitarian understanding of soteriology maintains a continuity between the objective and the subjective aspects of redemption.[14]

This cohesive and integrated understanding of salvation in general and of justification in particular is implicit in Muller's definition of subjective justification:

> Scholastic Protestantism distinguishes between the *actus gratiae* or *actus forensis* of objective justification (*iustificatio objectiva*) and the *actus iustificatorius*, the justificatory realization, or subjective justification (*iustificatio subjectiva*) of the believer. The former set of terms refers to the objective work of Christ and its effect, the remission of sin and the counting righteous of all who are in Christ; the latter set of terms refers to the inward, subjective recognition on the part of the believer that he is counted righteous in Christ and therefore freed from the condemnation of the law.[15]

For Muller, forensic justification itself involves a subjective facet, and this differentiation between *iustificatio objectiva* and *iustificatio subjectiva* allows for the distinction between, on the one hand, justification through and in Christ as the objective matrix from which the personal benefits of salvation derive and, on the other hand, justification as one of the personal benefits subjectively experienced through faith alone by those who have been united to Christ.[16] In general terms, the reality of the Father's forensic acquittal is used by the Spirit to impact subjectively the human person.[17] That means,

---

14. Zahl is convinced that, even though they do not neglect the intra-Trinitarian relations, the "New Testament authors as a whole are substantially more interested in the particular effects the Spirit has on human beings in the world, especially in salvation, in sanctification, and in mission" (*The Holy Spirit and Christian Experience*, 6)7.

15. Muller, *Dictionary of Latin and Greek Theological Terms*, 163. Owen similarly explains that God's *actus forensis* is twofold: initial in this life and complete at the day of judgment, adding that the "manifestation in this life respects either the *souls* and *consciences* of them that are justified, or others; that is, the church or the world." Yet "this *manifestation* of a man's own justification unto himself ... is not a *second justification* when it is attained; but only the application of the former [justification before God] unto his conscience by the Holy Ghost" (*The Works of John Owen*, 5:139).

16. Herman Witsius considers that God's sentence of justification "is intimated and insinuated *to the conscience* by the Holy Spirit; so that the believer knows, feels, and experiences, that his sins are forgiven." *The Economy of the Covenants between God and Man: Comprehending a Complete Body of Divinity* (Den Dulk Christian Foundation, 1990), 1:417.

17. Subjective/passive justification offers a way of avoiding one of the greatest challenges for a pneumatology of Christian experience, namely, according to Zahl, "the temptation to

considered as *iustificatio subjectiva*, forensic justification has *at least some* transformative consequences for the inner person.[18]

Third, attention must be given specifically to the central role of conscience in subjective justification. As it is experienced *in foro conscientiae*, subjective justification is distinguished from the ontological understanding of transformation implicit in the notion of infusion, both in Roman Catholic theology and in its Protestant formulations. The role of conscience allows for a subjective experiential element in justification without the need to introduce the notion of infusion and without downplaying or confusing other transformative benefits of redemption, such as regeneration and sanctification, or—as will be investigated later—adoption (though this also possesses a forensic element).

Recognizing the central place of conscience allows one to maintain a soteriological connection between theology proper and theological anthropology without coordinating righteousness exclusively with either and, consequently, without compelling a choice between the forensic/objective and the ontological/subjective dimensions. However, as will be explained more fully below, the experience of transformation should be viewed as a process with a beginning, a development, and (eschatologically) a completion. Although justification is received by and has effects on the conscience, transformation implies and entails more, namely a renewal of the whole human being, which requires that other soteriological and spiritual benefits gradually affect sinners emotionally, physically, intellectually, volitionally, and linguistically.

In the *iustificatio subjectiva* the Father's objective verdict of justification and the Spirit's subjective regenerating grace meet and intertwine with each

---

split theological-metaphysical claims about the Spirit's work in our *being* and in our *bodies* into discrete and only indirectly related spheres" (*The Holy Spirit and Christian Experience*, 135).

18. For Zahl, the relational change involved in justification is psychologically meaningful and experientially impactful: "To make such observations is not of course to conflate justification with salvation as a whole, or to reduce the meaning of justification for Paul to relational and experiential imagery alone. What they seem to indicate, however, is that there are good reasons to think of justification as something that is experienced as transformative, psychologically salient change. ... The point for present purposes is simply that there are good reasons to believe that to speak of 'justification' in Paul is to speak not least of how a particular dimension of God's saving action in the world comes to be experienced in concrete cases." "Beyond the Critique of Soteriological Individualism: Relationality and Social Cognition," *Modern Theology* 37, no. 2 (2021): 344-45.

other.[19] There is a mysterious and wonderful moment in which the objective benefits merited by the Mediator of the covenant of grace begin to become a subjective reality, namely when subjective justification is realized *in foro conscientiae*.[20] Bavinck writes:

> They [Reformed theologians] commonly assumed that, even if one could with some warrant speak of a justification in the divine decree, in the resurrection of Christ, and in the gospel, *active justification first occurred only in the internal calling before and until faith, but the intimation of it in human consciousness (in other words, passive justification) came into being only through and from within faith*. In this connection they did their utmost to keep the two parts as closely connected as possible and to assume only a logical, not a temporal, distinction between them.[21]

A few pages later, Bavinck is even more direct:

> Active justification already in a sense occurred in the proclamation of the gospel, in the external calling, but it occurs especially in the internal calling when God by his word and Spirit effectually calls sinners, convicts them of sin, drives them out toward Christ, and prompts them to find forgiveness and life in him. ... And when these persons, after first, as it were, going out to Christ (the direct act of faith), then (by a reflex act of faith) return to themselves and acknowledge with childlike gratitude that their sins too have been personally forgiven, then, *in that moment, the passive justification occurs by which God acquits*

---

19. In examining Melanchthon's "affective" explanation of justification, Zahl expresses that *"the experience of justification—the Spirit's gift of faith that consoles terrified hearts—is so closely interwoven with the experience of 'regeneration'—the Spirit's kindling of love and peace and new desires to follow God's law—that a strict distinction between the two simply cannot be maintained"* (*The Holy Spirit and Christian Experience*, 125, emphasis added).

20. Here, the prudent and humbling remarks of Berkouwer should be pondered: "Our reflection on internal grace and the ineffable operation of the Spirit leads us to the mystery of the work of God. At best the Church of the ages gave but faltering expression to what needed to be said in the matter. Something it had to say to preserve the comfort and purity of the Gospel of grace; but those who tried to push beyond this ineffability soon lapsed into language that is hard, into formulas that are rigid, and into a matter-of-factness that is alien to the miracle of grace" (*Faith and Sanctification*, 86).

21. Bavinck, *Reformed Dogmatics*, 4:203.

believers in their conscience and by his Spirit bears witness with their own spirit that they are children of God and heirs of eternal life.[22]

Without for an instant obliterating the objective dimension of justification, Bavinck concentrates on the experiential realization of justification *in nobis*, which begins to happen in a certain moment *in the conscience*, according to the purpose of the electing and saving grace of God in Christ. He writes: "Justification does not consist in a transcendent acquittal of the sinner on the part of God in the court of heaven but is an act that passes from one sphere to another, *is carried by the Holy Spirit into the consciousness of believers*."[23] Even if the imputation of Christ's perfect obedience and righteousness is objective, extrinsic, forensic and non-transformative, it is also experienced *inwardly* and *subjectively* as a perception and recognition on the part of the believers *in foro conscientiae*.

Zahl explores the affective and cognitive effects of the doctrines of the gospel. He takes as his case study the doctrine of justification in light of "the recent wave of criticism directed at 'forensic' soteriologies and the corresponding turn across a variety of traditions towards soteriologies of 'participation' and *theosis*."[24] According to Zahl, forensic justification "is traditionally contrasted with the broadly Thomistic position that the formal cause of justification is God's righteousness 'infused' within the baptized believer as the habit of charity."[25] "The most prominent line of critique," Zahl continues, "is that forensic models are thought to offer no satisfying way of connecting what is happening objectively *coram deo*, before God, with subjective human

---

22. Bavinck, *Reformed Dogmatics*, 4:219 (emphasis added). In considering subjective justification, Bavinck does not principally conceive of conscience in terms of the Thomistic notion of practical reason and *conscientia*. While in his *Reformed Ethics* Bavinck is closer to Aquinas in his understanding of conscience as *synderesis* (see 1:193–99), at this point in the *Reformed Dogmatics* he is closer to Calvin's notion of *sensus* and to a covenantal and perceptual conception of conscience.

23. Bavinck, *Reformed Dogmatics*, 4:225 (emphasis added).

24. Zahl, "On the Affective Salience of Doctrines," 434. Reversing the common axiom according to which forensic justification is purely extrinsic and fictional, Zahl proposes that the classical understanding of justification is characterized by an affective transformation that is in itself a form of participation; see *The Holy Spirit and Christian Experience*, 136–41.

25. Zahl, "On the Affective Salience of Doctrines," 435. For a brief analysis of neo-Thomism on justification and sanctification, see Zahl, *The Holy Spirit and Christian Experience*, 108–18.

experience in the world."²⁶ Focusing on this criticism,²⁷ Zahl underlines the affective and cognitive involvement of the conscience²⁸ as an example of the inward and subjective relevance of forensic justification:

> The event of coming to faith can be characterized as an imaginative shift in one's present and/or future relation to a perceived or postulated divine judgment. When the "doctrine" changes—in the case of forensic justification from something like "God judges sinners like me" to "in Christ God accepts me fully and will judge me no longer"—this entails a change in the "cognitive basis" of the emotion of terror [in the conscience]. Such a change, if it actually takes place, cannot but result in specific and plausible affective consequences—the muting of feelings of fear and the kindling of feelings of peace, joy, gratitude, and so on.²⁹

Through subjective justification the individual sinner begins to perceive with delight and with an astonishment that baffles the understanding the reality of the doctrine of the imputation of the extrinsic and alien righteousness of Christ. In this subjective sense, justification could be viewed

---

26. Zahl, "On the Affective Salience of Doctrines," 435. The issue at stake is not so much the relation between the objective and the subjective sides of salvation but rather the possibility of attributing any merit to humanity in relation to that salvation: "Classical Protestant theologies of forensic justification are indeed deeply concerned with the exclusion from soteriological consideration of any inner requirement of righteousness, of any inner subjective change that would be *formally necessary* to salvation. Although from the start theologians who held to a forensic view of justification usually took great pains to emphasize some form of inner renewal or 'fruit' consequent to justification or simultaneous with it—usually called sanctification—they took equal pains to separate that renewal formally from salvation itself" (*The Holy Spirit and Christian Experience*, 90-91).

27. Bavinck notes that this critique was incisively formulated by Robert Bellarmine and that it returns regularly in the works of all the critics of the Reformation doctrine of justification (*Reformed Dogmatics*, 4:212-14).

28. Reflecting Melanchthon's emphasis on conscience, Zahl mentions conscience a number of times in coming to this conclusion: "For Melanchthon the key to understanding forensic justification lies above all in understanding the powerful affective salience he perceives it to have for fearful human beings with troubled consciences" ("On the Affective Salience of Doctrines," 439).

29. Zahl, "On the Affective Salience of Doctrines," 441. "It makes psychological sense," affirms Zahl, "to think that when a person living in fear of judgment becomes convinced that God no longer stands in judgment over them on account of their sins—a position rendered emotionally as well as conceptually compelling through a particular kind of account of the atonement—they might well experience 'consolation' in their fear as well as affects of joy and gratitude and a new sensation of freedom and even empowerment" (*The Holy Spirit and Christian Experience*, 175). On the involvement of conscience, see Zahl, *The Holy Spirit and Christian Experience*, 126-36.

as somewhat transformative, being what Horton calls a "verdict that does what it says,"[30] in the sense that it *does* something *to* believers by causing them to become aware and recognize their personal participation in Christ's perfect obedience.

Concluding this first section on the justification of conscience, the effective declaration of objective justification brings about an affective and cognitive reversal as "the conscience becomes conscious" of that reality. Subjective justification is not a making righteous, in the sense of possessing personally the perfect righteousness of the Lord Jesus, but a conscious reception by faith of the gift of the imputed righteousness of Christ, a reception that in some measure contributes to a spiritual and psychological change in believers.

As indicated previously, the next investigation will be the benefit of adoption, which expands and extends what has begun to be experienced through the reception of the imputed righteousness of Christ received by faith.[31]

THE JUSTIFICATION OF CONSCIENCE AND THE CHERISHING OF ADOPTION

Subjective justification is accompanied by *the cherishing of adoption*.[32] It was affirmed earlier that the judicial nature of justification does not rule out, at least in general, a subjective influence because of the phenomenon of

---

30. See Horton, *Covenant and Salvation*, 243–66; Zahl, *The Holy Spirit and Christian Experience*, 164–71.

31. The insistence on the subjective reception of justification in the conscience is not meant to downplay that justification, adoption, and sanctification are all benefits that derive from union with Christ. The reality of union with Christ embraces all the various elements within the *ordo salutis*, avoiding the pitfall of attributing a hierarchical importance to some elements to the detriment of others. Instead, this subjective emphasis is an attempt to address the problems of complacency with theological abstraction and experiential vagueness signaled by Zahl: "Instead of talking, as the New Testament so often does, about the effects of the Spirit's work on real bodies in time, theologians revert instead to ontological language about union with Christ, about salvific participation in the Godhead, or about deification and *theosis*. Through these strategies, the concrete historical experience of the Christian in the world quietly slides out of view" (*The Holy Spirit and Christian Experience*, 71).

32. For the conceptual backdrop of the metaphor of adoption, see David B. Garner, *Sons in the Son: The Riches and Reach of Adoption in Christ* (P&R Publishing, 2016), 35–54; Joachim Jeremias, *New Testament Theology: The Proclamation of Jesus* (SCM Press, 1971), 61–67, 178–202; Timothy J. R. Trumper, "The Metaphorical Import of Adoption: a Plea for Realisation I: The Adoption Metaphor in Biblical Usage," *The Scottish Bulletin of Evangelical Theology* 14 (1996): 129–45; "The Metaphorical Import of Adoption: A Plea for Realisation II: The Adoption Metaphor in Theological Usage," *The Scottish Bulletin of Evangelical Theology* 15 (1997): 98–115. For a historical and theological account of adoption in the Reformed tradition, see Timothy J. R. Trumper, "An Historical Study of the Doctrine of Adoption in the Calvinistic Tradition" (PhD diss., University of Edinburgh, 2001),

affective salience that involves the conscience. These experiential effects are even more manifest in the case of adoption. Adoption deepens, intensifies, and develops the experience of redemption of conscience begun with subjective justification. The distinction between justification and adoption does not imply that transformation is something that pertains only to the latter as if the former should be limited to the extrinsic dimensions. Indeed, conscience is the place where the judicial/declarative and the ontological/ regenerative aspects of the *ordo salutis* meet, and this is true both in the case of justification and in the case of adoption.[33]

The following reflection will proceed, first, by considering the relation between justification and adoption. Secondly, attention will be devoted to the necessity of maintaining some experiential continuity between justification and adoption (and sanctification) in spite of their distinction. Third, some exegetical material will be examined to better explain how adoption is related to the Spirit's work in the conscience. Lastly, some concluding observations will be made about conscience's gradual experience of delight in adoption, thus paving the way for the discussion of the sanctification of conscience.

In discussing adoption, we encounter once again the distinction between the objective/active and the subjective/passive dimensions.[34] These two facets of adoption have implications for its relation to justification. Bavinck notes that sometimes "the adoption as children was mentioned as the second part of justification [as in Turretin] but others, such as Peter Martyr, preferred to consider this a fruit of justification."[35] The challenge here is not to let the

---

https://era.ed.ac.uk/handle/1842/6803; and Isomi Saito, "Divine Adoption in the Confessions of the Reformation Period" (PhD diss., Vrije Universiteit, 2016), https://research.vu.nl/en/ publications/divine-adoption-in-the-confessions-of-the-reformation-period-2, which at least in part seeks to correct the work of Trumper.

33. On the *ordo salutis* in Reformed theology, see Richard A. Muller, "Union with Christ and the *Ordo Salutis*: Reflections on Developments in Early Modern Reformed Thought," in *Calvin and the Reformed Tradition: On the Work of Christ and the Order of Salvation* (Baker Academic, 2012) 202-43; Andrew T. B. McGowan, "Justification and the *ordo salutis*," in *Justification in Perspective: Historical Developments and Contemporary Challenges*, 147-63; Berkouwer, *Faith and Justification*, 25-36.

34. See Bavinck, *Reformed Ethics*, 1:386. As in justification, although *in foro divino* believers do not become gradually more and more children of God, nevertheless *in foro conscientiae* they are brought progressively into a deeper and fuller experiential awareness of adoption.

35. Bavinck, *Reformed Dogmatics*, 4:224. Though more positive toward Vermigli, Trumper blames Turretin for loss of the distinctive meaning of adoption within the Reformed tradition; see "An Historical Study of the Doctrine of Adoption," 19, 117-18, 217, 251-52, 270, 367, 409; for a similar line of historical interpretation, see Garner, *Sons in the Son*, 30-31, 231-34.

interaction between justification and adoption drop out of sight.³⁶ The different ways to understand the experience of adoption depend on the perspective from which one looks at it, whether through the objective lens or through the subjective one: in the first case, adoption might look closer to justification, while in the second the tendency will be to view it related more to sanctification. However, the two sides should always be kept together so that "distinction" does not become "discontinuity."³⁷

In his definition, Muller notes the immediate connection between justification and adoption:

> Adoption of the believer as a child of God occurs as the *immediate* corollary and result of the forensic declaration of righteousness on account of faith. Those justified by the grace of Christ are *also* made co-heirs with him of the kingdom and are declared sons with Christ, because of their union with him.³⁸

---

36. In discussing the forensic (justification) and the renovative (sanctification), Garner adds the category of the "filial" by which, in his view, "Paul qualifies his entire soteriological paradigm." For Garner, justification is purely forensic and objective while sanctification is uniquely transformative, and this *duplex gratia* should be seen "as an expression of the adoption of the Son." Garner accords to adoption an all-embracing role: "In the *ordo salutis* adoption embraces the whole of what union with Christ manifests [and] clarifies and qualifies all the other benefits" so that adoption should be considered as a more comprehensive concept and as "*the* benefit of union with Christ." In this manner, justification and sanctification become "core subsets" of adoption, which is the all-inclusive benefit of the *ordo salutis* (*Sons in the Son*, 306-8). Even though interpreting adoption in more comprehensive terms has some plausibility, a hierarchical explanation of the benefits of union with Christ runs the risk of obscuring their unity and reciprocal interdependence, therefore an integrative explanation is to be preferred.

37. According to Ridderbos, even though justification and adoption have their specific significance in explaining the rich content of the gospel, scholars have "been able to say of these various central concepts *with a certain degree of justice* that they are only different figures for the same thing and are related to each other as concentric circles" (*Paul: An Outline of His Theology*, 197, emphasis added). Witsius similarly writes: "There is not any one word, any one similitude, borrowed from human affairs, that can sufficiently express or represent this most happy bond of love; which can hardly be explained by a great number of metaphors heaped together. To express tranquillity of conscience, the scripture calls it *peace*: to shew us the pleasantness of familiarity, it calls it *friendship*: and when it illustrates a right to the inheritance, it speaks of *adoption*" (*The Economy of the Covenants*, 1:442).

38. Muller, *Dictionary of Latin and Greek Theological Terms*, 27 (emphasis added). Although historical reasons compelled Turretin and others to concentrate on the forensic element of salvation, Turretin's view of adoption as the positive side of justification has the advantage of preserving the experiential continuity between the two and of not losing sight of the legal nature of adoption. See also the comments of Garner about Archibald Alexander Hodge's understanding of adoption as both legal and transformative (*Sons in the Son*, 296-97).

David B. Garner, meanwhile, recognizes the clear connection between adoption and sanctification:

> The first-century Roman adoptive practices and the theology of the Old Testament render ample resources for Paul to choose *huiothesia* for both the divine act *and* its enduring effects. ... Paul's concern is not only the *act* of adoption, but also the *state* of adoptive sonship, the full change that union with the resurrected Son of God affords.[39]

However, in order to avoid discontinuity between justification and adoption (as well as sanctification) the living and ongoing experience of adoption should be seen as combining and coordinating in a special way the declarative and extrinsic aspect of justification with its ontological consequences *in foro conscientiae*, thus influencing the process of sanctification.

To provide exegetical substance to these claims, it is helpful to look at a couple of passages from Romans. The first passage is Romans 8:15-16:

> For you did not receive the spirit of slavery to fall back into fear, but you have received the Spirit of adoption as sons, by whom we cry, "Abba! Father!" The Spirit himself bears witness with our spirit that we are children of God.

Among the key texts speaking of adoption (Rom 8:15, 23; 9:4; Gal 4:5; and Eph 1:5), it is only in the context of Romans 8:15 that we find a specific mention of the witness of the human spirit together with that of the divine Spirit.[40] This passage in particular indicates that Paul intertwines the objective/active

---

39. Garner, *Sons in the Son*, 50. However, Berkouwer insists that "there is never a stretch along the way of salvation where justification drops out of sight," rather genuine sanctification "stands or falls with this continued orientation toward justification and the remission of sins" (*Faith and Sanctification*, 77–78; see also Zahl, *The Holy Spirit and Christian Experience*, 196). By contrast, while apparently limiting justification (which he defines as "legal blessing") to the changed forensic and relational position of the sinner (thus losing sight of the subjective realization of justification *in foro conscientiae*), Garner insists that adoption is not merely relegated to judicial categories because it manifests the further soteriological aspect of transformation. In reaction to what he perceives as "forensic fixation," Garner concentrates so much on the transformative element of adoption that he creates too sharp a dichotomy between justification and adoption, so that they become insulated from each other (*Sons in the Son*, 72–74, 223–27, 301–11).

40. Moo, *The Epistle to the Romans*, 503. Benjamin B. Warfield believes that "however the text be read, the 'Spirit of God' and 'our spirit' are brought into pointed contrast in it, and are emphatically distinguished from one another." "The Spirit's Testimony to Our Sonship," in *Faith and Life* (Banner of Truth, 1974), 182. Indeed, because the Spirit of adoption cries (Gal 4:6), the human spirit cries as well (Rom 8:15).

witness of the calling, regenerating, and justifying Spirit with the subjective/passive witness of the receiving human spirit, so that once more what is determined *extra nos* is experienced *in nobis*.[41] Moreover, recalling that fear was previously affirmed as a manifestation of conscience and that witnessing was previously identified as one of the chief functions of conscience, the references to "witness" and to "fear" in Romans 8:15-16 have particular importance.

Even though Paul never explicitly mentions conscience in relation to adoption, his reference to "our spirit," which Thiselton takes to indicate the "person's innermost self,"[42] seems implicitly to reference the experiential realities of conscience and self-awareness.[43] In Romans 2:15—which does not mention the human spirit—the person's innermost self is described with reference to the heart, the conscience, and thinking and the same verb "to bear witness" or "to demonstrate to be true." In Romans 8:16 this verb describes the activity of the Spirit, but in Romans 2:15 it describes explicitly the activity of the human conscience. Thus, it seems probable that the broad concept of (human) "spirit" includes an indirect reference to the conscience, whose witness in Romans 8:16 interacts and responds to the witness of the Spirit.[44]

Along with the theme of witnessing, in Romans 8:15-16 fear is mentioned, which might be seen as leading indirectly to the reality of conscience. Fear

---

41. A number of commentators understand that the Spirit "bears witness *to*" our spirit rather than "bears witness *with*" our spirit; see Cranfield, *A Critical and Exegetical Commentary*, 1:403. However, even if the preposition "to" were grammatically correct, that by itself does not rule out the idea that the human spirit is subjectively affected by the Spirit's active testifying *to* believers that they are children of God. "It is of no importance for this," writes Warfield, "whether Paul says that the Spirit bears witness with or to our spirit; in either case he distinctly distinguishes the Spirit of God from our spirit along with which or to which it bears its witness. And not only so but this distinction is the very nerve of the whole statement; the scope of which is nothing other than to give the Christian, along with his human conclusions, a Divine witness" ("The Spirit's Testimony to Our Sonship," 182-83).

42. For an exegetical analysis of this understanding of the human "spirit," see Thiselton, *The First Epistle to the Corinthians*, 255-60.

43. Warfield explains the human spirit in terms of the conscience: "The Holy Spirit does not deliver His testimony save through and in confluence with the testimony of our consciences that we are God's children" ("The Spirit's Testimony to Our Sonship," 188). Commenting upon this passage, Witsius believes that "by *our spirit*, is understood, the mind and conscience of every believer, whereby he may be conscious of what passes in his own heart" (*The Economy of the Covenants*, 1:462-63).

44. Quoting from Origen's commentary on Romans, Kries shows that Origen identifies conscience, mentioned in 2 Corinthians 1:12, with the human spirit mentioned in 1 Corinthians 2:11 and Romans 8:16; see "Origen, Plato, and Conscience," 78-79.

is one of the primary manifestations of conscience. Regardless of how one explains the expression "spirit of slavery,"[45] the testimony of the Spirit of adoption generates in the conscience an affection that is the opposite of fear. Without entering into a detailed analysis of the second part of Romans and the Adam-Christology that characterizes it (see Rom 5:12-21), suffice it to say that Romans 8 has a number of ways to refer the reader back to Genesis 1-3, notably in Romans 8:18-23—the paragraph that immediately follows Paul's reflection on adoption. Within this redemptive-historical context, Paul mentioning the possibility of falling "back into fear" might be seen as alluding to the original fear experienced by humanity in the garden (see Gen 3:8-10). Moo's explanation of Romans 8:15-16 seems to mirror what happened in the story of Adam, even though he does not explicitly quote or refer to Genesis 3 at this point:

> Since Paul has pictured the law as bringing awareness of sin and the corresponding penalty of condemnation (see 3:20; 7:7-13), he probably alludes to the ministry of the law [producing] this inner sense of dread before God, the righteous judge.[46]

The references to the human spirit, the theme of witnessing, and the mention of fear all point to the workings of conscience.

The second relevant passage is Romans 9:1, which is the only other verse in the New Testament—besides Romans 8:16 and 2:15—where the verb "to bear witness" (συμμαρτυρέω) is used. In this passage, the verb is again related to both the conscience and the Spirit: "I am speaking the truth in Christ—I am not lying; my conscience bears me witness in the Holy Spirit" (Rom 9:1). Here Paul is not speaking of justification or adoption but of the gospel and Israel. However, as in the case of Romans 8:16, there is a double and intertwined simultaneous witness: that of the conscience and the Spirit. For Paul, the witness of the conscience by itself is not enough, and therefore, he appeals to the more reliable work upon his conscience by the Spirit, whose function

---

45. On the various options, see Garner, *Sons in the Son*, 115-23.

46. Moo, *The Epistle to the Romans*, 500. The reference to Genesis 3:8-10 becomes more evident if the expressions "spirit of slavery" and "fear" are understood as generated by the legal witness of the "*ruach* of the day" in Genesis 3:8 and as experienced by Adam in judgment in Genesis 3:10. For an interpretation of Genesis 3:8 as the theophanic presence of the judging Spirit, see Kline, *Images of the Spirit*, 97-131; Garner, *Sons in the Son*, 119-23.

is to witness (see John 15:26; Heb 10:15; 1 John 5:6). Calvin highlights the work of these two witnesses:

> By these words he calls his own conscience before the tribunal of God, for he brings in the Spirit as a witness to his feeling. He adduced the Spirit for this end, that he might more fully testify that he was free and pure from an evil disposition, and that he pleaded the cause of Christ under the guidance and direction of the Spirit of God.[47]

Thus, the implicit and indirect reference to conscience in Romans 8:16 and the more explicit mention in Romans 9:1 show that in justification and adoption conscience is involved in a profoundly affective way.

Lastly, it should be briefly stressed that—as in the case of subjective justification—the personal reception of adoption marks the beginning of an experience which conscience learns to taste and enjoy increasingly. The subjective side of adoption is present in the definition given by Witsius, who writes of "the Holy Spirit, operating those things *in* the elect, which are suitable to, and becoming [of] the sons of God, who love God, and are beloved by him."[48] He continues, "The Spirit of adoption discovers God to the believing soul, as a kind and indulgent Father; and by giving him assurance of the love of God, and sweetly cherishing the hope of future inheritance, makes him, with alacrity and generous emotions of a filial reverence, willingly to obey God, as an affectionate parent."[49] Witsius adds that this witness of the Spirit is experienced repeatedly in the Christian life:

> The Spirit of God does not leave himself *without witness* ... for he excites generous motions and the sweetest raptures in believers, and delights them with consolations so ravishing and ecstatical, and even exceeding all thought, that they cannot consider them, in any other light, but as so many testimonies of their adoption.[50]

---

47. Calvin, *Calvin's Commentaries*, 19:335. Most commentators see—both in Romans 8:16 and 9:1—a reference to the juridical need of two or three witnesses to provide legal evidence; see Moo, *The Epistle to the Romans*, 504, 556. If that is the case, there is yet another reason to affirm that the Spirit testifies so that the human spirit/conscience may follow the Spirit, with the result that the two testimonies become one.

48. Witsius, *The Economy of the Covenants*, 1:455 (emphasis added).

49. Witsius, *The Economy of the Covenants*, 1:456.

50. Witsius, *The Economy of the Covenants*, 1:466–67.

And with this—that is, with the experience of subjective justification and adoption—the boundary that introduces believers into the territory of sanctification is crossed because, as Witsius explains,

> The souls of the elect are never refreshed with the sweet consolation of the Spirit, but they are at the same time, inflamed with the love of God, and excited to the vigorous exercise of strict religion. *The same Spirit, who is the Comforter, is also, by the same act* [of adoption], *the Sanctifier.*[51]

SUMMARY

This chapter examined the realization of subjective justification, showing that the objective aspect of justification should not imply a dismissal of the subjective or experiential side, which directly connects to the process of the redemption of conscience. Moreover, this realization of subjective justification is accompanied by the inward realization of adoption. It was shown that through the benefits of justification and adoption conscience is involved in an affective way. The following chapter will address the sanctification of conscience.

---

51. Witsius, *The Economy of the Covenants*, 1:467 (emphasis added).

9

THE SANCTIFICATION OF CONSCIENCE

The sanctification of conscience is but one aspect of the process in which the Christian believer is sanctified. In sanctification, the believer increasingly experiences the reality of having been delivered from the kingdom of darkness and being transformed by the blessings of justification and adoption. This process of sanctification deepens and strengthens the subjective appropriation of justification and adoption, thus enabling believers to live more comprehensively in their love of God and neighbor. These three benefits of union with Christ are interwoven, and they influence each other experientially, such that sanctification is conceived of as a developing and deepening of the same experience that was sovereignly initiated at the point of effectual calling by the triune God and, on this basis, as a growing movement into holiness of life (cf. Phil 1:6).

Attending to this growing into holiness, and to the intimate interweaving of conscience with the emotions, this chapter will investigate the sanctification of conscience principally in its emotional dimensions. In the process, sanctification will be understood as an affective transformation resulting from a perceptual reversal or reconfiguration. At each point, the sanctification of the conscience will be explained in relation to the experiential realities of justification and adoption, on the basis that the Father reorders human life by subduing the feeling of guilt through justification in the Son and pacifying creaturely shame through the Spirit of adoption. As a consequence of this divine activity, there is also a progressive calming of fear and an increasing abandonment of hiddenness in the human person. In sanctification, the afflictive emotions engendered by the fall are reversed and progressively become their opposite through the gradual renewal of the *sensus divinitatis* and the ongoing restoration of spiritual delight.

This chapter will cover these three sections: the subduing of guilt; the pacifying of shame; and finally, the calming of fear and the abandoning of hiddenness. Of course, much more could be written about sanctification itself, such as about grieving the Spirit and repentance, mortification, the didactic role of the moral law, the practice of spiritual disciplines, and Christian formation in relation to the means of grace and to the life of the church. However, these themes all have a more indirect relation to conscience, while justification and adoption have a more immediate and evident impact on the sanctification of conscience.

In speaking of sanctification in progressive terms, it should not be forgotten that sanctification—in a similar way to justification and adoption— is also primarily an objective and indicative benefit of union with Christ.[1] Carson writes:

> In most conservative theological discussion, sanctification is the progressive purifying of the believer, the process by which he becomes increasingly holy after an instantaneous "positional" or "forensic" justification. But it is commonplace among Pauline scholars that although the term *sanctification* can have that force, it commonly refers to the initial setting aside of an individual for God at his conversion.[2]

It seems appropriate then that justification, adoption, and sanctification should always be understood in objective and subjective terms. Although, as important as it is to insist on their distinctiveness, their inseparability should be stressed with equal force, especially in their experiential dimensions. They are inseparable because they are bound together in the objective act of God by which he unites human creatures to his Son by the Spirit's effectual call. They are inseparable because justice, sonship, and sanctity belong to the person in Jesus Christ so that when individuals look to Christ by a direct act of faith, they return to themselves by a reflexive

---

1. Sanctification begins at the same time as conversion, and in sanctification there is a primary objective dimension in which God decisively sets sinners aside for himself. However, this objective act of God does not remain without a transition into human consciousness, ergo sanctification passively received also becomes a subjective experience; see Calvin, *Institutes*, 3.16.1.

2. Carson, *Exegetical Fallacies*, 45. For an exegetical analysis of the concept of positional sanctification, see Thiselton's comments on 1 Corinthians 1:2, 1:30, and 6:11 (*The First Epistle to the Corinthians*, 76–77, 190–95, 453–55).

act of faith, receiving at once the whole Christ and all that belongs to him. Consequently, these three are inseparable also because, when passively received by faith, all of them become at once subjective aspects of Christian identity. It is not therefore that justification (or justification and adoption taken together, depending on one's views) is purely extrinsic while sanctification (or adoption and sanctification) are purely intrinsic. Rather all three have both extrinsic and intrinsic dimensions. Finally, justification, adoption, and sanctification are inseparable insofar as all of them continue together to characterize Christian experience as it subjectively lives in union with Christ in a progressive way.

Dealing now directly with the theme of the chapter, subjective sanctification of conscience can be considered the result of a growing awareness of justification and a progressive cherishing of adoption that together diminish the afflictive realities of guilt, shame, fear and the urge to hide. Flowing from the experience of a developing subjective realization of justification and a deepening inward tasting of adoption, sanctification quietly but steadily effects the affective change through which the *sensus divinitatis* and the orientation of human delight begins and continues to be transfigured. This progressive refinement of the *sensus divinitatis* and the gradual ennoblement of spiritual delight is not realized by setting aside justification and adoption; rather, the new sensitivity and spiritual delight blossom and grow in the heart and in the conscience as they are nurtured and tended by the benefits of justification and adoption. Zahl writes:

> Insofar as Christians remain embedded in sin and subject to "the desires of the flesh" (Gal. 5:16), the mechanism by which the Spirit extricates them from this sin *continues* to follow the pattern established in justification. As in salvation, it is in the revelation of sin through critical encounter with the law that the "affective predicates" of effective encounter with divine grace are generated, intensified, and made salient. In turn, it is primarily in the context of these *affective predicates* that *desiderative attachments* to sin have a chance of beginning to change. That is, it is through specific instantiations of this soteriological pattern in bodies and in time that sin can plausibly come to be experienced as debilitating and a "torment" rather than

delightful, and repentance as "*sweet*," liberating, and joyous rather than as repressive and stultifying.³

It is evident that for Zahl there is continuity between what is experienced at the initial stage of the Christian life and what is experienced in progression. It is clear that sanctification involves an intensification of the *sensus divinitatis* and a deepening of spiritual delight, both of which begin to be transfigured in regeneration. As will be explored below, it is the realization of a renewed *sensus* and of inward delight that constitutes the sanctification of conscience, gradually delivering it from guilt, shame, fear, and the impulse to flee from God.

What is realized *in nobis* in this way, however, is always mediated by the indicative reality of the gospel *extra nos*. As Webster insists, this means that "a theology of conscience will describe the ultimate context of conscience as the fact that, in and as Jesus Christ, God has acted to effect the entire reordering of human life" and, correspondingly, a theology of conscience will "talk of the Holy Spirit as the repetition, the realizing and perfecting *in us* of the Father's verdict in the Son."⁴ It is the act of God in Jesus Christ that reorders human life by efficaciously and pleasantly repeating, through the Spirit, the verdict of justification, adoption, and holiness of the Son in the conscience of those who have been united to him. This promotes the progressive sanctification of believers that is experienced in terms of the subduing of guilt, the pacifying of shame, the calming of fear, and the abandoning of hiddenness.⁵

THE SANCTIFICATION OF CONSCIENCE CONSISTING IN THE SUBDUING OF GUILT

Theologically, it is not possible to conceive of guilt merely in terms of subjective psychology or individual morality, as simply a human phenomenon or, even worse, as an irrational emotion detrimental for the highest forms of human

---

3. Zahl, *The Holy Spirit and Christian Experience*, 195-96 (emphasis added). Even though Zahl does not mention adoption, its interrelatedness with justification makes his observations applicable to adoption as well.

4. Webster, "God and Conscience," 252-53 (emphasis added).

5. On this afflictive experience of conscience, see the penetrating observations of Stoker, *Conscience: Phenomena and Theories*, 157-81.

rationality.⁶ Understood covenantally, the feeling of guilt is an intrinsically religious fact, and according to Merold Westphal, "Guilt lies at the heart of religious concern and ... religion is regularly a means of solving the problem of guilt."⁷ Westphal understands guilt as "a form of self-consciousness" that nevertheless cannot be reduced to "an act of unconditioned self-positing," for "the voice of conscience is not a soliloquy," but it is "always a response to the other's attitude toward me."⁸ Recalling the episode of Nathan the prophet and David the king (2 Sam 12:7), Westphal explains guilt in covenantal terms:

> The voice which accusingly tells the self, Thou art the man, is in the first instance the other's voice. Guilt is an echo effect; for when that voice resounds off the walls of the self's inner life it has been transformed into the self's own voice. This fusion of voices is but another way of indicating that in guilt I recognize (even when I cannot bring myself to acknowledge) the justification of the other's judgment upon me. If we would keep guilt before us whole, we will have to preserve this unity of self-consciousness and other-consciousness.⁹

Given that guilt is a manifestation of human self-consciousness—understood primarily and covenantally in relation to God—the sanctification of the conscience requires that this inner afflictive sense of guilt be addressed.

The sanctification of conscience consists in the inversion of its own spontaneous awareness of the guilt *coram Deo* that is experienced *coram mundo*. It is here that justification interacts experientially with sanctification to effect the progressive transformation of believers. As the sense of guilt is related to the presence of indwelling sin, the sanctification of conscience deepens the subjective realization of justification in the Son, so that the reality of the believer's identification with Christ in his perfect righteousness and obedience gradually and persuasively subdues the feelings of guilt (see Gal 2:20; Phil 3:9).

---

6. For a phenomenological investigation of guilt in covenantal religion, see Merold Westphal, *God, Guilt, and Death: An Existential Phenomenology of Religion* (Indiana University Press, 1984), 69–89, 217–51.

7. Westphal, *God, Guilt, and Death*, 73.

8. Westphal, *God, Guilt, and Death*, 81–82.

9. Westphal, *God, Guilt, and Death*, 82. For more on the interpersonal and relational nature of moral emotions and their vertical relation to the Holy, see Steinbock, *Moral Emotions*, 12–14 and, with particular reference to guilt, 100–33.

In his treatise on justification, Owen sheds further light on this idea of the subduing of guilt as an aspect of sanctification when he considers the need for a continual realization of the justified state. He writes: "This *manifestation* of a man's own justification unto himself ... is not a *second justification* when it is attained; but only the application of the former [justification before God] unto his conscience by the Holy Ghost."[10] Owen observes that Christ's justice "doth take away *conscience condemning the sinner for sin*, with respect unto the curse of the law; but it doth not take away *conscience condemning sin in the sinner*,"[11] and from this experiential reality he asserts the need for a continued subjective realization of justification.[12] Far from being forgotten as something purely forensic and extrinsic that has nothing to do with sanctification, it appears that justification is experienced more and more in sanctification, as an aspect of sanctification, with the result that feelings of guilt are subdued so that the believer might continue to live for God. In other words, the *sensus divinitatis* and spiritual delight continue to be transformed in sanctification through a deeper application by the Spirit of the reality of Christ's righteousness to the heart.

The Letter to the Hebrews addresses this sanctification of conscience through the subduing of afflictive guilt. One problem dealt with by its author is that religious practices "cannot *perfect* the conscience of the worshiper" (Heb 9:9, emphasis added). Sinners who approach God with the desire to worship and serve him in holiness of life always have a "consciousness of sins" (Heb 10:2). And because of this awareness, even their religious practices become a "reminder of sins" (Heb 10:3). The remedy is for the worshiper to draw near to God to have their heart sprinkled so as to be cleansed "from a guilty conscience" (Heb 10:22 NIV). For this reason, Pierce observes that "conscience is the real obstacle to worship."[13] Until the problem of a

---

10. Owen, *The Works of John Owen*, 5:139.

11. Owen, *The Works of John Owen*, 5:146.

12. It is a pity that Owen does not dwell at least a little on the subjective aspect of the continuation of our justification: "We speak not of the sense and evidence of it unto our own soul unto peace with God ... but of the continuance of it in the sight of God." *The Works of John Owen*, 5:148. Witsius too alludes to this idea in terms of repetition: "And it is to be observed, that such a declaration [of justification] is often repeated" (*The Economy of the Covenants*, 1:417).

13. Pierce, *Conscience in the New Testament*, 101. Noticing that in Hebrews (apart from 13:8) conscience always has negative connotations referring to guilt, William A. Lane states that a "defiled conscience is an obstacle to the worship of God and calls for decisive purgation." *Hebrews 9–13*, Word Biblical Commentary (Word Books, 1991), 225.

guilty conscience is addressed, there cannot be any real progress in sanctification. A continued experience of justification is essential: the redemption of conscience must be experienced as a progressive realization of justification, which in sanctification gradually and sweetly reverses the sense of guilt and thus promotes personal holiness of life.

More specifically, Hebrews stresses that this subjective realization derives from a contemplation of its objective accomplishment in the reality of the atonement: "How much more will the blood of Christ, who through the eternal Spirit offered himself without blemish to God, purify our conscience from dead works to serve the living God" (Heb 9:14). In reflecting on the pressure exerted by the sense of guilt on conscience, and on the relation between justification and spiritual transformation, Owen stresses the sanctifying contribution of justification in the course of the Christian life through the purging of conscience. According to some, notes Owen, Hebrews is primarily referring to internal or inherent sanctification, but in contrast with this view he writes:

> But neither the sense of the word, nor the context, nor the exposition given by the apostle of this very expression, Heb. X.1, 2, will admit of this restrained sense. I grant it is included therein, but there is something else principally intended, namely, the expiation of sin, with our justification and peace with God thereon. ... It is "conscience" that it is said to be purged. Now conscience is the proper seat of the *guilt* of sin; it is that which chargeth it on the soul, and which hinder all approach unto God in his service with liberty and boldness, unless it is removed. ... To have the conscience purged, is to have its *condemning power for sin* taken away and cease.[14]

In other words, for Owen the sanctification of conscience consists in its being delivered by the subjective realization of justification from the afflictive feeling of guilt that burdens it, so that the soul is enabled to approach God in his service with liberty and boldness. Similarly, considering the story of the Christian doctrine of atonement in modern Europe, Zahl retrieves for the present time this same experiential understanding of sanctification:

---

14. John Owen, "An Exposition of the Epistle to the Hebrews with Preliminary Exercitations," in *The Works of John Owen* (Banner of Truth, 1991), 22:297.

Personal feelings of doubt, depression, anxiety, inner unrest, and rootlessness are understood to be closely connected to a sense of sin and guilt before God. A deeply emotional and individual conversion experience takes place which removes the negative affect and replaces it with powerful feelings of joy and purpose. The mechanism behind this event ... is the forgiveness of sins through the vicarious sacrifice of Jesus Christ. Importantly, however, the imputation of Christ's righteousness *coram deo*, and the non-imputation of sin, are utterly connected with particular inner feelings and a sensation of personal transformation at a particular time and place.[15]

In conclusion, the sanctification of conscience includes a still but steady appropriation of the reality of justification before God. In sanctification, the sinner's conscience is patiently and gently brought to see that, in Jesus Christ, God has acted so as to effect the entire reordering of human life in order that it experiences a progressive reversal of guilt and a new and growing consciousness of justification. However, as noted above, the process of sanctification also includes the new and deepening awareness of the reality of adoption, therefore the next section turns to the sanctification of conscience in relation to shame.

THE SANCTIFICATION OF CONSCIENCE CONSISTING IN THE PACIFYING OF SHAME

If in relation to guilt the sanctification of conscience is realized by a deepening awareness of Christ's imputed righteousness, then through the Spirit of adoption an increasing soothing of the sense of shame progressively sanctifies conscience. The sense of shame that afflicts the conscience is transfigured in a sentiment of filial awareness and assurance, and the human heart is made willing to live for God the Father, sanctifying his name, seeking his kingdom, and doing his will on earth.

---

15. Simeon Zahl, "Atonement," in *The Oxford Handbook of Theology and Modern European Thought* (Oxford University Press, 2013), 636-37. Even though Zahl is here thinking in terms of a conversion experience, his broad analysis of the experiential effects of the reality of Christ's atonement relates to sanctification as well.

Considering a prelapsarian condition without shame and a postlapsarian condition with shame, Dan Lé argues that shame is an experience that reveals a perceptual change in human consciousness:

> The couple [Adam and Eve] hide because they feel the *dis-ease* when thinking of facing God, for they know they have to give an account for disobeying the command the moment they meet God again. It is reasonable to consider that nakedness hints at the *dis-ease* caused by the broken state of the couple's relationship with God. In other words, the "sin and fall" motif employs *the dis-ease involved in the shame* of nakedness in order to indicate a broken spiritual relationship via an act of disobedience.[16]

According to Lé, the disease of shame experienced by humanity in the garden is an eminently subjective phenomenon that is at the same time other-oriented and relational.[17] Encompassing the human person in entirety, shame afflicts the individual with a general sense of self-depreciation that makes one feel inadequate, unworthy, and loathsome. This displeasure with oneself requires that, in order to be sanctified, conscience needs to experience an inversion of its instinctive fallen sense of unworthiness before God. This deep sense of displeasure is the focus of the work of the Spirit of adoption, who in the work of sanctification effects a gradual reduction of the sense of shame.

Because the covenant of works is our default human setting, according to Dane Ortlund, we have a "chronic tendency to function out of a subtle belief that our obedience strengthens the love of God." As a consequence,

> there is an entire psychological substructure that, due to the fall, is a near-constant manufacturing of relational leveraging, fear-stuffing, nervousness, score-keeping, neurotic controlling, anxiety-festering silliness that is not something we say or even think so much as something we exhale.[18]

---

16. Lé, *The Naked Christ*, 102 (emphasis added).

17. For a phenomenological investigation of the relational nature of shame, see Steinbock, *Moral Emotions*, 12–14, 67–99; Dan Zahavi, *Self and Other: Exploring Subjectivity, Empathy, and Shame* (Oxford University Press, 2014), 208–50.

18. Dane Ortlund, *Gentle and Lowly: The Heart of Christ for Sinners and Sufferers* (Crossway, 2020), 182, 185.

Given this "inveterate yet subtle proclivity to seek to leverage Christ's favor with our behavior," continues Ortlund, human creatures need instead to understand that

> God is rich in mercy means that your regions of *deepest shame and regret* are not hotels through which divine mercy passes but homes in which divine mercy abides. ... The battle of the Christian life is to bring your own heart into alignment with Christ's, that is, *getting up each morning and replacing your natural orphan mind-set with a mind-set of full and free adoption into the family of God through the work of Christ your older brother.*[19]

This "getting up each morning and replacing your natural orphan mind-set with a mind-set of full and free adoption" is the goal of the sanctifying work of the Spirit, as he progressively reconfigures the conscience. Through justification God releases the guilty from his negative verdict, and through adoption he welcomes them back home as beloved children. The growth of this awareness of being a beloved child is a further aspect of the sanctification of conscience, and this new awareness of sonship reverses the fallen sense of shame.

In Galatians 4:4-7 Paul coordinates the doctrines of the Trinity, the incarnation, and the covenant of works with those of the atonement (see Gal 3:13-14), justification, and adoption, relating all of them to the ongoing sanctification of believers:

> But when the fullness of time had come, God sent forth his Son, born of woman, born under the law, to redeem those who were under the law, so that we might receive adoption as sons. And because you are sons, God has sent the Spirit of his Son into our hearts, crying, "Abba! Father!" So you are no longer a slave, but a son, and if a son, then an heir through God.

In this passage, Paul focuses on the subjective consequences of justification and adoption, emphasizing the sanctifying effects that derive from the presence of the Spirit of adoption in the hearts of those who become God's children. Once again, the inseparability and the porous nature of the benefits

---

19. Ortlund, *Gentle and Lowly*, 179, 181.

of union with Christ in his justice, sonship, and holiness are evidenced here, as they are seen to be working together simultaneously, strengthening each other and making their impact felt in Christian experience.[20]

While stressing the forensic aspect of adoption, Owen also affirms that adoption is proclaimed by God not only before angels and Satan but inwardly, "*unto the conscience of the person adopted*":

> The Spirit of Christ testifies to the heart and conscience of a believer that he is freed from all engagements unto the family of Satan, and is become the son of God, Rom. viii. 14, 15; and enables him to cry "Abba, Father," Gal. iv. 6 ... testifying to his conscience his acceptance with God, enabling him to behave himself as a child.[21]

As believers are taken to a deeper experiential consciousness of their adoption, their sense of unworthiness and shame is progressively pacified through a growing awareness of their union with Christ. The result is that—as the Son in the days of his flesh was comforted and strengthened by the consciousness of the reality of his filial relation with the Father—believers are enabled to enjoy their belonging to "the household of God," "the Father of mercies and God of all comfort" (Eph 2:19; 2 Cor 1:3).

However, in spite of the continuing experience of justification and adoption, conscience remains at war in the arena of sanctification where, because of indwelling sin (especially in times of temptation), it must battle with its own crippling and ongoing sense of shame and alienation from God. Calvin is particularly aware that this conflict derives from conscience itself. After having considered first the peace experienced in the conscience by believers,[22] Calvin recognizes that in reality believers experience something other

---

20. The opinion that a legal model of the atonement is counterproductive in relation to the problem of shame is advanced, for example, in Pattison, *Shame*, 243-48 and Stockitt, *Restoring the Shamed*, 83-113. By contrast, Zahl affirms that the forensic understanding of the atonement has a powerful healing efficacy in relation to guilt and shame: "It makes psychological sense to think that when a person living in fear of judgment becomes convinced that God no longer stands in judgment over them on account of their sins—a position rendered emotionally as well as conceptually compelling through a particular kind of account of the atonement—they might well experience 'consolation' in their fear as well as affects of joy and gratitude and a new sensation of freedom and even empowerment" (*The Holy Spirit and Christian Experience*, 175).

21. John Owen, "Of Communion with God the Father, Son, and Holy Ghost, Each Person Distinctly, in Love, Grace, and Consolation," *The Works of John Owen* (Banner of Truth, 1966), 2:210-11.

22. Calvin, *Institutes*, 3.2.16.

than peace and assurance, and he relates this difficulty to the tension experienced within conscience:

> Surely, while we teach that faith ought to be certain and assured, we cannot imagine any certainty that is not tinged with doubt, or any assurance that is not assailed by some anxiety. On the other hand, we say that believers are in perpetual conflict with their own unbelief. Far, indeed, are we from putting their consciences in any peaceful repose, undisturbed by any tumult at all. ... But it is especially our conscience itself that, weighed down by a mass of sins, now complains and groans, now accuses itself, now murmurs secretly, now breaks out in open tumult. ... Yet these [temptations] are always directed to this objective: that, thinking God to be against us and hostile to us, we should not hope for any help from him, and should fear him as if he were our deadly enemy.[23]

In opposition to the turbulence of this struggle that Calvin so vividly depicts, holiness of life develops in sanctification through the progressive realization that we belong to God as our Father. Even though sin continues to burden our conscience, fresh awareness in the conscience of the reality of our adoption increasingly acts to dispel by grace the sense of shame and estrangement from God.

This fresh awareness is effected through the work of the Spirit of adoption, who assists in the practice of prayer as believers learn gradually to understand what it means to address God, crying, "Abba, Father!" (Rom 8:15). This cry of the believer is prompted by the sending of the Spirit of the Son "into [their] hearts" (Gal 4:6; see also Mark 14:36).[24] As well, the work of the Spirit of adoption is described by the forceful and vigorous verb κράζω ("to cry," "to call out"). The strength of the verb refers to the passionate affections which are raised within the human heart. Commenting on Galatians 4:6, Moo offers the following interpretation: "Paul perhaps uses a word picture to convey the deep and emotional reaction within the believer's heart

---

23. Calvin, *Institutes*, 3.2.17, 20.

24. Jeremias remarks that the "use of the everyday word *'abbā* as a form of address to God is the most important linguistic innovation on the part of Jesus. ... The complete novelty and uniqueness of *'Abbā* as an address to God in the prayers of Jesus shows that it expresses the heart of Jesus' relationship to God" (*New Testament Theology*, 36, 67).

to the joyful conviction, brought by God's Spirit, that we are, indeed, God's sons."[25] His comment on the same verb in Romans 8:15 is even more pertinent:

> The Spirit not only bestows "adoption" on us; he also makes us *aware* of this new relationship. ... In using the verb "crying out," Paul stresses that our *awareness* of God as Father comes not from rational consideration nor from external testimony alone but from a truth deeply felt and intensively experienced.[26]

It is this intense and intensifying owning of the status of adoption that is at the heart of the sanctification of believers. That is why in teaching the disciples to pray the Son instructed them to address God as "our Father in heaven" (Matt 6:9). Calvin considers prayer to be the chief exercise of faith "by which we daily receive God's benefits,"[27] and he relates it to the benefits of union with Christ and the ongoing experience of justification, adoption, and sanctification. In the introduction to his treatment of the Lord's Prayer, Calvin writes of our experience of adoption: "The Spirit of adoption, who seals the witness of the gospel in our hearts [Rom. 8:16], raises up our spirits to dare show forth to God their desires, to stir up unspeakable groanings [Rom. 8:26], and confidently cry, 'Abba! Father!' [Rom. 8:15]."[28] Calvin focuses on the christological dimension of the Lord's Prayer, highlighting that the gift of adoption dissipates our ingrained shame and distrust through prayerful contemplation of God's fatherly love:

> We ought to offer all prayer to God only in Christ's name, as it cannot be agreeable to him in any other name. For in calling God "Father," we put forward the name "Christ." With what confidence would anyone address God as "Father"? Who would break forth into such rashness as to claim for himself *the honor of a son* of God unless we had been adopted as children of grace in Christ? He, while he is the true Son, has of himself been given us as a brother that what he has of his own by nature may become ours by benefit of adoption if we embrace this

---

25. Douglas J. Moo, *Galatians*, Baker Exegetical Commentary on the New Testament (Baker Academic, 2013), 270.
26. Moo, *The Epistle to the Romans*, 502 (emphasis added).
27. Calvin, *Institutes*, 3.20.
28. Calvin, *Institutes*, 3.20.1.

great blessing with sure faith. ... Therefore God both calls himself our Father and would have us so address him. By the great sweetness of his name he frees us from all distrust, since no greater feeling of love can be found elsewhere than in the Father.[29]

Even though he does not develop this insight, it is interesting that Calvin relates adoption to a perceived sense of honor—the opposite of shame—and thus, he understands implicitly progressive sanctification in terms of a gradual healing of this sense of shame.

In conclusion, in the process of sanctification for those who have been built upon the chosen and precious cornerstone of Jesus Christ (Isa 28:16; Ps 118:22), shame has been reversed and transfigured into honor: "So the honor is for you who believe" (1 Pet 2:7).[30] Having considered how—in connection with justification and adoption—sanctification mitigates and appeases the guilt and shame of the conscience, the last section of this chapter will explore how conscience is sanctified in respect to the way in which the displeasure deriving from fear and the impulse to hide from God are progressively removed.[31]

---

29. Calvin, *Institutes*, 3.20.36 (emphasis added).

30. Karen H. Jobes observes that "Peter apparently takes his cue from the phrase of Isa. 28:16 LXX that those who trust in the Stone placed in Zion will never be put to shame, which he reads as a litotes strongly affirming the opposite of shame." *1 Peter*, Baker Exegetical Commentary on the New Testament (Baker Academic, 2005), 152; see also J. Ramsey Michaels, *1 Peter*, Word Biblical Themes (Word Books, 1988), 104.

31. Space does not allow for an exploration of how the practices of meditative reading of Scripture and contemplative prayer centering on justification and adoption promote sanctification. Roman Catholic scholar Joseph A. Fitzmyer devised a Pauline version of the *Spiritual Exercises* of Ignatius Loyola, in which the doctrines of justification and adoption have a foundational role in cultivating spiritual depth and maturity; see *Spiritual Exercises Based in Paul's Epistle to the Romans* (Paulist Press, 1995), 54–62, 78–90, 120–34. In this work, Fitzmyer advances a forensic model of the atonement that stresses its transformative potential (*Spiritual Exercises*, 57–61). Similarly, Zahl observes that "the vehemence of reactions against substitutionary and forensic models over the centuries has often obscured recognition of its sheer effectiveness in a wide variety of contexts and over many centuries." Even though "Protestant traditions are often thought to be less successful at aligning what is happening *coram deo* and *coram hominibus*," Zahl continues, "this is only partly true—preaching judicial models of the atonement in fact often maps quite closely to particular affective and embodied experiences" ("Atonement," 637, 652).

THE SANCTIFICATION OF CONSCIENCE CONSISTING IN THE CALMING OF FEAR AND THE ABANDONING OF HIDDENNESS

The biblical idea that seems to characterize the sanctification of conscience in Scripture in relation to fear and hiddenness is that of *parrēsía*, which describes a spiritual posture of openness, transparency, and humble and joyful confidence (see Phil 1:20). If—because of guilt and shame—fallen conscience relates to God by way of fear and the desire to hide, redeemed conscience learns by grace to respond to God's self-revelatory presence with a sense of calm assurance and serene openness.

Urging Roman Catholics to emulate Protestantism's earnest study of Scripture as God's truthful revelation,[32] Hans Urs von Balthasar elaborates in his Trinitarian theology of contemplative prayer a reflection on communion with God the Father, in the Son, and through the Spirit, in which he connects the experience of *parrēsía* to the doctrine of adoption and to the phenomenon of conscience. He stresses that it is in the context of meditative and contemplative prayer that conscience is sanctified as it benefits from *parrēsía*.[33] Balthasar first explains the meaning of *parrēsía* as a response to God:

> This *parrhesia* on our part [preceded by the objective openness of God] is the *open*, unconstrained and *childlike approach* to the Father, *neither ashamed nor fearing shame*. We come to him with heads held high, as those who have an innate right to be there and to speak. We may look into the Father's face *without fear*.[34]

Balthasar observes that *parrēsía* characterizes the attitudes of the adopted children of God in whom are dispelled the sense of shame and fear and (implicitly) the impulse to hide from God. Correspondingly, it encourages humble and confident openness. This twofold dynamic is a fundamental

---

32. Hans Urs von Balthasar, *Prayer* (Ignatius Press, 1986), 28.

33. Balthasar's work on a Trinitarian theology of contemplative prayer is a recent treasure in the literature. However, it should not be overlooked that Protestant theology shared much of what Balthasar writes, as can be evidenced, for instance, in Calvin's lengthy exposition of the Lord's Prayer (*Institutes*, 3.20.1-52); in John Owen's Trinitarian approach to communion with God (*The Works of John Owen*, 2:1-277); or in the almost forgotten volume (published originally in 1894) of Presbyterian pastor Benjamin M. Palmer, *Theology of Prayer as Viewed in the Religion of Nature and in the System of Grace* (Sprinkle Publications, 1980).

34. Balthasar, *Prayer*, 46 (emphasis added).

aspect of the progressive sanctification of conscience,³⁵ and Balthasar later relates *parrēsía* to the resultant transfigured awareness of the conscience:

> The fact that the truth, the love, and the whole life of God is open to us is only the other side of man's election, calling, justification and glorification by God. Seen in this way is the immense, stupendous gift of grace given to men of a "good conscience." It was our shame that brought Christ to the cross, the shame (for which we could never atone) of our lack of love for God and our fellow men. ... All attempts to overcome this inability through "works" were fruitless: *God himself had to cleanse us in the blood of his Son and give us a good conscience*, that "confidence [*parrēsía*] to enter the sanctuary" (Heb. 10:19). Peace with God in a good conscience is such an incomprehensible gift of grace—because it fundamentally overthrows all the laws of ethics—that *the person involved literally does not know what is happening to him*. By rights, in any way, he ought to have a bad conscience; his heart accuses him.³⁶

According to Balthasar, by rights—that is, with respect to the law—human beings ought to have only a bad conscience. But by redemption, human conscience is subjectively turned upside down by the gift of *parrēsía*,³⁷ a new awareness that quiets fear and calls the believer out of hiddenness. Consequently, the gracious gift of a good conscience transforms fear and the impulse to hide into a new awareness characterized by assurance and openness.

It is interesting to connect Balthasar's observations on the interaction between conscience and *parrēsía* (in reference to Heb 10:19) with some comments by Owen. *Parrēsía*, according to Owen, aims at removing two things:

---

35. It is clear that what Balthasar writes echoes what was noted above concerning guilt and shame. However, the reason for including Balthasar at this point is his specific reflection on the transformative impact of *parrēsía* on conscience.

36. Balthasar, *Prayer*, 47 (emphasis added).

37. Since *parrēsía* is a gift of grace, it possesses, as noted by Heinrich Schlier, a "peculiarly objective character" that brings again to the fore the dynamism between the passive/objective and the active/subjective dimensions of grace. One has *parrēsía* not primarily as a subjective attitude, "but as the appropriation of something already there," for *parrēsía* "is given with the blood of Jesus ([Heb] 10:19)." "παρρησία, παρρησιάζομαι," in *Theological Dictionary of the New Testament*, 5:884.

First, *A bondage frame of spirit*. ... This legal diffidence and distrust in our approaches unto God, which shuts up the heart, straitens the spirit, and takes away the liberty with him as father, is now by Christ removed and taken away, Gal. iv.4-6 ... whereby, also, we receive the adoption of children, and therewithal the Spirit of Christ, to treat with God with the liberty, boldness, and ingenuity of children, crying "Abba, Father." ... Secondly, *A disbelief of acceptation*, arising from a sense of our own unworthiness. From an apprehension of God's greatness and terror there arises a dread in persons under the law; and from the consideration of their own vileness there arises distrust in sinners, accompanied with fear and despondency, as though there were no hope for them.[38]

For Owen, *parrēsía* reverses the sense of afflictive fear and estrangement that the individual experiences before God. More specifically, Owen relates *parrēsía* to a new kind of perception of the conscience. Affirming that in Hebrews 10:22 the expression "full assurance of faith" includes what in other places is meant by *parrēsía* (cf. Heb 10:19), Owen writes that by virtue of the process of ongoing sanctification we gain the confidence to enter into God's sanctuary with a conscience that is not only once, but continually, being purified:

Hereby are "our hearts sprinkled from an evil conscience"; [1] *Originally*, in the communication of regenerating, sanctifying grace; [2] *Continually*, in fresh applications of the virtue of the blood of Christ, for the taking away of the defilement by internal, actual sin.[39]

For Owen, as well as for Balthasar, confidence and assurance characterize the experience of sanctification through the transformative purification of the conscience.

---

38. John Owen, "An Exposition of the Epistle to the Hebrews with Preliminary Exercitations," in *The Works of John Owen* (Banner of Truth, 1991), 20:429-30.

39. *The Works of John Owen*, 22:513. Lane emphasizes that "the association of παρρησία with a purged conscience was a distinctive and new development in the use of the word," and relating this dynamic to sanctification, he adds, "Only when the heart has been purged from the defilement of a smiting conscience can it be renewed in fullness of faith and sincerity toward God" (*Hebrews 9-13*, 283).

Balthasar—in common with Calvin, Owen, and Bavinck[40]—finally unites the objective side (*extra nos*) of redemption with its subjective (*in nobis*) appropriation and makes the newly experienced *parrēsía* of the conscience the place where they meet:

> The openness of the *objective* path to the Father is the openness of the *subjective* heart (the "good conscience"). ... At this point hearing the word, i.e., Christian contemplation, reveals its basic presupposition, which is *inseparably both objective and subjective*: on the one hand the openness of divine truth to man, and on the other the openness of the human spirit and heart for this truth. The latter depends on the former.[41]

Once again, in these observations by Balthasar not only are the objective and the subjective sides of redemption kept united, but they are both related to the conscience.

SUMMARY

This chapter has argued that the sanctification of conscience is accomplished by a gradual subjective transformation in which the afflictive emotions of guilt, shame, fear, and the impulse to hide are reversed in order to become progressively their opposite. It has claimed that the Reformed understanding of the objective and subjective aspects of justification, adoption, and sanctification offers a plausible description of the inward transformation of the human conscience that conforms both to scriptural evidence and to human

---

40. From time to time, Balthasar blames Protestant theology for neglecting the subjective, aesthetical, and contemplative side of redemption. For example, he considers the responses of John of the Cross and Pascal to the objective emphasis of Reformation theology, claiming that they responded with a radically personal, experimental, and psychological piety in which they accentuated a personal experience of faith in objective as well as subjective terms; see *The Glory of the Lord*, vol. 3 of *Studies in Theological Style: Lay Styles*, (T&T Clark, 1984), 105-7. See, however, the assessment on the aesthetical and contemplative orientation of Reformed theology by Belden C. Lane, *Ravished by Beauty: The Surprising Legacy of Reformed Spirituality* (Oxford University Press, 2011). Tom Schwanda explores the contemplative and mystical piety of Bavinck in "Soul Recreation: Spiritual Marriage and Ravishment in the Contemplative-Mystical Piety of Isaac Ambrose" (PhD diss., Durham University, 2009), 283-99, http://etheses.dur.ac.uk/55/. Indeed, it is remarkable that Bavinck—with a measure of continuity with the monastic tradition—devotes significant attention to meditative and contemplative practices as remedies for the pathologies of the Christian life; see *Reformed Ethics*, 1:415-93.

41. Balthasar, *Prayer*, 48 (emphasis added).

experience. In this connection, a forensic understanding of the atonement possesses explanatory power in relation to what happens *in foro conscientiae* and to the way in which there begins and continues a progressive renovation of the conscience through a repeated subjective experience of justification, adoption, and sanctification that, in turn, prompts the believer to live for God's glory. And since—again in the words of Balthasar—"there is in principle no need for any special way or effort to rise from nature to supernature,"[42] this experiential transformation of conscience fits very well with the notion of a change that occurs in an affective way. This change results in a cognitive transformation of feelings of overwhelming guilt, crippling shame, devouring fear, and the urge to hide that culminates in experiential *parrēsía*. This gift, bestowed to the human conscience, confers instead a trusting openness and secure confidence before God and other human beings.

However, as Calvin and Owen pointed out so well, conscience must struggle with the problem of indwelling sin to the very end. In this life, the battle is never won. Therefore, it is time now to turn to the blessed hope of a perfected conscience in the consummated new creation.

---

42. Balthasar, *Prayer*, 45.

10

THE PERFECTING OF CONSCIENCE

Up to this point, conscience has been presented not simply as a capacity for moral judgments but especially in aesthetical terms of perception and awareness (*sensus*) for perceiving the divine.[1] Following this trajectory, the perfected conscience will be explained in terms of heightened awareness.

According to Thiselton, glorified humanity will be characterized by three key features:

> (1) First, *Christ's* own sufferings, death, and resurrection will permeate everything. They will provide the lens through which everything else is seen. ... (2) Secondly, the "spiritual body," or mode of existence after resurrection, as marked by the character and action of the Holy Spirit, will *embrace* our experience of God to a degree hitherto unimaginable. (3) Third, just as prayer on earth was *by* the Holy Spirit, *through* Jesus Christ the Son, *to* God the Father (Rom. 8:26-27), this *Trinitarian* process will move from faith to sight, and we shall participate in it with heightened awareness.[2]

This brief closing chapter will consider each of these features of glorified humanity with specific attention to the conscience, albeit in a slightly different order.[3] It will analyze, first, the notion of heightened awareness, then proceed, second, to look at perfected conscience as Christic—that is, through a christological lens—and conclude by contemplating the Trinitarian dimension of conscience's eschatological transformation.

---

[1]. Commenting on the affective nature of the *sensus* in Calvin, Helm points out that this aspect of Calvin's epistemology "is perhaps closer to the aesthetic and moral appreciation of a work of art than it is to the sort of understanding that operates in natural science" (*John Calvin's Ideas*, 240).

[2]. Thiselton, *The Last Things*, 205-6.

[3]. Space does not allow for an extended analysis of eschatological conscience; therefore, this final part of the theology of conscience can only be developed in outline by way of suggestion.

PERFECTED CONSCIENCE AS HEIGHTENED AWARENESS

Conceiving of conscience as *sensus*—that is, as a capacity for nonphysical perception and awareness—leads to it being brought to perfection in terms of the complete purification and perfect actualization of such a capacity. The renewal of the *sensus divinitatis* and the restoration of spiritual delight will be made whole in glorification, and the human person will experience an unfettered awareness of God's very presence. Thiselton's reference to "heightened awareness" is helpful in describing the eschatological transformation of conscience: conscience will experience a "perfected awareness" because the eschatological *sensus* will be without spot or wrinkle or any such thing and will instead be completely holy (see Eph 5:27). It will be the same human conscience and not something added to human nature. However, heavenly conscience will surpass by far—to a degree thus far unimaginable—conscience as experienced on earth. Theissen uses the expression "expansion of consciousness" in speaking of the cognitive reconstruction of the inner person that takes place eschatologically:

> In 1 Cor. 15:44-45, Paul stresses that the pneumatic is to be understood as a goal, not as origin—that is, the pneumatic human being is not the primeval one of Genesis 1-2 but rather Christ, the new man. ... If the conferral of the Pneuma signifies *an expansion of consciousness beyond the familiar "psychic" limits*, this, according to Paul, is not an expansion of consciousness that points only to the depths of our origin but rather one that points to the future.[4]

These expressions—"perfected awareness," "heightened awareness," and "expansion of consciousness"—should be understood not in a static and fixed sense but as a dynamic and growing experience. These terms refer to the so-called *visio beatifica*, indicating that they have to do with the experience of a transfigured humanity. According to Muller, the *visio Dei* should be understood in terms of "the saints' new perception of God." He writes that the *visio* is "*cognititio Dei clara et intuitiva*, a clear and intuitive knowledge of God, an inward *actus*."[5] Therefore, what changes at the consummation is not that God

---

4. Theissen, *Psychological Aspects of Pauline Theology*, 365 (emphasis added).
5. Muller, *Dictionary of Latin and Greek Theological Terms*, 327.

will relate to human creatures in his essence and consequently produce a change in humanity, but rather the human capacity for awareness of God will be made perfectly able to apprehend God as he reveals himself to human creatures as far as their own glorified but still finite humanity will allow.

This transformed capacity for perceiving God represents a radical departure from the current human predicament within which—to use Calvin's phrasing again—in feeling God human beings feel him not.[6] As things now stand, despite being somewhat aware of God, human awareness not only proves to be inadequate for an unencumbered perception of God but also, because of the fall, paradoxically produces a sense of separation from God. Anselm shares Calvin's frustration, and using the language of the spiritual senses, he articulates the human incapacity for an adequate affective knowledge of God in the present in spite of the experience of redemption:

> Still, O Lord, you are hidden from my soul in your light and happiness, and so it lives in darkness and misery. It *looks* around but it does not see your *beauty*. It *listens*, but it does not hear your *harmony*. It *smells*, but it does not perceive your *fragrance*. It *tastes*, but it does not know your *savor*. It *touches*, but it does not sense your *softness*. For you have these qualities in you, O Lord God, in your own ineffable way; and you have given them in their own perceptible way to the things you created. But *the senses of my soul have been stiffened, dulled, and obstructed by the long-standing weakness of sin*.[7]

Both Calvin's sorrow and Anselm's lament (see Rom 8:18–25) express the Christian longing and anticipation for the time when the "the spirits of the righteous [will be] made perfect" (Heb 12:23). Pointing to the innermost selves of people, the word "spirits" in this verse encompasses all human inward capacities and dispositions, including conscience (as suggested in the previous exegesis of Rom 8:15–16). In Christ, humanity after the eschaton will in this perfection experience through the Spirit an awareness of and delight in God that are characterized by a perfectly clear, free, and confident conscience. The fullness of human life in the new creation will dispel any deficiency in

---

6. See Calvin, *Calvin's Commentaries*, 19:167.

7. Anselm of Canterbury, *Proslogion with the Replies of Gaunilo and Anselm* (Hackett, 2001), 17 (emphasis added).

and inconsistency between our *cognitio Dei* and our *amor Dei*, so that glorified conscience will experience a perfect *fruitio* (enjoyment, delight) *Dei*.

In commenting on Hebrews 12:23, Owen considers the future perfection of the human mind in the presence of God:

> Our minds, *in their essential powers and faculties*, shall be enabled *to comprehend and acquiesce* in this glory of Christ. ... This is vision or sight. Here we walk by faith; there, by sight. And *this sight is not an external aid*, like a glass helping the weakness of the visive faculty to see things afar off; but *it is an internal power, or an act of the internal power of our minds*, wherewith they are endowed in a glorified state. Hereby we shall be able to "see him face to face,—to see him as he is," in a direct comprehension of his glory. ... Hereunto the whole glory of Christ is clear, perspicuous, and evident; which will give us eternal acquiescency therein.[8]

Even though Owen mentions human powers in a general way, his reference to a perfected acquiescence implicitly points to the full delight and uncontaminated compliance of our conscience, which will be completely delivered from the afflictive sense of guilt, fear, and shame, and from the consequent impulse to hide. Having been perfectly transfigured, conscience will possess an awareness that does not lack transparency and innocence and be able to acquiesce joyfully to the glory of God.

Integrating the experiences of *cognitio Dei* and *amor Dei* that flow into the realization of a perfect *fruitio Dei*, Turretin speaks of the perfecting of the delight of conscience:

> In order to understand more fully that most blissful state, we think the three things are to be united which inseparably cohere with each other in happiness: sight, love, joy. From these effloresces that ineffable glory with which the blessed will shine for ever on account of their fruition of the supreme good. For as that happiness is the full and ultimate perfection of the soul and all its faculties, so it requires the operation of all the powers, every imperfection having been removed (i.e., perfect vision, and from it supreme joy and consolation). Sight

---

8. Owen, *The Works of John Owen*, 1:406-7 (emphasis added).

contemplates God as the supreme good; love is carried out towards him, and is most closely united with him; and joy enjoys and acquiesces in him. Sight perfects the intellect, love the will, joy the conscience.[9]

For both Owen and Turretin, the final transfiguration of conscience consists in the experience of a perfected sense of delight and acquiescence in God.

In the previous chapter, *parrēsía* was described as a gift of grace that—along with justification, adoption, and sanctification—reverses conscience's fallen orientation, and it was observed that before glorification the experience of *parrēsía* is related to a good conscience (see 1 John 3:20-21). However, *parrēsía* is only a partial experience in the present. At the eschaton, in the consummated new creation, *parrēsía* will be a completed condition that Christians will enjoy perfectly. In this respect, 1 John 2:28 relates the perfect *parrēsía* that will be subjectively received by believers when Christ returns to the problem of shame, which is one of the ongoing miseries experienced even by redeemed conscience. In the day of judgment, Christians will have a full *parrēsía*—that is, a perfect freedom, confidence, and openness of conscience in Christ (see 1 John 4:17). At that point, as indicated by Owen and Turretin, the spirits of the righteous will be made perfect in relation to their conscience because they will be enabled to experience a perfected sense of delight and acquiescence in God such that conscience, being perfectly and generously aware of God, will not be afflicted by any impulse to recoil and withdraw from God's presence.[10]

---

9. Francis Turretin, *Institutes of Elenctic Theology* (P&R Publishing, 1997), 3:609.

10. Recalling what was discussed earlier regarding conscience cooperating with other human capacities, this heightened awareness of perfected conscience should not be emphasized to the point of overlooking the participation of all of humanity in the event of glorification: the emotions, body, reason, will, and language will all be at once perfected along with conscience so that the fullness of the human creature, the total person, is glorified and all faculties will interact and cooperate together without any hindrance so as to make possible pure human communion with God. For an extended exegetical analysis of humanity's resurrection life in the Spirit in its totality, see Thiselton, *The First Epistle to the Corinthians*, 1275-92.

PERFECTED CONSCIENCE AS CHRISTIC CONSCIENCE

The definitive transformation of conscience described in the previous section will be determined through union with the humanity of Jesus Christ as God's true image: as Christ has been resurrected and glorified so also will be those who are one with him (see 1 Cor 6:17; Rom 8:17). This christological focus is important for considering the perfection of conscience, as Webster highlights:

> Conscience is thus eschatological, oriented to that which I have been made through Christ and which, through the power of the Holy Spirit, I am becoming. ... The perfection and unconditional character of conscience has nothing to do with the inviolability of my ethical ego, and everything to do with the fact that, in conscience, I am accosted by the call of the future secured for me in Christ and held out to me as the only future in which I can be who I am.[11]

As argued previously, the justice, sonship, and holiness of Christ—as well as the Son's own *parrēsía*—are the realities that determine the subjective reversal of conscience's fallen orientation, experienced partially now in redemption and perfectly to come in consummation.[12] The image of the righteous and holy Son of God shapes the perfected awareness of those who have been united to him and conformed to his image. At the last, the subjectivity of redeemed humanity will correspond to the subjectivity of the second Adam. Having been conformed to Christ's own *sensus*, conscience will experience a new and fully transformed perception and awareness—a perfect *fruitio*—in relation to God. Indeed, if union with Christ in his justice, sonship, and holiness begins a transformation of human subjectivity in the present, in its vale of tears, the perfect awareness of union with him in glory will complete the transformation of the human *sensus divinitatis* and *sensus iudicii*.

Recalling the notion of covenantal vocation, Vos makes the following observations concerning the last Adam:

> *Jesus most assuredly had a vocational consciousness of self.* ... The Messianic consciousness is of a peculiarly unifying and comprehensive character. It might in this respect be compared to a single-track

---

11. Webster, "God and Conscience," 259.
12. See the discussion above on the justification and sanctification of conscience.

mind. All else entering into it is inevitably held in subordination and subservience to its one regnant purpose. It straightway assumes dominance in the mental world wherein it has once found lodgement.[13]

It should be noted once more—this time in relation to the last Adam—that this vocational awareness is not restricted merely to ethical consciousness or related only to the moral duty of obedience to a law (whether natural or revealed), even as it is true that the consciousness of Christ "harboured in itself the strong, acute *sense* of that responsibility to the divine will which was the noblest fruit of the Old Testament religion."[14] Instead, before being a *sensus iudicii*, the consciousness of Jesus is first and foremost a deepest and purest *sensus divinitatis*. Moreover, this *sensus* is not simply focused on the present, but rather, as Vos insists, it has an eschatological character:

> Jesus being consciously the Messiah, his whole manner of thinking and feeling could not be otherwise than steeped in ... an atmosphere in which the currents of air from this world and from the world to come constantly intermingled, with the stronger steady blowing towards the future.[15]

This objective orientation of the consciousness of Jesus toward the heavenly kingdom and perfect communion with God (see John 1:1–3; 16:28; 17:1–5) aligns with a corresponding subjective experience. Vos explains:

> The religious states of mind have in their subjective aspect no separate existence of their own, but entwine themselves around the outward acts of God, to which they are a response and by which they are cultivated in continuance. The subjective is nowhere lacking. ... But it always keeps in the closest touch with what God has done outside the subjectivity.[16]

As the consciousness of believers after the resurrection will be in the image of the covenantal awareness of the Lord Jesus, the saints too will enjoy

---

13. Geerhardus Vos, *The Self-Disclosure of Jesus: The Modern Debate about the Messianic Consciousness* (George H. Doran Company, 1926), 13 (emphasis added).
14. Vos, *The Self-Disclosure of Jesus*, 16 (emphasis added).
15. Vos, *The Self-Disclosure of Jesus*, 19.
16. Vos, *The Self-Disclosure of Jesus*, 19.

a full and perfect *parrēsía* of conscience before the Father—in the Son and by the Spirit. The *parrēsía* of the Son will become finally the *parrēsía* of the sons and daughters (see Eph 3:12). In this sense, redeemed conscience will be perfected in human creatures in being brought to be like the conscience of the person of Christ, our "older brother."[17]

PERFECTED CONSCIENCE AS SHARING IN THE TRINITARIAN LIFE

Lastly, the perfected union and identification between the person of Christ and redeemed humanity will fully engage human consciousness in the Trinitarian life of God. This theology of conscience has proposed that what ultimately determines the nature of conscience is the essential life of the triune God. Thus understood, conscience is not merely the competence to form moral judgments; it is particularly a capacity for responsiveness to divine alterity and its implicit call to reciprocity, determined by the consciousness of the presence of the divine other and his prerogatives. Coming from God and reaching back to the reality of the Trinitarian communion of the divine persons, conscience, at the final consummation, will be brought entirely back to God and enter into a perfect reciprocal relationship with the divine persons. This is not an essential fellowship of any kind. However, it is a mode of participation in the divine life that remains within the limits of the finite nature of human creatures and that corresponds in a finite way to the fellowship between the persons of the Trinity. In this sense, the *imago Dei* revealed as *imago Christi* will be discovered to be nothing less than a human *imago Trinitatis*.

Owen is emphatic in asserting that redeemed humanity *already* has communion *distinctly* with God the Father, God the Son, and God the Holy Spirit in this present age. This "communion," writes Owen, "is the mutual communication of such good things as wherein the persons holding that communion are delighted, bottomed upon some union between them." Our communion with God, he continues, "consisteth in his *communication of himself unto us, with our returnal unto him* of that which he requireth and accepteth, flowing

---

17. As will be briefly stated in the conclusion, space does not allow for a deeper reflection here on the ways in which the experience of a perfected conscience will be brought to the likeness of Christ's experience of conscience in his humanity.

from that *union* which in Jesus Christ we have with him." This communion is *"initial and incomplete,* in the firstfruits and dawnings of that perfection which we have here in grace," but also *"perfect and complete,* in the full fruition of his glory and total giving up of ourselves to him, resting in him as our utmost end; which we shall enjoy when we see him as he is."[18] Although in his treatise Owen explores in detail only the initial and incomplete communion with the triune God in this present life, he clearly alludes to the distinct Trinitarian dimension of this participation in the communion of the triune God.

Horton, drawing on the work of Walter J. Ong, suggests in this connection that a special emphasis should be placed on the verbal nature of this communion, which derives from the communicative dynamism of Trinitarian coinherence itself.[19] Ong himself observes:

> An oral-aural theology of revelation through the Word of God would entail an oral-aural theology of the Trinity, which could explicate the "intersubjectivity" of the three Persons in terms of communication conceived of as focused (analogously) in a world of sound rather than in a world of space and light. ... The communication of the Persons with one another is typically treated in terms of *circumcessio,* a "sitting-around-in." ... This latter is patently a concept based on a visual analogy with strong tactile and kinesthetic components. These concepts ... have profoundly aided understanding and should certainly be respected, *but their awkwardness shows the strain under which visual analogies must operate when one is speaking of conscious awareness or of presence as such.*[20]

Following Ong's trajectory of thought, it seems that verbal and auditory analogies may operate more naturally in relation to conscious awareness and presence of otherness.[21] His observations—especially his connection

---

18. Owen, *The Works of John Owen,* 2:8–9. For a contemporary perspective on the Christian life as existence in the Trinity, see Daniel A. Keating, "Trinity and Salvation: Christian Life as an Existence in the Trinity," in Gilles and Levering, *The Oxford Handbook of the Trinity,* 442–53.

19. Horton, *Covenant and Salvation,* 303–4.

20. Walter J. Ong, S. J., *The Presence of the Word: Some Prolegomena for Cultural and Religious History* (Yale University Press, 1967), 180–81 (emphasis added).

21. For more reflection on these matters, see Horton, *The Christian Faith,* 80–94.

between an oral-aural Trinitarian theology and conscious awareness and presence—fit well with what has been noted above concerning conscience interacting with and exhibiting itself in linguistic form and particularly well with the point that conscience becomes a voice (that is, a human response to a call coming from another). A substantial benefit of a conscious awareness that is intrinsically verbal and auditory is that it provides a Trinitarian theology both free in principle from abstractness and speculation and fundamentally experiential and participatory. The verbal and auditory world of sound appears to be more conducive to intersubjectivity, while the intellectual act of theorizing, contemplating, gazing, and comprehending is prone to remaining more private, autonomous, and self-enclosed. The reality of conscience as a spontaneous and insuppressible voice of response to a call coming from another compels one to be confronted and to confront the divine as well as the human other.

More specifically, the ectypal linguistic awareness of perfected conscience is an image—however distant—of the archetypal intra-Trinitarian dialogical life shared by the divine persons. Vern Poythress refers to this intra-Trinitarian linguistic dynamism as follows:

> The New Testament indicates that the persons of the trinity speak to one another. ... Not only is God a member of a language community that includes human beings, but the persons of the Trinity function as members of a language community among themselves. Language does not have as its sole purpose human-human communication, or even divine-human communication, but also divine-divine communication.[22]

This communicative reality of the life of the immanent Trinity and of the dialogical reciprocity of the divine persons seems to support the dialogical model of conscience advanced here.[23] Such a model of conscience is reflected

---

22. Vern S. Poythress, *In the Beginning Was the Word: Language, A God-Centered Approach* (Crossway, 2009), 18; see also Vern S. Poythress, *The Mystery of the Trinity: A Trinitarian Approach to the Attributes of God* (P&R Publishing, 2020), 103–25.

23. This perspective on the archetypal intra-Trinitarian dialogical life is shared by some Roman Catholic theologians, such as Romano Guardini and Hans Urs von Balthasar, who have been influenced by Christian philosophers, such as Ferdinand Ebner, and Jewish thinkers, such as Martin Buber; see also Silvano Zucal, "Filosofia dialogica e dottrina trinitaria," in *Elaborare*

in the dialogical character of biblical revelation that, through the words and acts of God, calls the human creature to respond to that call.[24]

SUMMARY

In the new creation perfected conscience will be experienced as an expansion of consciousness, transcending the psychic and spiritual limitations known in the present life, even though human creatures will not transcend their humanity. Rather, conscience will have been brought in conformity to the subjectivity of the last Adam, Jesus Christ, so that it is enabled to participate in the life of the triune God with full awareness, bringing human creatures to the amazed and glorious acknowledgment of the inexhaustible fountain of every good who is the triune God himself.

---

l'esperienza di Dio: Atti del convegno "La Trinità," May 2009, https://mondodomani.org/teologia/zucal2011.htm.

24. See Kevin J. Vanhoozer, "Word of God," in *Dictionary for Theological Interpretation of the Bible*, ed. Kevin J. Vanhoozer et al. (Baker Books, 2005), 850–54.

CONCLUSION

This work has sought to develop a theology of conscience following a redemptive trajectory, focusing on the creation, the fall, the redemption, and the perfection of conscience. All of this was constantly referred to theology proper and the consequential theological anthropology flowing from it. This conclusion offers a brief summary of the argument it has presented and an indication of further avenues for possible research.

The principal aim of this study has been to engage in a theological renovation of conscience, explaining it in relation to God and within the drama of salvation, as was originally proposed by Webster.[1] From the biblical data of Scripture, a theological explanation of conscience was offered, constructed upon a Trinitarian foundation and within the framework of a covenantal superstructure. As a result, conscience was not primarily analyzed phenomenologically, in itself, but in the context of the witness of Scripture, as coming from and being subordinated to God. Particular attention was paid to the Old Testament, for in considering existing literature, it was found that the presence of conscience in the Old Testament is usually treated briefly and superficially. Starting the investigation with the Old Testament raised the matter of conscience's creation, which led to finding in Scripture evidence of its presence before the fall. As an external work of God, created conscience was also explained as arising in some manner "from and correspond[ing] to his [God's] inner life."[2] That consideration stimulated a theological explanation of the function and nature of conscience in terms of covenant, especially in relation to the reality of God's own Trinitarian existence.

In the course of the theological analysis of fallen and redeemed conscience, what emerged was the inward and subjective significance of conscience. As this inward and subjective phenomenon, conscience was explained in light

---

1. See Webster, "God and Conscience," 233, 57.
2. Webster, "Life in and of Himself," 23.

of Calvin's *sensus divinitatis* and *sensus iudicii* and interpreted as a nonphysical perceptual awareness operating concurrently with other human capacities. More precisely, it was proposed that human creatures experience conscience as a subjective and immediate covenantal perception and awareness of God in relation to his calling of humanity. The subjective significance of conscience became particularly relevant in the discussion of justification in which, while the notion of infusion was rejected, it was affirmed that the realization of *iustificatio subjectiva* in *foro conscientiae* offers a plausible way to see the subjective potential of the doctrine of forensic justification. Besides the resultant subjective effects of justification, attention was devoted to the renovation of conscience as an evaluative and aesthetical reversal of the corruption of the *sensus* by the experiential reception and gradual realization of adoption and sanctification along with the experiential grace of *parrēsía*. Finally, the spiritual transformation and perfection of conscience that will take place at the consummation in the new creation was explored.

In suggesting further research possibilities that arise from this theology of conscience, three areas for future study might be noted—biblical, theological, and pastoral.

First, there is a need for further research in biblical studies. Although this book offered substantial exegetical material to demonstrate the reality and the presence of conscience throughout the Scriptures, especially in the Old Testament, a more comprehensive and integrated biblical theology of conscience might still be developed. In this regard, the usually atomized and fragmented results of biblical exegesis related to conscience could be brought together in a full phenomenological analysis based on biblical evidence. Such an exegetical endeavor would require one to address the particular passages that speak explicitly about conscience as well as excavate its concealed presence within different literary genres, under various metaphorical expressions, and its impact upon human experiences.

Second, there are a series of theological topics reflecting upon conscience that are worthy of further research. Perhaps the three most important are creation, covenant, and the Trinity. In terms of conscience and creation, this work has observed that conscience is usually considered in relation to sin and salvation.[3] However, Webster's proposal that "conscience is … the amazed

---

3. This is evidenced, for example, in Stoker's phenomenological exploration of conscience, in which he thinks of conscience especially as a guilty conscience and as showing its presence in

acknowledgment of moral and theological truth"[4] might be brought into closer conversation with the doctrine of creation *ex nihilo*. This would involve recognizing that conscience also refers to the amazed acknowledgment of truth prior to and apart from the experience of sin and personal evil. After all, if conscience will be perfected in the new creation, this means that conscience—as expanded and free awareness—can be experienced apart from evil and personal sin (being Christ without sin, a christological investigation of Christ's experience of conscience in his humanity would be welcome, as it appears to be a topic that is not treated with any depth). In respect to conscience and covenant, the phenomenon of conscience deserves a more comprehensive anthropology in relation to both the covenant of works and the covenant of grace. As this work explained, especially in discussing redeemed conscience, the covenantal history of redemption is closely integrated with the experience of conscience through the realities of law and gospel. Further attention to these aspects of the covenant would lead to a deeper theological understanding of conscience. Most importantly, in respect to conscience and the Trinity, future research might explore the relationships between theological anthropology and divine being in order to generate further insights on human conscience that do not enclose its phenomenology simply within ethical boundaries. In particular, the conscious and communicative reciprocal awareness that exists among the divine persons resonates profoundly with Calvin's notion of the human conscience as *sensus*, a capacity given to human creatures that allows for much more than simply forming moral judgments but indicates the ongoing nature of personal communication.

Finally, in relation to ecclesiology and pastoral theology a retrieval of an appropriately biblical and covenantal understanding of conscience may bear promise for dealing with the perennial psychological and spiritual maladies that afflict human beings, as well as with the spiritual formation of conscience. In pastoral practice the strict relation between conscience and the afflictive experiences of guilt, fear, shame, and hiddenness suggests that the traditional ways of addressing these disrupting states that are offered

---

generating isolation, alienation, shame, remorse, fear, and anger toward oneself. The conclusion of Stoker is that "genuine phenomena of conscience are such moral and religious phenomena as exhibit an experience of a real personal relationship to evil, or, more concisely, *genuine conscience is the real inner revelation of personal evil*" (*Conscience: Phenomena and Theories*, 228).

4. Webster, "God and Conscience," 254–55.

by Christian wisdom cannot be discarded as psychologically irrelevant and obsolete. Furthermore, the notion of conscience as *sensus*—that is, as spontaneous nonphysical perceptual awareness rather than as a rational facet of practical reason—might be of assistance in approaching people with mental limitations and disabilities, for even though the intellect and the will might be impaired, the more immediate subjective awareness of the *sensus* still opens a door for communion with God.[5] Meanwhile in Christian education, a realization of the uniqueness and the function of the role of conscience is a great encouragement for the Christian preacher and the Christian teacher as conscience guarantees them that in some way their labors are never in vain. As an indestructible bridge between God and humanity, conscience is an ever-present point of contact that in spite of sin and evil cannot be completely silenced.[6] In respect of preaching and teaching, the covenantal and Trinitarian approach to conscience developed here could be deepened and refined by exploring the relationships between conscience, habits of language, and the theology of sound.[7] These avenues (and others as well) for possible research will certainly contribute to the needed "repair work ... to accomplish the theological renovation of conscience."[8]

TEN THESES ON CONSCIENCE

In concluding this investigation of human conscience, several fundamental truths should be kept in mind. These truths have authority for the church and for professing Christians today. Today, we need a trustworthy account of the nature and function of human conscience, an account which is not founded on the changing opinions of mortals but founded on the immortal

---

[5]. On the remarkable spontaneous responsiveness of mentally disabled people, see Jean Vanier, *Our Life Together* (HarperCollins, 2007); Frances Young, *Arthur's Call: A Journey of Faith in the Face of Severe Learning Disability* (SPCK, 2014); Young, *God's Presence: A Contemporary Recapitulation of Early Christianity* (Cambridge University Press, 2013), 92–201; Amos Yong, *Theology and Down Syndrome: Reimagining Disability in Late Modernity* (Baylor University Press, 2007). For a more general introduction to the subject, see Brian Brock and John Swinton, eds., *Disability in the Christian Tradition: A Reader* (Eerdmans, 2012).

[6]. See Stoker, *Conscience: Phenomena and Theories*, 16–64.

[7]. See Rowan Williams, *The Edge of Words: God and the Habits of Language* (Bloomsbury, 2012); Stephen H. Webb, *The Divine Voice: Christian Proclamation and the Theology of Sound* (Brazos Press, 2004).

[8]. Webster, "God and Conscience," 233.

witness of the Word of God. Therefore, the following affirmations are to be pondered in our hearts.

1. The whole Bible attests to the reality of conscience from the very beginning.

2. Theological and pastoral reflection should locate any discourse on conscience primarily in the context of the doctrine of creation and only secondarily as related to the doctrine of sin and salvation.

3. Human conscience is best understood in light of the immanent life of the triune God who should not be investigated only in strictly moral terms.

4. Conscience should be regarded as a nonphysical perceptual awareness according to Calvin's notion of *sensus divinitatis*.

5. Because human conscience is fallen and affected by the corruption of sin, it cannot be trusted as the authoritative and ultimate spiritual and moral guide of human beings.

6. The Spirit prepares conscience for a spiritual renewal by the word working in conviction and illumination.

7. Although conscience may be convicted by the law and illuminated by the gospel, that is not enough; to be redeemed, conscience needs to be regenerated and made alive.

8. Since in regeneration conscience is renewed in its capacity for spiritual delight, the benefits of justification and adoption are experienced by conscience in an affective way.

9. The affective impact of justification and adoption has a major role in the sanctification of conscience.

10. Glorified humanity will experience a perfected conscience that will share in Christ's own sinless conscience through the power of the Spirit.

TEN THESES ON CONSCIENCE EXPLAINED

1. THE WHOLE BIBLE ATTESTS TO THE REALITY OF CONSCIENCE FROM THE VERY BEGINNING.

The presence of conscience is pervasive in the whole of Scripture, from beginning to end. The fact that the Hebrew language does not have a term corresponding either to συνείδησις or *conscientia* does not justify the assertion that the notion of conscience originated in Greco-Roman culture. The lack of certain words in Scripture does not imply that a specific reality or concept—such as conscience—is anachronistically read back into earlier literature, having been derived from a later usage originating in different cultures and languages.

2. THEOLOGICAL AND PASTORAL REFLECTION SHOULD LOCATE ANY DISCOURSE ON CONSCIENCE PRIMARILY IN THE CONTEXT OF THE DOCTRINE OF CREATION AND ONLY SECONDARILY AS RELATED TO THE DOCTRINE OF SIN AND SALVATION.

God created human beings with a conscience capable of witnessing, legislating, and summoning positively and negatively. In creation, conscience was bestowed on human beings as positive and indicative of theological and moral truth, even though potentially it could operate as a negative awareness in relation to obligation and condemnation. Instead of being limited to the negative role of conscience, theological and pastoral reflection also should develop the positive capacities of conscience in order to give full significance to its essential and immutable mediating character in the relation between the triune God and human creatures. The significance of a positive approach to conscience is made even more clear by the fact that the Lord Jesus was without sin and unaffected by the fall and yet his conscience was active and functioning.

3. HUMAN CONSCIENCE IS BEST UNDERSTOOD IN LIGHT OF THE IMMANENT LIFE OF THE TRIUNE GOD WHO SHOULD NOT BE INVESTIGATED ONLY IN STRICTLY MORAL TERMS.

By the triune God calling creation into being through the medium of his covenant-generating word, conscience has been formed in such a way as to be a covenantal awareness—that is, a perception that makes the human person capable of responding to God's covenantal vocation. Scripture approaches anthropology from the perspective of vocation in order to place human beings before their life's calling in a comprehensive manner, and conscience is a hearing and an answer in which the human person attends to God's calling. However, if in creation from himself the triune God gives himself, then conscience as covenantal awareness and vocational perception reflects in some manner God's inner life. In fact, the reality of the *imago Dei* defines the identity of human creatures so that it could be said that the identity of human beings is ontologically derivative of the essential inner identity of the triune God.

4. CONSCIENCE SHOULD BE REGARDED AS A NONPHYSICAL PERCEPTUAL AWARENESS ACCORDING TO CALVIN'S NOTION OF *SENSUS DIVINITATIS*.

Conscience operates in cooperation and concurrence with other human capacities in the form of a basic awareness that is cognitive in nature. The fact that the operations of conscience are not isolated from those of other human capacities shows that there is no human faculty that in itself can be considered in a special way to actualize the *imago Dei*. Moreover, before being moral, the cognitive perceptions of conscience are religious—that is, God-oriented—because the covenant relation to God is central to what it means to be human. This understanding reflects Calvin's notion of conscience as a *sensus* producing an awareness of God, his will, and his judgments in contrast with other intellectualistic or voluntaristic conceptions of conscience. As a consequence of his radical belief about the noetic effects of sin, Calvin's view of conscience as *sensus* precludes the human person from any measure of autonomy in the realms of religion and morality.

5. BECAUSE HUMAN CONSCIENCE IS FALLEN AND AFFECTED BY THE CORRUPTION OF SIN, IT CANNOT BE TRUSTED AS THE AUTHORITATIVE AND ULTIMATE SPIRITUAL AND MORAL GUIDE OF HUMAN BEINGS.

Because of sin and its corruption, our conscience—as the whole of our humanity—has been depraved from its original state of integrity, becoming ineffectual in delivering a trustworthy self-knowledge and being an accomplice in our manipulative self-deception through which we persuade ourselves of the false goodness of that which is not God (i.e., what is true, righteous, and beautiful). Since usually the concept of the noetic effects of sin is not applied to conscience in a substantial manner, theological reflection has tended to view conscience in too optimistic terms. Therefore, even though conscience—as the other human capabilities and faculties—did not completely cease to function, it lost its capacity and sensitivity to the extent that it cannot be effective in its proper office in relation to God.

6. THE SPIRIT PREPARES CONSCIENCE FOR A SPIRITUAL RENEWAL BY THE WORD WORKING IN CONVICTION AND ILLUMINATION.

The distinction between conviction and illumination indicates that conscience—besides being convicted of what it already, in some ongoing and limited sense and in spite of the fall, knows by nature (namely, the covenant of works or the law)—receives in redemption additional gospel light, or a new awareness beyond what it can perceive and agree with naturally (namely, the covenant of grace). And because of its relation to this evangelical illumination, the convicting application of the law needs similarly to be conceived of as spiritual, supernatural, and special, not so much to go above and beyond the natural operations of conscience but rather because of the need to address the fallenness of the sinner and the sinner's need for grace, pardon, and justification. In other words, saving or redeeming conviction is different from the operations of natural conscience in that is wholly a divine work, a spiritual work that only the Spirit can accomplish by relating it through illumination to the message concerning the person and mission of Jesus Christ.

7. ALTHOUGH CONSCIENCE MAY BE CONVICTED BY THE LAW AND ILLUMINATED BY THE GOSPEL, THAT IS NOT ENOUGH; TO BE REDEEMED, CONSCIENCE NEEDS TO BE REGENERATED AND MADE ALIVE.

Regeneration consists in the restoration of created nature—that is, in the renovation and repair of all those powers and activities in which it consists. Therefore, in regeneration it is the same created and fallen conscience that is made alive by the Spirit through the word, not the infusion of an additional ability that bypasses natural and fallen human capacities. More specifically, in regeneration it is conscience as *sensus* that is renewed, and this divine work reactivates the human capacity for truthful perception. The experience of regeneration does not respond only to the problems of the darkness of the mind and/or the bondage of the will and therefore does not engender only new thoughts and desires, but it is also a reorienting of the evaluative powers of the human creature. This reorientation results in a renewed capacity of the *sensus* for spiritual delight or affective cognition.

8. SINCE IN REGENERATION CONSCIENCE IS RENEWED IN ITS CAPACITY FOR SPIRITUAL DELIGHT, THE BENEFITS OF JUSTIFICATION AND ADOPTION ARE EXPERIENCED BY CONSCIENCE IN AN AFFECTIVE WAY.

The experiential grasping of justification is nourishment for piety toward God because justification is not a declaration that God pronounces to himself but in the human consciousness. This dialogical dimension of justification shows that even if the imputation of Christ's perfect obedience and righteousness is objective, extrinsic, forensic, and non-transformative, it is also experienced inwardly and subjectively as an affective perception and delightful recognition on the part of believers in the conscience. These experiential effects are even more apparent in the case of adoption. Adoption deepens, intensifies, and develops the affective experience of the redemption of conscience that began with the subjective reception of justification.

9. THE AFFECTIVE IMPACT OF JUSTIFICATION AND ADOPTION HAS A MAJOR ROLE IN THE SANCTIFICATION OF CONSCIENCE.

The sanctification of conscience is an affective transformation resulting from a perceptual reversal or reconfiguration due to the experiential realities of justification and adoption. It is in this way that the Father reorders human life by subduing the feeling of guilt through justification in the Son and pacifying creaturely shame through the Spirit of adoption. As a consequence of this divine activity, there also is a progressive calming of fear and an increasing abandonment of hiddenness in the human person. Thus, in the sanctification of conscience the afflictive emotions engendered by the fall are reversed and progressively become their opposite through the gradual renewal of the *sensus divinitatis* and the ongoing restoration of spiritual delight.

10. GLORIFIED HUMANITY WILL EXPERIENCE A PERFECTED CONSCIENCE THAT WILL SHARE IN CHRIST'S OWN SINLESS CONSCIENCE THROUGH THE POWER OF THE SPIRIT.

The renewal of conscience (the *sensus divinitatis*) and the restoration of spiritual delight will be made whole in glorification so that the human person will experience an unfettered awareness of God's very presence and a perfected sense of delight and acquiescence in God. A perfected conscience will reflect Christ's conscience, because Christ's humanity—which includes his conscience—is determinative of perfected humanity. In other words, the conscience of the first Adam will be transfigured according to the conscience of the last Adam. As a result, the perfected union and identification between the person of Christ and redeemed humanity will fully engage human consciousness in the Trinitarian life of God from which it derived its origin.

BIBLIOGRAPHY

Abraham, William J. "Analytical Philosophers of Religion." In Gravilyuk and Coakley, *The Spiritual Senses*.

Adams, Nicholas, George Pattison, and Graham Ward, eds. *The Oxford Handbook of Theology and Modern European Thought*. Oxford University Press, 2013.

Aland, Barbara, Kurt Aland, Johannes Karavidopoulos, Carlo M. Martini, and Bruce M. Metzger, eds. *The Greek New Testament*. Deutsche Bibelgesellschaft, 2001.

Alexander, Archibald. *Outlines of Moral Science*. Charles Scribner, 1854.

Allen, Michael, ed. *Theological Commentary: Evangelical Perspectives*. T&T Clark, 2011.

———. "Toward Theological Theology: Tracing the Methodological Principles of John Webster." *Themelios* 41, no. 2 (2016): 217-37.

———. "Toward Theological Anthropology: Tracing the Anthropological Principles of John Webster." *International Journal of Systematic Theology* 19, no. 1 (2017): 6-29.

———. "Reason." In Allen and Swain, *A Companion to the Theology of John Webster*.

Allen, Michael and R. David Nelson, eds. *A Companion to the Theology of John Webster*. Eerdmans, 2021.

Allen, Michael and Scott R. Swain. *Reformed Catholicity: The Promise of Retrieval for Theology and Biblical Interpretation*. Baker Academic, 2015.

———, eds. *Christian Dogmatics: Reformed Theology for the Church Catholic*. Baker Academic, 2016.

———. "Obedience of the Eternal Son." *International Journal of Systematic Theology* 15, no. 2 (2013): 114-34.

Alston, William P. *Perceiving God: The Epistemology of Religious Experience*. Cornell University Press, 1991.

Alter, Robert. *Ancient Israel—The Former Prophets: Joshua, Judges, Kings, Samuel, and Kings—A Translation with Commentary.* W. W. Norton, 2013.

———. *The Book of Psalms: A Translation with Commentary.* W. W. Norton, 2007.

Anselm of Canterbury. *Proslogion with the Replies of Gaunilo and Anselm.* Hackett, 2001.

Aquinas, Thomas. *Summa Theologica.* Translated by the Fathers of the English Dominican Province. Benziger Bros., 1947–1948.

Ash, Christopher. *Discovering the Joy of a Clear Conscience.* P&R Publishing, 2012.

Audi, Robert. *Moral Perception.* Princeton University Press, 2013.

Ayres, Lewis. *Nicaea and Its Legacy: An Approach to Fourth-Century Trinitarian Theology.* Oxford University Press, 2004.

Bach, Kent. "Self-Deception." In McLaughlin, Beckermann, Walter, *The Oxford Handbook of Philosophy of Mind.*

Backus, Irena. "Calvin's Concept of Natural Law and Roman Law." *Calvin Theological Journal* 38 (2003): 7–26.

Badgett, Jonathan P. "Undermining Moral Self-Deception with the Help of Puritan Pastoral Theology." *Journal of Spiritual Formation and Soul Care* 11, no. 1 (2018): 23–38.

Bagnoli, Carla. *Morality and the Emotions.* Oxford University Press, 2011.

Ballor, Jordan J., David S. Sytsma, and Jason Zuidema. *Church and School in Early Modern Protestantism: Studies in Honor of Richard Muller on the Maturation of a Theological Tradition.* Brill, 2013.

Balthasar, Hans Urs von. *Prayer.* Ignatius Press, 1986.

Balthasar, Hans Urs von. *Studies in Theological Style: Lay Styles.* Vol. 3, *The Glory of the Lord.* T&T Clark, 1984.

Balz, Horst and Gerhard Schneider, eds. *Exegetical Dictionary of the New Testament.* 3 vols. Eerdmans, 1990–1993.

Barr, James. *The Semantics of Biblical Language.* Oxford University Press, 1961.

Baschera, Luca. "Ethics in Reformed Orthodoxy." In Selderhuis, *A Companion to Reformed Orthodoxy.*

Bartholomew, Craig G. "A God for Life, and Not Just for Christmas! The Revelation of God in the Old Testament Wisdom Literature." In Helm and Trueman, *The Trustworthiness of God.*

Bauckham, Richard and Carl Mosser, eds. *The Gospel of John and Christian Theology*. Eerdmans, 2008.

Baugh, Steven M. *Ephesians*. Evangelical Exegetical Commentary. Lexham Press, 2016.

Baugus, Bruce P. *The Roots of Reformed Moral Theology: A Study of the Historical Background of an Ecclesial Tradition of Moral Instruction*. Reformation Heritage Books, 2022.

Bavinck, Herman. *Reformed Dogmatics*. 4 vols. Baker Academic, 2003, 2004, 2006, 2008.

———. *Reformed Ethics*. Vol. 1, *Created, Fallen, and Converted Humanity*. Baker Academic, 2019.

———. "Conscience." *Bavinck Review* 6 (2015), https://bavinckinstitute.org/review/tbr6-2015/.

———. "Foundation of Psychology." *Bavinck Review* 9 (2018), https://bavinckinstitute.org/tag/psychology/.

———. *The Philosophy of Revelation*. Baker Books, 1979.

———. *Saved By Grace: The Holy Spirit's Work in Calling and Regeneration*. Reformation Heritage Books, 2008.

Baylor, Michael G. *Action and Person: Conscience in Late Scholasticism and the Young Luther*. Brill, 1977.

Baylor, T. Robert. "He Humbled Himself: Trinity, Covenant, and the Gracious Condescension of the Son in John Owen." In Bird and Harrower, *Trinity without Hierarchy*.

Beach, J. Mark. "The Doctrine of the *Pactum Salutis* in the Covenant Theology of Herman Witsius." *Mid-America Journal of Theology* 13 (2002): 101-42.

Beale, Gregory K. *The Book of Revelation*. Eerdmans, 1999.

———. *The Temple and the Church's Mission: A Biblical Theology of the Dwelling Place of God* InterVarsity Press, 2004.

———. *We Become What We Worship: A Biblical Theology of Idolatry*. InterVarsity Press, 2008.

———. *A New Testament Biblical Theology: The Unfolding of the Old Testament in the New*. Baker Academic, 2011.

———. *Redemptive Reversals and the Ironic Overturning of Human Wisdom*. Crossway, 2019.

Beeke, Joel R. and Mark Jones. *A Puritan Theology: Doctrine for Life.* Reformation Heritage Books, 2012.

Berkhof, Louis. *Systematic Theology.* Banner of Truth, 1958.

Berkouwer, Gerrit C. *Man: The Image of God.* Eerdmans, 1962.

———. *Faith and Sanctification.* Eerdmans, 1952.

———. *Faith and Justification.* Eerdmans, 1954.

Berlin, Adele and Marc Zvi Brettler, eds. *The Jewish Study Bible.* Oxford University Press, 2004.

Billings, J. Todd. "John Calvin's Soteriology: On the Multifaceted 'Sum' of the Gospel." *International Journal of Systematic Theology* 11, no. 4 (2009): 428–47.

Bird, Michael and Scott Harrower, eds., *Trinity without Hierarchy: Reclaiming Nicene Orthodoxy in Evangelical Theology.* Kregel Publications, 2019.

Boda, Mark J. *A Severe Mercy: Sin and Its Remedy in the Old Testament.* Eisenbrauns, 2009.

———. *The Heartbeat of Old Testament Theology: Three Creedal Expressions.* Baker Academic, 2017.

Bonhoeffer, Dietrich. *Creation and Fall: A Theological Interpretation of Genesis 1–3.* Macmillan, 1966.

———. *Ethics.* Macmillan, 1955.

Bosman, Philip. *Conscience in Philo and Paul.* Mohr Siebeck, 2003.

Boston, Thomas. *Human Nature in its Fourfold State.* Banner of Truth, 1964.

Brock, Brian and John Swinton, eds. *Disability in the Christian Tradition: A Reader.* Eerdmans, 2012.

Brunner, Emil and Karl Barth. *Natural Theology: Comprising "Nature and Grace" by Professor Dr. Emil Brunner and the reply "No!" by Dr. Karl Barth.* Wipf & Stock, 2002.

Butler, Joseph. *Fifteen Sermons and Other Writings on Ethics.* Edited by David McNaughton. Oxford University Press, 2017.

Calvin, John. *Institutes of the Christian Religion.* Edited by John T. McNeill. Westminster Press, 1960.

———. *Calvin's Commentaries.* 22 vols. Baker Books, 1996.

———. *Sermons on the Epistle to the Ephesians.* Banner of Truth, 1973.

Cancrini, Antonia. *Syneidesis: Il tema semantico della "conscientia" nella Grecia antica.* Edizioni dell'Ateneo, 1970.

Carson, D. A. "Systematic Theology and Biblical Theology." Pages 89-104 in New Dictionary of Biblical Theology: Exploring the Unity & Diversity in Scripture. Edited by T. Desmond Alexander, Brian S. Rosner, D.A. Carson, and Graeme Goldsworthy. IVP Academic, 2000.

———. "Theological Interpretation of Scripture: Yes, But ..." In Allen, *Theological Commentary*.

———. *Exegetical Fallacies*. Baker Books, 1996.

———. *The Gospel according to John*. Eerdmans, 1991.

———. *The Gagging of God: Christianity Confronts Pluralism*. Apollos, 1996.

Carter, Craig A. *Contemplating God with the Great Tradition: Recovering Trinitarian Classical Theism*. Baker Academic, 2021.

Casarella Peter J., "Culture and Conscience in the Thought of Jospeh Ratzinger, Pope Benedict XVI." In Hammond and Alvare, *Christianity and the Laws of Conscience*, 265-284.

Chalmers, Thomas. *The Expulsive Power of a New Affection*. Edited by Rev. William Hannah. Thomas Constable, 1855.

Charnock, Stephen. *Discourses Upon the Existence and Attributes of God*. 2 vols. Baker Books, 1979.

———. *The New Birth*. Banner of Truth, 1986.

Clark, Stephen R. L. "The Classical Origins of Natural Theology." In Manning, *The Oxford Handbook of Natural Theology*.

Clark, R. Scott. "Christ and the Covenant: Federal Theology in Orthodoxy." In Selderhuis, *A Companion to Reformed Orthodoxy*.

Collicut, Joanna. "Discernment and the Psychology of Perception." In McGrath, *The Open Secret: A New Vision for Natural Theology*.

Cortez, Marc. *Theological Anthropology: A Guide for the Perplexed*. T&T Clark, 2010.

Cotterell, Peter and Max Turner. *Linguistics and Biblical Interpretation*. InterVarsity Press, 1989.

Courcelle, Pierre. *Connais-toi toi-même: De Socrate à Saint Bernard*. Études augustiniennes, 1974-1975.

Cranfield, Charles E. B. *A Critical and Exegetical Commentary on the Epistle to the Romans*. 2 vols. T&T Clark, 1975, 1979.

Crisp, Oliver D. "A Christological Model of the *Imago Dei*." In Farris and Taliaferro, *The Ashgate Research Companion to Theological Anthropology*.

Crisp, Oliver D. and Fred Sanders, eds. *Locating Atonement: Explorations in Constructive Dogmatics*. Zondervan, 2015.

Crisp, Oliver D. and Michael C. Rea. *Analytic Theology: New Essays in the Philosophy of Theology*. Oxford University Press, 2009.

Cross, Richard. "Thomas Aquinas." In Gravilyuk and Coakley, *The Spiritual Senses*.

Cuddy, Cajetan. "St. Thomas Aquinas on Conscience." In Hammond and Alvare, *Christianity and the Laws of Conscience*.

D'Avenia, Marco. *La conoscenza per connaturalità in S. Tommaso d'Aquino*. Edizioni Studio Domenicano, 1992.

Davidson, Ivor J. "Introduction." In Webster, *The Culture of Theology*.

Davies, Brian and Eleonore Stump. *The Oxford Handbook of Aquinas*. Oxford University Press, 2012.

Davis, Robert Glenn. *The Weight of Love: Affect, Ecstasy, and Union in the Theology of Bonaventure*. Fordham University Press, 2017.

Dowey, Edward A., Jr. *The Knowledge of God in Calvin's Theology*. Eerdmans, 1994.

Duncan, J. Ligon, III. "The Covenant Idea in Irenaeus of Lyons: An Introduction and Survey." In Pipa and Willborn, *Confessing Our Hope*.

Elshof, Gregg A. Ten. *I Told Me So: Self-Deception and the Christian Life*. Eerdmans, 2009.

Emery, Gilles. *The Trinitarian Theology of Saint Thomas Aquinas*. Oxford University Press, 2004.

Emery, Gilles and Matthew Levering, eds. *The Oxford Handbook of the Trinity*. Oxford University Press, 2011.

Farris, Joshua R. and Charles Taliaferro, eds. *The Ashgate Research Companion to Theological Anthropology*. Ashgate Publishing, 2015.

Fee, Gordon D. *1 and 2 Timothy, Titus*. Understanding the Bible Commentary Series. Hendrickson Publishers, 1984.

Fergusson, David. *The Providence of God: A Polyphonic Approach*. Cambridge University Press, 2018.

Fesko, John V. *The Covenant of Works: The Origins, Development, and Reception of the Doctrine*. Oxford University Press, 2020.

———. *The Trinity and the Covenant of Redemption*. Christian Focus Publications, 2016.

———. "Reformed Orthodoxy on Imputation: Active and Passive Justification." *Perichoresis* 14, no. 3 (2016): 61-80.

———. "Introduction." In Vos, *Natural Theology*.

Firth, David G. *1 and 2 Samuel*. Apollos Old Testament Commentary. Apollos, 2009.

Fitzmyer, Joseph A. *Spiritual Exercises Based in Paul's Epistle to the Romans*. Paulist Press, 1995.

Flint, Thomas P. *Christian Philosophy*. Notre Dame University Press, 1990.

Fox, Michael V. *Proverbs 10-31: A New Translation with Introduction and Commentary*. Anchor Yale Bible Commentaries. Yale University Press, 2009.

———. *Proverbs 1-9: A New Translation with Introduction and Commentary*. Anchor Yale Bible Commentaries. Yale University Press, 2010.

Fulton, Rachel. "Taste and See that the Lord Is Sweet Ps. 33:9: The Flavor of God in the Monastic West." *The Journal of Religion* 86, no. 2.1 (April 2006): 169-203.

Gabrill, Stephen G. *Rediscovering the Natural Law in Reformed Theological Ethics*. Eerdmans, 2006.

Garner, David B. *Sons in the Son: The Riches and Reach of Adoption in Christ*. P&R Publishing, 2016.

Gathercole, Simon J. "A Law unto Themselves: The Gentiles in Romans 2.14-15 Revisited." *Journal for the Study of the New Testament* 85 (2002), 27-49.

Goldingay, John. *Old Testament Theology*. Vol. 2, *Israel's Faith*. InterVarsity Press, 2006.

———. *Psalms*. 3 vols. Baker Academic, 2006-2008.

Goodwin, Thomas. *The Works of Thomas Goodwin*. Vols. 6 and 10. Tanski Publications, 1996.

Gorsky, Jonathan. "Conscience in Jewish Tradition." In Hoose, *Conscience in World Religions*.

Gravilyuk, Paul and Sarah Coakley, eds. *The Spiritual Senses: Perceiving God in Western Christianity*. Cambridge University Press, 2012.

Grogan, Geoffrey W. "The Old Testament Concept of Solidarity in Hebrews." *Tyndale Bulletin* 49, no. 1 (1998): 162.

Guthrie, George H. *2 Corinthians*. Baker Exegetical Commentary on the New Testament. Baker Academic, 2015.

Hafemann, Scott J. and Paul R. House, eds. *Central Themes in Biblical Theology: Mapping Unity in Diversity*. Baker Academic, 2007.

Hammond, Jeffrey B. and Helen M. Alvaré, eds. *Christianity and the Laws of Conscience: An Introduction*. Cambridge University Press, 2021.

Hengel, Martin. "The Prologue of the Gospel of John as the Gateway to Christological Truth." In Bauckham and Mosser, *The Gospel of John and Christian Theology*.

Hodge, Charles. *Systematic Theology*. 3 vols. Eerdmans, 1989.

Hofmann, Rudolf. "Conscience." In *Sacramentum Mundi: An Encyclopedia of Theology*. Vol. 1. Herder and Herder, 1968.

Hoose, Jayne, ed. *Conscience in World Religions*. University of Notre Dame Press, 1999.

Kline, Meredith G. *Kingdom Prologue: Genesis Foundation for a Covenantal Worldview*. Wipf & Stock, 2006.

———. *Images of the Spirit*. Wipf & Stock, 1999.

Hahn, Scott W. *Kinship by Covenant: A Canonical Approach to the Fulfillment of God's Saving Promises*. Yale University Press, 2009.

Harris, Bruce F. "ΣΥΝΕΙΔΗΣΙΣ Conscience in the Pauline Writings." *Westminster Theological Journal* 24, no. 2 (1962).

Harris, Harriet A. "Should We Say that Personhood Is Relational?" *Scottish Journal of Theology* 41, no. 2 (1998): 214–34.

Harris, Murray J. *Preposition and Theology in the Greek New Testament*. Zondervan, 2012.

Hasselink, John. "Calvin, Theologian of Sweetness." *Calvin Theological Journal* 37, no. 2 (November 2002), 318–32.

Helm, Paul. *John Calvin's Ideas*. Oxford University Press, 2004.

———. "Nature and Grace." In Svensson and VanDrunen, *Aquinas among the Protestants*.

———. *Human Nature from Calvin to Edwards*. Reformation Heritage Books, 2018.

———. *The Divine Revelation: The Basic Issues*. Regent College Publishing, 2004.

———. *Calvin at the Centre*. Oxford University Press, 2010.

Helm, Paul and Carl Trueman, eds. *The Trustworthiness of God: Perspectives on the Nature of Scripture*. Apollos, 2002.

Hendriksen, William. *A Commentary on the Gospel of John: Commentary on Chapters 7–21*. Banner of Truth, 1959.

Hoffmann, Tobias. "Conscience and *Synderesis*." In Davies and Stump, *The Oxford Handbook of Aquinas*.

Holmes, Stephen R. *The Quest for the Trinity: The Doctrine of God in Scripture, History and Modernity*. InterVarsity Press, 2012.

Horton, Michael S. *The Christian Faith: A Systematic Theology for Pilgrims on the Way*. Zondervan, 2011.

———. *Covenant and Eschatology: The Divine Drama*. Westminster John Knox, 2002.

———. *Lord and Servant: A Covenantal Christology*. Westminster John Knox, 2005.

———. *Calvin on the Christian Life: Glorifying and Enjoying God Forever*. Crossway, 2014.

———. *Covenant and Salvation: Union with Christ*. Westminster John Knox, 2007.

———. *Justification*. Vol. 1. Zondervan, 2018.

Howard, Jason J. *Conscience in Moral Life: Rethinking How Our Convictions Structure Self and Society*. Rowan & Littlefield, 2014.

Hugenberger, Gordon P. *Marriage as a Covenant: Biblical Law and Ethics as Developed from Malachi*. Brill, 1994.

Hughes, Philip E. *The Second Epistle to the Corinthians*. The New International Commentary on the New Testament. Eerdmans, 1962.

Husbands, Mark and Daniel J. Treier, eds. *Justification: What's at Stake in the Current Debates*. InterVarsity Press, 2004.

Jackendoff, Ray. *Patterns in the Mind: Language and Human Nature*. Basic Books, 1994.

———. *Language, Consciousness, Culture: Essays on Mental Structure*. MIT Press, 2007.

Jaeger, H., S. J. "L'examen de conscience dans le religions nonchrétienne et avan le christianisme." *Numen* 6, no. 3 (1959): 175–233.

Jenson, Matt. *The Gravity of Sin: Augustine, Luther and Barth on "homo incurvatus in se."* T&T Clark, 2006.

Jeon, Jeong Koo. *Biblical Theology: Covenants and the Kingdom of God in Redemptive History*. Wipf & Stock, 2017.

Jeremias, Joachim. *New Testament Theology: The Proclamation of Jesus.* SCM Press, 1971.

Jewett, Robert. *Paul's Anthropological Terms: A Study of Their Use in Conflict Settings.* Brill, 1971.

Jobes, Karen H. *1 Peter.* Baker Exegetical Commentary on the New Testament. Baker Academic, 2005.

Johnson, Aubrey R. *The Vitality of the Individual in the Thought of Ancient Israel.* University of Wales Press, 1964.

Johnson, Dennis E. "The Function of Romans 7:13-25 in Paul's Argument for the Law's Impotence and the Spirit's Power, and Its Bearing on the Identity of the Schizophrenic 'I.'" In Tipton and Waddington, *Resurrection and Eschatology.*

Käsemann, Ernst. *Commentary on Romans.* Eerdmans, 1980.

Keating, Daniel A. "Trinity and Salvation: Christian Life as an Existence in the Trinity." In Emery and Levering, *The Oxford Handbook of the Trinity.*

Keil, C. F. and F. Delitzsch. *Commentary on the Old Testament.* 10 vols. Eerdmans, 1986.

Kelly, Douglas F. *Systematic Theology: Grounded in Holy Scripture and Understood in the Light of the Church.* Vol. 1, *The God Who Is: The Holy Trinity.* Christian Focus Publications, 2008.

Kilby, Karen. "Perichoresis and Projection: Problems with Social Doctrines of the Trinity." *New Blackfriars* 81, no. 956 (2000): 432-45.

King, David M. "The Affective Spirituality of John Owen." *The Evangelical Quarterly,* 68, no. 3 (1996): 223-33.

Kiuchi, Nobuyoshi. *The Purification Offering.* Sheffield Academic, 1987.

Knight, George W., III. *The Pastoral Epistles.* Eerdmans, 1992.

Köstenberger, Andreas J. and Scott R. Swain, *Father, Son and Spirit: The Trinity in John's Gospel.* Apollos, 2008.

Kries, Douglas. "Origen, Plato, and Conscience (*Synderesis*) in Jerome's Ezekiel Commentary." *Traditio* 57 (2002): 67-83.

Krokos, Jan. *Conscience as Cognition: Phenomenological Complementing of Aquinas's Theory of Conscience.* Peter Lang, 2013.

Kuyper, Abraham. *The Work of the Holy Spirit.* Eerdmans, 1946.

Lane, Belden C. *Ravished by Beauty: The Surprising Legacy of Reformed Spirituality.* Oxford University Press, 2011.

Lane, William A. *Hebrews 9–13*. Word Biblical Commentary. Word Books, 1991.

Langdon, Douglas C. *Conscience and Other Virtues*. Pennsylvania State University Press, 2001.

Lapsley, Jacqueline E. "Shame and Self-Knowledge: The Positive Role of Shame in Ezekiel's View of the Moral Self." In Odell and Strong, *The Book of Ezekiel*.

Lé, Dan. *The Naked Christ: An Atonement Model for a Body Obsessed Culture*. Wipf & Stock, 2012.

Lehmann, Paul L. *Ethics in a Christian Context*. Westminster John Knox, 2006.

Levenson, Jon D. *Sinai and Zion: An Entry into the Jewish Bible*. HarperCollins, 1985.

———. *The Love of God: Divine Gift, Human Gratitude, and Mutual Faithfulness in Judaism*. Princeton University Press, 2016.

Levering, Matthew. *The Abuse of Conscience: A Century of Catholic Moral Theology*. Eerdmans, 2021.

Lewis, Clive S. *Studies in Words*. Cambridge University Press, 1960.

Lillback, Peter A. *The Binding of God: Calvin's Role in the Development of Covenant Theology*. Baker Academic, 2001.

Lincoln, Andrew T. *Truth on Trial: The Lawsuit Motif in the Fourth Gospel*. Hendrikson, 2000.

Lints, Richard. *Identity and Idolatry: The Image of God and Its Inversion*. InterVarsity Press, 2015.

Long, D. Stephen. *The Perfectly Simple Triune God: Aquinas and His Legacy*. Fortress Press, 2016.

Longenecker, Richard N. *The Epistle to the Romans*. Eerdmans, 2016.

Lottin, Odon. "Syndérèse et conscience aux XIIe et XIIIe siècles." In *Psychologie et morale aux XIIe et XIIIe siècles: table chronologique des écrits et leur influence littéraire*. Vol. 2. J. Duculot, 1948.

Manning, Russell Re, ed. *The Oxford Handbook of Natural Theology*. Oxford University Press, 2013.

McConnell, T. Mark. "From 'I Have Done Wrong' to 'I Am Wrong': (Re)Constructing Atonement as a Response to Shame." In Crisp and Sanders, *Locating Atonement*.

McCormack, Bruce L. "What's at Stake in Current Debates over Justification." In Husbands and Treier, *Justification: What's at Stake in the Current Debates*. InterVarsity Press, 2004.

———, ed. *Justification in Perspective: Historical Developments and Contemporary Challenges*. Baker Academic, 2006.

———. "*Iustitia aliena*: Karl Barth in Conversation with the Evangelical Doctrine of Imputed Righteousness." In McCormack, *Justification in Perspective*.

McGowan, Andrew T. B. "Justification and the *ordo salutis*." In McCormack, *Justification in Perspective*.

McGrath, Alister E. *The Open Secret: A New Vision for Natural Theology*. Blackwell, 2008.

———. *Christian Theology: An Introduction*. Blackwell, 1994.

———. *Emil Brunner: A Reappraisal*. John Wiley & Sons, 2014.

McGinn, Colin. "Imagination." In McLaughlin, Beckermann, and Walter, *The Oxford Handbook of Philosophy of Mind*.

McGuckin, John A. "Conscience in Early Christian Thought." In Hammond and Alvare, *Christianity and the Laws of Conscience*.

McInroy, Mark J. "Origen of Alexandria." In Gravilyuk and Coakley, *The Spiritual Senses*.

———. "Karl Rahner and Hans Urs von Balthasar." In Gravilyuk and Coakley, *The Spiritual Senses*.

McLaughlin, Brian P. Ansgar Beckermann, and Sven Walter, eds. *The Oxford Handbook of Philosophy of Mind*. Oxford University Press, 2009.

Michaels, J. Ramsey. *1 Peter*. Word Biblical Themes. Word Books, 1988.

Milgrom, Jacob. *Leviticus 1-16*. Anchor Yale Bible Commentaries. Yale University Press, 1991.

———. *Leviticus 23-27*. Anchor Yale Bible Commentaries. Yale University Press, 2001.

Moberly, Robert W. L. *The Theology of the Book of Genesis*. Cambridge University Press, 2009.

Molnar, Paul D. *Divine Freedom and the Doctrine of the Immanent Trinity: In Dialogue with Karl Barth and Contemporary Theology*. Bloomsbury, 2017.

Montanari, Antonio, ed. *I sensi spirituali: Tra anima e corpo*. Edizioni Glossa, 2012.
Moo, Douglas J. *The Epistle to the Romans*. The New International Commentary on the New Testament. Eerdmans, 1996.
———. *Galatians*. Baker Exegetical Commentary on the New Testament. Baker Academic, 2013.
Morris, Leon. *The Gospel according to John*. Eerdmans, 1971.
Muller, Richard A. *Dictionary of Latin and Greek Theological Terms Drawn Principally from Protestant Scholastic Theology*. Baker Books, 1985.
———. *Post-Reformation Reformed Dogmatics: The Rise and Development of Reformed Orthodoxy, ca. 1520–1725*. Vol. 2. Baker Academic, 2003.
Muller, Richard A. *Calvin and the Reformed Tradition: On the Work of Christ and the Order of Salvation*. Baker Academic, 2012.
Nelson, R. David, Darren Sarisky, and Justin Stratis, eds. *Theological Theology: Essays in Honour of John Webster*. T&T Clark, 2015.
Novak, David. *Covenantal Rights: A Study in Jewish Political Theory*. Princeton University Press, 2000.
———. *Natural Law in Judaism*. Cambridge University Press, 1998.
Nussbaum, Martha C. *Upheavals of Thought: The Intelligence of Emotions*. Cambridge University Press, 2001.
O'Brien, Peter T. *The Letter to the Ephesians*. Pillar New Testament Commentary. Eerdmans, 1999.
Odell, Margaret S. and John T. Strong, eds. *The Book of Ezekiel: Theological and Anthropological Perspectives*. Society of Biblical Literature, 2000.
O'Donovan, Oliver. *The Ways of Judgment*. Eerdmans, 2005.
Ong, Walter J. *The Presence of the Word: Some Prolegomena for Cultural and Religious History*. Yale University Press, 1967.
Ortlund, Dane. *Gentle and Lowly: The Heart of Christ for Sinners and Sufferers*. Crossway, 2020.
Otto, Randall E. "The Use and Abuse of Perichoresis in Recent Theology." *Scottish Journal of Theology* 54 (2001): 366–84.
Owen, John. *The Works of John Owen*. 22 vols. Banner of Truth, 1965–1991.
Pak, Joseph K. "Self-Deception in Current Philosophical Discussions and Its Importance in Theology." *International Journal of Philosophy and Theology* 4, no. 1 (2016): 13–21.

Palmer, Benjamin M. *Theology of Prayer as Viewed in the Religion of Nature and in the System of Grace*. Sprinkle Publications, 1980.

Pannenberg, Wolfhart. *Anthropology in Theological Perspective*. T&T Clark, 1985.

Pattison, Stephen. *Shame: Theory, Therapy, Theology*. Cambridge University Press, 2000.

Perler, Dominik, ed. *The Faculties: A History*. Oxford University Press, 2015.

Perkins, Harrison. *Catholicity and the Covenant of Works: James Ussher and the Reformed Tradition*. Oxford University Press, 2020.

Perkins, William. *The Works of William Perkins*. Vol. 8. Edited by Joel R. Beeke and Derek W. H. Thomas. Reformation Heritage Books, 2019.

Pierce, Claude A. *Conscience in the New Testament: A Study of Syneidesis in the New Testament; in the Light of Its Sources, and with Particular Reference to St. Paul; with Some Observations Regarding Its Pastoral Relevance Today*. SCM Press, 1955.

Pipa, Joseph A. and C. N. Willborn, eds. *Confessing Our Hope: Essays Celebrating the Life and Ministry of Morton H. Smith*. Southern Presbyterian Press, 2004.

Plantinga, Alvin. *Warranted Christian Belief*. Oxford University Press, 2000.

Pope, Marvin H. *Job*. The Anchor Bible. Doubleday, 1965.

Potts, Timothy C. *Conscience in Medieval Philosophy*. Cambridge University Press, 1980.

Poythress, Vern S. *In the Beginning Was the Word: Language, A God-Centered Approach*. Crossway, 2009.

Poythress, Vern S. *The Mystery of the Trinity: A Trinitarian Approach to the Attributes of God*. P&R Publishing, 2020.

Rad, Gerhard von. *Wisdom in Israel*. SCM Press, 1972.

Ratzinger Joseph, *On Conscience*. San Francisco: Ignatius Press, 2007.

Rendtorff, Rolf. *The Covenant Formula: An Exegetical and Theological Investigation*. T&T Clark, 1998.

Ridderbos, Herman. *Paul: An Outline of His Theology*. Eerdmans, 1975.

———. *The Gospel of John: A Theological Commentary*. Eerdmans, 1997.

Ricoeur, Paul. *Figuring the Sacred: Religion, Narrative, and Imagination*. Edited by Mark I. Wallace. Augsburg Fortress, 1995.

———. *Oneself as Another*. University of Chicago Press, 1992.

Roberts, Robert C. *Emotions: An Essay in Aid of Moral Psychology*. Cambridge University Press, 2003.

———. *Spiritual Emotions: A Psychology of Christian Virtues*. Eerdmans, 2007.

———. *Emotions in the Moral Life*. Cambridge University Press, 2013.

Rowland, Christopher. "Natural Theology and the Christian Bible." In Manning, *The Oxford Handbook of Natural Theology*.

Saito, Isomi. "Divine Adoption in the Confessions of the Reformation Period." PhD diss., Vrije Universiteit, 2016. https://research.vu.nl/en/publications/divine-adoption-in-the-confessions-of-the-reformation-period-2.

Salvioli, Marco. "Il fascino discreto di un tema marginale: I sensi spirituali in Tommaso d'Aquino." In Montanari, *I sensi spirituali: Tra anima e corpo*.

Sanday, William and Arthur C. Headlam. *A Critical and Exegetical Commentary on the Epistle to the Romans*. T&T Clark, 1902.

Sanders, Fred. *The Triune God*. Zondervan, 2016.

———. "The Trinity." In Webster, Tanner, and Torrance, *The Oxford Handbook of Systematic Theology*.

Sarna, Nahum M. *The JPS Torah Commentary: Genesis*. Jewish Publication Society, 1989.

———. *The JPS Torah Commentary: Exodus*. Jewish Publication Society, 1991.

Sarna, Nahum M. "The Psalm for the Sabbath Day Ps 92." *Journal of Biblical Literature* 81, no. 2 (1962), 155–68.

Schaff, Philip, ed. *The Creeds of Christendom*. Vol. 3, *The Evangelical Protestant Creeds*. Baker Books, 1993.

Schwanda, Tom. "Soul Recreation: Spiritual Marriage and Ravishment in the Contemplative Mystical Piety of Isaac Ambrose." PhD diss., Durham University, 2009. http://etheses.dur.ac.uk/55/.

Schliesser, Eric. *Sympathy: A History*. Oxford University Press, 2015.

Selderhuis, Herman J., ed. *A Companion to Reformed Orthodoxy*. Brill, 2013.

Senner, Jordan. *John Webster: The Shape and Development of His Theology*. T&T Clark, 2022.

Sklar, Jay. *Sin, Impurity, Sacrifice, Atonement: The Priestly Conceptions*. Sheffield Phoenix, 2015.

Silva, Moisés. *Biblical Words and Their Meaning: An Introduction to Lexical Semantics*. Zondervan, 1983.

Simmer, Julia. *Synaesthesia: A Very Short Introduction.* Oxford University Press, 2019.

Sorabji, Richard. *Moral Conscience through the Ages.* Oxford University Press, 2014.

Spicq, Ceslas. "La conscience dans le Nouveau Testament." *Revue Biblique* 47 (1938).

Spijker, Willem van't. "Extra nos and in nobis by Calvin in a Pneumatological Light." In *Calvin and the Holy Spirit: Papers and Responses Presented at the Sixth Colloquium on Calvin and Calvin Studies.* Edited by Peter De Klerk. Calvin Studies Society, 1989.

Steinbock, Anthony J. *Moral Emotions: Reclaiming the Evidence of the Heart.* Northwestern University Press, 2014.

Stiebert, Johanna. *Construction of Shame in the Hebrew Bible.* Sheffield Academic, 2002.

Stockitt, Robin. *Restoring the Shamed: Towards a Theology of Shame.* Cascade Books, 2012.

Stoker, Hendrik G. *Conscience: Phenomena and Theories.* University of Notre Dame Press, 2018.

Strohm, Paul. *Conscience: A Very Short Introduction.* Oxford University Press, 2011.

Sudduth, Michael. "The Contribution of Religious Experience to Dogmatic Theology." In Crisp and Rea, *Analytic Theology.*

Svensson, Manfred and David VanDrunen. *Aquinas among the Protestants.* John Wiley & Sons, 2018.

Swain, Scott R. "The Covenant of Redemption." In Allen and Swain, *Christian Dogmatics.*

Sweeney, Marvin A. *TANAK: A Theological and Critical Introduction to the Jewish Bible.* Fortress Press, 2012.

Sytsma, David S. "The Logic of the Heart: Analyzing the Affections in Early Reformed Orthodoxy." In Ballor, Sytsma, and Zuidema, *Church and School.*

Tangney, June P. and Ronda L. Dearing. *Shame and Guilt.* Guildford Press, 2002.

Theissen, Gerd. *Psychological Aspects of Pauline Theology.* T&T Clark, 1987.

Thiselton, Anthony C. *The First Epistle to the Corinthians.* The New International Greek Testament Commentary. Eerdmans, 2000.

———. *The Last Things: A New Approach.* SPCK, 2012.

Thrall, Margaret. "The Pauline Use of Συνείδησις." *New Testament Studies* 14 (1967).

Tipton, Lane G. and Jeffrey C. Waddington. *Resurrection and Eschatology: Theology in Service of the Church.* P&R Publishing, 2008.

Torrance, Alexis. "Conscience in the Early Church Fathers." In Hammond and Alvare, *Christianity and the Laws of Conscience.*

Torrance, David W. and Thomas F. Torrance, eds. *Calvin's New Testament Commentaries.* Vol. 4. Eerdmans, 1959-1972.

Trueman, Carl R. *John Owen: Reformed Catholic, Renaissance Man.* Ashgate Publishing, 2007.

———. "Illumination." In Vanhoozer, Bartholomew, Treier, and Wright, *Dictionary for Theological Interpretation of the Bible.*

Trumper, Timothy J. R. "The Metaphorical Import of Adoption: A Plea for Realisation I: The Adoption Metaphor in Biblical Usage." *The Scottish Bulletin of Evangelical Theology* 14 (1996), 129-45.

———. "The Metaphorical Import of Adoption: A Plea for Realisation II: The Adoption Metaphor in Theological Usage." *The Scottish Bulletin of Evangelical Theology* 15 (1997), 98-115.

———. "An Historical Study of the Doctrine of Adoption in the Calvinistic Tradition." PhD diss., University of Edinburgh, 2001. https://era.ed.ac.uk/handle/1842/6803.

Turretin, Francis. *Institutes of Elenctic Theology.* 3 vols. P&R Publishing, 1992, 1996, 1997.

Van den Brink, Gijsbert. "Social Trinitarianism: A Discussion of Some Recent Theological Criticisms." *International Journal of Systematic Theology* 16, no. 3 (2014): 331-50.

VanDrunen, David. *Divine Covenants and Moral Order: A Biblical Theology of Natural Law.* Eerdmans, 2014.

———. "Medieval Natural Law and the Reformation: A Comparison of Aquinas and Calvin." *American Catholic Philosophical Quarterly* 80, no. 1 (2006), 77-98.

———. "Conscience and Natural Law in Scripture." In Hammond and Alvare, *Christianity and the Laws of Conscience.*

VanGemeren, Willem A., ed. *New International Dictionary of Old Testament Theology and Exegesis.* 5 vols. Paternoster Press, 1996.

Vanhoozer, Kevin J. *The Drama of Doctrine: A Canonical-Linguistic Approach to Christian Theology.* Westminster John Knox, 2005.
———. *First Theology: God, Scripture and Hermeneutics.* InterVarsity Press, 2002.
———, ed., *The Cambridge Companion to Postmodern Theology.* Cambridge University Press, 2003.
———. "Ezekiel 14: 'I, The Lord, Have Deceived That Prophet.' " In Allen, *Theological Commentary.*
———. "Word of God." In Vanhoozer, Bartholomew, Treier, and Wright, *Dictionary for Theological Interpretation of the Bible.*
Vanhoozer, Kevin J., Craig G. Bartholomew, Daniel J. Treier, and N. T. Wright, eds. *Dictionary for Theological Interpretation of the Bible.* Baker Books, 2005.
Vanier, Jean. *Our Life Together.* HarperCollins, 2007.
Van Til, Cornelius. *Christian Apologetics.* P&R Publishing, 1976.
Vos, Geerhardus. *Biblical Theology: Old and New Testament.* Eerdmans, 1948.
———. *Grace and Glory: Sermons Preached in the Chapel of Princeton Theological Seminary.* Banner of Truth, 1994.
Vos, Geerhardus. *Redemptive History and Biblical Theology: The Shorter Writings of Geerhardus Vos.* Edited by Richard B. Gaffin Jr. P&R Publishing, 2001.
———. *The Self-Disclosure of Jesus: The Modern Debate about the Messianic Consciousness.* George H. Doran, 1926.
———. *Natural Theology.* Reformation Heritage Books, 2019.
Waltke, Bruce K. and Cathi J. Fredricks. *Genesis: A Commentary.* Zondervan, 2001.
Ward, Timothy. *Words of Life: Scripture as the Living and Active Word of God.* InterVarsity Press, 2009.
———. *Word and Supplement: Speech Acts, Biblical Texts, and the Sufficiency of Scripture.* Oxford University Press, 2002.
Warfield, Benjamin B. *Calvin and Augustine.* P&R Publishing, 1980.
———. *Biblical and Theological Studies.* P&R Publishing, 1968.
———. *Faith and Life.* Banner of Truth, 1974.
Waters, Guy Prentiss, J. Nicholas Reid, and John R. Muether, eds. *Covenant Theology: Biblical, Theological, and Historical Perspectives.* Crossway, 2020.

Webb, Stephen H. *The Divine Voice: Christian Proclamation and the Theology of Sound*. Brazos Press, 2004.

Wenham, Gordon J. *Genesis 1–15*. Word Biblical Commentary. Thomas Nelson, 1987.

Webster, John B. *Word and Church: Essays in Christian Dogmatics*. T&T Clark, 2001.

———. *The Domain of the Word: Scripture and Theological Reasoning*. T&T Clark, 2012.

———. *Confessing God: Essays in Christian Dogmatics II*. T&T Clark, 2005.

———. "Theologies of Retrieval." In Webster, Tanner, and Torrance, *The Oxford Handbook of Systematic Theology*.

———. "The Human Person." In Vanhoozer, *The Cambridge Companion to Postmodern Theology*.

———. *The Culture of Theology*. Edited by Ivor J. Davidson and Alden C. McCray. Baker Academic, 2019.

———. *God without Measure: Working Papers in Christian Theology*, 2 vols. T&T Clark, 2016.

———. *Confronted by Grace: Meditation of a Theologian*. Lexham Press, 2015.

———. "Creation Out of Nothing." In Allen and Swain, *Christian Dogmatics*.

Webster, John, Kathryn Tanner, and Iain Torrance, eds. *The Oxford Handbook of Systematic Theology*. Oxford University Press, 2007.

Weinfeld, Moshe. "The Covenant of Grant in the Old Testament and in the Ancient Near East." *Journal of the American Oriental Society* 90 (1970): 184–203.

Welch, Edward T. *Shame Interrupted: How God Lifts the Pain of Worthlessness and Rejection*. New Growth Press, 2012.

Westberg, Daniel. "The Influence of Aquinas on Protestant Ethics." In Svensson and Vandrunen, *Aquinas among the Protestants*.

Westphal, Merold. "Taking Paul Seriously: Sin as an Epistemological Category." Pages 200–26 in *Christian Philosophy*. Edited by Thomas P. Flint. University of Notre Dame Press, 1990.

———. "Taking St. Paul Seriously: Sin as an Epistemological Category." In Flint, *Christian Philosophy*.

———. *God, Guilt, and Death: An Existential Phenomenology of Religion*. Indiana University Press, 1984.

Wilder, William N. "Illumination and Investiture: The Royal Significance of the Tree of Wisdom in Genesis 3." *Westminster Theological Journal* 68, no. 1 (2006), 51-69.

Williams, Anna N. *The Divine Sense: The Intellect in Patristic Theology.* Cambridge University Press, 2007.

Williams, Rowan. *The Edge of Words: God and the Habits of Language.* Bloomsbury, 2012.

Williamson, Paul R. *Sealed with an Oath: Covenant in God's Unfolding Purpose.* Intervarsity Press, 2007.

Willis, Wendell. "Conscience in the New Testament." In Hammond and Alvare, *Christianity and the Laws of Conscience*.

Witsius, Herman. *The Economy of the Covenants between God and Man: Comprehending a Complete Body of Divinity.* 2 vols. Den Dulk Christian Foundation, 1990.

Wolff, Hans Walter. *Anthropology of the Old Testament.* SCM Press, 1973.

Wolterstorff, Nicholas. *Divine Discourse: Philosophical Reflections on the Claim that God Speaks.* Cambridge University Press, 1995.

Wood, William D. "Reason's Rapport: Pascalian Reflections on the Persuasiveness of Natural Theology." *Faith and Philosophy* 21, no. 4 (2004): 519-32.

——. *Blaise Pascal on Duplicity, Sin and the Fall: The Secret Instinct.* Oxford University Press, 2013.

Woolsey, Andrew A. *Unity and Continuity in Covenantal Thought: A Study in the Reformed Tradition to the Westminster Assembly.* Reformation Heritage Books, 2012.

Wright, Nicholas T. *Paul in Fresh Perspective.* Fortress Press, 2005.

——. *The Day the Revolution Began: Reconsidering the Meaning of Jesus' Crucifixion.* HarperOne, 2016.

——. *The Climax of the Covenant: Christ and the Law in Pauline Theology.* T&T Clark, 1991.

——. *History and Eschatology: Jesus and the Promise of Natural Theology.* SPCK, 2019.

——. *John for Everyone: Part 2, Chapters 11-21.* SPCK, 2002.

Yong, Amos. *Theology and Down Syndrome: Reimagining Disability in Late Modernity.* Baylor University Press, 2007.

Young, Edward J. *A Commentary on Daniel.* Banner of Truth, 1949.

Young, Frances. *Arthur's Call: A Journey of Faith in the Face of Severe Learning Disability.* SPCK, 2014.

———. *God's Presence: A Contemporary Recapitulation of Early Christianity.* Cambridge University Press, 2013.

Zachman, Randall C. *The Assurance of Faith: Conscience in the Theology of Martin Luther and John Calvin.* Westminster John Knox, 2005.

Zahavi, Dan. *Self and Other: Exploring Subjectivity, Empathy, and Shame.* Oxford University Press, 2014.

Zahl, Simeon. *The Holy Spirit and Christian Experience.* Oxford University Press, 2020.

———. "On the Affective Salience of Doctrines." *Modern Theology* 31, no. 3 (2015): 428-44.

———. "Non-Competitive Agency and Luther's Experiential Argument Against Virtue." *Modern Theology* 35, no. 2 (2019), 199-222.

———. "Beyond the Critique of Soteriological Individualism: Relationality and Social Cognition." *Modern Theology* 37, no. 2 (2021), 336-61.

———. "Atonement." In Adams, Pattison, and Ward, *The Oxford Handbook of Theology and Modern European Thought.*

Zucal, Silvano. "Filosofia dialogica e dottrina trinitaria." *Elaborare l'esperienza di Dio: Atti del convegno "La Trinità."* May 26-28, 2009. Accessed on June 1st 2021. https://mondodomani.org/teologia/zucal2011.htm.

SUBJECT INDEX

A

Abandonment of hiddenness, 207-8, 210, 221, 225, 247
Abimelech, 38, 104-5
  fear of God, 104-5
  innocence of, 38, 104
Accountability
  before God, 51, 61-62, 65-67, 95
  covenantal, 62, 66-67, 95
  moral, 51, 99
  see also: Judgment, divine
Adam, 147, 151, 152, 168, 170, 175, 203
  and conscience, 29, 44, 46, 51, 58-60, 62-63, 66
  and Eve, 44-48, 53, 58-60, 62-63, 66
  and fear, 44, 51, 53, 63-64
  and marriage covenant, 66-67
  and shame, 44-48, 53, 63
  second, 170
Adoption, 160, 189, 193, 198-205, 207, 214, 216-19, 222, 225, 247
  awareness of, 214, 216, 218
  benefit of, 207, 214, 217, 225, 247
  co-heirs with Christ, 200
  divine act, 201
  relation to justification, 199-201
  subjective experience, 207, 216, 225, 247
Affection(s), 162, 169, 178-83
  kindling of, 184
  love implanted upon, 179
  movement of inner self, 169
  renewal of, 179
  see also Emotions
Affective knowledge, 183-85

Affective salience, 15
Alienation from God, 55, 64, 136, 137
Amen, 187
  Adam's protological, 59
Analytical thinking, 166
Ancient Near East, 52, 102
Anknüpfungspunkt, 168
Anthropology,
  Covenantal, 14
  Theocentric, 11
  theological, 1, 12, 23, 30, 92-93, 120, 133
  see also Human nature; *Imago Dei*
Apostates, 138, 139
Aquinas, Thomas
  affective knowledge, 184-85
  and Calvin, 119-22, 124-25
  conscientia, 118-119, 122
  natural law, 119, 121-22
  spiritual senses, 183
  synderesis, 117-20, 122
Atonement, 39, 46-47, 180, 213, 217
  forensic understanding, 217, 220, 225
  vicarious sacrifice, 214
Augustinian notion, 154
  disordered love, 154
Authority
  of conscience, 65-66, 94-95, 116
  of God, 36, 65-66, 94-95
Awareness, 92-99, 109-10, 116, 122-33, 227, 239, 245
  conscious, 236-37
  of divine judgment, 65, 123
  of God, 29, 32, 35-36, 44, 53, 62, 92, 97, 102, 105, 109-11, 116, 120, 122-33, 229, 231

perfected, 229–30, 234
   religious and moral, 29, 32–33, 35–36, 44, 54, 59, 102, 109–11

B

Belgic Confession, 44, 51, 152, 180
Biblical anthropology, 156
Biblical literacy, 18
Biblical reasoning, 116
Blood of Christ, 213, 222
Body, and conscience, 37, 43, 59, 96, 100, 107–8, 114, 116, 133
Bondage of the will, 140, 154, 160, 178
Branding, 138
Brokenness, spiritual, 34

C

Cain, 102–3, 106, 117
Calling, 167, 171, 176–77, 195, 207, 222, 235, 237–38, 241, 245
   effectual, 176–77, 192, 195
   external, 195
   general, 171
   internal, 195
   special, 169, 171, 176
   see also Effectual calling
Callousness, 137–39, 141, 153, 157
Calvin, John
   and Aquinas, 119–22, 124–25
   knowledge of God, 140–44, 147
   on adoption, 219–20
   on conscience, 13, 24, 33–34, 36, 47–48, 57–58, 61–62, 65, 93–94, 103, 108, 111, 117, 119–27, 129–33, 140, 143, 157, 165–66, 168, 177, 192, 204, 217–18, 230, 239, 245
   on faith, 185
   on illumination, 171
   on indwelling sin, 225
   on prayer, 219
   on regeneration, 171, 176, 179, 185
   sensus divini iudicii, 65, 123, 126–27, 129
   sensus divinitatis, 13, 22, 24, 58, 65, 93, 123, 126–27, 129–32, 207, 209–10, 234, 239, 245

synderesis, abandonment of, 119–21
Canons of Dort, 180
Capacities, human, 28–29, 32, 43, 51, 61, 65–66, 92, 94–99, 101, 105, 110, 114, 116, 120, 122, 125, 127–28, 132–33
   cooperation of, 93, 95, 99–116, 122, 132–33
   holistic view, 95–97, 116, 132
Cauterization, 138–39
Christ, Jesus, 147, 151, 160, 163, 168, 169, 170, 180, 185, 189, 190, 191, 192, 193, 195, 197, 198, 200, 203, 204
   Adam-Christology, 151, 203
   conformity to, 234, 238, 248
   consciousness of, 235
   image of, 233–34, 236
   imputed righteousness, 160, 196, 197
   last Adam, 234, 238, 248
   objective work of, 160, 168, 175, 189, 191
   person and mission, 162, 163, 168
   righteousness of, 211, 214
   union with, 198, 200, 201
Christian anthropology, 1
Christian experience, 207–9, 217
Christian identity, 209
Christian philosophy, 135
Christic conscience, 227, 233
Church Fathers, 135, 139, 151
Cognitio insita, 129, 132
Cognitive imagination, 156
Commandment of life, 44, 46, 60, 63, 109
Common grace, 173
Common notions of God, 152, 174
Communicative act of God, 176
Community, role in sin, 40–41
Communion with God, 221, 233, 235–36
   initial/incomplete, 236
   mutual communication, 236
   perfect/complete, 236
   trinitarian dimension, 236
   verbal nature, 236
Conscience, 135–205
   accusing, 42, 57, 66, 104, 109, 114, 212, 218, 222

acquitted, 169
affective transformation, 207, 225, 247
and affections, 162, 169, 178-82
and body, 37, 43, 59, 96, 100, 107-8, 114, 116, 133
and emotions, 44, 51, 55, 93, 96, 98-107, 114, 116, 132-33
and imagination, 155-56
and language, 31-32, 35, 37-44, 93, 96, 99, 101, 103, 105, 108, 110, 114-16, 120, 133
and law, 135, 151, 161, 162, 163, 165-69, 190, 203
and thinking, 32, 35, 43, 93-94, 96, 99, 105, 108-14, 116, 121-22, 125, 129-30, 132-33
and will, 59, 61, 93-94, 96, 99, 103, 113-14, 116, 120, 133
as created reality, 28-29, 31, 43, 57, 61, 65-66, 68, 95, 125-26, 132, 136, 169, 173
as *sensus*, 136, 138, 139, 141, 143, 144, 146, 148, 150, 151, 152, 154, 157, 160, 161, 163, 165, 172, 173, 177, 178, 183, 186, 187
authority of, 65-66, 94-95, 116
awakening of, 28, 45, 55, 94, 107
biblical attestation, 13, 15-16, 243-44
condemning, 212-13
conviction of, 160, 161-67, 168, 169
covenantal, 9-11, 24, 210-11, 234, 239, 244-45
created, 15, 20-21, 23, 239, 243-44
definition of, 28, 31-32, 35, 43-44, 51, 55, 57, 61, 65, 92-93, 97-99, 116, 122-23, 125-33
depraved, 24, 136-39
dialogical model, 238
eschatological, 227, 233
experience of, 28, 31, 43-44, 55, 93, 96-99, 102, 104-5, 109, 113-14, 116, 120, 123-24, 126-33
faculty, as a, 29, 95, 97-99, 116, 120, 132

fallen, 2, 24, 28-29, 43, 46, 59, 92-133, 135-57, 161, 163, 166, 169, 215, 221, 230, 234, 239, 245
finite, 136
good, 28, 57, 61, 118, 222-25, 232
guilty, 212, 225
heavenly, 229
hinders self-knowledge, 140-52, 157
illumination of, 160, 161-63, 167-70
in Old Testament, 15-19, 23, 29, 31-44, 55, 57, 99, 102, 104, 106-8, 110-11, 113-16, 140
in Paul, 16-19, 138-39, 141-52, 169, 199-204
in relation to God, 15, 21-22, 28-29, 32, 34-36, 45, 47-48, 51, 53, 55, 57-68, 94-95, 97, 102, 104-6, 108-11, 113-16, 120-33
in Romans, 140-52, 169, 199, 201-4
incapable of self-scrutiny, 136, 153-57
inward transformation, 225
justification of, 13-14, 24, 160, 189-205
legislating, 57, 65-68, 95, 112
manifestation of, 29, 31-55, 57, 61, 99, 101, 105-8, 114-16
mediator, as, 94, 116, 122, 132
moral judgments, 13, 227, 235
nature of, 23, 29-31, 57, 61, 68, 93, 100, 102, 110, 113, 116, 120, 123-25, 129, 132-33
nonphysical perceptual awareness, 93, 125-33, 135
objective/subjective aspects, 224-25
obstacle to worship, 212
operations of, 135, 136
perfected, 25, 225, 227, 229, 231-33, 235, 238, 243, 248
positive mode, 28-29, 57-58, 61, 65-66
prelapsarian, 28-29, 44, 57-68, 99, 109, 118, 122-23, 130
preparation of, 160, 161-70
primal awareness of God, 135
probity of, 136, 140
purification of, 213, 224, 229

redeemed, 24, 157, 160, 161, 163, 169, 173, 178, 187, 189, 198, 201, 221, 233, 235, 240, 246
regeneration of, 160, 171, 172, 173–87, 240, 246
renovation of, 225, 240, 246
sanctification of, 160, 205
seared, 138, 139
secret instinct of, 155, 157, 176
self-review process, 135
summoning, 57, 61–65, 68, 95, 108, 112
theology of, 2–7, 12, 15–16, 20, 210, 227, 235, 239
voice of, 210–11, 237
witness of, 136, 143, 144, 163, 164, 166, 168, 169, 202–4
witnessing, 29, 35, 57–61, 65, 95, 105, 107–8, 112
Conscientia, 31, 44, 117–19, 121–22, 124
see also Aquinas, Thomas; *Synderesis*
Consciousness
  covenantal, 62, 95, 97, 103–4, 106, 116, 122, 125, 132
  expansion of, 229, 238
  messianic, 234
  moral, 29, 32–33, 35–36, 44, 54, 59, 102, 109–11
  of Christ, 235
  of God, 29, 32, 35–36, 44, 53, 62, 92, 97, 102, 105, 109–11, 116, 120, 122–23, 125–33, 176–77
  of justification, 214
  of sin, 28–29, 40–43, 46, 51, 53, 55, 102, 107, 109, 113
  of sins, 212
  self-consciousness, 28, 32–33, 35–36, 46, 54, 59, 62, 109, 114
Contemplative prayer, 220–21, 224
Contrition, 34, 42
Conversion, 208, 214
Conviction, 160, 161–67, 168, 169, 171, 172, 178
  by law, 161, 162, 167, 169, 171
  of natural conscience, 160
  of sin, 161, 162, 164, 168

saving or redeeming, 163
spiritual, 164
see also Illumination
Coram Deo, 45, 192, 196, 211, 214
Coram mundo, 192
Corruption, complete, 93, 120
see also Fall, the; Noetic effects of sin; Sin
Covenant, 3, 10, 150, 151, 163, 166, 168, 169, 175, 191, 195
  history, 3, 11
  of creation/works, 65, 94–95, 103, 111
  of grace, 152, 166, 168, 169, 175, 195
  of marriage, 66–67
  of vocation, 92, 95, 97, 101, 103–4, 106, 109, 116, 122, 125, 132–33, 164, 168
  of works, 150, 152, 163, 164, 166, 169, 175, 215, 241, 246
  theology, 9–11, 14, 23, 94
  vocation, 234, 245
Covenant theology, 169
Created conscience, 28–30, 31, 43, 57–68, 95, 109, 125–26, 132
Creation, 135, 136, 141–45, 150, 157, 161, 163, 164, 166, 170, 172, 173, 176, 182, 183, 187
  as ethical act, 52
  conscience in, 239, 241, 243–44
  doctrine of, 13, 15, 20–21, 23, 241, 243–44
  ex nihilo (out of nothing), 20, 28–29, 68
  goodness of, 58–60
  new, 170, 172, 173, 176, 191, 225, 231, 238, 240
  order of, 9, 28, 52, 54, 60, 111, 128, 130, 164
  original knowledge of God, 140
  revelation in, 141–45, 150
  see also Doctrine of creation
Creatures, accountability of, 62

D

Darkness of understanding, 137, 154, 160, 178
Dead works, 213

Debased mind, 148, 149, 150, 152
Delight, spiritual, 160, 173, 178–87
  in God, 180, 185, 186
  restoration of, 173, 178–87
  see Spiritual delight
Depravity, total, 136, 137, 141
Desire, 140, 152, 157, 160, 165, 178, 187
  idolatrous, 152, 157
Dialogue, internal, 36, 115
Discernment, 35, 48, 109, 121, 126, 128
  good and evil, 48, 109, 121
Disordered love, 154, 156
Divine grace, 209
Divine light, 167
Divine mercy, 216
Divine requirement, 190
Doctrine of creation, 28–29, 43, 57–68, 95, 109, 111, 125–26, 132
Doctrine of fall, 28, 43, 58, 61–62, 93, 109, 117, 120, 122, 125, 130, 132
Double grace, 190

E

Eden, 28, 47, 53, 60, 64, 121, 130
Effectual calling, 176–77, 192, 195, 207
  see also Calling
Election, 222
Emotions, 43, 51, 55, 93, 96, 98–107, 114, 116, 132–33, 137, 138, 162, 165, 169, 181, 197, 204
  moral, 51, 93, 96, 98–101, 104, 115
  see also Fear; Guilt; Shame
Enlightenment, 98
Epicureanism, 143
Epistemological category, sin as, 135
Epistemology of love, 143
Eschatological transformation, 227, 229
Eschatology, 15, 25, 59–60, 64
Estrangement from God, 218, 224
Ethical conduct, 13, 148
Ethical judgment, 33, 35, 57, 61, 65, 114
Evangelical illumination, 163, 167, 168, 169, 171
Evaluative fall, 154, 157
Evaluative powers, 160, 178

Eve, see Adam and Eve
Evil, 137
Exegesis, 18, 28–29, 31, 43, 57, 93, 117, 120
Experience
  of conscience, see Conscience, experience of
  subjective, 31, 39–40, 42, 44, 55, 97, 100–101, 106, 116, 122, 125, 132
Experiential knowing, 144
Experiential *parrēsía*, 225
Extra nos, 160, 171, 175, 191, 192, 202, 210
Eyes, opening of, 46, 109

F

Face, 102, 106
Faculty, conscience as a, 29, 95, 97–99, 116, 120, 132
  thick sense, 97–98
  thin sense, 97–98
Faith, 139, 150, 160, 164, 167, 169, 177, 180, 183, 185, 189, 193, 195, 197, 200
  assurance of, 218, 224
  certainty of, 218
  chief exercise, 219
  gift of, 185
  in Christ, 193, 197, 200
  objective, 185
  reflex act of, 195
  walk by, 231
Fall, the, 28–29, 43–44, 46, 51, 53, 57, 59, 61–64, 93, 98–99, 109, 117, 120, 122, 125, 130, 132, 135, 136, 137, 138, 139, 140, 141, 145, 153, 154, 155, 156, 157, 160, 161, 163, 164, 166, 173, 174, 176, 177, 199, 202, 203
  cognitive consequences of, 154, 160
  doctrine of, see Doctrine of fall
  evaluative effects of, 154
  noetic effects of, 136, 142, 147, 154, 160, 172
  of conscience, 135–57
Fallen conscience, 28–29, 43, 46, 59, 92–133
Fear, 31, 44, 47, 51–54, 55, 59–60, 62–65, 93, 100–101, 104–5, 109–10, 113,

116, 122, 125, 130, 132, 136, 140, 160, 179, 197, 199, 202–3
afflictive, 224
calming of, 207–8, 210, 221, 225, 247
delivered from, 232
dispelled, 222
filial, 63–64
filial awareness, 214
of God, 35, 49, 51–52, 54, 63–64, 104–5, 110, 114, 123
quiets, 223
Feeling, 137, 138, 144, 147, 151, 152, 155, 179, 186, 197
see also Emotions
Fiats of creation, 28
Finitude, 136, 153
Forensic justification, 175, 189, 191, 192, 193, 196, 197, 200, 201, 208, 212, 225, 240
see also Justification
Forgiveness of sins, 214
Foro conscientiae, 160, 192, 195, 196, 198, 199, 201
Foro divino, 160, 189, 191, 196, 199
Fruitio Dei, 231, 232, 234
Function of conscience, 29, 30–31, 57–68, 95, 110, 112, 122, 125, 132
Futility of mind, 137, 152

G

Garden of Eden, see Eden
General revelation, 143–47, 150, 164
insufficiency of, 145
Gentiles, 111–12, 137, 144, 149
Gifford Lectures, 143
Gladness, 60
Glorification, 222, 227, 229, 231–33, 248
Glory of God, see God, glory of
God, 135–205 (*passim*)
as Creator, 20, 21, 28–29, 36, 52, 57–60, 62, 95, 103, 111, 127, 130, 136, 161, 163, 164, 169
as Father, 160, 169, 180, 189, 192, 195, 199, 204

as Judge, 35, 48, 51, 54, 107, 111, 123, 135, 197, 203
as Legislator, 21, 65, 94
attributes of, 60
awareness of, 229, 231
communion with, see Communion with God
coram Deo, 211
covenant Lord, 14, 18, 151
divine grace, 209
fatherly love, 219
glory of, 46, 58–60, 62, 95, 113, 127, 225, 231–32
imago Dei, 236, 245
knowledge of, 28, 35, 37, 52, 57–58, 60–62, 65, 95, 103, 105, 109–11, 121, 123, 125–32, 136, 139, 140–54, 161–65, 170, 174, 176, 185
knowledge of, see Knowledge of God
love of, 207
peace with, 213, 222
presence of, 44, 47, 51, 53–55, 58, 60, 63, 104, 106, 125–26, 128, 130–32, 229, 235–37
reordering human life, 207, 210, 214
self-revelation, 4, 6, 8, 221
Triune, see Trinity
visio Dei, 230
voice/sound of, 51, 62–63, 128
Good, 154, 156, 157, 160, 174, 177, 178, 183
perception of, 57, 109, 113, 118–19
Goodness of creation, 58–60
Gospel, 4, 22, 135, 160, 161, 162, 163, 164, 165, 166, 167, 168, 169, 170, 171, 172, 176, 180, 185, 187, 189, 190, 195, 203
and law, 2, 135, 160, 162, 167, 168, 185
light, 160, 161, 163, 167, 169, 170
message, 162, 163, 168
promise of grace, 169
Grace, 145, 150, 160, 163, 167, 169, 172, 175, 176, 177, 179, 185, 187, 192, 195, 200
common, 173
covenant of, 152, 166, 168, 169, 175, 195
means of, 163

of Christ, 167, 185, 200
Greek philosophy, 148
Guilt, 28, 31, 39-44, 46-48, 51, 53-55,
    59-60, 62-66, 93, 100-104, 106-7,
    109, 112-14, 123, 130-31, 138, 160,
    171
  afflictive, 207, 210, 212-13, 225
  covenantal, 210
  delivered from, 232
  feeling of, 31, 39-44, 46, 53, 100-104,
    112-13, 207, 210-11
  objective, 39, 41, 46
  reversal of, 214, 225
  subduing of, 207-8, 210-12, 225, 247
  subjective, 39-40, 42, 46, 102

H

Hands/Palms, 31, 37-38, 55, 107
  innocence of, 38
  moral judgment of, 37-38
Hardening of heart, 35
Hardness of heart, 137, 138
Harmony
  prelapsarian, 28, 46, 58
  with God, 28-29, 46, 51, 58
Heart, 31-36, 37-38, 44-45, 51, 55, 62,
    65, 96, 102, 104, 107, 109, 111-12,
    114-15, 120, 126, 137, 138, 140, 147,
    148, 149, 150, 152, 155, 156, 162, 166,
    168, 179, 183, 195, 197, 202
  as seat of conscience, 32, 35
  beating/striking of, 32-33, 45, 114
  callous, 137
  clean/pure, 34, 112
  contrite, 34
  darkened, 147
  deceitful, 152-53
  foolish, 147
  hardness of, 35, 137, 138
  law written on, 65, 111-12, 120
Heavenly lawsuit, 164
Heidelberg Catechism, 180
Heilsgeschichtlich scheme, 152
Hiddenness, 31, 44, 53-55, 59-60, 62-64,
    106, 109, 136, 160
  abandonment of, 207-8, 210, 221, 225,
    247
  calls from, 223
  impulse to hide, 209, 220, 222, 225, 232
Holiness
  of life, 207, 213, 218
  of Son, 210, 234
  personal, 213
Holy Spirit, 4, 8-10, 14, 21, 24, 160,
    161-73, 175, 176, 178-82, 184, 185,
    187, 189, 191, 192, 193, 195, 196,
    199, 201-5
  action in conscience, 160, 161-70, 171,
    172, 189, 193, 195, 196, 199, 201-5
  action of, 227
  and affections, 162, 179, 184
  and Word, 160, 161, 163, 164, 165, 168,
    171, 172, 173, 175, 176, 178, 180, 181,
    187, 189, 195
  conviction by, 161-67, 168, 169, 240, 246
  illumination by, 160, 161-63, 167-70,
    240, 246
  in adoption, 199, 201-5
  in justification, 189, 191, 192, 193, 195
  in regeneration, 162, 171, 172, 173, 175,
    176, 178-82, 184, 185, 187
  mission of, 180, 184
  power of, 233, 248
  spirit of adoption, 207, 214, 216, 218-19,
    247
  witness of, 164, 168, 169, 195, 199, 201-4
  see also Illuminatio evangelica;
    Illuminatio legalis
Honor, 219-20
Human capacity, 136, 137, 138, 141, 144,
    147, 149, 152, 157, 160, 167, 172, 173,
    175, 176, 178, 179, 181, 183, 184,
    186, 187
  for self-scrutiny, 136, 153-57
  for sympathy, 137, 138
  for transparency, 136, 140-52, 153
  to evaluate truth, 157
Human depravity, 136
  see also Depravity, total
Human identity, 140, 148, 152, 181

imago Dei, 136, 148, 152
Human nature, 28, 43, 92, 94-95, 97, 100, 116, 132
  see also Anthropology, theological; Imago Dei
Human powers, 137, 143, 144, 147, 160, 172, 173, 178
  corruption of, 137
Human self-knowledge, 136, 140-52, 153
Human spirit, 201-4
Human sympathy, 138
Humanity
  consciousness of, 208, 227, 229-30, 235-38
  finite nature, 230, 236
  glorified, 227, 229-30, 243, 248
  reordering life, 207, 210, 214
  subjectivity of, 234
Huiothesia, 201

I

Idolatry, 49, 54, 107, 109, 137, 140, 146-48, 152, 153, 156, 157
  and self-deception, 153
  consequences of, 148
Ignorance, 137
Illumination, 160, 161-63, 167-70, 171, 172, 173, 178, 187
  illuminatio evangelica, 161, 167, 168, 169, 171
  illuminatio legalis, 161, 162, 163, 167, 169, 171
  of conscience, 160, 161-63, 167-70
  of understanding, 162
  spiritual, 172
  see also Conviction; Holy Spirit
Imago Christi, 236
Imago Dei, 23, 24, 65, 92, 94-95, 103, 116, 136, 148, 152, 160, 175, 236, 245
  covenantal understanding, 95
  holistic understanding, 95-96
Imago Trinitatis, 236
Imagination, 155-56, 157, 169
  and conscience, 96, 101, 113-14, 128
  cognitive, 156

corruption of, 156
  sensory, 156
Immediacy of perception, 128-32
  absolute, 131
  mediated, 128-29, 131
Immoral conduct, 137
Imperative, moral, 65, 66
Imputability, 97
Imputation, 160, 196, 197
  of righteousness, 160, 196, 197
Imputed righteousness, 211, 214
In nobis, 160, 175, 191, 192, 196, 202, 210, 224
Incarnation, 8, 173, 180
Indicative, moral, 58, 65
Indwelling sin, 211, 217, 225
Infusion, 173, 174, 175, 187, 189, 192, 196
  of righteousness, 189
Innocence
  of Abimelech, 38, 104
  original, 46, 53, 58, 60-61, 63, 109, 130
  state of, 57, 60-61, 63, 98, 109, 130
Innocent self-scrutiny, 136, 153-57
Intellect, 137, 145, 147, 148, 155, 181, 184, 185, 186, 187
  see also Reason; Thinking
Internal moral auditing, 135
Intuition, moral, 96, 105, 109, 123, 129
Inward transformation (conscience), 225
Israel, 33, 37, 49, 52, 66, 95, 103, 105-6, 147, 152, 160, 203

J

Jesus Christ, 46, 54, 61, 95
  conscience of, 61
  last Adam, 49, 61, 95
Job, conscience of, 35, 38
Judgment
  divine, 33, 35, 48-49, 51, 54, 65, 104, 107, 111, 123
  ethical, 33, 35, 57, 61, 65, 114
  moral, 34, 35, 37-38, 104
Justice, divine, 35-36, 46-47, 49, 104-5

Justification, 48, 135, 160, 163, 170, 173, 175, 189–205, 207–9, 212–14, 216–17, 222, 225, 232, 240, 247
- active, 160, 189, 191, 192, 195
- and adoption, 160, 189, 193, 198–205
- appropriation of, 214
- benefit of, 207, 225, 247
- by faith, 163
- consciousness of, 214
- forensic, 175, 189–93, 196, 197, 200, 201, 208, 212, 225, 240
- objective, 22, 24, 160, 189–98, 200, 202
- objective/subjective, 207–9, 211–14, 225, 240, 247
- of conscience, 160, 189–205
- passive, 160, 189–92, 195
- relation to sanctification, 190–91
- subjective, 13–14, 22, 24, 160, 189–93, 195–99, 201, 202, 205
- *see also* Adoption; Forensic justification; Sanctification

K

Kidneys, 31, 36–37, 44–45, 55, 96, 107
- as seat of conscience, 36
- God searching, 36, 44

Knowing, 40, 105, 109–10

Knowledge
- affective, 183, 184
- experiential, 144, 165
- moral, 155
- natural, 162, 164
- of God, *see* God, knowledge of
- of oneself, *see* Human self-knowledge
- saving, 165
- supernatural, 162

Knowledge of God, 28, 35, 37, 52, 57–58, 60–62, 65, 95, 103, 105, 109–11, 121, 123, 125–32
- experiential, 105, 109, 123–24, 127–32
- innate, 118, 120, 122, 125, 127–29
- propositional, 123, 129–32
- *see also Sensus divinitatis*

L

Language, 137, 140, 147, 148, 152, 154, 156, 182, 183, 195, 198
- and conscience, 31–32, 35, 37–44, 93, 96, 99, 101, 103, 105, 108, 110, 114–16, 120, 133
- covenantal, 151
- sensory-organ-malfunction, 146–47

Last Adam, 234, 238, 248

Law, 135, 148–52, 160–69, 180, 182, 190, 193, 195, 203, 208, 212, 216, 235, 241, 246
- and conscience, *see* Conscience and law
- and gospel, *see* Gospel and law
- conviction by, *see* Conviction by law
- delight in, 149, 150
- first use of, 166
- God's righteous decree, 151
- Moses, 166
- natural, *see* Natural law
- of creation, 164
- of God, 49, 65, 68, 103, 111–12, 118–19, 121
- of the mind, 151
- righteous requirement of, 151
- written in heart, 65, 111–12, 120, 149, 150

Legal declaration, 189

Legislating conscience, 57, 65–68, 95, 112

Liberty and boldness, 213, 223

Linguistic expressions of conscience, 31, 39, 55

Living water, 165

Lord's Prayer, 219

Love, 137, 140, 143, 154, 156, 160, 179, 180, 185, 195, 204, 207, 215, 219–20, 222, 231–32
- disordered, 154, 156
- epistemology of, 143
- of God, 140, 160, 179, 180, 185, 195, 204
- of self, 137
- perfect, 64

M

Manifestation of conscience, 29, 31–55, 57, 61, 99, 101, 105–8, 114–16
Marriage, covenant of, 66–67
Mediator, 174, 175, 195
Meditation, 115–16
Meditative prayer, 220–21
Memory, and conscience, 96, 112–13
Metaphors for conscience
  hands/palms, 31, 37–38, 55, 107
  heart, 31–36, 37–38, 44–45, 51, 55, 62, 65, 96, 102, 104, 107, 109, 111–12, 114–15, 120, 126
  kidneys, 31, 36–37, 44–45, 55, 96, 107
Methodological presuppositions, 4
Mind, 32, 58, 95, 108, 112, 115, 126, 133, 137, 139, 140, 141, 145, 147, 148–53, 154, 155, 156, 157, 162, 164, 167, 169, 171, 172, 175, 177, 178, 179, 181, 185
  callousness of, 139
  debased, 148, 149, 150, 152
  futility of, 137, 152
  guiding faculty, 178
  illumination of, 162, 167, 169, 171, 172, 175, 177, 187
  see also Reason; Thinking
Monastic tradition, 183
Moral agency, 135
Moral callousness, 139, 152, 153
Moral consciousness, 135, 186
Moral emotions, 51, 93, 96, 98–101, 104, 115, 138
  see also Fear; Guilt; Shame
Moral judgment, 155
  see also Ethical judgment
Moral law, 149, 151, 208
  see also Law, of God; Natural law
Moral order, 51, 54, 68
Moral sentiment, 155
Moral theology, 2
Mortification, 208
Mysticism, 187

N

Nakedness, 45–46, 48, 53, 55, 109
Natural conscience, 161, 163, 164
Natural existence, 136, 140
Natural instinct, 143
Natural knowledge, 162, 164
Natural law, 3, 16, 51, 65, 103, 111, 117–23
  Aquinas on, 119, 121–22
  Calvin on, 119–23
Natural religion, 5
Natural revelation, *see* General revelation
Natural theology, 3, 143, 145
Nature and grace, 145, 175
Nature of conscience, 29–31, 57, 61, 68, 93, 100, 102, 110, 113, 116, 120, 123–25, 129, 132–33
New birth, 165, 176, 181
Noetic effects of sin, 24, 93, 120–22, 124, 136, 142, 147, 154, 160, 172
  see also Corruption, complete; Fall, the; Sin
Nonphysical perception, 143, 144, 147, 161, 173
Nonphysical perceptual awareness, 93, 125–33
Nudity, *see* Nakedness

O

Obedience, 151, 196, 204
Objective justification, *see* Justification, objective
Objective revelation, 141, 142, 151
Objective sanctification, 208, 225
Obligation, moral, 51, 58, 61, 65–67, 95, 109, 127, 130
Old Testament, 147, 153, 156, 201
  conscience in, 15–19, 23, 29, 31–44, 55, 57, 99, 102, 104, 106–8, 110–11, 113–16
  linguistic expressions, 31, 39, 55, 99
Ontological transformation, 175, 192
Openness, 221, 223–25
Oral-aural theology, 236–37

Ordo salutis, 198, 199, 200
Original integrity, 137
Orphan mind-set, 216
Owen, John
 on adoption, 217
 on affections, 162, 178-79
 on communion, 236
 on conscience, 162, 165, 172, 178
 on conviction, 162, 164, 165
 on illumination, 161, 162, 163, 167, 168, 172
 on indwelling sin, 225
 on justification, 163, 191, 193, 212-13
 on *parrēsía*, 223-24
 on regeneration, 162, 171, 172, 173, 175, 176, 178-79, 183

P

Pacifying of shame, 207-8, 210, 214, 225, 247
Parrēsía, 221-25, 232-35, 240
 completed condition, 233
 experiential, 225
 gift of grace, 223, 232
 of Son, 234-35
 spiritual posture, 221
Participatio Christi, 196
Passive justification, *see* Justification, passive
Passivity, 166, 181
Pastoral theology, 153
Patristic theology, 3, 18, 139, 140, 151, 183
Paul (Apostle), 35, 58, 61, 93, 105, 110-12, 208, 211, 216, 229
 on conscience, 16-19, 58, 61, 105, 110-12
 on fear of the Lord, 105
 on law and Gentiles, 111-12
Peace with God, 213, 217-18, 222
Pentecost, 8
Perception, 135, 143, 144, 145, 147, 151, 152, 154, 155, 157, 160, 161, 165, 168, 169, 172, 173, 177, 178, 180, 181, 182, 183, 185, 186, 187, 196, 197
 divine, 125-32
 immediacy of, 128-32

 moral, 97, 105, 109-10, 122-23, 125, 186
 nonphysical, 93, 125-33, 135, 143, 144, 147, 161, 173, 229, 239, 245
 of God, 135, 143, 144, 151, 152, 161, 165, 168, 169, 172, 177, 180, 182, 183, 185, 187, 230
 of good and evil, 57, 109, 113, 118-19
 reversal of, 207, 225, 247
 sense, 143, 144
 spiritual, 161, 182
 wise, 172
Perceptual awareness, 135
Perfected conscience, *see* Conscience, Perfected
Perfection, original, 59, 129
Person, whole, 95-97, 105-7, 112, 120
Personal holiness, 213
Philosophy of mind, 153
Piety, 190
Positional sanctification, 208
Practical reason, 152, 166, 196
Prayer, 208, 218-21, 227
 Abba Father, 216, 218, 223
 contemplative, 220-21
 Lord's Prayer, 219
Preaching, 168, 171, 175, 184, 189
Predestination, 195
Prelapsarian state, *see* Conscience, prelapsarian; Innocence, original;
Presence of God, 144, 157, 168, 181, 182
 see also God, presence of
Priestly literature (Leviticus), 39-43, 101-2
Primal awareness of God, 135
Probity of conscience, 136, 140
Progressive sanctification, 160, 208, 210, 213, 220, 222
 see also Sanctification
Prophets, 49, 54
Prosoponic exegesis, 8
Protestant theology, 173, 189, 192, 193, 196
Psychology (moral), 12
Punishment, 36, 43, 55, 64

see also Judgment, divine
Pure heart, 34, 112
Purification offering, 39, 101
Puritan pastoral theology, 153

Q
Qohelet (Preacher), 35

R
Reason, 32, 65, 94, 96, 105, 108-9, 111, 115, 117-25, 128, 133, 145, 148, 150, 154, 155, 166, 167, 168, 172, 177, 181, 183, 185
  fall of, 154
  human, 150, 167, 168, 183
  practical, 118-19, 122, 124, 133
  speculative, 118
  speculative processes of, 150
  see also Thinking
Redeemed conscience, *see* Conscience, redeemed
Redemption, 3, 5, 10-12, 23, 28, 46, 98, 122, 135, 145, 146, 150, 160, 161, 163, 168, 169, 170, 172, 173, 175, 176, 177, 181, 182, 183, 187, 189, 192, 193, 198, 199, 213, 222-25, 234, 239-40, 246
  drama of, 2, 4, 8, 15, 135
  economy of, 145, 150, 163
  of conscience, *see* Conscience, redeemed
Redemptive reversals, 160
Reformation, 153, 162, 164, 175, 180, 197
Reformed Dogmatics, 160, 168, 173, 175, 176, 177, 180, 189, 191, 192, 193, 195, 196, 197, 199
Reformed ethics, 196, 199
Reformed theology, 136, 137, 160, 161, 166, 169, 171, 173, 185, 189, 190, 195, 198, 199
  conscience in, 136
  illumination in, 161, 169
  justification in, 189, 190
  regeneration in, 173
Reformed understanding, 225

Regeneration, 160, 162, 163, 164, 165, 171-87, 189, 190, 191, 192, 195, 210, 224, 240, 246-47
  and justification, 190, 191, 192, 195
  as renewal of sensus, 173-177
  as restoration of delight, 173, 178-87
  cognitive benefits of, 177
  of conscience, *see* Conscience, regeneration of
Rejoicing, 60-61
Relationality, 157
Religious insensitivity, 139
Remorse, 33, 42, 43, 46
Repentance, 34, 103, 208-9
Reprobate, 171, 185
Resurrection of Christ, 189, 192, 195
Retrieval theology, 7
Retribution, divine, 35, 49, 52
  see also Judgment, divine
Revelation, 141-145, 150, 161, 162, 163, 164, 166, 168, 169, 171, 172, 176, 182, 185
  general, *see* General revelation
  general/natural, 52, 62, 111, 125, 127-28, 131-32
  in creation, 28, 52, 111, 126-28, 130-32
  natural, *see* General revelation
  objective external, 141-42
  of creation, *see* Creation, revelation in
  special, 4-6, 8, 52, 62, 98, 101, 129, 131, 146, 164, 167
  subjective, 28, 126-27, 132
  see also Word of God
Righteousness, 28, 35, 37-38, 49, 53, 60, 105, 110, 113, 115, 125, 135, 149, 151, 152, 157, 160, 164, 189, 190, 191, 192, 193, 196, 197, 198, 200
  imputed, 160, 196, 197
  inherent, 191
  of Christ, 160, 196, 197
  of God, 189, 190, 191, 196
Righteousness of Christ, 211, 214
Roman Catholic theology, 192

S
Sabbath, 58-60

Sacraments, 168
Sacrifices, 34, 39, 41, 101-2, 106
Salvation, 28, 66, 98, 128-29, 135, 145,
    160-63, 165-169, 171-73, 175-77,
    189-93, 196-97, 201
  drama of, 2, 4, 8, 135
  experiential knowledge of, 165
  history of, 172
  objective side of, 175, 196
  subjective side of, 175, 192, 196
Sanctification, 160, 187, 189-93, 196-97,
    200-201, 205, 207-10, 212-14, 217,
    220, 222, 224-25, 232, 240, 247
  affective transformation, 207, 225, 247
  and justification, 190-91
  of conscience, 160, 205, 207-210,
    212-14, 217, 221-22, 224-25, 240,
    247
  objective/subjective, 207-9, 225
  positional, 208
  progressive, 160, 208, 210, 213, 220, 222
Saul (king), 32-33
Scholasticism, 18, 93, 117-22, 124
Scripture, 4-7, 10, 15-16, 23, 28-29, 31-32,
    43-45, 51, 57, 62, 96, 100, 102, 107,
    111, 117, 120, 122, 137, 145, 151, 160,
    169, 182, 185, 190, 192, 204 Self,
    135, 137, 140, 153-57, 169, 173, 181,
    193, 202
Self-awareness, *see* Awareness, self-
  awareness
Self-consciousness, *see* Consciousness,
  self-consciousness
Self-deception, 93, 153-57
  idolatrous, 153
  morally culpable, 156
Self-evaluation, 22, 38, 106, 110
Self-judgment, 48
Self-knowledge, 93
Self-persuasion, 156
Self-scrutiny, 136, 153-57
  incapable of innocent, 136, 153-57
Sensus, 93, 98, 117, 121-25, 127-33, 227,
    229, 234-35, 239, 241, 245-47

divinitatis, 13, 22, 24, 58, 65, 93, 123,
    126-27, 129-32, 136, 139, 143-44,
    146, 148, 150-52, 154-55, 157,
    160-61, 163, 165, 172-73, 176-79,
    181, 183, 186-87, 207, 209-10, 212,
    229, 234, 239, 245, 247-48
  in Calvin, 143, 155, 157, 165, 177, 179
  in Plantinga, 177, 179
  iudicii, 13, 123, 126-27, 129, 187, 233-34,
    240
  renewal of, 173-77, 229, 247-48
  repairing of, 177, 179
  restoration of, 207, 229, 247-48
Sense perception, 143-44
Sensibility, spiritual, 160, 173
Sensitivity, 138-39, 141, 152-53, 157, 181,
    202
  religious, 139
Sensory imagination, 156
Servant Songs (Isaiah), 49
Shame, 31, 44-51, 53-55, 59-60, 62-66, 93,
    100-101, 105-7, 109, 117, 136, 138,
    160, 207, 209-10, 214-17, 220, 222,
    225, 232-33, 247
  and conscience, 44-51, 53, 55, 63,
    100-101, 105-7
  creaturely, 207
  delivered from, 232
  godward orientation, 45, 49-50
  healing of, 220
  in Genesis, 44-48, 50
  in Prophets, 49
  in Psalms, 49
  in Proverbs, 50
  pacifying of, 207-8, 210, 214, 225, 247
  reversed, 220, 225
Sin, 24, 28-29, 34, 39-44, 46-48, 51, 53-55,
    57-58, 61-66, 93, 98, 101-4, 106-7,
    109, 111-14, 118-23, 130-31, 135-37,
    139-42, 144-47, 150, 152-54, 156-
    57, 160-62, 164, 168, 171-78, 180,
    191-92, 195, 197, 201, 203, 211-12,
    214, 217, 225, 239, 245
  as epistemological category, 135

awareness/consciousness of, 28–29, 40–43, 46, 51, 53, 55, 102, 107, 109, 113
bondage of, 140
consciousness of, 212
conviction of, 161–62, 164, 168
corruption of, 239, 245
dead in, 178
effects of, *see* Corruption, complete; Fall, the; Noetic effects of sin
heinousness of, 180
indwelling, 211, 217, 225
power of, 135, 144–47, 150
sense of, 214
unintentional, 39–40
Sinful humanity, 137, 140, 146
Slavery, spirit of, 199, 203
Son of God, 162, 173, 180, 184, 201
Sonship, 208, 216, 234
Soteriology, 13, 15, 21, 23, 24, 177, 190, 193, 196–98, 200–201
Soul, 33, 94
Special revelation, *see* Revelation, special
Spirit, human, 34, 96
Spirit, *see* Holy Spirit
Spiritual anesthesia, 160
Spiritual delight, *see* Delight, spiritual
Spiritual disciplines, 208
Spiritual illumination, 172
Spiritual perception, 161, 182
Spiritual senses, 182–84
Steadfast spirit, 34
Subjective justification, *see* Justification, subjective
Subjective sanctification, 209, 225
Subjectivity, 14, 142–43, 192, 207–9, 212–14, 216–17, 224–25, 233–35, 238, 240, 247
Sympathy, 137–38, 148, 151
Synderesis, 29, 93, 117–25, 183, 196
  Aquinas on, 117–20, 122
  Calvin's abandonment of, 119–21
  infallibility of, 29, 118–20
Scholastic notion, 29, 93, 117–19

T

Taste, 172, 182–86, 204
  spiritual, 172, 182–86, 204
Temptation, 113
Theological anthropology, 192
Theology of conscience, 2–7, 12, 15–16, 20, 135, 149, 160, 169, 210, 227, 235, 239
Theosis, 196, 198
Thinking, 32, 35, 43, 93–94, 96, 99, 105, 108–114, 116, 121–22, 125, 128–30, 132–33
  and conscience, 32, 35, 43, 93–94, 96, 99, 105, 108–14, 116, 121–22, 125, 129–30, 132–33
  inferential, 102, 108, 110, 118, 122, 124–25, 133
  spontaneous reflection, 108–9
Thoughts, accusing/excusing, 112, 114
Torah, *see* Law
Total depravity, *see* Depravity, total
Transformation, 207, 225, 227, 233, 240, 247
  affective, 207, 225, 247
  cognitive, 225
  eschatological, 227
  of conscience, 207, 225, 233, 240, 247
Transparency in self-knowledge, *see* Human self-knowledge, lack of transparency
Transgression, *see* Sin Trinitarian soteriology, 190, 193
Trinity, 48, 98, 129, 132–33, 141, 184, 190, 192–93, 207, 216, 235–38, 241, 243–45
  communicative dynamism, 236
  dialogical life, 237
  imago Trinitatis, 236
  participation in life, 235–36, 238
  triune God, 3, 7–9, 18, 20, 21, 207, 235–36, 238, 241, 243–45
Trust in God, 49, 63–64
Truth, 140, 143, 145–47, 152–57, 160, 165, 172, 176, 178, 180, 184–85, 203

aversion to, 154
suppression of, 140, 145
witness to, 57-58, 111

U

Understanding, 29, 32, 35, 46, 50, 52, 96, 100, 108, 110, 115, 117-18, 120-21, 123, 127, 130, 132, 137, 139, 144, 147-48, 150-51, 154, 160, 162, 167, 172, 174-75, 178, 184-85, 197
see also Reason; Thinking
darkened, 137, 154, 160, 178
illumination of, 162
Unfaithfulness, covenantal, 41, 106
Union with Christ, 198, 200-201, 207-8, 217, 233-34
benefits of, 207-8, 217
Unworthiness, 215, 217, 223

V

Verbum alienum, 167
Verbum externum, 168
Verbum internum, 168
Vicarious sacrifice, 214
Visio Beatifica, 230
Visio Dei, 25, 230
Vocation, covenantal, *see* Covenant of vocation
Voice of conscience, 210-11, 237
Voice of God, *see* God, voice/sound of
Volition, *see* Will

W

Whole Christ, 209
Will, 59, 61, 93-94, 96, 99, 103, 113-14, 116, 120, 125, 133, 137, 140, 152, 154-55, 157, 160, 162, 165, 172, 174-75, 178-81, 183, 185, 187, 190, 192
and conscience, 59, 61, 93-94, 96, 99, 103, 113-14, 116, 120, 133
bondage of, 140, 154, 160, 178
conversion of, 179
fall of, 154
ruling faculty, 178
Wisdom, 35, 46, 50-52, 105, 110, 115, 125
divine, 50, 52
literature, 35, 51-52, 110, 115, 140
Witness of conscience, *see* Conscience, witnessing to God's truth, 57-58, 111
evaluative fall, 154, 157
secret instinct, 155, 157, 176
Word of God, 4, 5, 8, 10, 44, 51, 62, 96, 103, 106, 116, 160-65, 168-76, 178, 180-87, 189, 195
and Spirit, *see* Holy Spirit and Word as means of grace, 163
convicting power, 164
in regeneration, 171-73, 175-76, 178, 180181, 187
Worship, 102-3

Y

YHWH (Yahweh), *see* God

NAME INDEX

A

Alexander, Archibald, 186
Allen, Michael, 7, 12, 13, 23, 172
Alston, William, 128-29, 131
Alter, Robert, 33-35, 47, 115-16, 183
Anselm, 230-31
Aquinas, Thomas, 13, 92, 117-25, 133, 183-85
Ash, Christopher, 22
Augustine, 65, 111, 117, 121

B

Balthasar, Hans Urs von, 221-24
Barr, James, 18
Barth, Karl, 168, 191
Baschera, Luca, 22
Baugh, Steven, 137, 138
Bavinck, Herman, 11-16, 21, 28-29, 47, 55, 61, 65-66, 93-95, 100, 111-12, 118, 126-27, 160, 167, 175, 177, 180, 189, 191-93, 195-97, 199
Beale, Gregory K., 54, 146-47, 160
Bellarmine, Robert, 197
Berkouwer, Gerrit C., 68, 95-96, 111, 120, 190, 192, 195, 201
Bernard of Clairvaux, 183-84
Boda, Mark J., 19, 39, 41-42
Bonhoeffer, Dietrich, 28, 46-47
Brunner, Emil, 168
Boston, Thomas, 23

C

Calvin, John, 1, 12, 13, 33-34, 36, 47-48, 57-58, 61-62, 65, 92-94, 103, 108, 111, 117, 119-27, 129-33, 138, 140-44, 146-47, 151, 55, 157, 160, 165-66, 168, 171, 76, 177, 179, 180, 183, 185, 190, 192, 204
Cancrini, Antonia, 17, 19, 138
Carson, Donald A., 4-7, 18, 19, 164, 208
Chalmers, Thomas, 160
Charnock, Stephen, 126, 175-76
Chisholm, Robert, 36
Clark, Stephen R. L., 145
Cortez, Marc, 11, 12, 16, 19
Cotterell, Peter, 18
Courcelle, Pierre, 140
Cranfield, C. E. B., 111, 141-42, 145, 146, 147, 148, 202
Cross, Richard, 183

D

D'Avenia, Marco, 124, 183, 185
Delitzsch, Franz, 35, 59-60
Dowey, Edward A. Jr., 28, 95, 123, 126-27, 185

F

Fee, Gordon, 138
Fesko, John V., 160
Flint, Thomas P., 135
Fox, Michael V., 50-52, 110-11, 115
Fulton, Rachel, 183

G

Garner, David B., 198, 200-201, 203
Goldingay, John, 32, 36, 49, 59, 115
Goodwin, Thomas, 135, 173-75
Grabill, Stephen, 122-23

H

Harris, Murray J., 142
Helm, Paul, 120, 127, 129-32, 140, 145, 177, 185
Hendriksen, William, 164
Hodge, Charles, 11
Horton, Michael, 4-7, 10-12, 14, 28, 47, 51, 168, 172, 173, 175, 180, 198, 236
Howard, Jason, 97-99, 101, 122
Hugenberger, Gordon, 66-67

J

Jackendoff, Ray, 17, 115
Jeremias, Joachim, 218
Jerome, 117
Jewett, Paul, 94, 112
Jobes, Karen H., 220
John of Damascus, 151
Johnson, Aubrey R., 32, 37, 106
Johnson, Dennis E., 149
Josiah, King, 103

K

Käsemann, Ernst, 141
King, David M., 179
Kline, Meredith G., 9, 48, 51, 53-54, 58, 65, 203
Knight III, George W., 138, 139
Kries, Douglas, 117, 202
Krokos, Jan, 117-18
Kuyper, Abraham, 175

L

Lane, William A., 212, 223
Lé, Dan, 215
Lehmann, Paul, 2
Levenson, Jon D., 64
Levering, Matthew, 2, 9
Lewis, C.S., 31, 123-24
Lints, Richard, 95, 103
Longenecker, Richard N., 141, 142, 144, 145
Luc, Alex, 32
Luther, Martin, 111, 120-21

M

Martyr, Peter, 199
McCormack, Bruce L., 173, 175, 190, 191
McGinn, Colin, 156
McGrath, Alister E., 168
McInroy, Mark J., 182
McLaughlin, Brian P., 153
Melanchthon, Philip, 195, 197
Milgrom, Jacob, 39, 42-43, 101-102
Moberly, Robert W. L., 19
Moo, Douglas J., 141, 144, 145, 148-52, 201, 203-4, 218-19
Morris, Leon, 61
Muller, Richard A., 161, 162, 169, 171, 189, 193, 200, 230

O

O'Brien, Peter T., 138
O'Donovan, Oliver, 18
Ong, Walter J., 236-37
Origen, 182, 202
Ortlund, Dane, 215-16
Owen, John, 9, 28, 96, 112, 128, 161-68, 171-76, 178-79, 183, 191, 193, 212-13, 217, 220, 223-25, 231-33, 236

P

Pak, Joseph K., 153
Pannenberg, Wolfhart, 16, 55, 64, 100-101
Pascal, Blaise, 145, 154-55, 157, 176, 180
Perkins, William, 22
Peter Martyr Vermigli, 199
Pierce, Claude A., 16, 18-19, 138, 139, 212
Plantinga, Alvin, 177, 179, 180
Potts, Timothy C., 16, 18, 20
Poythress, Vern S., 237

Q

Quintilian, 57

R

Rad, Gerhard von, 44, 52, 110, 115, 125, 140
Rahner, Karl, 182
Ratzinger, Jospeh, 121
Ricouer, Paul, 2, 79-80
Ridderbos, Herman N., 149, 150, 165, 200
Rowland, Christopher, 145

S

Salvioli, Marco, 183
Sand, Alexander, 148-49
Sanday, William, 141
Sanders, Fred, 8
Sarna, Nahum M., 46, 51, 53-54, 59, 67, 102, 104-5, 109-10, 113, 131
Schliesser, Eric, 138
Silva, Moisés, 18
Sklar, Jay, 39-43
Sorabji, Richard, 1, 19
Spicq, Ceslas, 18-19
Spijker, Willem van't, 175
Stoker, Hendrik G., 13, 17, 19, 186
Strohm, Paul, 1
Sweeney, Marvin A., 9

T

Ten Elshof, Gregg A., 153
Theissen, Gerd, 170, 229
Thiselton, Anthony C., 16, 22, 202, 227, 229
Torrance, Thomas F., 135, 139, 151, 165
Trueman, Carl R., 167
Trumper, Timothy J. R., 198-99
Turretin, Francis, 11, 199-200, 232-33
Turner, Max, 18

V

VanDrunen, David, 16, 51, 63, 111, 119
Vanhoozer, Kevin J., 5, 10, 17, 153, 167, 176
Van Til, Cornelius, 62
Vos, Geerhardus, 3, 4, 9, 60, 127-28, 130, 145-46, 234-35

W

Waltke, Bruce, 46
Ward, Timothy, 4, 5, 7, 8, 10
Warfield, Benjamin B., 64, 176-77, 180, 185, 187, 201-2
Webster, John B., 2, 5-7, 9, 11-13, 17, 18, 20- 23, 28, 45, 51-52, 62, 92, 94, 100-101, 116, 128, 135-36, 153, 163, 167, 169, 172-73, 181, 190, 210, 233, 239, 241-42
Welch, Edward T., 48
Westphal, Merold, 135, 210-11
Witsius, Herman, 193, 200, 202, 204-5
Wolff, Hans Walter, 32-34, 36-37
Wood, William, 145, 154-57, 176, 180
Wright, Nicholas T. (N.T.), 143, 150, 152, 164

Y

Young, Edward J., 107

Z

Zachman, Randall C., 57, 120, 124, 127, 166-68
Zahl, Simeon, 12, 14-15, 160, 162, 180, 185, 187, 190-93, 195-98, 201, 209, 213-14, 217, 220

SCRIPTURE INDEX

—

Old Testament

Genesis

Reference	Page
1	27, 59
1–2	228
1–3	51, 203
1:3	170
1:31	58, 59
2	27
2:16–17	63
2:19–20	63
2:21	63
2:22–23	63
2:23	66, 67
2:24	67
2:25	44, 45
3	46, 50, 63, 203
3:7	44, 46
3:7–10	109
3:7a	48
3:8	44, 53, 54, 63
3:8–10	203
3:10	44, 53, 63
3:12	47
3:13	47
4:5	102
11:6	113
14:22	37
20:1–2	104
20:3	38
20:3–5	104
20:5	38
20:6–7	104
20:8	104
20:9	104
20:11	104
22:1	106
29:14	67
31:11	106
41:9	112
43:3	106
43:5	106
46:2	106

Exodus

Reference	Page
3:4	106
7:3	35
14:8	37
24:7	103
39:43	58

Leviticus

Reference	Page
1–3	101
4–5	101
4:13–14	39
4:22–23	39, 40
4:27–28	39, 40
6:2–5	39, 41
6:4	42
9	102
16	102
23	102
26:36	103

Numbers

Reference	Page
5:6–7	41
15:30	37
20:9–11	37
28–29	102

Deuteronomy

Reference	Page
4:12	50
5:22–23	50
28:58	103

Joshua

Reference	Page
1:8	103, 116

Judges

Reference	Page
9:2–3	67

1 Samuel

Reference	Page
3:4	106
21:13	183
23:16	37
24:4–5	32

2 Samuel

Reference	Page
5:2	67
12:7	211
14:24	106
19:13	67
21:1	42, 44
24:10	33, 114

1 Kings

17:18 112
19:12 50

2 Kings

22:8 103
22:11 103
22:13 103
22:19 103

1 Chronicles

11:1 67

Ezra

9:1-3 106
9:6................................ 106

Nehemiah

1:6-7 107

Job

8:3-6 38
9 38
9:2.................................. 38
9:3a 38
9:20-21........................... 38
9:22................................ 38
9:30-31a 38
20:3 103
23:16 103
27:6 35

Psalms

1:2 115
4:4 .... 33, 115
6:1-2 107
7:9 36
11:2 34
14:1 34
16:7 37
16:11 37
17:3 .... 33, 113
22:5 49
24:4 .... 34, 38
25 112
25:2-3 49
25:6-7 112
25:11 112
25:20 49
26:2 36
27:8 115
29 .... 50, 63
31:1 49
31:17 49
33:6-9 10
34:8 .... 59, 183
34:11 52
34:19 43
37:30 .... 115, 116
38 107
38:1 112
38:2-11........................... 43
38:18-19 43
46:10 148
51 34
51:3 .... 34, 110
51:5 112
51:10 34
51:17 34
57:7 34
63:6 116
71:1 49
71:24 115
73:13 38
73:21-22.......................... 37
79:8 112
92 .... 59, 60
92:1 .... 59, 60
92:2 60
92:4-5 60
92:7-14 60
92:8 60
92:15 60
93-99 9
95:8 35
102:4-11 43
103:20-22 62
114:7 9
115:5-7 147
118:22 220
119:5-6a 49
119:70 35
119:80 34
139:1-3 xvii
139:13 36
148 .... 9, 62
149:3 43

Proverbs

2:5 .... 52, 110
2:17 66
2:21-22 52
3:19-20 51
8:7 115
8:22-31 51
10:5 50
12:4 50
14:31 51
14:35 50
17:2 50
17:5 51
19:26 50
28:14 35
29:15 50
30:1 52
30:7-9 113
30:32 114
31:1 52

Ecclesiastes

1:17 35
3:1 35

3:1–8 35	59:11 115	16:8 66
3:11 35		16:52 49
3:16 35	Jeremiah	16:63 112
3:17 35	2 147	36:32 49
	2:5 147	
Isaiah	4:29 54	Daniel
1:29 49	10:14 49	5:3–4 107
2:10 54	17:9 153	5:5 107
2:19 54	17:14 43	5:6 107
6:8 106	23:39 106	5:7 107
6:9–13 146	48:31 115	9:4–19 107
7:4 103	50:2 49	9:6–8 49
13:7 37	51:17 49	
28:16 220	51:46 103	Hosea
30:5 49	51:47 49	10:6 49
31:4 115		10:8 54
38:14 115	Ezekiel	
42:17 49	1:7 117	Micah
43:18 112	1:24 50	3:7 49
44:9 49	1:25 50	Malachi
45:16 49	1:28 50	2:14 66

New Testament

Matthew	John	Acts
6:9 219	1:1–3 233	17:27 143
10:20 169	1:4 127	Romans
	1:13 181	
Mark	1:14–18 168	1 .... 77, 92, 147, 149
4:9 182	3:5–6 165	1:1–4 168
14:36 218	3:18–19 169	1–2 110
	4:10 165	1:18 140
Luke	7:37 166	1:18–20 111
1:38 106	8:46 61	1:18–32 141
10:21 61	12:47–48 169	1:19 .... 65, 141, 142, 143
15:11–32 161	15:26 204	1:19–21 150
23:26–29 54	16:8 .... 165, 171	1:20 .... 111, 125, 141, 150
23:30 54	16:8–11 .... 164, 169	1:20–21 144
	16:28 233	1:21 .... 142, 145, 146
	17:1–5 233	1:21–25 147

1:22-23 148	8:26 219	Philippians
1:24-27 148	8:26-27 227	1:6 207
1:28 .... 148, 149	9:1 .... 58, 203, 204	1:20 221
1:32 ...... 65, 111, 150, 151, 152	9:4 201	3:9 211
2 77	10:17 168	
2:11 111	11:36 20	1 Timothy
2:12 111		1:19 139
2:14 .... 65, 84, 111	1 Corinthians	4:1 138
2:14-15 .... 110, 111, 112,	6:17 232	4:1-2 139
148, 150, 152	15:44-45 .... 170, 228	4:2 .... 138, 139
2:15 .... 58, 115, 202, 203		
2:16 111	2 Corinthians	Hebrews
2:26 151	1:3 217	6:4-5 .... 182, 185
3:19-20 111	1:12 .... 58, 105	6:4-6 172
3:20 203	2:14 182	9:9 212
5:12-21 .... 151, 203	4:2 105	9:14 213
5:13-14 152	4:6 170	10:1 213
5:16 151	5:11 105	10:2 .... 102, 212, 213
5:18 .... 151, 191	5:17 .... 170, 191	10:3 212
5:21 191		10:7 106
7 149	Galatians	10:15 204
7:6 162	2:19-21 169	10:19 .... 222, 223
7:7-13 203	2:20 211	10:22 .... 102, 212
7:7-25 150	3:1 168	12:23 .... 229, 230
7:10 152	3:8-14 168	
7:21-25 149	3:13-14 216	1 Peter
7:22 151	4:4-5 168	1:12 169
7:22-23 149	4:4-6 223	2:3 183
7:23 149	4:4-7 216	2:7 220
8 203	4:5 201	
8:3 168	4:6 .... 217, 218	1 John
8:4 151	5:16 209	1:1 182
8:14 217	6:15 .... 170, 191	2:28 231
8:15 .... 217, 218, 219		3:20-21 231
8:15-16 .... 201, 202,	Ephesians	4:17 231
203, 229	1:5 201	4:18 64
8:16 .... 203, 219	1:18 182	5:6 204
8:17 232	2:19 217	
8:18-23 203	3:12 234	Revelation
8:18-25 229	4:17-19 137	2:23 36
8:23 201	4:18 138	6:15-16 54
	5:27 228	